EFFECTIVE LEGAL WRITING

FOR LAW STUDENTS AND LAWYERS

FOURTH EDITION

By

GERTRUDE BLOCK

Lecturer and Writing Specialist Emeritus
University of Florida College of Law

Westbury, New York
THE FOUNDATION PRESS, INC.
1992

Library of Congress Cataloging-in-Publication Data

Block, Gertrude.
    Effective legal writing : for law students and lawyers / by
Gertrude Block. — 4th ed.
        p.   cm.
    Includes index.
    ISBN 0–88277–964–8
    1. Legal composition. I. Title.
KF250.B56 1992
808'.06634—dc20   91–44818

Block Legal Writing 4th Ed. FP

TABLE OF CONTENTS

TABLE OF CONTENTS

TABLE OF CONTENTS

INTRODUCTION

"Reading maketh a full man, speaking a ready man, writing an exact man."

Francis Bacon's words are especially important in the practice of law. Yet too many lawyers practice law without knowing how to write effectively. Author and law professor David Melinkoff has said that many lawyers can't write because they learned the law before they learned English. Thus they "hoard words as a squirrel hoards nuts— without thinking what to keep and what to drop." *

Another lawyer, Supreme Court Justice Anthony Scalia, chided lawyers for making the law more unintelligible than it should be by writing in "legal English," which they believe means writing "as pompously as possible, using words and phrases that have long since disappeared from normal English." **

This edition of my book, like the previous editions, is intended to help students learn to write effectively about the law as they come to understand it and to help legal professionals write more effectively. I have tried to make my book "user-friendly" by teaching the principles of effective writing simply and clearly.

A recent encounter with a former student, now a practicing lawyer, was especially gratifying to me because it gave me reason to think that I had achieved my objective. The lawyer told me that late one night she was reading in bed, and when her husband asked what book she was reading, she said it was the copy of *Effective Legal Writing* that she had used as a law student. "Why on earth are you reading that?" he asked—and she answered, "Because it's fun to read."

Now some people would deny that any "how-to" book could be fun to read. But in writing my book I have tried to make the learning process as pleasant as possible. And this fourth edition should be even more "user-friendly" than before.

Chapter One is a new chapter, designed to de-mystify court opinions and to make the writing of case briefs less onerous. New, too, is an expanded chapter on legal reasoning (Chapter Four) to guide students through the processes of analogizing and synthesizing cases. Chapter Five, dealing with the preparation of inter-office memoranda of law, has been expanded, and a new chapter (Chapter Six) has been added, showing students how to prepare appellate briefs.

---

* At an American Bar Association workshop, August 1984; reported in *The Gainesville Sun*, August 4, 1984.

** At the 92nd annual meeting of the Colorado Bar Association, September 17, 1990.

Finally, the last chapter contains questions that lawyers, judges, and others have submitted over the years to be answered in my columns on legal writing that appear in a number of state law journals and newspapers. Many of these same questions may also occur to you; you will find them answered in Chapter Nine.

With regard to the subject of "sexist language," specifically the use of the masculine pronoun (*he*), editors and authors sometimes resort to cumbersome devices to convey the intention to include women in the masculine pronoun. (Consider, for example, the Revised Statutes of Canada (1952), which state, "Words importing male persons include female persons and corporations.") I have declined to use such disclaimers and have instead chosen to balance the referent pronouns: half the time I have used *he* and the other half *she*. I have also tried to avoid the problem by altering the construction of sentences where it might otherwise appear. (See page 62 for suggestions about avoiding "sexist" language.)

One caveat: This book is not intended to teach the substance or doctrines of any area of law. Although the legal rules accompanying the hypothetical writing problems in Chapter Eight are sound, they should not be considered legally sufficient for any purpose except to teach essential legal writing skills.

My thanks to the secretaries of the University of Florida, who have guided me through the throes of learning to use my word processor, to Gwen Reynolds and Marguerite Baker, for their kind assistance; to Michael Giordano and Leanne Pflaum, who ably provided the chapter on appellate writing, and to my husband, Seymour Block, who unfailingly serves as sounding board and adviser. Any shortcomings are my own responsibility.

SOME LEGAL DEFINITIONS

Included in the list below are definitions of some of the legal words and phrases you will need to know as law students, lawyers, and paralegals. The list is not exhaustive; consult your law dictionary for terms you do not find. Included here are terms not ordinarily used in lay language, terms whose meanings differ from their lay meanings, and "law Latin" terms. Words defined elsewhere in this book and Latin terms in general use are omitted from the list.

action: Shorthand for "cause of action"; for example, a court action to obtain relief, a judicial remedy to enforce or protect a right, or a proceeding by a plaintiff against a defendant to enforce an obligation of the defendant to the plaintiff.

Actus non facit reum, nisi mens sit rea: *An act does not make one guilty, unless he has a guilty mind.* (For crime, there must be both act and evil intent.)

adhesion contract: A contract drafted by the stronger party, then presented for acceptance to the weaker party, who has no power to modify its terms.

ad litem: (Latin: *For the suit.*) A "guardian ad litem" is a guardian appointed to represent a person who is incapable of acting on his own behalf.

advance sheets, advance pamphlets: Paperback publications printed and distributed as soon as possible after a judicial decision, in order that the information be available before it appears in a bound volume. (**Slip laws** are similar publications of acts passed by a legislative body.)

affirmative defense: A defense which does more than deny the plaintiff's allegations; it also brings forth new allegations.

aforethought: Arrived at beforehand; a premeditated.

allegation: A statement that a party to a lawsuit intends to prove.

amicus curiae: (Latin: *A friend of the court.*) One who interposes in a legal action.

appellant: The party who appeals to a higher court from the judgment against himself in a lower court, sometimes called "petitioner."

appellee: The party against whom a case is appealed from a lower court to a higher court, sometimes called "respondent."

assumpsit: A common law action to recover damages for the nonperformance of a contract.

attractive nuisance: A condition on one's premises that is dangerous to children and yet so alluring to them that they may enter.

bad faith: The opposite of "bona fide" (in good faith): motivated by ulterior motives or by furtive intent.

beyond a reasonable doubt: The proof required of the prosecutor in criminal proceedings.

breach: Violation of a duty; the breaking of an obligation.

burden of evidence: The duty of one party to produce evidence to meet or present a prima facie case.

burden of proof: The duty to establish in the trial the truth of a proposition or issue by the amount of evidence required.

case: A controversy to be decided in a court of justice.

case law: The law set forth in the decisions of appellate courts, that is, in cases that have been decided.

case in point: A previously decided case that is similar in important respects to the one now being decided.

case system: Analysis of actual cases that have been decided, the method used in many law school courses to teach law students.

causa sine qua non: (Latin: *cause without which nothing.*) The determining cause, without which a result would not have occurred.

cause: An action or suit; sometimes used synonymously with "case."

caveat: (Latin: *Let him beware.*) Used in phrases like "caveat emptor," (let the buyer beware).

certiorari: Literally, *to be made certain,* a writ of review or inquiry by an appellate court re-examining an action of an inferior tribunal or to enable the appellate court to obtain further information in a pending cause.

change of venue: The removal of a suit for trial from one county to another.

charged with crime: Accused of a crime, either formally or informally.

chattels: Movable property, in contrast to real estate.

chose: From Old French: a *thing.* An item of personal property, a chattel.

civil action: An action to enforce a civil right, as distinguished from a criminal action.

class action: An action brought on behalf of a class of persons by one or more nominal plaintiffs.

clean hands doctrine: The principle by which the court of equity requires that one who comes to it for relief must not be guilty of wrongful conduct.

clear and convincing evidence: A degree of proof higher than that of preponderance of the evidence and lower than that of evidence beyond a reasonable doubt.

color: Mere semblance of a legal right.

common law: Legal rules, principles, and usage that rest upon court decisions rather than upon statutes or other written declarations.

condition precedent: A condition that must occur before something else comes into effect.

contract: (Williston) An agreement upon sufficient consideration to do or refrain from doing a particular lawful thing.

conversion: A wrongful act of dominion over another's property.

convict: (verb) To find a person guilty of the crime charged.

court of last resort: The highest court to which a case may be taken, from which no appeal can be made.

criterion: The test on which a judgment or a decision is based.

damage: Harm resulting from illegal invasion of a legal right.

damages: Compensation imposed by the law to one who has suffered harm due to another's wrongdoing.

decision: The conclusion reached by a court in adjudication of a case, or the decision reached by arbitration; sometimes synonymous with judgment.

declaratory judgment: A decision stating the rights and duties of the parties, but involving no relief as a result.

de facto: (Latin: *from the fact.*) In fact or reality, as contrasted with de jure, *by right or by law.*

defamation: Libel or slander.

degree of care: A standard, testing conduct to decide whether the conduct is negligent.

degree of proof: The amount of evidence required in action to establish the truth of an allegation.

de minimis non curat lex: (Latin: *The law is not concerned with trifles.*)

demurrer: A statement that even if the facts as stated are true, their legal consequences do not require that the action proceed further.

detriment: (in contract law) Some forbearance on the part of one party, as consideration for the contract.

devise: A testamentary gift of real estate.

doctrine: A rule or principle of law developed by court decisions.

due care: The care that a person of ordinary prudence would take in similar circumstances.

due process of law: A course of legal proceedings according to the rule of justice established to enforce and protect private rights.

earnest money: A payment of part of the purchase price to bind the contract.

ejusdem generis: (Latin: *of the same kind.*)

embezzlement: The fraudulent appropriation of property or money entrusted to one person by another.

encumbrance: A hindrance or impediment that burdens or obstructs the use of land.

entirety: The whole as distinguished from a part, as used to refer to the joint estate of spouses.

equal protection: Generally refers to the guaranty under the Fourteenth Amendment to the Constitution that all persons should enjoy the same protection of the law.

equity: A principle which provides justice when ordinary law may be inadequate.

escheat: The reversion or forfeiture of property to the government because persons who have a legal claim to it are absent.

establish: In evidence, to settle a disputed or doubtful fact.

estop: (From Old French: *to stop up*.) To bar, preclude, prohibit.

except: (verb) To object; to take exception to a court order or ruling.

facial: Pertaining to the language on the face of a document, pleading, statute, or writ.

for cause: For legal cause, as in the challenge of a juror.

four corners: The entire face of a document; thus, the construction of a document itself, as a whole.

frivolous: So unmeritorious as to require no argument to convince the court of this fact.

fungible goods: Goods of a kind in which all units are identical.

fundamental error: In appellate practice, an error so material as to render a judgment void.

garnish: To warn, summon, or notify.

good cause: Substantial legal reason.

good faith: Sincere motivation or behavior lacking fraud or deceit.

guardian: One entrusted by law with the control and custody of another person or estate.

guilty mind: Criminal intent (Latin: *mens rea.*)

harmless error: In appellate practice, error committed during the trial below, but not prejudicial to the rights of the party assigning it, and because of which, therefore, the court will not reverse the judgment below.

hostile possession: Possession of land under a claim of exclusive right.

hypothetical fact situation: A fictional legal problem, postulated by law professors, in order to sharpen their students' analytical skills.

Id.: Abbreviation of "idem," (Latin: *the same.*)

i.e.: Abbreviation of "id est," (Latin: *that is.*)

in absentia: (Latin: *In [someone's] absence.*)

in banco: (Latin: *On the bench*); that is, when all judges are sitting.

inferior: With less legal power, subordinate.

in jure: (Latin: *in law.*)

injuria: (Latin: *a wrong*); a violation of a legal right.

in personam: (Latin: *involving the person.*)

in rem: (Latin: *involving the matter or thing.*)

inter alia: (Latin: *among others.*)

in toto: (Latin: *in total*); altogether, wholly.

ipso facto: (Latin: *by that fact.*)

lessee: One who has leased property from another; tenant.

lessor: One who has leased property to another; landlord.

lex talionis: The law of retaliation.

malfeasance: Legal misconduct; an act that is legally wrong.

material (adjective): Important, of the essence.

matter: Those facts that constitute the entire ground or a part of the ground for an action or a defense.

misfeasance: The doing of a lawful act in an unlawful manner.

moiety: A part of something. (From Old French: moiete; *half.*)

moot question: (1) an academic question; (2) a question which has lost significance because it has already been decided, or for other reasons.

mortgagee: One to whom a mortgage is made.

mortgagor: One who takes out a mortgage on his property.

natural person: A real person, in contrast to a corporation.

negligence per se: (Latin: *negligence in itself*); negligence as defined by the law.

nolo contendere: (Latin: *I do not wish to contend.*)

nonfeasance: The failure to act, when action is legally required.

n.o.v.: Abbrevation of Latin: "non obstante veredicto," *notwithstanding the verdict.*

notorious possession: Possession of real property openly.

nudum pactum: (Latin: *a bare pact*); thus a promise lacking consideration.

nullity: Something that has no legal effect.

parol: Oral, as contrasted to "in writing."

patent ambiguity: Obvious upon ordinary inspection; contrasts with "latent ambiguity."

per curiam: (Latin: *by the court*); as a whole.

person: Either an individual or an organization, e.g., a corporation.

per stirpes: (Latin: *by class*); distribution according to the share a deceased ancestor would have taken.

plaintiff: The party bringing an action.

precatory words: Words expressing desire rather than command.

prejudicial: Detrimental to one party in a dispute.

preponderance of evidence: The greater weight and value of the evidence adduced.

presumption: An assumption about the existence of a fact; a presumption may be either rebuttable or irrebuttable (conclusive).

prima facie case: A cause of action sufficiently established to justify a favorable verdict if the other party to the action does not rebut the evidence.

probable cause: Reasonable cause.

proximate cause: That event or occurrence which produces the injury, and without which the injury would not have occurred.

punitive damages: Damages beyond compensatory damages, imposed to punish the defendant for his act.

quantum meruit: (Latin: *As much as it is worth*); the amount deserved.

question of fact: A question for the jury to decide, upon conflicting evidence.

question of law: A question about the law affecting the case, for the judge to decide.

recovery: The amount a claimant receives as a result of a judgment.

remedy: The means of enforcing a legal right or redressing a legal injury.

res: (Latin: *thing*); matter.

res ipsa loquitur: (Latin: *The thing speaks for itself.*)

res judicata: (Latin: *The thing having been adjudicated.*) The earlier judgment thus bars a second action.

respondeat superior: (Latin: *The superior is responsible.*) The doctrine that imposes liability upon an employer for the acts of his employees in the course of their employment.

rule: A statement of law that will henceforth act as precedent; a principle established by authority.

satisfaction: Performance of the terms of an agreement; discharge of an obligation.

scienter: (Latin: *knowingly.*) Often means defendant's "guilty knowledge."

seasonable: Within the agreed time or at the agreed time. If no time is stipulated, a "reasonable" time.

seisin: Possession coupled with the right of possession.

strict construction: Narrow or literal construction of language.

sui generis: (Latin: *of its own kind*); thus the only one of its kind.

tort: A wrong, for which a civil action is a remedy, outside of contract law.

tortfeasor: One who commits a tort; a wrongdoer.

vicarious liability: The imposition of liability upon one person for the acts of another.

*

EFFECTIVE LEGAL WRITING

FOR LAW STUDENTS AND LAWYERS

*

Chapter One

Understanding Court Opinions and Writing Case Briefs

As undergraduates you learned what you needed to know by studying in textbooks. As law students you learn what you need to know by studying in casebooks. That difference symbolizes the difference in the two types of learning. Because our legal system is grounded in caselaw, to learn how it works you must be able to understand and use the caselaw found in casebooks. That understanding does not always come easily. As Supreme Court Justice Cardozo once said, "Cases do not unfold their principles for the asking. They yield up their principles slowly and painfully." *

Nevertheless your ability to understand and analyze court opinions is crucial to your academic and professional success, for you will need to interpret the court opinions you read and to apply their reasoning to subsequent controversies. Because all other legal skills are grounded on this ability, this first chapter shows you how to read and understand court opinions and how to write case briefs.

I. How to Read and Understand Court Opinions

From the day you enter law school to the day you graduate, and probably for your entire legal career, you will spend much of your time reading court opinions. Your textbooks are called casebooks because they are composed largely of court opinions that decide appellate cases. You will need to understand how these opinions are organized and what they mean. The following opinion (*Creel v. S.A. Tarver & Son Tractor Co.*) is typical of the opinions you will read in reporters.** The opinions you read in your casebooks may be shortened versions.

In the reporter, the first four parts of the opinion make up the heading or caption. (See numbers (1) to (4) marked on the accompanying opinion.) Part (1) is the title of the case, which includes the names of the parties involved. The first-named party is the appellant (or petitioner) who is bringing

---

* In *The Nature of the Judicial Process*, p. 29 (Yale University Press, 1921).

** *Reporters* is the name given to collections of court opinions that are published in a set of volumes. *Official* reporters are those published under the authority of the government; *unofficial* reporters are published by private companies. Both official and unofficial court reporters are reliable as authority.

When your professors refer to an appellate court opinion, they may sometimes call it a *case* or a *decision*. This terminology will not confuse you if you understand that either term may be synonymous with *opinion*.

1

the case to the appellate court in order to "appeal" the decision of the lower court. The second party named is the appellee (or respondent), who is in court in response to the request of the appellant. In the case below, Creel is the appellant and S.A. Tarver and Son Tractor Co., Inc., et al., are the appellees.

The caption includes also the docket number of the case, assigned by the court (2), the name of the court deciding the case (3), and the date it was decided (4).

The next three paragraphs (in this opinion, one long and two single-sentence paragraphs) summarize the opinion (5). This part of the opinion is called the syllabus or prefatory statement. Be aware that this summary was written by the authors of the reporter, not by the court that decided the case. Therefore you should not cite the syllabus as authority—or read it instead of the opinion. (This mistake has occurred. There is on record a case in which an erroneous headnote was cited and accepted as law for many years before someone discovered the error.)

Notice that in this case the appellate decision was "affirmed as amended," and that Judge Carter concurred with the decision and gave his own reasons. You will find his one-paragraph concurrence at the end of the opinion. Sometimes concurring opinions are much more lengthy, and often there are dissenting opinions as well. If so, the dissenting opinions follow the concurring opinions and both follow the majority opinions.

The next two sections of the opinion, (6) and (7) contain the headnotes. In this opinion section (6) contains six case headnotes. The numbers 1 through 6 are West Key numbers and refer to digest topics to aid you in further researching the law on the stated subjects. For example, Key number 1 is labeled "Trial," and you will note as you read the opinion that when a paragraph refers to that key number, the number is bracketed to show where, within the opinion, that subject appears. In the headnote paragraph 1, following "Trial," a key symbol is followed by numbers 250, 267(1), and 295(1). These numbers refer to relevant West digest topics so that you can research the subject further. (You will learn how to use the digests in your legal research course.)

Next in the headnotes (7) are listed the names of the attorneys who represented the parties to the appeal, the names of the judges who tried the case and the name of the judge who wrote the opinion. In this opinion, a one-sentence statement follows, which briefly states what issues the court had to decide. This issue statement is often omitted from the summary and the issues are stated only in the body of the opinion.

The main part of the opinion (8) is (in this opinion) labeled "Facts." The opinion contains 17 paragraphs of facts.* In paragraphs 1 and 2, the court states the key facts of the case as well as what the plaintiff requested in the

---

* The paragraphs are not numbered in the actual opinion. I have numbered them to make reference to each paragraph easier.

trial court and what the jury decided. The final sentence of the second paragraph tells the reader why the plaintiff has appealed the lower court decision.

In paragraph 3, the court considers the plaintiff's appeal to reverse the lower court decision on the ground that the judge refused to give the jury the plaintiff's requested charge containing the phrase "reasonable medical possibility." In paragraphs 4, 5, 6, and 7, the appellate court dismisses the plaintiff's request to reverse the trial court's decision on this ground, reasoning (in paragraph 5) that the trial court did not err in refusing to give the requested charge, and (in paragraph 6) that even if it had erred, that error would not be "reversible." (That is, such an error would not be reason for the appellate court to overturn the jury verdict.) In paragraph 7, the court concludes that, as to the jury instructions, they "adequately informed the jury of the plaintiff's burden of proving his [*sic*] case by a preponderance of the evidence." In other words, the court says that the plaintiff loses on that part of her appeal.

Paragraphs 8 and 9 discuss plaintiff's next claim: the trial court erred when it refused to allow her to question the medical experts regarding the language "reasonable medical possibility." In paragraph 8, the appellate court rejects this claim of error and adds in paragraph 9, that even if the trial court did err in this respect, that error was "harmless" (i.e., not detrimental to the plaintiff).

Finally, in paragraphs 10 through 17, the appellate court deals with the plaintiff's complaints that the jury erred by awarding her inadequate money for general damages, by awarding only a part of the medical expenses she claimed, and by failing to make an award for her future medical expenses. In all these claims, the appellate court finds for the plaintiff, after carefully explaining (in paragraph 11) that generally appellate courts do not disturb jury decisions on the amount of money awarded unless the jury has abused its discretion, and will even then only raise or lower the award to an amount "reasonably within the discretion of the jury."

A short digression is in order here to explain why the appellate court took pains to make this point clear. It did so because appellate courts are not permitted to reverse trial court decisions on matters of fact, only on matters of law. The amount of damages awarded the plaintiff becomes a matter of law only if the jury abused its discretion by awarding the plaintiff much too much or much too little in damages, that is (in the case at hand) by awarding her less in damages than is permissible as a matter of law. The court is, in effect, justifying its reversal of the trial court decision by saying that the jury decision was "unreasonable."

Paragraphs 12, 13, and 14, then, explain the court's reason for considering the damages award to be "unreasonable" under the law. The court details the evidence leading to its conclusion, in paragraph 15, that the plaintiff was awarded too little for general damages, and decides that an increase in the amount of general damages is necessary to reach "the lowest amount reasonable within the jury's discretion."

With regard to the plaintiff's claim that the jury erred in awarding her only a part of her medical expenses, in paragraph 16 the court agrees and explains why, in view of the facts, it has reached that conclusion. The court then awards her $5,083.73 additional for past medical expenses and, because the record shows that the plaintiff will require further medical treatment, the court allows her an extra $1,500 for that purpose.

The final paragraph, 17, sums up the amendments the appellate court has made to the lower court judgment, and affirms the lower court judgment "in all other respects." The court's decision is then stated, as a new paragraph, in capital letters (part (9)).

All that remains is for the judge who joins in the majority opinion as to its result, but who differs slightly in the manner of arriving at that result, to state his reasons for differing, in part (10). Thus the opinion ends.

But this explanation should not end without two additional points. The first is that the opinion illustrates the way courts reason from precedent (discussed, also, elsewhere in the book). Notice that (beginning in paragraph 4 of the facts) this appellate court cites to previous Louisiana cases after stating a rule of law. In paragraph 5, *Mart v. Hill* is cited for the rule that the test for determining the causal relationship between an accident and subsequent injuries is whether the plaintiff has proved that it was more probable than not that the injuries were due to the accident. Also in paragraph 5, *Wells v. Allstate Ins. Co.* is cited for the rule that mere possibility of a causal connection is not sufficient. Because these two rules have been articulated by previous appellate courts in Louisiana, they are binding for this court.

As you read the opinion, you will notice that these two and other Louisiana appellate court opinions are referred to as precedent for the conclusions of this court. That is the use of precedent in action.

The second point: courts and reporter editors, like the rest of us, make mistakes. This court (or the reporter) has made two. The first was in paragraph 7, where the plaintiff was referred to as "his" and the second in paragraph 11, in the phrase "abused its much discretion." That language is not idiomatic English; the line was probably intended to read, "unless the trier of fact much abused its discretion." Gremlins creep into copy. You should be aware of their possible presence and avoid compounding errors by mistakenly quoting them. If you have to quote the erroneous usage, follow it with [*sic*].

A TYPICAL APPELLATE OPINION:

①

Pamela Kay CREEL

v.

S.A. TARVER & SON TRACTOR CO., INC., et al.

②   No. CA 87 1308.

③ Court of Appeal of Louisiana, First Circuit.

④   Dec. 20, 1988.

⑤

Victim of automobile accident sued driver's employer and employer's insurer for injuries allegedly sustained. The 22nd Judicial District Court, Parish of St. Tammany, James R. Strain, Jr., J., entered jury verdict of $30,000 in favor of victim, and victim appealed. The Court of Appeal, LeBlanc, J., held that: (1) trial court properly refused to permit victim to question medical experts concerning reasonable medical possibility that her injuries were caused by accident, and (2) general damage award of $20,000 was inadequate and would be increased to $30,000 in light of injuries and pain experienced by victim.

Affirmed as amended.

Carter, J., concurred and assigned reasons.

1. Trial ⟐250, 267(1), 295(1)

Judge in jury trial is not required to give precise instructions submitted by parties, but must give instructions which properly reflect law applicable in view of facts present; adequacy of jury instructions must be determined in light of instructions as a whole.

2. Damages ⟐185(1)

Test for determining causal relationship between accident and subsequent injuries is whether plaintiff proved through medical and lay testimony that it was more probable than not that injuries were caused by accident; mere possibility of causal connection is insufficient.

3. Appeal and Error ⟐1064.1(1)

Appellate courts exercise great restraint in overturning jury verdict on basis of erroneous jury instructions.

4. Evidence ⟐547.5

In suit brought by victim of automobile accident, trial court properly refused to allow victim to question medical experts concerning "reasonable medical possibility" that her injuries were caused by accident; proper line of inquiry was whether there was reasonable medical probability of causal connection between accident and injuries.

5. Appeal and Error ⟐1004.1(1), 1151(2, 3)

Damages ⟐96, 104, 119

Trier of fact is given much discretion in fixing amount of damages due, and this determination will not be disturbed on appeal unless trier of fact abused its discretion, and then only to extent of raising or lowering damage to lowest or highest amount which is reasonably within discretion of jury.

6. Damages ⟐132(15)

General damage award of $20,000 for victim of automobile accident was insufficient and would be increased to $30,000; as a result of injuries sustained in accident victim was no longer able to participate in physical activities such as jogging and exercising, wiring of jaw required victim to eat restricted diet of soft foods for approximately nine weeks and suffer extreme

⑥

⑥ soreness and episodes of intense pain in her jaw, and victim also suffered severe laceration of lower lip which was very painful injury and from headaches, dizziness and nausea as well as depression because of her inability to resume former level of physical activity.

---

⑦ Elisabeth Ramirez & Robert Anderson, Jr., Covington, Joseph McMahon, Jr., New Orleans, for plaintiff-appellant.

Edward Levert, Jr., New Orleans, Pierre Livaudais, Covington, for defendants-appellees.

Before CARTER, LANIER and LeBLANC, JJ.

LeBLANC, Judge.

The issues presented in this personal injury case concern a requested jury instruction, the exclusion of certain testimony and quantum.

⑧ ──────→ FACTS

On the morning of September 27, 1985, plaintiff, Pamela Creel, was injured in a collision between her automobile and a vehicle driven by David Passman during the course and scope of his employment with defendant, S.A. Tarver & Son Tractor Co. ¶ 1 Plaintiff sustained a blow to her chin, a two inch laceration of her lower lip and a blow to her knee in the collision. She was taken to the emergency room at St. Tammany Parish Hospital complaining primarily of pain to her jaw and face. After an examination, she was x-rayed, sutured with five stitches to her lip and released that afternoon. Since the accident, plaintiff has consulted several doctors and dentists regarding complaints of pain to her head, jaw, lip, teeth, chest, back and right knee.

The present suit was filed by plaintiff against Tarver & Son and its insurer, Sen- ¶ 2 try Insurance, seeking damages for personal injuries, lost wages and medical expenses. After a trial, the jury returned a special verdict awarding plaintiff $20,-000.00 for general damages, $7,800.00 for lost wages and $10,408.55 in medical ex-

penses. In accordance with this verdict, the district court rendered judgment in favor of plaintiff, against defendants, in the ¶ 2 amount of $38,208.55. Plaintiff has appealed, alleging that the trial court erred in its jury instructions and that the jury verdict was inadequate in several respects.

Before the jury in this case was instructed, plaintiff's attorney requested that the judge include a charge stating that if a victim is in good health before an accident ¶ 3 and, after the accident, a disabling injury manifests itself and there is a reasonable medical possibility of a causal connection between the injury and the accident, it is presumed, subject to rebutting evidence, that the accident caused the disabling injury. The trial court agreed to give this charge if the words "reasonable medical possibility" were changed to "reasonable medical certainty". Plaintiff's attorney indicated a preference to omit the charge entirely, rather than agree to this substitution. Consequently, the trial court did not give the requested charge.

[1] The judge in a jury trial is not required to give the precise instructions submitted by either party, but must give instructions which properly reflect the law ¶ 4 applicable in view of the facts present. The adequacy of jury instructions must be determined in light of the instructions as a whole. *Laborde v. Velsicol Chemical Corp.*, 474 So.2d 1320 (La.App. 3d Cir. 1985), *writ denied*, 480 So.2d 738 (1986).

[2] In this case, the trial court did not err in refusing to give the charge requested by plaintiff. The test for determining the causal relationship between an accident and subsequent injuries is whether the ¶ 5 plaintiff proved through medical and lay testimony that it was *more probable than not* that the injuries were caused by the accident. *Mart v. Hill*, 505 So.2d 1120 (La.1987). The mere possibility of a causal connection is insufficient. *Wells v. Allstate Ins. Co.*, 510 So.2d 763 (La.App. 1st Cir.), *writ denied*, 514 So.2d 463 (1987).

[3] Finally, even if it was error for the trial court to refuse to give the requested ¶ 6 charge, we do not believe such error would

¶6 be reversible. Appellate courts exercise great restraint in overturning a jury verdict on the basis of erroneous jury instructions. *Cuccia v. Cabrejo*, 429 So.2d 232 (La.App. 5th Cir.), *writ denied*, 434 So.2d 1097 (1983). The pertinent inquiry in making such a determination is whether the jury was misled to such an extent as to prevent it from doing justice. *Cuccia, supra.* The manifest error standard of review may not be ignored unless the instructions were so incorrect or inadequate as to preclude the jury from reaching a verdict based on the law and facts. *Laborde, supra.*

¶7 After examining the jury instructions in their entirety, we believe that they adequately informed the jury of the plaintiff's burden of proving his case by a preponderance of the evidence. We do not believe such error would have been of sufficient gravity to preclude the jury from reaching a verdict based on the law and facts of this case.

¶8 [4] Plaintiff also contends that the trial court erred in refusing to allow her to question the medical experts concerning the "reasonable medical *possibility*" that her injuries were caused by the accident. The trial court sustained defendants' objection to this line of questioning on the basis that the proper inquiry was whether there was any reasonable medical *probability* of a causal connection between the accident and injuries. We find no error in the trial court's ruling, agreeing that the proper inquiry was whether a reasonable medical probability of causation existed rather than a reasonable medical possibility of causation. The "possibility" of a causal connection is in itself of little probative value. *Cf. Wells v. Allstate, supra.*

¶9 Even if the trial court's refusal to allow this line of questioning was error, we find it was harmless error. From our review of Dr. Bradford's [1] proffered testimony, we do not believe its exclusion was prejudicial to plaintiff because this testimony was basi-

cally cumulative. *Cf. Royle v. Casualty Reciprocal Exchange*, 486 So.2d 271, 276 (La.App. 3d Cir.), *writ denied*, 489 So.2d 250 (1986). Accordingly, this assignment of error is without merit.

¶10 [5, 6] Finally, plaintiff complains that the jury erred in awarding an inadequate amount for general damages, in awarding only a portion of the medical expenses she claimed and in failing to make an award for future medical expenses.

¶11 The trier of fact is given much discretion in fixing the amount of damages due. *Scott v. Hosp. Serv. Dist. No. 1*, 496 So.2d 270 (La.1986); *Coco v. Winston Industries, Inc.*, 341 So.2d 332 (La.1976). This determination will not be disturbed on appeal unless the trier of fact abused its much discretion, and then only to the extent of raising it (or lowering it) to the lowest (or highest) amount which is reasonably within the discretion of the jury. *Id.*

¶12 In this case, plaintiff enjoyed good health and was physically active before the accident. Although she had had prior problems with her knee, she had been asymptomatic for several years prior to the accident. Immediately thereafter, she began having pain and swelling in her right knee, which necessitated an arthroscope on January 2, 1986. Plaintiff is no longer able to participate in physical activities such as jogging and exercising, which she previously had enjoyed. The accident clearly aggravated plaintiff's pre-existing knee condition.

¶13 Shortly after the accident, it also became necessary for wire loops to be placed on plaintiff's teeth as a result of the injuries she sustained to her teeth and jaw; these loops were not completely removed until February of 1986. Accordingly, she was restricted to a diet of soft foods for approximately nine weeks. Plaintiff experienced extreme soreness in her jaw and on several occasions experienced episodes of intense pain. In May, 1986, she was prescribed a transcutaneous electric nerve stimulation

1. We note that our review on this issue is limited only to the proffered testimony of Dr. Bradford. Since plaintiff did not proffer the testimony of any of the other doctors, she is precluded from now complaining of the "exclusion" of the other doctors' testimony on this issue. *McLean v. Hunter*, 495 So.2d 1298, 1305 (La.1986).

ℛ 13

(TENS) unit to help relieve the pain in her jaw. Although the TENS unit relieved much of her pain, at the time of trial, plaintiff continued to experience problems with pain and locking of her jaw, due to arthritis in the left temporomandibular joint of her jaw, a condition aggravated by the accident.

ℛ 14

Additionally, plaintiff also suffered a severe laceration to her lower lip, which was a very painful injury. For a time after the accident, she suffered from headaches, dizziness and nausea, as well as depression because of her inability to resume her former level of physical activity. Plaintiff also sustained a bad bruise of the chest wall, which was sore and caused her pain for several months.

ℛ 15

Considering all of the evidence, we conclude that the jury abused its discretion in awarding plaintiff only $20,000.00 in general damages. In view of the particular facts of this case, we find that $30,000.00 was the lowest amount reasonably within the jury's discretion. We therefore increase plaintiff's award for general damages to this amount.

ℛ 16

Plaintiff also complains that the jury erred in awarding her only a portion of the medical expenses she incurred relative to her knee and orthodontic problems. We agree. As discussed above, although at least a portion of plaintiff's condition was pre-existent, she was asymptomatic for several years prior to the accident. The record establishes that the claimed medical expenses were necessitated by the injuries she sustained and the aggravation of pre-existing conditions resulting from the accident. Plaintiff is therefore entitled to an additional sum of $5,083.73 for past medical expenses incurred in the treatment of her knee injury and orthodontic problems. The record also establishes that a magnetic resonance imaging test and an arthroscopy, resulting in combined costs of $1,500.00, were recommended as further treatment of plaintiff's temporomandibular joint syndrome.

ℛ 17

For the above reasons, we amend the judgment of the lower court to award plaintiff the additional amounts of $10,000.00

ℛ 17

for general damages, $5,083.73 for past medical expenses and $1,500.00 for future medical expenses. The judgment is affirmed in all other respects. Appellees are to pay all costs of appeal.

⑨

AMENDED AND, AS AMENDED, AFFIRMED.

CARTER, J., concurs.

⑩

CARTER, Judge, concurring.

I respectfully submit that although the result reached is correct, I believe that the plaintiff's burden of proof is not as set forth by the majority, but is as set forth in *Wisner v. Illinois Central Gulf Railroad, et al.*, 537 So.2d 740 (La.App. 1st Cir.1988).

II. How to Brief Cases

As law students, besides being able to read and understand court opinions, you need to know how to "brief" those opinions. As you have already learned, your professors often call court opinions *cases*. Thus, when you are told to brief a *case* you will be expected to prepare a concise outline of a court opinion.

A. Why Briefing Cases Is Important

First, and of foremost importance to you as a law student, brief cases because your professor will expect you to do so. When you are called on in class your professor will assume that you are relying on your case brief as you answer questions about any aspect of the court opinion. With the case brief before you, you can answer quickly and competently. Without a case brief, you may struggle to respond because you cannot quickly put into words your understanding of the opinion.

Second, brief cases because the case briefs will be valuable to you when you study for final examinations. Your case brief will contain the vital elements of the case so you can avoid re-reading the entire opinion. It is true that "canned briefs" are available, but these are no substitute for the "from scratch" variety you prepare yourself. Canned briefs may also contain errors, so you cannot depend upon their accuracy. They are useful, however, as a comparison with your own case briefs. If there are discrepancies between yours and the canned brief, you can re-check the opinion to find out why.

Third, the ability to brief cases is a basic legal skill that can be learned only through practice. Each time you exercise that skill your analytical ability will improve. With improvement, you will find that you can understand and analyze cases quickly and efficiently.

B. How to Organize and Prepare a Case Brief

You have already discovered that professors disagree about what a case brief should contain. So do the authors of legal texts. The important thing to remember is that the number of categories your brief contains is far less important than *that* you brief. The outline that follows contains nine categories, probably the most any professor will ask you to include. After you learn what belongs in each category, you can reduce the number as it suits your purpose. Probably *every* brief should include the following: facts, legal theory, issue(s), holding, reasoning, and rule.

To prepare a case brief, carefully read the opinion to be briefed and list the categories your brief will contain on the left side of a legal-sized sheet of paper, leaving room opposite each category to insert relevant data from the opinion. Then re-read the opinion, listing in the margin of the opinion where in your outline you will enter the data. Concisely summarize the data and transfer to the proper position. Try to retain the crucial terms the court used in the opinion. If you don't understand all of the legal terminology in the opinion, look it up in a legal dictionary and footnote your case brief with the definitions. (See, for example, the *Transatlantic Financing Corporation* brief, below, at page 13.)

C. The Categories of a Case Brief

1. Parties; their relationship; how the matter reached this court (procedural posture)
2. Legal theories (cause(s) of action and defense)
3. Facts
4. Relief requested
5. Issue(s)
6. Holding(s) and disposition
7. Reasoning
8. Resulting legal rule(s)
9. Dictum (dicta)

Here is an explanation of each item:

1. *Parties; their relationship; how the matter reached this court (procedural posture):*

The names of the parties usually appear in the caption at the beginning of the opinion. Their relationship also appears there, the plaintiff(s) first, followed, after the *v.* (for *versus*), the defendant(s). When multiple parties are involved, list only the last name of the first litigant on each side. These are the names that appear in the body of the opinion. Even in captions reading, *In re* . . . or *In the Matter of* . . . there are at least two opposing parties, and their names should appear in your brief. In this section of your brief, indicate as well the status of each party, e.g., *employer* and *employee, appellant* and *appellee, petitioner* and *respondent.*

In "how the matter reached this court," briefly note any prior proceedings and explain why this court is now involved. Most of the cases you will brief are appellate court cases whose previous history appears at the beginning of the opinion. The headnote (syllabus) also contains this information, but be aware that errors may be present in this material since notes that precede the opinion are written by the reporter, not by the judge who wrote the opinion. A story, perhaps apocryphal, is told of a legal principle established over the years by *stare decisis,* whose original citation was from an erroneous headnote, the information never having appeared in the opinion itself!

2. *Legal theories (cause(s) of action and defense):*

These are the legal rules that form the basis of the plaintiff's claim. The plaintiff always advances one or more legal theories in order to obtain his desired objective. The defendant may also advance one or more legal theories if, instead of merely denying the validity of the plaintiff's cause of action, he raises a separate claim (an affirmative defense).

3. *Facts:*

The fact section of your brief contains a succinct summary of the salient information, often called *key facts,* of the opinion. Key facts are those facts upon which the court based its holding. Thus facts that could be omitted or altered without changing the decision are not key facts. (For example, in *Transatlantic Financing Corporation v. United States,* at 13, below, the fact that the Egyptian government had nationalized and taken over operation of the Suez Canal is not a key fact, since it could be deleted without changing the opinion of the court; however, the fact that the Suez Canal had been closed to traffic as a result of the takeover is a key fact.)

    4.   *Relief requested:*

The plaintiff states here what he hopes to achieve by going to court, his *remedy.* In the cases briefed below, the relief requested is in the form of money. The kind of relief requested was a key fact in *Transatlantic Financing Corporation* (below), the court stating that the plaintiff's theory of relief was inappropriate.

    5.   *Issue(s):*

Issues are the precise legal questions that must be resolved by the court in order to reach its decision in the case under consideration. Often the issues are expressly stated in the opinion. If they are not, you can identify them by reading the court's holding and the reasons given to support it. The complete issue is the rule of law applied to the key facts of the case at hand. The issue question must be answerable by *yes* or *no.* It can be posed either as a direct or indirect question. The indirect question begins with *whether* and ends with a period. The direct question begins with a verb (e.g., *is, does, has*) and ends with a question mark.

    6.   *Holding(s) and disposition:*

The holding is stated as the court's affirmative or negative response to the issue. In its entirety, the holding contains the rule of law that was applied and the key facts of the case. In your own briefs of case opinions, however, you will probably include only a short answer to the issue (i.e., *yes* or *no*) because you have already completely stated the rule of law and key facts in the *issue* statement.

The disposition is whatever the court says it will do procedurally as a result of its holding. The disposition usually comes at the end of the opinion, stated in a few words (e.g., *vacated and remanded*).

    7.   *Reasoning:*

In its reasoning, the court justifies its holding on each issue. When the case presents more than one issue, the court may intermingle the reasoning behind its holding on several issues, but you should separate the court's statements so as to apply its reasoning to each issue. To identify the reasoning of the court, look for its reasons for agreeing with one party and disagreeing with the other, for accepting some legal precedents and rejecting others, for extending or limiting other courts' opinions. Also look for the court's citation of enacted law and its interpretation of the intent of that law.

    8.   *Resulting legal rule(s):*

The legal rule is a broad statement of principle developed by or applied in *this* decision. The rule may then become precedent for analogous cases, in future decisions. Few decisions enunciate a new legal rule; many cite a rule previously developed, which was applied in the case at hand. This item and item 9, which follows, are often omitted from briefs, but they are helpful in placing the case under consideration into perspective with respect to cases that have preceded or will follow it.

    9.   *Dictum (dicta):*

Dictum (the plural of which is dicta) is official but incidental and gratuitous language, unnecessary to the decision of the case under consideration. Since courts are supposed to reach decisions only on the narrow questions before them, decisions theoretically should not contain dicta, but they sometimes do. You will recognize as dictum any statement a court makes based on facts other than those presented in *this* controversy, or any conclusion a court reaches based upon law not applicable to *this* controversy. You should identify dictum because later courts may agree with the view expressed as dictum, although dictum is not binding on subsequent court decisions any more than the minority decision is binding. (In *Transatlantic Financing Corporation,* for example, the dictum expressed by the court could result in a future court's extending this court's holding.)

D. Sample Case Briefs of Actual Opinions.

    On the following pages there are three actual court opinions. Each opinion is followed by a case brief of the opinion, written by a student. Later, in Chapter Four, you will find a chart that the student prepared from her case briefs. She used the chart to prepare a case synthesis of the three cases. The synthesis is on page 14. The three court opinions are

    (1) **Transatlantic Financing Corporation v. United States**

        (In *Transatlantic,* the appellant sought payment from the United States for costs resulting from appellant's ship's diversion from its normal route to its destination, due to Egypt's closing of the Suez Canal.)

    (2) **American Trading and Production Corporation v. Shell International Marine LTD**

        (In *American Trading,* the appellant sought additional compensation for transporting cargo from Texas to India via an alternate route due to Egypt's closing of the Suez Canal.)

    (3) **Northern Corporation v. Chugach Electric Association**

        (In *Northern Corporation,* the appellant sought to recover costs it incurred when it attempted and failed to complete its contract to repair and protect a dam, as required by the appellee.)

TRANSATLANTIC FINANCING CORPORATION v. UNITED STATES *

United States Court of Appeals, District of Columbia Circuit, 1966.
363 F.2d 312.

J. SKELLY WRIGHT, CIRCUIT JUDGE:

This appeal involves a voyage charter between Transatlantic Financing Corporation, operator of the SS CHRISTOS, and the United States covering carriage of a full cargo of wheat from a United States Gulf port to a safe port in Iran. The District Court dismissed a libel filed by Transatlantic against the United States for costs attributable to the ship's diversion from the normal sea route caused by the closing of the Suez Canal. We affirm.

On July 26, 1956, the Government of Egypt nationalized the Suez Canal Company and took over operation of the Canal. On October 2, 1956, during the international crisis which resulted from the seizure, the voyage charter in suit was executed between representatives of Transatlantic and the United States. The charter indicated the termini of the voyage but not the route. On October 27, 1956, the SS CHRISTOS sailed from Galveston for Bandar Shapur, Iran, on a course which would have taken her through Gibraltar and the Suez Canal. On October 29, 1956, Israel invaded Egypt. On October 31, 1956, Great Britain and France invaded the Suez Canal Zone. On November 2, 1956, the Egyptian Government obstructed the Suez Canal with sunken vessels and closed it to traffic.

On or about November 7, 1956, Beckmann, representing Transatlantic, contacted Potosky, an employee of the United States Department of Agriculture, who appellant concedes was unauthorized to bind the Government, requesting instructions concerning disposition of the cargo and seeking an agreement for payment of additional compensation for a voyage around the Cape of Good Hope. Potosky advised Beckmann that Transatlantic was expected to perform the charter according to its terms, that he did not believe Transatlantic was entitled to additional compensation for a voyage around the Cape, but that Transatlantic was free to file such a claim. Following this discussion, the CHRISTOS changed course for the Cape of Good Hope and eventually arrived in Bandar Shapur on December 30, 1956.

Transatlantic's claim is based on the following train of argument. The charter was a contract for a voyage from a Gulf port to Iran. Admiralty principles and practices, especially stemming from the doctrine of deviation, require us to imply into the contract the term that the voyage was to be performed by the "usual and customary" route. The usual and customary route from Texas to Iran was, at the time of contract, via Suez, so the contract was for a voyage from Texas to Iran via Suez. When Suez was closed this contract became impossible to perform. Consequently, appellant's argument continues, when Transatlantic delivered the cargo by going around the Cape of

* I am grateful to Susan Katcher, of the University of Wisconsin Law School East   Asian Legal Studies Center, for her helpful comments regarding this opinion.

Good Hope, in compliance with the Government's demand under claim of right it conferred a benefit upon the United States for which it should be paid in *quantum meruit.*

The doctrine of impossibility of performance has gradually been freed from the earlier fictional and unrealistic strictures of such tests as the "implied term" and the parties' "contemplation." It is now recognized that " 'A thing is impossible in legal contemplation when it is not practicable; and a thing is impracticable when it can only be done at an excessive and unreasonable cost.' " The doctrine ultimately represents the ever-shifting line, drawn by courts hopefully responsive to commercial practices and mores, at which the community's interest in having contracts enforced according to their terms is outweighed by the commercial senselessness of requiring performance. When the issue is raised, the court is asked to construct a condition of performance based on the changed circumstances, a process which involves at least three reasonably definable steps. First, a contingency—something unexpected—must have occurred. Second, the risk of the unexpected occurrence must not have been allocated either by agreement or by custom. Finally, occurrence of the contingency must have rendered performance commercially impracticable. Unless the court finds these three requirements satisfied, the plea of impossibility must fail.

The first requirement was met here. It seems reasonable, where no route is mentioned in a contract, to assume the parties expected performance by the usual and customary route at the time of contract.[4] Since the usual and customary route from Texas to Iran at the time of contract was through Suez, closure of the Canal made impossible the expected method of performance. But this unexpected development raises rather than resolves the impossibility issue, which turns additionally on whether the risk of the contingency's occurrence had been allocated and, if not, whether performance by alternative routes was rendered impracticable.

Proof that the risk of a contingency's occurrence has been allocated may be expressed in or implied from the agreement. Such proof may also be found in the surrounding circumstances, including custom and usages of the trade. The contract in this case does not expressly condition performance upon availability of the Suez route. Nor does it specify "via Suez" or, on the other hand, "via Suez or Cape of Good Hope."[7] Nor are there provisions in

4. Uniform Commercial Code § 2–614, comment 1, states: "Under this Article, in the absence of specific agreement, the normal or usual facilities enter into the agreement either through the circumstances, usage of trade or prior course of dealing." So long as this sort of assumption does not necessarily result in construction of a condition of performance, it is idle to argue over whether the usual and customary route is an "implied term." The issue of impracticability must eventually be met. One court refused to imply the Suez route as a con-

tract term, but went on to rule the contract had been "frustrated." Carapanayoti & Co. Ltd. v. E.T. Green Ltd., [1959] 1 Q.B. 131. The holding was later rejected by the House of Lords. Tsakiroglou & Co. Ltd. v. Noblee Thorl G.m.b.H., [1960] 2 Q.B. 348.

7. In Glidden Company v. Hellenic Lines, Limited, 2 Cir., 275 F.2d 253 (1960), the charter was for transportation of materials from India to America "via Suez Canal or Cape of Good Hope, or Panama Canal," and the court held performance was not

the contract from which we may properly imply that the continued availability of Suez was a condition of performance. Nor is there anything in custom or trade usage, or in the surrounding circumstances generally, which would support our constructing a condition of performance. The numerous cases requiring performance around the Cape when Suez was closed, indicate that the Cape route is generally regarded as an alternative means of performance. So the implied expectation that the route would be via Suez is hardly adequate proof of an allocation to the promisee of the risk of closure. In some cases, even an express expectation may not amount to a condition of performance.[9] The doctrine of deviation supports our assumption that parties normally expect performance by the usual and customary route, but it adds nothing beyond this that is probative of an allocation of the risk.[10]

"frustrated." In his discussion of this case, Professor Corbin states: "Except for the provision for an alternative route, the defendant would have been discharged, for the reason that the parties contemplated an open Suez Canal as a specific condition or means of performance." 6 Corbin, supra, § 1339, at 399 n. 57. Appellant claims this supports its argument, since the Suez route was contemplated as usual and customary. But there is obviously a difference, in deciding whether a contract allocates the risk of a contingency's õccurrence, between a contract specifying no route and a contract specifying Suez. We think that when Professor Corbin said, "Except for the provision for an alternative route," he was referring, not to the entire *provision*—"via Suez Canal or Cape of Good Hope" etc.—but to the fact that *an alternative route* had been provided for. Moreover, in determining what Corbin meant when he said "the parties contemplated an open Suez Canal as a specific condition or means of performance," consideration must be given to the fact, recited by Corbin, that in *Glidden* the parties were specifically aware when the contract was made the Canal might be closed, and the promisee had refused to include a clause excusing performance in the event of closure. Corbin's statement, therefore, is most accurately read as referring to cases in which a route is specified after negotiations reflecting the parties' awareness that the usual and customary route might become unavailable. Compare Held v. Goldsmith, 153 La. 598, 96 So. 272 (1919).

9. Uniform Commercial Code § 2–614(1) provides: "Where without fault of either party . . . the *agreed* manner of delivery . . . becomes commercially impracticable but a commercially reasonable substitute is available, such substitute performance

must be tendered and accepted." (Emphasis added.) Compare Mr. Justice Holmes' observation: "You can give any conclusion a logical form. You always can imply a condition in a contract. But why do you imply it? It is because of some belief as to the practice of the community or of a class, or because of some opinion as to policy. . . ." Holmes, *The Path of the Law*, 10 Harv.L.Rev. 457, 466 (1897).

10. The deviation doctrine, drawn principally from admiralty insurance practice, implies into all relevant commercial instruments naming the termini of voyages the usual and customary route between those points. 1 Arnould, *Marine Insurance and Average*, § 376, at 522 (10th ed. 1921). Insurance is cancelled when a ship unreasonably "deviates" from this course, for example by extending a voyage or by putting in at an irregular port, and the shipowner forfeits the protection of clauses of exception which might otherwise have protected him from his common law insurer's liability to cargo. See Gilmore & Black, supra Note 8, § 2–6, at 59–60. This practice, properly qualified, see *id.* § 3–41, makes good sense, since insurance rates are computed on the basis of the implied course, and deviations in the course increasing the anticipated risk make the insurer's calculations meaningless. Arnould, supra, § 14, at 26. Thus the route, so far as insurance contracts are concerned, is crucial, whether express or implied. But even here, the implied term is not inflexible. Reasonable deviations do not result in loss of insurance, at least so long as established practice is followed. See Carriage of Goods by Sea Act § 4(4), 49 Stat. 1210, 46 U.S.C. § 1304(4); and discussion of "held covered" clauses in Gilmore & Black, supra, § 3–41, at 161. Some "deviations" are required. E.g., Hirsch Lumber Co. v. Weyerhaeuser Steamship Co., 2 Cir.,

If anything, the circumstances surrounding this contract indicate that the risk of the Canal's closure may be deemed to have been allocated to Transatlantic. We know or may safely assume that the parties were aware, as were most commercial men with interests affected by the Suez situation, see The Eugenia, supra, that the Canal might become a dangerous area. No doubt the tension affected freight rates, and it is arguable that the risk of closure became part of the dickered terms. Uniform Commercial Code § 2–615, comment 8. We do not deem the risk of closure so allocated, however. Foreseeability or even recognition of a risk does not necessarily prove its allocation. Compare Uniform Commercial Code § 2–615, Comment 1; Restatement, Contracts § 457 (1932). Parties to a contract are not always able to provide for all the possibilities of which they are aware, sometimes because they cannot agree, often simply because they are too busy. Moreover, that some abnormal risk was contemplated is probative but does not necessarily establish an allocation of the risk of the contingency which actually occurs. In this case, for example, nationalization by Egypt of the Canal Corporation and formation of the Suez Users Group did not necessarily indicate that the Canal would be blocked even if a confrontation resulted. The surrounding circumstances do indicate, however, a willingness by Transatlantic to assume abnormal risks, and this fact should legitimately cause us to judge the impracticability of performance by an alternative route in stricter terms than we would were the contingency unforeseen.

We turn then to the question whether occurrence of the contingency rendered performance commercially impracticable under the circumstances of this case. The goods shipped were not subject to harm from the longer, less temperate Southern route. The vessel and crew were fit to proceed around the Cape. Transatlantic was no less able than the United States to purchase insurance to cover the contingency's occurrence. If anything, it is more reasonable to expect owner-operators of vessels to insure against the hazards of war. They are in the best position to calculate the cost of performance by alternative routes (and therefore to estimate the amount of insurance required), and are undoubtedly sensitive to international troubles which uniquely affect the demand for and cost of their services. The only factor operating here in appellant's favor is the added expense, allegedly $43,972.00 above and beyond the contract price of $305,842.92, of extending a 10,000 mile voyage by approximately 3,000 miles. While it may be an overstatement to say that increased cost and difficulty of performance never constitute impracticability, to justify relief there must be more of a variation between expected cost and the cost of performing by an available alternative than is present in this case, where the promisor can legitimately be presumed to have accepted some

233 F.2d 791, cert. denied, 352 U.S. 880, 77 S.Ct. 102, 1 L.Ed.2d 80 (1956). The doctrine's only relevance, therefore, is that it provides additional support for the assumption we willingly make that merchants agreeing to a voyage between two points expect that the usual and customary route between those points will be used. The doctrine provides no evidence of an allocation of the risk of the route's unavailability.

degree of abnormal risk, and where impracticability is urged on the basis of added expense alone.[15]

We conclude, therefore, as have most other courts considering related issues arising out of the Suez closure,[16] that performance of this contract was not rendered legally impossible. Even if we agreed with appellant, its theory of relief seems untenable. When performance of a contract is deemed impossible it is a nullity. In the case of a charter party involving carriage of goods, the carrier may return to an appropriate port and unload its cargo, The Malcolm Baxter, Jr., 277 U.S. 323, 48 S.Ct. 516, 72 L.Ed. 901 (1928), subject of course to required steps to minimize damages. If the performance rendered has value, recovery in *quantum meruit* for the entire performance is proper. But here Transatlantic has collected its contract price, and now seeks *quantum meruit* relief for the additional expense of the trip around the Cape. If the contract is a nullity, Transatlantic's theory of relief should have been *quantum meruit* for the entire trip, rather than only for the extra expense. Transatlantic attempts to take its profit on the contract, and then force the Government to absorb the cost of the additional voyage. When impracticability without fault occurs, the law seeks an equitable solution, and *quantum meruit* is one of its potent devices to achieve this end. There is no interest in casting the entire burden of commercial disaster on one party in order to preserve the other's profit. Apparently the contract price in this case was advantageous enough to deter appellant from taking a stance on damages consistent with its theory of liability. In any event, there is no basis for relief.

Affirmed.

15. See Uniform Commercial Code § 2-615, comment 4: "Increased cost alone does not excuse performance unless the rise in cost is due to some unforeseen contingency which alters the essential nature of the performance." See also 6 Corbin, supra, § 1333; 6 Williston, supra, § 1952, at 5468.

16. Appellant seeks to distinguish the English cases supporting our view. The Eugenia, supra, appellant argues, involved a time charter. True, but it overruled The Massalia, supra Note 14, which involved a voyage charter. Indeed, when the time charter is for a voyage the difference is only verbal. See Carver, *Carriage of Goods by Sea* 256–257 (10th ed. 1957). More convincing is the argument that *Tsakiroglou & Co. Ltd.*, supra Note 4, involved a contract for the sale of goods, where the seller agreed to a C.I.F. clause requiring him to ship the goods to the buyer. There is a significant difference between a C.I.F. contract and voyage or time charters. The effect of delay in the former due to longer sea voyages is minimized, since the seller can raise money on the goods he has shipped almost at once, and the buyer, once he takes up the documents, can deal with the goods by transferring the documents before the goods arrive. See *Tsakiroglou & Co. Ltd.*, supra Note 4, [1960] 2 Q.B. at 361. But this difference is not so material that impossibility in C.I.F. contracts is unrelated to impossibility in charter parties. It would raise serious questions for a court to require sellers under C.I.F. contracts to perform in circumstances under which the sellers could be refused performance by carriers with whom they have entered into charter parties for affreightment. See The Eugenia, supra, [1964] 2 Q.B. at 241. Where the time of the voyage is unimportant, a charter party should be treated the same as a C.I.F. contract in determining impossibility of performance.

These cases certainly are not distinguishable, as appellant suggests, on the ground that they refer to "frustration" rather than to "impossibility." The English regard "frustration" as substantially identical with "impossibility." 6 Corbin, supra, § 1322, at 327 n. 9.

Case Brief

1.   Parties/their relationship/how matter reached this court: Transatlantic Financing Corporation, Plaintiff/Appellant/Charter Operator v. United States, Defendant/Appellee/Charterer. Appeal from dismissal of a libel action[a] by the United States District Court for the District of Columbia. 363 F.2d 312 (1966).

2.   Legal theories:

    Breach of contract, under:

    (1) Doctrine of deviation: The usual and customary route between points is implied into commercial contracts in which the termini of the voyage are named.

    (2) Doctrine of impossibility: A thing is legally impossible when it can be done only at an excessive and unreasonable cost.

    (3) Quantum meruit: When contract becomes a nullity, recovery "for the amount deserved" is the proper remedy.

3.   Facts: In July 1956, Egypt nationalized and took over the operation of the Suez Canal. In October 1956, a contract was executed between Transatlantic and the United States for a voyage from the United States to Iran. No route was stipulated in the contract, although the usual route for such a voyage was through the Suez Canal. When Egypt closed the Suez Canal to traffic in November 1956, Transatlantic delivered the cargo by travelling around the Cape of Good Hope.

4.   Relief requested: Additional compensation of $43,972.00 above the contract price, representing the added cost to the appellant over its expected cost of performing its contract by its usual route.

5.   Issues:

    (1) Does the doctrine of deviation imply as a term of this contract a voyage by the usual and customary route?

    (2) Under the doctrine of impossibility, did the closing of the Suez Canal render performance by the charter-operator legally impossible?

    (3) If so, did the charter-operator confer an in *quantum meruit* benefit upon the charterer by delivering the cargo by an alternate, more costly route?

6.   Holding and Disposition:

    (1) No. The doctrine of deviation does not imply as a term of this contract a voyage by the usual and customary route.

a. Libel: an initial pleading in a suit in admiralty, equivalent to a petition.

(2) No. The doctrine of impossibility does not apply if the charter-operator is able to deliver the cargo by an alternate, more costly route.

(3) No. In *quantum meruit* benefit does not apply when the charter-operator has collected its contract price, and seeks only additional compensation.

7. Reasoning:

1. The doctrine of deviation is inapplicable, for the Suez route was not a condition of the contract.

2. For a contract to be rendered legally impossible, three conditions must prevail:

   (1) a contingency must occur;

   (2) the risk of the contingency must have been allocated as a term of the contract by agreement or by custom;

   (3) the occurrence of the contingency must render performance commercially impracticable.

   Here, only the first requirement is met. Regarding (2), no express condition of performance via the Suez Canal is a term of this contract, nor is there a constructive condition of performance either in custom or trade usage or in the surrounding circumstances generally. Nor is condition (3) present, for the crew was not subject to harm from the longer route, the vessel and crew were fit to proceed around the Cape, and appellant could have purchased insurance as easily as appellee to protect against the unexpected occurrence.

8. Legal rule:

   For legal impracticability to be based upon added cost alone, there must be significant variation between the expected and the actual cost, with no presumption that appellant accepted and could have insured against contingency.

9. Dicta:

   (1) Even an expressed expectation that the route would be via the Suez Canal may not amount to a condition of performance. (U.C.C. § 2–614(1) cited in footnote.)

   (2) If anything, owner-operators of vessels can be more reasonably expected to insure against the hazards than those who hire their services since owner-operators are in the best position to calculate the cost of performance by alternate routes and to estimate the cost of the insurance required.

AMERICAN TRADING AND PRODUCTION CORP. v. SHELL INTERNATIONAL MARINE LTD.

United States Court of Appeals, Second Circuit, 1972.
453 F.2d 939.

MULLIGAN, CIRCUIT JUDGE:

This is an appeal by American Trading and Production Corporation (hereinafter "owner") from a judgment entered on July 29th, 1971, in the United States District Court for the Southern District of New York, dismissing its claim against Shell International Marine Ltd. (hereinafter "charterer") for additional compensation in the sum of $131,978.44 for the transportation of cargo from Texas to India via the Cape of Good Hope as a result of the closing of the Suez Canal in June, 1967. The charterer had asserted a counterclaim which was withdrawn and is not in issue. The action was tried on stipulated facts and without a jury before Hon. Harold R. Tyler, Jr. who dismissed the claim on the merits in an opinion dated July 22, 1971.

We affirm.

The owner is a Maryland corporation doing business in New York and the charterer is a United Kingdom corporation. On March 23, 1967 the parties entered into a contract of voyage charter in New York City which provided that the charterer would hire the owner's tank vessel, WASHINGTON TRADER, for a voyage with a full cargo of lube oil from Beaumont/Smiths Bluff, Texas to Bombay, India. The charter party provided that the freight rate would be in accordance with the then prevailing American Tanker Rate Schedule (ATRS), $14.25 per long ton of cargo, plus seventy-five percent (75%), and in addition there was a charge of $.85 per long ton for passage through the Suez Canal. On May 15, 1967 the WASHINGTON TRADER departed from Beaumont with a cargo of 16,183.32 long tons of lube oil. The charterer paid the freight at the invoiced sum of $417,327.36 on May 26, 1967. On May 29th, 1967 the owner advised the WASHINGTON TRADER by radio to take additional bunkers at Ceuta due to possible diversion because of the Suez Canal crisis. The vessel arrived at Ceuta, Spanish Morocco on May 30, bunkered and sailed on May 31st, 1967. On June 5th the owner cabled the ship's master advising him of various reports of trouble in the Canal and suggested delay in entering it pending clarification. On that very day, the Suez Canal was closed due to the state of war which had developed in the Middle East. The owner then communicated with the charterer on June 5th through the broker who had negotiated the charter party, requesting approval for the diversion of the WASHINGTON TRADER which then had proceeded to a point about 84 miles northwest of Port Said, the entrance to the Canal. On June 6th the charterer responded that under the circumstances it was "for owner to decide whether to continue to wait or make the alternative passage via the Cape since Charter Party Obliges them to deliver cargo without qualification." In response the owner replied on the same day that in view of the closing of the Suez, the WASHINGTON TRADER would proceed to

Bombay via the Cape of Good Hope and "[w]e [are] reserving all rights for extra compensation." The vessel proceeded westward, back through the Straits of Gibraltar and around the Cape and eventually arrived in Bombay on July 15th (some 30 days later than initially expected), traveling a total of 18,055 miles instead of the 9,709 miles which it would have sailed had the Canal been open. The owner billed $131,978.44 as extra compensation which the charterer has refused to pay.

On appeal and below the owner argues that transit of the Suez Canal was the agreed specific means of performance of the voyage charter and that the supervening destruction of this means rendered the contract legally impossible to perform and therefore discharged the owner's unperformed obligation (Restatement of Contracts § 460 (1932)). Consequently, when the WASHINGTON TRADER eventually delivered the oil after journeying around the Cape of Good Hope, a benefit was conferred upon the charterer for which it should respond in *quantum meruit.* The validity of this proposition depends upon a finding that the parties contemplated or agreed that the Suez passage was to be the exclusive method of performance, and indeed it was so argued on appeal. We cannot construe the agreement in such a fashion. The parties contracted for the shipment of the cargo from Texas to India at an agreed rate and the charter party makes absolutely no reference to any fixed route. It is urged that the Suez passage was a condition of performance because the ATRS rate was based on a Suez Canal passage, the invoice contained a specific Suez Canal toll charge and the vessel actually did proceed to a point 84 miles northwest of Port Said. In our view all that this establishes is that both parties contemplated that the Canal would be the probable route. It was the cheapest and shortest, and therefore it was in the interest of both that it be utilized. However, this is not at all equivalent to an agreement that it be the exclusive method of performance. The charter party does not so provide and it seems to have been well understood in the shipping industry that the Cape route is an acceptable alternative in voyages of this character.

The District of Columbia Circuit decided a closely analogous case, Transatlantic Financing Corp. v. United States, 124 U.S.App.D.C. 183, 363 F.2d 312 (1966). There the plaintiff had entered into a voyage charter with defendant in which it agreed to transport a full cargo of wheat on the CHRISTOS from a United States port to Iran. The parties clearly contemplated a Suez passage, but on November 2, 1956, the vessel reduced speed when war blocked the Suez Canal. The vessel changed its course in the Atlantic and eventually delivered its cargo in Iran after proceeding by way of the Cape of Good Hope. In an exhaustive opinion Judge Skelly Wright reviewed the English cases which had considered the same problem and concluded that "the Cape route is generally regarded as an alternative means of performance. So the implied expectation that the route would be via Suez is hardly adequate proof of an allocation to the promisee of the risk of closure. In some cases, even an express expectation may not amount to a condition of performance." Transatlantic Financing Corp. v. United States, supra, 363 F.2d at 317 (footnote omitted).

Appellant argues that *Transatlantic* is distinguishable since there was an agreed upon flat rate in that case unlike the instant case where the rate was based on Suez passage. This does not distinguish the case in our view. It is stipulated by the parties here that the only ATRS rate published at the time of the agreement from Beaumont to Bombay was the one utilized as a basis for the negotiated rate ultimately agreed upon. This rate was escalated by 75% to reflect whatever existing market conditions the parties contemplated. These conditions are not stipulated. Had a Cape route rate been requested, which was not the case, it is agreed that the point from which the parties would have bargained would be $17.35 per long ton of cargo as against $14.25 per long ton.

Actually, in *Transatlantic* it was argued that certain provisions in the P. & I. Bunker Deviation Clause referring to the direct and/or customary route required, by implication, a voyage through the Suez Canal. The court responded "[a]ctually they prove only what we are willing to accept—that the parties expected the usual and customary route would be used. The provisions in no way condition performance upon non-occurrence of this contingency." Transatlantic Financing Corp. v. United States, supra, 363 F.2d at 317 n. 8. We hold that all that the ATRS rate establishes is that the parties obviously expected a Suez passage but there is no indication at all in the instrument or *dehors* that it was a condition of performance.

This leaves us with the question as to whether the owner was excused from performance on the theory of commercial impracticability (Restatement of Contracts § 454 (1932)). Even though the owner is not excused because of strict impossibility, it is urged that American law recognizes that performance is rendered impossible if it can only be accomplished with extreme and unreasonable difficulty, expense, injury, or loss.[1] There is no extreme or unreasonable difficulty apparent here. The alternate route taken was well recognized, and there is no claim that the vessel or the crew or the nature of the cargo made the route actually taken unreasonably difficult, dangerous or onerous. The owner's case here essentially rests upon the element of the additional expense involved—$131,978.44. This represents an increase of less than one third over the agreed upon $417,327.36. We find that this increase in expense is not sufficient to constitute commercial impracticability under either American or English authority.

Mere increase in cost alone is not a sufficient excuse for non-performance (Restatement of Contracts § 467 (1932)). It must be an "extreme and unreasonable"[2] expense (Restatement of Contracts § 454 (1932)).[3] While in the *Transatlantic* case supra, the increased cost amounted to an increase of

---

1. This is the formula utilized in the Restatement of Contracts § 454 (1932).

2. The Restatement gives some examples of what is "extreme and unreasonable"—Restatement of Contracts § 460, Illus. 2 (tenfold increase in costs) and Illus. 3 (costs multiplied fifty times) (1932); compare § 467, Illus. 3. See generally G. Gris-

more, Principles of the Law of Contracts § 179 (rev. ed. J.E. Murray 1965).

3. Both parties take solace in the Uniform Commercial Code which in comment 4 to Section 2–615 states that the rise in cost must "alter the essential nature of the performance. . . ." This is clearly not the case here. The owner relies on a further

about 14% over the contract price, the court did cite with approval [4] the two leading English cases Ocean Tramp Tankers Corp. v. V/O Sovfracht (The Eugenia), [1964] 2 Q.B. 226, 233 (C.A.1963) (which expressly overruled Société Franco Tunisienne D'Armement v. Sidermar S.P.A. (The Messalia), [1961] 2 Q.B. 278 (1960), where the court had found frustration because the Cape route was highly circuitous and involved an increase in cost of approximately 50%), and Tsakiroglou & Co. Lt. v. Noblee Thorl G.m.b.H., [1960] 2 Q.B. 318, 348, aff'd, [1962] A.C., 93 (1961) where the House of Lords found no frustration though the freight costs were exactly doubled due to the Canal closure.[5]

Appellant further seeks to distinguish *Transatlantic* because in that case the change in course was in the mid-Atlantic and added some 300 miles to the voyage while in this case the WASHINGTON TRADER had traversed most of the Mediterranean and thus had added some 9000 miles to the contemplated voyage. It should be noted that although both the time and the length of the altered passage here exceeded those in the *Transatlantic,* the additional compensation sought here is just under one third of the contract price. Aside from this however, it is a fact that the master of the WASHINGTON TRADER was alerted by radio on May 29th, 1967 of a "possible diversion because of Suez Canal crisis," but nevertheless two days later he had left Ceuta (opposite Gibraltar) and proceeded across the Mediterranean. While we may not speculate about the foreseeability of a Suez crisis at the time the contract was entered, there does not seem to be any question but that the master here had been actually put on notice before traversing the Mediterranean that diversion was possible. Had the WASHINGTON TRADER then changed course, the time and cost of the Mediterranean trip could reasonably have been avoided, thereby reducing the amount now claimed. (Restatement of Contracts § 336, Comment *d* to subsection (1) (1932)).

In a case closely in point, Palmco Shipping Inc. v. Continental Ore Corp. *(The "Captain George K"),* [1970] 2 Lloyd's L.Rep. 21 (Q.B.1969), *The Eugenia,* supra, was followed, and no frustration was found where the vessel had sailed to a point three miles northwest of Port Said only to find the Canal

sentence in the comment which refers to a severe shortage of raw materials or of supplies due to "war, embargo, local crop failure, unforeseen shutdown of major sources of supply or the like, which either causes a marked increase in cost. . . ." Since this is not a case involving the sale of goods but transportation of a cargo where there was an alternative which was a commercially reasonable substitute (see Uniform Commercial Code § 2–614(1)) the owner's reliance is misplaced.

4. Transatlantic Financing Corp. v. United States, supra, 363 F.2d at 319 n. 14.

5. While these are English cases and refer to the doctrine of "frustration" rather than "impossibility" as Judge Skelly Wright

pointed out in *Transatlantic,* supra, 363 F.2d at 320 n. 16 the two are considered substantially identical, 6 A. Corbin, Contracts § 1322, at 327 n. 9 (rev. ed. 1962). While *Tsakiroglou* and *The Eugenia* are criticized in Schegal, Of Nuts, and Ships and Sealing Wax, Suez, and Frustrating Things—The Doctrine of Impossibility of Performance, 23 Rutgers L.Rev. 419, 448 (1969), apparently on the theory that the charterer is a better loss bearer, the overruled *Sidermar* case was previously condemned in Berman, Excuse for Nonperformance in the Light of Contract Practices in International Trade, 63 Colum.L.Rev. 1413, 1424–27 (1963).

blocked. The vessel then sailed back through the Mediterranean and around the Cape of Good Hope to its point of destination, Kandla. The distances involved, 9700 miles via the initially contemplated Canal route and 18,400 miles actually covered by way of the Cape of Good Hope, coincide almost exactly with those in this case. Moreover, in *The "Captain George K"* there was no indication that the master had at anytime after entering the Mediterranean been advised of the possibility of the Canal's closure.

Finally, owners urge that the language of the "Liberties Clause," Para. 28(a) of Part II of the charter party[6] provides explicit authority for extra compensation in the circumstances of this case. We do not so interpret the clause. We construe it to apply only where the master, by reason of dangerous conditions, deposits the cargo at some port or haven other than the designated place of discharge. Here the cargo did reach the designated port albeit by another route, and hence the clause is not applicable. No intermediate or other disposition of the oil was appropriate under the circumstances.

Appellant relies on C.H. Leavell & Co. v. Hellenic Lines, Ltd., 13 F.M.C., 76, 1969 A.M.C. 2177 (1969) for a contrary conclusion. That case involved a determination as to whether surcharges to compensate for extra expenses incurred when the Suez Canal was closed after the commencement of a voyage, were available to a carrier. The Federal Maritime Commission authorized the assessment since the applicable tariffs were on file as provided by section 18(b) of the Shipping Act (46 U.S.C. § 817(b)) and also on the basis of Clause 5 of the bill of lading which is comparable to the Liberties

---

6. "28. Liberty Clauses. (a) In any situation whatsoever and wheresoever occurring and whether existing or anticipated before commencement of or during the voyage, which in the judgment of the Owner or Master is likely to give rise to risk of capture, seizure, detention, damage, delay or disadvantage to or loss of the Vessel or any part of her cargo, or to make it unsafe, imprudent, or unlawful for any reason to commence or proceed on or continue the voyage or to enter or discharge the cargo at the port of discharge, or to give rise to delay or difficulty in arriving, discharging at or leaving the port of discharge or the usual place of discharge in such port, the Owner may before loading or before the commencement of the voyage, require the shipper or other person entitled thereto to take delivery of the Cargo at port of shipment and upon their failure to do so, may warehouse the cargo at the risk and expense of the cargo; or the owner or Master, whether or not proceeding toward or entering or attempting to enter the port of discharge or reaching or attempting to reach the usual place of discharge therein or attempting to discharge the cargo there, may discharge the cargo into depot, lazaretto, craft or other place; or the Vessel may proceed or return, directly or indirectly, to or stop at any such port or place whatsoever as the Master or the Owner may consider safe or advisable under the circumstances, and discharge the cargo, or any part thereof, at any such port or place; or the Owner or the Master may retain the cargo on board until the return trip or until such time as the Owner or the Master thinks advisable and discharge the cargo at any place whatsoever as herein provided or the Owner or the Master may discharge and forward the cargo by any means at the risk and expense of the cargo. The Owner may, when practicable, have the Vessel call and discharge the cargo at another or substitute port declared or requested by the Charterer. The Owner or the Master is not required to give notice of discharge of the cargo, or the forwarding thereof as herein provided. When the cargo is discharged from the Vessel, as herein provided, it shall be at its own risk and expense; such discharge shall constitute complete delivery and performance under this contract and the Owner shall be freed from any further responsibility. For any service rendered to the cargo as herein provided the Owner shall be entitled to a reasonable extra compensation."

Clause in issue here, except for the language which authorized the carrier to "proceed by any route. . . ." (*Leavell,* supra, 13 F.M.C. at 81, 1969 A.M.C. at 2182). This is the very language relied upon by the Commission in finding the surcharge appropriate (*Leavell,* supra, 13 F.M.C. at 89, 1969 A.M.C. at 2191) where the carrier proceeded to the initially designated port of destination via the Cape of Good Hope. Utilization of an alternate route contemplates berthing at the contracted port of destination. There is no such language in the clause at issue. Its absence fortifies the contention that the Liberties Clause was not intended to be applicable to the facts in litigation here.

Matters involving impossibility or impracticability of performance of contract are concededly vexing and difficult. One is even urged on the allocation of such risks to pray for the "wisdom of Solomon." 6 A. Corbin, Contracts § 1333, at 372 (1962). On the basis of all of the facts, the pertinent authority and a further belief in the efficacy of prayer, we affirm.

Case Brief

1. Parties/their relationship/how matter reached this court: American Trading and Production Corporation, Plaintiff/Appellant/Owner v. Shell International Marine LTD., Defendant/Appellee/Charterer. Appeal from a judgment of U.S. District Court for the Southern District of New York, which had dismissed the claim. 453 F.2d 939 (1972).

2. Legal theories:

   Breach of Contract:

   (1) In *quantum meruit* liability for benefit conferred upon charterer by owner's performance by other than agreed-upon methods, since contract was legally impossible to perform.

   (2) Commercial impracticability excused owner from performance because delivery had to be performed by a more expensive alternate route.

   (3) "Liberties Clause" of the contract provides explicit compensation for owner's extra costs due to his longer voyage.

3. Facts: Owner entered into a contract of a voyage charter with Charterer to hire Owner's tank vessel to deliver oil from Texas to India, the freight rate to be in accordance with the prevailing rate schedule, with an additional charge per ton for passage through the Suez Canal. Closing of Suez Canal resulted in decision to travel to India via the Cape of Good Hope, resulting in a voyage of 18,095 miles instead of 9,709 miles. Owner billed $131,978.44 in extra costs.

4. Relief requested: Owner seeks $131,978.44 in extra compensation from Charterer, for additional transportation costs due to Suez Canal closing.

5. Issues:

> (1) Was contract legally impossible to perform, subsequent delivery by owner thus conferring upon charterer a benefit for which it should respond in *quantum meruit?*
>
> (2) Was owner excused from performance on the theory of commercial impracticability?
>
> (3) Did the Liberties clause of the charter party provide explicit compensation for the owner's additional costs?

6. Holdings:

> (1) No. No in *quantum benefit* is due since owner's contract was not legally impossible to perform.
>
> (2) No. Owner was not excused from performance due to commercial impracticability.
>
> (3) No. The Liberties' Clause of the contract does not apply where cargo reaches the designated port.

Disposition of case: Lower court dismissal affirmed.

7. Reasoning:

> (1) In order for benefit in *quantum meruit* to be obtained, the parties to the contract must have contemplated or agreed that the Suez passage was to be the exclusive method of performance. No such agreement was a part of the contract here. The Cape route is well understood in the shipping industry to be an acceptable alternative route. (Citation to Transatlantic Financing Corporation, as "closely analogous.")
>
> (2) The theory of commercial impracticability is premised upon only extreme or unreasonable difficulty, expense, injury or loss resulting from performance. No such circumstances present here, only an increased cost to owner of less than one-third of the contracted price for performance of the contract, an amount insufficient to constitute commercial impracticability.
>
> (3) The Liberties Clause applies only where the master, because of dangerous conditions, deposits the cargo at a port other than the one designated. Here the cargo did reach the designated port, although by another route. Hence, the clause is inapplicable here.

8. Legal rules:

> (1) For in *quantum meruit* liability to lie, parties must have agreed in contract that the specific method of performance be one which subsequently became legally impossible to perform.
>
> (2) For commercial impracticability to apply, cost of performance must be extremely and unreasonably in excess of that contemplated, or there must be unreasonable difficulty or injury caused by performance. Increased cost of one-third above the contract-

　　ed price is not sufficient to constitute commercial impracticability.

9.　Dicta: None

NORTHERN CORPORATION v. CHUGACH ELECTRIC ASSOCIATION

Supreme Court of Alaska, 1974.
518 P.2d 76.

BOOCHEVER, JUSTICE.

We are here presented with issues concerning the alleged impossibility of performing a public contract. Northern Corporation (hereafter referred to as Northern), appellant and cross-appellee, entered into a contract with Chugach Electric Association (hereafter Chugach), appellee and cross-appellant, on August 3, 1966 for the repair and protection of the upstream face of the Cooper Lake Dam. The contract was awarded to Northern on the basis of its low bid in the sum of $63,655.

The work to be performed was described as follows:

It is required that the upstream face of Cooper Lake Dam be regraded and riprap and filter layer stone quarried, hauled and placed on the upstream face and all other appurtenant work accomplished as required, all in accordance with these plans and specification [sic]. There are about 1750 cubic yards of filter material and 3950 cubic yards of riprap to be placed. The Contractor shall furnish all labor, equipment, materials, etc. required for this project.

The contract called for completion of the work within 60 days of notice to proceed, which was given on August 29, 1966.

The major expense in performing the contract was to be the procurement and placing of riprap. The bidders on the contract were advised with respect to quarry areas from which rock could be obtained:

A quarry area, with suitable rock outcropping on the stream bank, has been located approximately 2500 feet downstream from the dam. A haul road will have to be constructed, either down the stream bed or along the left bank. The quarry area is shown on the vicinity map.

．．．

The Contractor may, at his option, select a quarry different from the site shown on the drawings. In this event, the Contractor shall pay the costs of all tests required to verify the suitability of the rock for this project.

Northern first discovered boulders in the stream bed which would be more economical than the designated quarry and received permission to use this source. According to Northern, approximately 20 percent of the contract requirements were fulfilled before Northern exhausted the supply located in the stream bed. Then in the first week of September, Northern moved to the designated quarry site and commenced shooting rock. On September 19, 1966, Northern wrote to Chugach informing them that the rock in the designated quarry was unusable, but was directed in a letter the following day from Chugach's engineering firm to proceed with further blasting and exploration of the designated areas. By September 27, however, Chugach conceded that suitable rock was not available at the designated site and reformed the agreement accordingly.

Alternate quarry sites were found at the opposite end of the lake from the dam. As a result of negotiations, Chugach wrote to Northern on September 27, 1966 authorizing completion of the contract by use of these alternate quarry sites. The authorization provided for amendments to reflect the circumstance that suitable rock was not available in the stream bed for mining, nor in the quarry which had been designated in the original contract documents. Paragraph 3 of the letter of authorization specified:

> Rock will be quarried in suitable sizes and quantities to complete the project and will be stockpiled in or near the quarry, or quarries, mentioned above for transport across Cooper Lake to the dam site when such lake is frozen to a sufficient depth to permit heavy vehicle traffic thereon.

The contract price was increased by $42,000. Subsequently, the contract was formally amended in accordance with the September 27, 1966 authorization. Work commenced in the new quarry in October 1966; and within about 30 days, all of the required rock was drilled and shot.

Although there is some question as to who first suggested it or how it came about, it was the agreement of the parties that the rock from the new quarry site would be transported in winter across the ice of Cooper Lake. In December 1966, Northern cleared a road on the ice to permit deeper freezing of the ice. By the time the ice was thought to be sufficiently thick to begin hauling, however, a water overflow on the ice one to two feet in depth prohibited crossings by the trucks. Northern complained to Chugach of unsafe conditions on the lake ice, but Chugach insisted on performance. In March 1967, one of Northern's Euclid loaders went through the ice and sank, and a small crawler tractor subsequently broke through but was recovered. Neither incident involved loss of life. Despite these occurrences, Chugach and its engineering firm continued to insist on performance, threatening default. On March 27, 1967, Chugach again threatened to consider Northern in default unless they immediately commenced hauling operations. Northern attempted to commence operations but continued to meet with difficulties, finally ceasing operations on March 31, 1967, apparently with the approval of Chugach.

On January 8, 1968, Chugach advised Northern that it would consider Northern in default unless all rock was hauled by April 1, 1968. On January 20, Northern informed Chugach that they were returning to Cooper Lake, and wrote on January 30 that they anticipated favorable conditions to start hauling rock on January 31. The ice conditions were apparently different from those encountered in 1967—there was very little snow cover and no overflow problem. The ice varied from 23½ inches to 30 inches thick, and for several days the temperature had been 30 degrees below zero and clear.

On February 1, 1968, Northern started hauling with half-loaded trucks; but within the first few hours, two trucks with their drivers broke through the ice, resulting in the death of the drivers and loss of the trucks. Northern at this point ceased operations; and on February 16, 1968, informed Chugach that it would make no more attempts to haul rock across the lake. On March 28, 1968, Northern advised Chugach that it considered the contract terminated for impossibility of performance.

Northern commenced legal action against Chugach in September 1968, seeking recovery for costs incurred in attempted completion of the contract less revenues received. The case was tried in superior court without a jury in December 1971. Northern contended that in the original contract there were express and implied warranties that the designated quarry contained sufficient quantities of suitable rock for the job, and that breach of the warranties entitled Northern to damages. In the alternative, Northern argued that the modified contract was impossible of performance, justifying an award to Northern of reasonable costs incurred in attempted performance. Chugach counterclaimed, contending that it overpaid Northern for work performed under the contract, and that it was entitled to liquidated damages for the period between the date of completion specified in the amended contract and the date of its termination by Northern. The superior court discharged the parties from the contract on the ground of impossibility of performance, but denied both parties' claims for damages and attorney's fees. From that decision, Northern appeals and Chugach cross-appeals.

The issues on this appeal may be summarized as follows:

1. Is Northern entitled to damages for breach of alleged express and implied warranties contained in the original contract pertaining to available quantities of rock?

2. In the alternative, was the contract as modified impossible of performance?

3. If the modified contract was impossible of performance, is Northern entitled to reasonable costs incurred in endeavoring to perform it?

4. Is Chugach entitled to liquidated damages for delays in performance of the contract, and to costs and attorney's fees? [1]

Our analysis of the events preceding the lawsuit leads us to the conclusion that the dispositive issues pertain to the question of impossibility of performance. It appears clear to us that the original agreement between Chugach and Northern was superseded as a result of Chugach's letter to Northern, dated September 27, 1966, and the subsequent formal amendment of the contract in accordance therewith. The amendment recognized that the quarries originally specified did not provide a sufficient quantity of riprap. The original contract price of $63,655 was increased by $42,000 to cover the additional costs incurred and to be incurred by Northern in exploration of the quarry originally

1. Chugach's contention that it overpaid Northern has apparently been abandoned on appeal.

designated, in securing rock at the redesignated quarries, in hauling the rock to the dam site, in stockpiling it, and in cleaning up the redesignated quarry areas. The amendment was executed by both parties to the contract. Since the amendment provided for the additional costs incurred by Northern as a result of the absence of a suitable rock supply at the quarry originally designated, we need not concern ourselves with whether express or implied warranties were breached with reference to the quantity of rock available at the originally designated quarry.[2] There is no contention here that the amended contract did not designate quarries containing suitable quantities of rock.

IMPOSSIBILITY

The focal question is whether the amended contract was impossible of performance. The September 27, 1966 directive specified that the rock was to be transported "across Cooper Lake to the dam site when such lake is frozen to a sufficient depth to permit heavy vehicle traffic thereon," and the formal amendment specified that the hauling to the dam site would be done during the winter of 1966–67. It is therefore clear that the parties contemplated that the rock would be transported across the frozen lake by truck. Northern's repeated efforts to perform the contract by this method during the winter of 1966–67 and subsequently in February 1968, culminating in the tragic loss of life, abundantly support the trial court's finding that the contract was impossible of performance by this method.

Chugach contends, however, that Northern was nevertheless bound to perform, and that it could have used means other than hauling by truck across the ice to transport the rock. The answer to Chugach's contention is that, as the trial court found, the parties contemplated that the rock would be hauled by truck once the ice froze to a sufficient depth to support the weight of the vehicles. The specification of this particular method of performance presupposed the existence of ice frozen to the requisite depth. Since this expectation of the parties was never fulfilled, and since the provisions relating to the means of performance was clearly material,[3] Northern's duty to perform was discharged by reason of impossibility.[4]

---

2. See Cooperative Refinery Ass'n v. Consumers Public Power Dist., 190 F.2d 852, 856–857 (8th Cir.1951); Johnson v. Mosley, 179 F.2d 573, 588 (8th Cir.1950); In re Swindle, 188 F.Supp. 601, 604 (D.Or. 1960).

3. The initial contract price was $63,655. Performing by the alternative method (barging) would have cost an additional $59,520.

4. Restatement of Contracts § 460 (1932) provides in pertinent part:

Where the existence of a specific thing . . . is, either by the terms of a bargain or in the contemplation of both parties, necessary for the performance of a prom-

ise in the bargain, a duty to perform the promise . . . is discharged if the thing . . . subsequently is not in existence in time for seasonable performance. . . .

In accord with this rule is Texas Co. v. Hogarth Shipping Co., 256 U.S. 619, 629–630, 41 S.Ct. 612, 65 L.Ed. 1123, 1130 (1921); Parrish v. Stratton Cripple Creek Min. & Development Co., 116 F.2d 207 (10th Cir. 1940), cert. denied, 312 U.S. 698, 61 S.Ct. 738, 85 L.Ed. 1132 (1941); see especially Kansas, Oklahoma & Gulf Railway Co. v. Grand Lake Grain Co., 434 P.2d 153 (Okl. 1967).

Discharge of a party for impossibility of performance abates the severity of the old

There is an additional reason for our holding that Northern's duty to perform was discharged because of impossibility. It is true that in order for a defendant to prevail under the original common law doctrine of impossibility, he had to show that no one else could have performed the contract.[5] However, this harsh rule has gradually been eroded, and the Restatement of Contracts [6] has departed from the early common law rule by recognizing the principle of "commercial impracticability". Under this doctrine, a party is discharged from his contract obligations, even if it is technically possible to perform them, if the costs of performance would be so disproportionate to that reasonably contemplated by the parties as to make the contract totally impractical in a commercial sense.[7] This principle was explicated in Natus Corp. v. United States,[8] where the Court of Claims, although holding that the defense was not justified on the facts of that case, went on to explain:

> In taking this position, we readily concede that the doctrine of legal impossibility does not demand a showing of actual or literal impossibility. Removed from the strictures of the common law, "impossibility" in its modern context has become a coat of many colors, including among its hues the point argued here—namely, impossibility predicated upon "commercial impracticability." This concept—which finds expression both in case law . . . and in other authorities . . . is grounded upon the assumption that in legal contemplation something is impracticable when it can only be done at an excessive and unreasonable cost. As stated in Transatlantic Financing Corp. v. United States . . .:
>
> > . . . The doctrine ultimately represents the ever-shifting line, drawn by courts hopefully responsive to commercial practices and mores, at which the community's interest in having contracts enforced according to their terms is outweighed by the commercial senselessness of requiring performance . . . [citations omitted].[9]

Sec. 465 of the Restatement also provides that a serious risk to life or health will excuse nonperformance.[10]

common law doctrine that not even objective impossibility excused performance; see Annot., 84 A.L.R.2d 12, 22 (1962).

5. See generally 84 A.L.R.2d at 35–36.

6. Restatement of Contracts § 454 (1932) states:

Definition of Impossibility.

In the Restatement of this Subject impossibility means not only strict impossibility but impracticability because of extreme and unreasonable difficulty, expense, injury or loss involved.

7. For example, one California case applied this result where it was about ten times as expensive to perform as was contemplated by the parties. Mineral Park Land Co. v. Howard, 172 Cal. 289, 156 P. 458 (1916).

8. 371 F.2d 450, 178 Ct.Cl. 1 (1967).

9. Id. at 456. See also Transatlantic Financing Corp. v. United States, 124 U.S. App.D.C. 183, 363 F.2d 312 (1966).

10. Restatement of Contracts § 465 states:

When Apprehension of Impossibility Excuses Beginning or Continuing Performance.

(1) Where a promisor apprehends before or during the time for performance of a promise in a bargain that there will be such impossibility of performance as would discharge or suspend a duty under the promise or that performance will seriously jeopardize his own life or health or that of others, he is not liable, unless a contrary intention is manifested or he is

Alaska has adopted the Restatement doctrine whereby commercial impracticability may under certain circumstances justify regarding a contract as impossible to perform. In Merl F. Thomas Sons, Inc. v. State,[11] this court was confronted with an appeal from a grant of summary judgment against a contractor who alleged in defense of nonperformance that the contemplated means of performing a clearing contract was to move equipment across the ice on the Susitna River from Talkeetna to the job site. Due to thin ice, this means of performance was impossible. Despite the state's contention that the equipment could be transported across the ice at Hurricane, some 70 miles to the north, we reversed the grant of summary judgment, holding that the contractor's allegation that all parties contemplated that equipment would be moved across the ice at Talkeetna raised a question of fact material to the defense of impossibility of performance. We quoted with approval Professor Williston's analysis of the concept of impossibility:

> The true distinction is not between difficulty and impossibility. As has been seen, a man may contract to do what is impossible, as well as what is difficult. The important question is whether an unanticipated circumstance, the risk of which should not fairly be thrown upon the promisor, has made performance of the promise vitally different from what was reasonably to be expected (footnote omitted).[12]

In the case before us the detailed opinion of the trial court clearly indicates that the appropriate standard was followed. There is ample evidence to support its findings that "[t]he ice haul method of transporting riprap ultimately selected was within the contemplation of the parties and was part of the basis of the agreement which ultimately resulted in amendment No. 1 in October 1966," and that that method was not commercially feasible within the financial parameters of the contract. We affirm the court's conclusion that the contract was impossible of performance.[13]

guilty of contributing fault, for failing to begin or to continue performance, while such apprehension exists, if the failure to begin or to continue performance is reasonable.

(2) In determining whether a promisor's failure to begin or to continue performance is reasonable under the rule stated in Subsection (1), consideration is given to

(a) the degree of probability, apparent from what he knows or has reason to know, not only of such impossibility but of physical or pecuniary harm or loss to himself or to others if he begins or continues performance, and

(b) the extent of physical or pecuniary harm or loss to himself or to others likely to be incurred by attempting performance as compared with the amount of harmful consequences likely to be caused to the promisee by non-performance.

11. 396 P.2d 76 (Alaska 1964).

12. Id. at 79, quoting from 6 Williston, Contracts § 1963 at 5511 (rev. ed. 1938).

13. Affirmance of this holding disposes of Chugach's contention that it was entitled to liquidated damages for delay. Only if the contract were held to be possible to perform could a right to damages for delay arise, for otherwise the legal duty to perform would be discharged.

DAMAGES

The court below found that the decision to utilize the alternate riprap source and the ice haul method of transporting it "was the joint decision of the parties reached in arm's length bargaining and was mutually agreed." Because adequate evidence supports that finding, the cases appellant cites permitting a contractor to recover under an implied warranty of specifications theory are not applicable. Since Chugach did not unilaterally specify the ice haul method, it no more warranted that method than did Northern.

Commencing in February 1967, Northern both orally and by letter began to question the feasibility of the ice haul method. On March 16, it advised of the loss of its Euclid loader, and suggested that an alternate method of hauling the rock be considered and the contract modified. Northern requested authority to demobilize its equipment so as to reduce continuing rental costs. On March 21, 1967, Northern asked to be released from responsibility for loss of life or equipment if an attempt was to be made to haul rock across the lake. On March 22, 1967, it stated:

> We cannot morally require any employee of ours or of our subcontractor's [sic] to operate equipment on the ice any longer this spring. We feel extremely fortunate that we did not lose a life when we lost the L–30 Loader. . . . We are ready to negotiate an alternate method of hauling the rock. . . .

Subsequently, an additional letter was sent, emphasizing in detail the impossibility of hauling rock across the ice.

Despite Northern's verbal and written protestations, Chugach implacably insisted on performance of the contract as agreed upon. Repeated demands by Chugach culminated in a January 1968 letter threatening to declare Northern in default, and to take such further steps against its surety as might be necessary, unless all rock was hauled by April 1. As a result, the final and ultimately fatal, effort was undertaken in February.

It is Northern's contention that if it is not entitled to recover under an implied warranty theory, it should be awarded compensation under the so-called "changes" clause of the contract. Under that clause, Chugach reserved the right to make changes in the contract plans and specifications; but if the cost of the project to Northern was increased as a result of the modification, the contract price would be increased by an amount equal to the reasonable cost thereof.[14]

14. Art. I, sec. 2, of the Chugach–Northern contract specifies:

Changes in Construction. The Owner, acting through the Engineer and with the approval of the Administrator, may from time to time during the progress of the construction of the Project, make such changes, additions to or subtractions from the Plans and Specifications which are part of the Proposal as conditions may warrant; provided, however, that if substantial change in the construction to be done shall require an extension of time, a reasonable extension will be granted if the Bidder shall make a written request therefor to the Owner within ten days after any such change is made. If the cost of the Project to the Bidder to

Under comparable clauses in government contracts, contractors have been awarded their additional costs in endeavoring to meet faulty specifications that were impossible to comply with, even when such costs were incurred prior to a negotiated modification. For example, in Hol–Gar Mfg. Corp. v. United States [15] the Government solicited proposals for the manufacture and delivery of electric generator sets in accordance with an elaborate set of specifications drafted by the Air Force Air Research and Development Command. On the basis of Hol–Gar's proposal, a fixed-price contract was negotiated. Upon testing, pre-production samples were found not to comply with the Government specifications. At subsequent meetings, Hol–Gar's representative stated that they did not believe that the engine which they had selected could meet the Government's performance requirements, and that the specifications should be changed to permit a substituted engine. The contract was then amended, relaxing the size and weight limitations in the existing specifications. Hol–Gar submitted a claim for costs incurred in trying to perform within the requirements of the original specifications. It had initially been agreed that if, as a result of testing, changes in the specifications were required, such changes were to be processed in accordance with the "changes" clause of the contract (which was very similar to the "changes" clause of the Chugach contract). The court held:

> Since the necessity for the change was not due to plaintiff's fault, but to faulty specifications, an equitable adjustment requires that plaintiff be paid the increase in its costs over what they would have been had no change been required.

The Armed Services Board of Contract Appeals has recognized the correctness of the allowance of costs incident to an attempt to comply with defective specifications. See, e.g., J.W. Hurst & Son Awnings, Inc., 59–1 BCA ¶ 2095 at 8965 (1959), where the Board stated:

> . . . Where, as here, the change is necessitated by defective specifications and drawings, the equitable adjustment to which a contractor is entitled must, if it is to be equitable, i.e., fair and just, include the costs which it incurred in attempting to perform in accordance with the defective specifications and drawings. Under these circum-

make the change shall be increased or decreased, the contract price shall be amended by an amount equal to the reasonable cost thereof in accordance with a construction contract amendment signed by the Owner and the Bidder and approved by the Administrator, but no claim for additional compensation for any such change or addition will be considered unless the Bidder shall have made a written request therefor to the Owner prior to the commencement of work in connection with such change or addition. The reasonable cost of any increase or decrease in the contract price covered by contract amendment as outlined above, in the ab-

sence of other mutual agreement, shall be computed on the basis of the direct cost of materials, f.o.b. the site of the Project, plus the direct cost of labor necessary to incorporate such materials into the Project (including actual cost of payroll taxes and insurance, not to exceed ten percent of payroll cost of labor), plus fifteen percent of the direct cost of materials and labor. Labor cost shall be limited to the direct costs for workmen and foremen. Costs for Bidder's main office overhead, job office overhead and superintendence shall not be included.

15. 360 F.2d 634, 175 Ct.Cl. 518 (1966).

stances the equitable adjustment may not be limited to costs incurred subsequent to the issuance of the change orders [citations omitted].[16]
In Maxwell Dynamometer Co. v. United States,[17] the Court of Claims relying on *Hol–Gar,* also found that the plaintiff was entitled to recover increased costs and expenses which were incurred in attempting to comply with a specification requirement that was impossible to meet.[18]

Closely analogous to the Chugach situation is the decision of the Armed Services Board of Contract Appeals in *Landsverk Electrometer Co.*[19] A manufacturer of dosimeters entered into a contract, thinking that an electrical leakage requirement could be met; but recognizing that it would be necessary for him to "stretch the state of the art" to comply. When, after vain attempts, the contractor advised the Government that it could not meet the specification, the Government relaxed the specification. Although it was held that the contractor was not entitled to extra compensation for the work performed in attempting to meet the specifications before notification to the Government, because the parties had contemplated the necessity of substantial research efforts to meet the required specifications and the contractor had not expended substantially more effort to that end than it was reasonable to anticipate, the Board went on to state:

> There was here no insistence by the Government that the contractor perform, or continue to try to perform, in the face of the contractor's protests that performance was impossible and it should be relieved of its obligation to meet that portion of the specification. On the contrary, within two hours of the appellant's telling the Government that it had become convinced that it simply was unable to perform to the upgraded specification, the Government relaxed the specification and permitted performance at the old, lower level. Had the Government, after it had, or should have, become aware that performance could not be achieved, continued to direct further efforts by a contractor, that direction would certainly constitute a compensable change in the contract, the understanding of the parties [sic].[20]

Unlike the Government in the *Landsverk* case, Chugach continued to demand performance, and we hold that its insistence after it was, or should have been, aware that performance could not be accomplished by the ice haul method constituted, in effect, a compensable change in the contract. Notions of equity and fairness compel this result. If liability for increased costs under the "changes" clause of Government contracts has been predicated on the defectiveness of Government specifications, of which the Government has no actual knowledge, then surely one must hold Chugach liable here, for it had

---

16. Id. at 638. The court additionally based its decision on a finding of breach of implied warranty of the specifications. Judge Davis in concurring, however, evaluated the record as indicating that neither party warranted the specifications, a situation analogous to that of Chugach and Northern.

17. 386 F.2d 855, 181 Ct.Cl. 607 (1967).

18. See also Bell v. United States, 404 F.2d 975, 186 Ct.Cl. 189 (1968); Jack Heller, Inc., 72–1 BCA ¶ 9341 (ASBCA 1972).

19. 67–2 BCA ¶ 6649 (ASBCA 1967).

20. Id. at p. 30,823.

been informed not once but repeatedly that the contract was impossible of performance by the ice haul method.

If Chugach, on being advised of the unfeasibility of the ice haul method, and of its hazards to life and property, had issued a change order prior to the fatal accident of February 1968 but at some time after it knew or should have known that performance was impossible, Northern would have been entitled to the extra costs incurred by it in seeking to perform by the impossible method after Chugach had, or should have, become aware of this impossibility. In fact, Chugach apparently recognized this principle of law, for it had agreed earlier to pay Northern an additional sum for its abortive efforts to obtain rock from the initially-designated quarry. Once alerted to the impossibility of performance by the agreed-upon ice haul method, Chugach's adamant insistence on such performance and its refusal to issue a change order should not be permitted to bar Northern's claim under the "changes" clause. It would indeed be anomalous to hold Chugach liable for such extra costs previously incurred if it belatedly provided for a change order after ascertaining the impossibility of utilizing an ice road, while absolving it from such liability when it continued to insist on an impossible and highly hazardous performance. Despite the fact that no change order was actually issued by Chugach, we hold that it should be held liable for Northern's increased costs incurred after such time as Chugach was reasonably placed on notice that it was not feasible to perform the contract by means of the ice haul method. At that time, it should either have agreed to a termination of the contract or issued a change order providing for some other method of hauling the rock. Those costs incurred by Northern thereafter in its vain attempts to perform the impossible in accordance with Chugach's demands should have been recompensed.

The case is remanded for further proceedings in accordance with this opinion. Upon remand, the court should determine when Chugach knew or should have known of the impossibility of performance by the ice haul method; and if that date is ascertained to be prior to the actual termination of the contract, Northern should be awarded its costs incurred thereafter, the amount to be determined in accordance with the "changes" clause of the contract.[21]

Affirmed in part, reversed in part and remanded.

ERWIN and FITZGERALD, JJ., not participating.

Case Brief

1. Parties/their relationship/how matter reached this court: Northern Corporation, Appellant/Contractor v. Chugach Electric Association, Appellee/Owner. The Superior Court, Third Judicial District, Anchorage, discharged parties from contract on ground of impossibil-

21. Our decision makes it unnecessary to consider Chugach's contention on its cross-appeal that because it was the prevailing party, it was entitled to costs and attorney's fees.

ity of performance, but denied both parties' claims for damages and attorney's fees.   Contractor appeals and owner cross-appeals.

2.   Legal theories relied upon:

(Appellant) (1) Breach of warranty: Express and implied warranties that the designated quarry contained enough rock for the job; thus breach of warranties entitles appellant to damages.

(Appellant) (2) (Alternatively) Impossibility of contract: The modified contract was impossible to perform, justifying an award to appellant of reasonable costs incurred in attempted performance.

(Appellant) (3) Change of contract: The increase in costs to appellant constitutes a compensable change in contract under the changes clause of the contract.

(Appellee) (1) Breach of contract: Liquidated damages for delays in performance of the contract and for costs and attorney's fees.

3.   Facts: Appellant and appellee entered into a contract for the procurement and hauling of rock from a designated area within a quarry, the rock to be transported across a specified lake to a certain dam site when the lake had frozen enough to permit heavy vehicle traffic.   When suitable rock was not found at the originally-designated site, the agreement was reformed to permit a new site and the contract price was increased by $42,000.   All the required rock was procured and prepared for transporting.   Although both parties had agreed that the rock was to be transported across the lake, appellant soon discovered that the ice was too thin to permit this arrangement, appellant losing a loader and a tractor through the ice.   Nevertheless, appellee insisted upon performance, threatening, in January 1968, to hold appellant in default of contract unless the rock was transported by April 1, 1968.   On February 1, 1968, appellant began hauling rock with half-loaded trucks; nevertheless two trucks and their drivers broke through the ice, resulting in the death of the drivers and the loss of the trucks.   Appellant then ceased operations, informing appellee that it would make no more attempts to haul rock and that it considered the contract terminated for impossibility of performance.

4.   Relief requested: Recovery by appellant for costs incurred in the attempted completion of the contract, less revenues received.   Appellee counter-claimed, contending that it had overpaid appellant for work performed under the contract and thus was entitled to liquidated damages for the period between the date of completion specified in the amended contract and the date of its termination by appellant. (Appellee's claim of overpayment was abandoned on appeal.)

5.   Issues:

(1) Is appellant entitled to damages for breach of alleged express and implied warranties contained in the original contract pertaining to available quantities of rock?

(2) (Alternatively) was the contract as modified impossible of performance? [a]

(3) If the modified contract was impossible of performance, is appellant entitled to reasonable costs incurred in attempting to perform it?

(4) Is appellee entitled to liquidated damages for delays in performance of the contract and costs and attorney's fees?

6.   Holding:

(1) No. Appellant is not entitled to damages where the contract was formally amended by later letter.

(2) Yes. The contract as modified was impossible to perform when appellant suffered loss of life and property in attempting to perform the contract.

(3) Yes. Because the contract was impossible to perform, appellant is entitled to reasonable costs incurred by attempting to perform it and for attorney's fees.

(4) Previous holdings make it unnecessary to consider this issue.

Disposition of Case: Lower court decision affirmed in part (Issues 1 and 2), reversed in part (Issue 3), and remanded.

7.   Reasoning:

(Issue 1) Since the original agreement was superseded by an amendment executed by both parties to the contract and since the amendment provided for additional costs incurred by the appellant, the court need not be concerned with whether warranties were breached with reference to the quantity of rock available at the originally-designated quarry. Appellant does not contend that the amended contract did not designate quarries containing suitable quantities of rock.

(Issue 2) Since the contract specified that the rock be hauled across the ice by truck, and since this method required ice frozen deeply enough to support such passage, and since this unfulfilled provision was material to its performance, appellant's duty to perform was discharged by reason of impossibility. Appellant is also excused under the principle of commercial impracticability, which has superseded the original harsh rule of impossibility. Under the doctrine of commercial impracticability, a party is excused from contract performance if an unanticipated circumstance, the risk of which should not be borne by the promisor, has made performance

a.   Court calls this the "focal issue."

of the contract vitally different from what could reasonably have been expected.

(Issue 3) Upon remand, the Court should determine when appellee knew or should have known performance was impossible and if that date preceded actual termination of the contract, appellant should be awarded costs incurred thereafter. Notions of equity and fairness entitle appellant to its extra costs incurred in seeking to perform by the required but impossible method after such time as appellee was reasonably placed on notice that it was not feasible to perform the contract by the means required.

(Issue 4) See Holding, above.

8. Legal Rules:

   (1) The doctrine of impossibility has been expanded to include the principle of commercial impracticability.

   (2) A party to a contract is entitled to recover increased costs incurred in attempting to comply with a specific requirement in the contract that is impossible to meet, if such requirement is insisted upon by the other party to the contract.

9. Dicta: None

The student who prepared these three case briefs used the briefs to prepare the synthesis chart on page 145. She then used the chart to write a synthesis of the opinions. The synthesis is on pages 141–143.

Chapter Two

Grammar and Meaning

"The student ought to carefully reperuse what he has written [and to] correct . . . every error of orthography and grammar. A mistake in either is unpardonable." (From John Marshall's letter to his grandson, December 7, 1834. The Nation, LXXII, Feb. 7, 1901.)

Grammar may be boring to learn, but it is important to know. It is, in fact, the basis of all effective writing. You will never be praised for good grammar, but you will surely be censured for its absence. And if your excellent reasoning is couched in ungrammatical language, don't expect to get the credit for it that you deserve.

Of course, there is more to effective writing than standard grammar. To write well you need appropriate style and organization, and good analysis. But the *sine qua non* of writing is good grammar. Your clients will depend on it; courts will expect it. If your grammar is substandard, expect to be embarrassed.

Take, for example, the following case, in which the issue was whether the indictment under which the defendant was charged was legally adequate. The indictment read, in part:

- The store building there situated, the property of M . . . A . . ., in which store building was kept for sale valuable things, to-wit: goods, ware and merchandise unlawfully, feloniously and burglariously did break and enter, with intent the goods, wares and merchandise of said M . . . A . . . then and there being in said store building unlawfully, feloniously and then and there being in said store building burglariously to take, steal and carry away [various items] . . . the said [defendant] having been twice previously convicted of felonies . . . [The remainder of the indictment charges the defendant with being a recidivist.]

The defendant demurred and presented as expert witness an English teacher who testified that, consistent with English grammatical rules, the indictment did not charge the defendant with doing anything.

The judge agreed with the defendant that under the rules of good English, the district attorney's indictment charged "goods, ware and merchandise" with breaking and entering, or that, alternatively, the indictment was a "largely unintelligible effort" to describe "the store building" as the perpetrator of the crime. Certainly, said the judge, the indictment failed to charge the defendant with any crime. Thus, under the rules of standard English, the defendant should go free. Reluctantly, however, the judge held the indictment legally (though not grammatically) adequate, adding:

40

- Establishment of a literate bar is a worthy aspiration. 'Tis without doubt a consummation devoutly to be wished. Its achievement, however, must be relegated to means other than reversal of criminal convictions justly and lawfully secured. The assignment of error is rejected.

But other courts have held against drafters of contracts containing incorrect grammar. In one such case the court scolded the insurance company policy drafter:

- [T]he language [of this policy] follows no well-recognized grammatical rules. Elemental rules of sentence construction were totally ignored in the drafting of the clause upon which the Appellant relies. Any student of law or composition assigned to draft language to accomplish the Appellant's goal of creating a clause to exclude coverage, in the situation presented in this case, would probably receive a failing grade if he presented the contract clause found in the Appellant's policy. It would have been very easy for the Appellant to set forth its intent in a clear and succinct manner. It certainly has not done so in this situation.

Even a minor grammatical error like a missing comma can lead to defeat in court. One court held that the absence of a single comma permitted a plaintiff trucking company to ship beyond a 100–mile limit, although both the plaintiff and the defendant intended the contract to limit shipping to 100 miles.

For law students, poor grammar may lower grades. Law professors, like other people, often unconsciously assume that grammatical—and even spelling—errors indicate inadequate thinking. I have seen that happen so often that I've given it a name: the "can't even" theory. The professor's reasoning process goes something like this: "This student can't even write in standard English. How can he (or she) possibly resolve complex legal problems?" So the writer of a final examination that contains grammar and spelling errors may be handicapped even before the professor considers the ideas presented.

Finally, grammatical correctness is important in legal writing for two more reasons: (1) so that your readers can focus on what you are saying, not on how badly you are saying it; and (2) so that your readers can understand what you mean—even if they would rather not.

You will find that correct grammar is not hard to learn. Much of what follows in this chapter you already learned once, long ago, and you will find the re-discovery of old rules a pleasant experience.

I. Some Definitions of Grammatical Terms

Defined below are some of the terms that appear in this book. Grammatical definitions are risky, however, because grammarians disagree about them. For example, the traditional definition of a sentence is that it is a group of words conveying a complete thought, but this definition leaves out more sentences than it includes, and it has been rejected by modern grammarians. Even among modern grammarians, there is no consensus regarding the definition of a sentence; I have read at least 10 definitions, the simplest (and least helpful) being that it is a group of words between a capital letter and a period! So take the definitions offered below with a grain of salt. Do not memorize them; just use them to aid you in understanding the discussions in this book.

Verbs: Verbs are sometimes called the action words of a sentence. An important function of verbs is that they indicate what the subject of the sentence is doing. Finite verbs contain tense, mood, and voice. Sentences must contain finite verbs. For example, the first sentence below contains a past tense finite verb. The second locution is not a sentence; it is a sentence fragment because it contains no finite verb, only a present participle of a verb:

- The girl walked down the street. (Finite verb, complete sentence.)
- The girl walking down the street. (No finite verb, sentence fragment.)

Tense:

When you think of **tense,** think of **time.** **Verbs** can express three main time divisions (past, present, and future). In English only two tenses, present and past, are indicated in the verb itself. Other time indications are added with helping words. For example,

- Present Tense: walk; throw, is thrown
- Past Tense: walked; threw, was thrown
- Future Tense: will walk, shall walk; will throw, shall throw, will be thrown, shall be thrown
- Present Perfect Tense: have (has) walked; have (has) thrown, have (has) been thrown
- Past Perfect Tense: had walked; had thrown, had been thrown
- Future Perfect Tense: will have walked, shall have walked; will have thrown, shall have thrown, will have been thrown, shall have been thrown

Mood: English verbs can indicate three moods, indicative, imperative, and subjunctive.

- **Indicative:** used in statements and questions.
  - He has left. Are you going?
- **Imperative:** used in commands, directions, requests.
  - Stop doing that!
  - Go four blocks east.
  - Get me an eraser.
- **Subjunctive:** used to express conditions contrary to fact, following words of command or desire, and in a few idiomatic sayings.

- (Condition contrary to fact) If the plaintiff **were** present, we could proceed.

- (Following command) He requires that dress code **be** observed.

- (Following desire) She is eager that the facts **be** known.

- (Idioms) Heaven **forbid**! Far **be** it from me to object! Come what **may** . . .

Voice: Verbs may be either active or passive in voice.

- **Active voice:** John **threw** the ball to Jean.

Note that the active voice verb has a **subject** (John) and an **object** (ball).

- **Passive voice:** The ball **was thrown** to Jean by John.

When you change the verb to passive voice, you move the former *object* to the *subject* slot, and the former subject becomes the *object* of a preposition (or is often deleted). For the desirability of using active verbs, see pages 100–102.

Nouns: Nouns usually denote persons, places, things, actions, or qualities. They can be **count** (apples, chairs) or **non-count** (happiness, information). They can be **common** (man, idea) or **proper** (Buffalo, John Jones). They can be **concrete** (trees, table) or **abstract** (irony, love). Nouns function in sentences as subjects (the *sun* is shining), objects (visit *Russia*), indirect objects (Give *John* the book) and objects of prepositions (Listen to the *music*).

Pronouns: These substitute for nouns and function like nouns. The most common kinds are **personal pronouns** (*I, you, he, she, it, we, and they*); **indefinite pronouns** (*anyone, anybody, anything, someone, somebody, something, everyone, everybody, everything*); and **relative pronouns** (*who/whom, which, that*).

Adjectives: These modify nouns and pronouns, and should be placed near the words they modify. Some examples of adjectives are:

- The *uncooperative* witness

- A *just* claim

- A *directed* verdict

Note: Usually adjectives precede the nouns they modify (as they do above). But when the modifying language is more than one word, put it after the noun it modifies; compare:

- An attractive nuisance

- A nuisance attractive to children.

Adverbs: They modify verbs or adjectives, other adverbs, and many other words. Adverbs often state *where, how, when,* or *how often.* Some examples are:

- An *extremely* old contract.
- He needs the answer *now.*
- She is *very* pleasant to work with.
- They *seldom* need help.

Sentence: A group of words that conveys an idea and contains a subject and a predicate. However, when such a group of words is preceded by a subordinator, it is not a sentence but a subordinate (dependent) clause.

Subjects: Nouns and pronouns can be subjects. Phrases and gerunds are sometimes subjects too.

- The defense *attorney* persuaded the jury. (Noun subject)
- *Someone* entered the house without permission. (Pronoun subject)
- *Almost unbelievable* is how he got in. (Phrase subject)
- *Seeing* is believing. (Gerund subject)

Predicate: The part of a sentence that expresses something about the subject. The predicate of a sentence always includes a finite verb and sometimes includes other components.

- The defendant *collapsed.* (Verb as predicate)
- The prosecuting attorney *questioned the witness.* (Verb plus object as predicate)

Clause: A group of words containing a subject and a predicate, and conveying an idea. If the clause can stand alone as a sentence, it is called an independent (main) clause; if it can not, it is called a dependent (subordinate) clause.

- The plaintiff applauded the decision; the defendant deplored it. (Each clause is **independent.**)
- Although the plaintiff applauded the decision, the defendant deplored it. (The first clause is **dependent;** the second clause is **independent.**)

Subordinators: Words that, when they introduce a clause, make it a dependent (subordinate) clause. Some subordinators are *when, if, after, whereas, although, while, because, since, that, which, whoever, whichever.*

Coordinators: Words that join **independent** (main) clauses. These include **coordinating conjunctions,** *e.g., and, but, for, nor, or, so;* **correlatives** (coordinating conjunctions in pairs), e.g., *both . . . and; either . . . or; not only . . . but also;* and **conjunctive adverbs,** *e.g., however, moreover, nevertheless, consequently, thus, furthermore, therefore.*

Phrase: A group of related words that lack either a subject or a predicate, or both. Some phrases are:

- John, the defendant's counsel, . . . (no predicate)
- Lacking the proper evidence, . . . (no subject)
- Without further ado, . . . (no subject, no predicate).

II. Punctuation

A. When to Use a Comma

If you don't know the rules, you probably rely on guesswork in using commas. Guessing will work some of the time, because your vocal intonation and pauses ("sentence contour") help you decide where commas belong. But guesswork is not infallible, and what usually happens is that if you don't know the rules you will omit commas where they belong and put them in where they don't belong. The following constructions require commas; if a construction does not appear here, it probably needs no comma. One good rule to follow: never separate the subject of a sentence from its predicate unless you have a good reason—like one of the ones listed below.

Use a comma:

1. **Before coordinating conjunctions** (and, but, or, for, nor . . .) that join independent clauses:

- The defense was inadequate, and an appeal is probable.
- The landlord was not liable for the defect, for he was unaware of it.
- The Socratic method of teaching is pedagogically stimulating, but it has drawbacks.

2. **After dependent clauses,** when they precede independent clauses:

- Although she has retired, [dependent clause] she is still active. [independent clause]
- Before the defendant is sentenced, [dependent clause] the court considers mitigating circumstances.

Note: When the dependent clause follows the independent clause, use a comma if the dependent clause is fairly long, but if the dependent clause is short, no comma is necessary:

- The landlord was not liable for the tenant's injury, since at common law he had no duty to repair the tenant's apartment.
- The jury retired to deliberate after the trial ended.

3. **Following other introductory language:**

   a. **Introductory phrases:**

- Although nearly 80, he still practiced law.

b. **Transitional phrases:**

- On the other hand, the victim suffered no damages.

c. **Interjections:**

- Amazingly, there were no injuries.
- Consequently, the claim failed.
- However, it is too late to consider another plan.

4. **To separate items in a series:**

- Stolen during the armed robbery were credit cards, checks, and cash of an unknown amount.

Note: If you omit the final comma in a series, you may confuse your reader. For example:

- The plaintiff turned over all his holdings, houses and lands.

Were houses and lands his total holdings? A comma makes clear the facts that his holdings included more than houses and lands:

- The plaintiff turned over all his holdings, houses, and lands.

The next two sentences illustrate the same point:

- The government has announced the capture of five smugglers, three women, and two youths. (Ten persons, five smugglers.)
- The government has announced the capture of five smugglers, three women and two youths. (Five persons, five smugglers.)

Even the omission of a single comma sometimes makes it impossible for the reader to decide what grouping of items the drafter intended. Here is the way the First Restatement of Torts defined assault:

- An act other than the mere speaking of words which, directly or indirectly, is a legal cause of putting another in apprehension of an immediate and harmful or offensive contact.

Without a comma to guide you, you cannot tell whether the person's apprehension must be of an immediate and harmful, or offensive contact, or an immediate, and harmful or offensive contact. As you know from your torts class, the apprehension must be immediate, and of a harmful or offensive contact, and the definition should be punctuated to reflect that meaning:

- An act other than the mere speaking of words which, directly or indirectly, is a legal cause of putting another in apprehension of an immediate, and harmful or offensive contact.

5. **To separate non-restrictive relative clauses:**

- Professor Mary Smith, who is a member of this faculty, is on sabbatical at present.

Note: For more on relative clauses, see pages 53–60.

6. **To set off appositives:**

- John Jones, the lieutenant-governor, is a graduate of this law school.

7. **To set off interrupters** (words, phrases, clauses):
   - It is up to Congress, not the courts, to change the law.

Note: Commas are sometimes crucial. Compare:
   - The defendant said the witness lied.
   - The defendant, said the witness, lied.

8. **To punctuate geographical names, dates, and addresses:**
   - My address is 222 Fischer Street, Gainesville, Florida.
   - Summer term began on June 22, 1987.

B. When to Use a Semi–Colon

When you have two ideas that could be sentences, but you want to indicate a closer relationship between them than would be shown by two sentences, you might choose a semi-colon. Or to indicate less relationship between two independent clauses than shown by a comma, you might choose a semi-colon.

Use a semi-colon:

1. **To join two independent clauses** (instead of a period):
   - The elements of battery were all present; it was a prima facie case.

2. **As a substitute for a comma** (to join two independent clauses separated by a coordinating conjunction):
   - The suggestion has been made before; but I am not going to follow it.

3. **To join two independent clauses** (when you use a conjunctive adverb between them):
   - The jury decision was inconsistent with the facts; therefore an appeal is probable.
   - An important witness was out of the country; however, the trial took place without her.
   - The recent typhoon was a tragedy; nevertheless, it taught an important lesson.

Note: Decide whether to place a comma *after* the conjunctive adverb by saying the sentence out loud and listening for a pause in your voice at that position.

4. To separate components when a list already contains commas:
   - In attendance at the meeting were the firms of Abel, Baker and Crony; Gargle, Koff and Sneaze; and Mountain, Hill and Valley.

5. To separate items in a list introduced by a colon:
   - The following elements of assault are present: (1) the act was intentional and unconsented to; (2) the gesture caused reasonable apprehension of an imminent and harmful touching; and (3) the actor was unprivileged to make the gesture.

(The numbering of three or more items in a list, as was done in (5), is not necessary grammatically, but helpful stylistically.)

Note: Use a comma instead of a semi-colon, if you like, to link short clauses, parallel in construction and closely related. For example, "That was his last speech, it was also his best."

C. When to Use a Colon

The colon is another handy mark of punctuation that is largely ignored by law students except as part of the salutation in business letters (Dear Attorney Smith:). As it does in the salutation, the colon signals to the reader that more on the subject is to come.

- Both the public and criminals suffer from overcrowded jails: the public because criminals are often released prematurely; the criminals because the quality of life suffers in overcrowded prisons.
- Upon examining the contents of the glove compartment, officers found: 30 quaaludes; 10 syringes; one rubber hose; 20 packages of marijuana.

Note: When the items in the list are short, numbering them is probably not necessary; if you prefer, you can also separate them with commas instead of semi-colons.

D. When to Use a Dash

In a word: sparingly. The dash is too unspecific and informal for legal writing. Used excessively, moreover, it makes your writing seem gushy. Choose instead commas, semi-colons, or colons. To indicate parenthetical material, parentheses are also acceptable.

- The witness, a police officer, testified for the plaintiff.
- It was clear (despite evidence to the contrary) that the witness would not change her testimony.

E. When to Use a Possessive Apostrophe

Before learning how to use the possessive apostrophe, learn where *not* to use it.

1. Generally, avoid the possessive apostrophe to indicate possession in inanimate nouns.* Use the longer form instead, called the periphrastic possessive. For example, write

- the roof of the house (*not* the house's roof)
- the contents of the course (*not* the course's contents)
- the winner of the dispute (*not* the dispute's winner)
- the long form of the possessive (*not* the possessive's long form).

* This rule does not apply to informal, colloquial writing.

Like most rules, this one has an exception: certain well-known phrases like "for argument's sake" are acceptable. And group nouns composed of human beings use the possessive apostrophe. For example,

- the committee's policy (but "the policy of the committee" is also acceptable.)
- the corporation's profits (but "the profits of the corporation" is also acceptable.)
- the alumni association's program (but "the program of the alumni" is also acceptable).

2. Omit the possessive apostrophe in possessive personal pronouns. For example, the following are correct forms:

- The book is hers.
- The decision is theirs.
- The dog is ours.
- The luggage is yours.

3. Now for where the possessive apostrophe *is* used:

- In most singular animate nouns, add 's to form the possessive:
- the author's words
- the dog's tail
- Joe's house
- the professor's class.

In plural animate nouns ending in an *s* or *z* sound, add the possessive apostrophe after the final letter:

- boys' caps
- professors' classes
- ladies' clubs
- geniuses' problems

In one-syllable singular animate nouns that end in an *s* or a *z* sound, add 's:

- the boss's request
- the horse's legs
- James's appointment

In singular nouns of more than one syllable, add only an apostrophe:

- Euripedes' plays
- Moses' leadership
- Socrates' death

But in nouns in which the second *s* or *z* sound is pronounced, add 's:

- Louise's deposition
- Horace's hearing
- Alice's book

You may use the periphrastic possessive, if you prefer, for animate nouns, but not for proper nouns. That is, you can say "the classes of the professor," but not, "the book of Alice."

The following compounds add 's to form the possessive:

everybody's	someone's
anybody's	no one's
somebody's	everyone's
nobody's	anyone's

When two or more nouns are used to denote possession, only the last noun in the series takes the possessive form when possession is shared by all members of the group. For example:

- John, Mary, and Bill's property (joint ownership)
- Mary and Paul's will (only one will)
- Joe and Joan's tax form (joint filing)

But when separate possession is indicated, every noun in the list must take the possessive form:

- John's, Mary's, and Bill's property (three pieces of property)
- Mary's and Paul's wills (two separate wills)
- Joe's and Joan's tax forms (separate filing)

F.   When to Use a Hyphen

The decision of when and where to use hyphens is as much stylistic as it is grammatical. The discussion of hyphens appears here instead of in Chapter Three mainly because this is where readers probably expect to find it. Generally speaking, use hyphens for three reasons: (1) to express the idea of the unity of two or more words; (2) to avoid ambiguity; and (3) to prevent mispronunciation. Examples follow.

1.   **Hyphenate to indicate the unity of two or more words.** This rule applies to adjectives and to nouns. First, **adjectives:**

- A well-known legal rule
- A six-member law firm
- A value-added tax
- An open-and-shut case
- Four- five- and six-page pleadings
- Black-letter law

Note that in all these examples, the hyphenated adjectives modify their noun **together,** not singly. An **exception** to the rule is when the modifiers are an adverb-adjective combination and the adverb ends in **-ly:**

- An unusually negligent act
- An increasingly severe sentence
- A suddenly appearing witness

Applying the rule of unity to nouns, you should realize that hyphenation of nouns represents one stage in a process. What happens is that when two or more nouns begin to be used together, first they are considered two separate words, then they are (usually) hyphenated, and finally they become one word. This is what has happened in the following words:

First	**Later**	**Currently**
ice box	ice-box	icebox
ball park	ball-park	ballpark
mail man	mail-man	mailman
racquet ball	racquet-ball	racquetball

Because hyphenation in these compounds represents only a stage, you may disagree with the final item (current usage) in this list. Perhaps, in your usage, you still hyphenate racquetball. If so, feel free to do so; you are making a stylistic choice. English usage is more conservative than American usage, so you will find words still hyphenated in British English that Americans write as one word. Winston Churchill, who is said to have hated hyphens, urged English writers to avoid them: "My feeling is that you may run [words] together or leave them apart, except when nature revolts."

Even American writers continue to use hyphens in certain titles, for example:

- Attorney-at-law
- Editor-in-chief
- Commander-in-chief
- President-elect

The final word is that there is **no arbitrary rule** about the hyphenation of two or more words to indicate their unity. As a native speaker (and reader), you may rely on your instincts to guide your own usage.

2. **Hyphenate to avoid ambiguity.** Here the rule is based, not upon style, but upon common sense. In each of the examples below, the lack of a hyphen would result in a change of meaning:

- A little-used sailboat (*compare* a little used sailboat)
- A hard-working attorney (*compare* a hard working attorney)
- Extra-judicial duties (*compare* extra judicial duties)
- Three-quarter-hour intervals (*compare* three quarter-hour intervals)
- A re-formed contract (*compare* a reformed contract)
- Re-covered office furniture (*compare* recovered office furniture)

3. **Hyphenate to avoid mispronunciation.** Notice that in the examples, above, hyphens change the pronunciation of the phrase as well as its meaning. You may wish to retain the hyphen in words like loop-hole, co-worker, and public-house, to avoid the pronunciation *pho, cow* and *cho.* Even American writers, less concerned than English writers with the possible mispronunciation of non-hyphenated words, usually hyphenate *de-ice, de-emphasize,*

re-issue, and *re-analysis.*   Only fairly recent is the omission of the hyphen following the prefix *co-,* when it is followed by a vowel, as in *co-educational, co-ordinal, co-incide.*   You can choose to retain or remove the hyphen following *co-* and other prefixes, like *non-, ex-, pro-,* and *anti-.*   With suffixes, like *-less,* frequency and familiarity are also the deciding factors.   Thus, you would not hyphenate *harmless, careless,* or *meaningless;* but you might hyphenate *brain-less* or *ambition-less.*

4.   The rule regarding the hyphenation of compound numbers and fractions is more precise.   **Hyphenate compound numbers from twenty-one to ninety-nine and hyphenate fractions used as modifiers:**

- Twenty-five members attended.
- Ninety-five percent of those questioned responded.
- A one-third vote of the registrants (*Compare:* One third of those registered voted.)
- A two-thirds majority (*Compare:* A majority of two thirds).

Finally, it is easier to decide when *not* to hyphenate.

Do not hyphenate when modifiers follow nouns:

- A thirty-page brief (*but* a brief of thirty pages)
- A well-known legal principle (*but* a legal principle that is well known)
- A vehicle-operator mileage restriction (*but* a mileage restriction for vehicle operators)
- A for-adults-only film (*but* a film for adults only)

G.   When and Where to Use Quotation Marks

The modern tendency is to use quotation marks sparingly.   Omit quotation marks around **common nicknames, biblical references, proverbs, well-known literary quotations,** or **commonly known facts,** available in numerous sources.   Here are illustrations of these:

- Bob insisted that Dick be available to attend the meeting.
- Let the dead bury their dead.
- Still waters run deep.
- The criminal should be hoist with his own petard.
- Benjamin Franklin was the oldest delegate at the 1787 Constitutional Convention.

When you quote single words or short phrases, use quotation marks, but no commas if they are an integral part of the sentence in which they appear:

- What was meant by the term "insurance agent" in an insurance code was decided by the meaning of the language in an employment security act.

Place quotation marks around each word or phrase in a series, and place periods and commas inside quotation marks:

- Courts apply the rule of *noscitur a sociis* (Latin for "it is known by its associates"), when two words appear together and ordinarily have a similar meaning. When applied, the *noscitur a sociis* rule results in the general word being limited and qualified by the word with the narrower meaning. Courts apply this "fallible aid," however, only when the document in question contains "doubtful words," "some ambiguity," or "a question of legislative intent."

In the above paragraph, notice that the commas and the period are placed inside the quotation marks. This is correct American usage. In American usage, colons and semi-colons are placed outside the final quotation marks, and question marks and exclamation points are placed inside the quotation marks if they are part of the quoted material and outside if they are not.

The following four sentences illustrate American usage:

- Mary said, "I am going out."
- Mary said, "I'm going," but she was unable to go.
- Mary asked, "Where are you going?"
- Mary asked, "Where are you going?"; but I did not answer.

British usage differs in that all quotation marks are placed according to whether they are part of the quoted material.

H. How to Recognize and Punctuate Relative Clauses

1. What is a relative clause?

In Section IIA (above), discussing comma use, you read that non-restrictive relative clauses were constructions requiring commas. But what is a relative clause? It is a clause introduced by the relative pronouns *that, which, who (whom, whose)*, modifying an antecedent noun or pronoun. The following are relative clauses:

- The book **that** I forgot to bring . . .
- The lecture **which** Professor Grummby gave . . .
- The language, **which** she remembered verbatim . . .
- The attorney, **who** had won the case . . .
- The plaintiff **whose** contract had been breached . . .
- The defendant to **whom** she had sent the letter . . .

2. How to decide whether a relative clause is restrictive or non-restrictive:

To distinguish between restrictive relative clauses and non-restrictive relative clauses, consider the following pair of sentences. The first sentence contains a restrictive relative clause; the second, a non-restrictive relative clause.

- The member of this faculty who is on sabbatical at present is Professor Mary Smith.
- Professor Mary Smith, who is a member of this faculty, is on sabbatical at present.

In the first sentence, the relative pronoun *who* introduces a clause that explains which faculty member is on sabbatical at present. The grammatical explanation traditionally given is that a restrictive relative clause "defines or restricts" the meaning of the language it follows. Here, the member of the faculty is "defined" by the language that *who* introduces. By contrast, in the second sentence, Mary Smith is defined by the language in her own clause, and the language following the relative pronoun *who* merely adds more information about her. Thus, the second sentence is a non-restrictive relative clause, and it is enclosed by commas.

3. The "which one" test:

An easy test to decide whether a relative clause is restrictive or non-restrictive is whether the clause in question answers the question "which one." In the first sentence, "who is on sabbatical at present" answers the question "which one" (which faculty member?). In sentence 2, we already *know* which faculty member. She is defined in her own clause by name and title.

The next two sentences contain relative clauses. Can you apply the "which one" test to explain the punctuation of each sentence?

- The judge rebuked the attorney who had left the courtroom.
- The judge rebuked the attorney, who had left the courtroom.

You are right if you decided that the first sentence needs no punctuation because it contains a restrictive relative clause. That clause ("who left the courtroom") answers the question, "Which attorney left the courtroom?"; and the absence of a comma indicates that more than one attorney was present in the courtroom. In the second sentence, however, it is clear by the comma after *attorney* that only one attorney was present in the courtroom. Therefore the question "which one?" is irrelevant, and the clause is non-restrictive.

To return to the sentence excerpts that were given in Section H., 1 (above) as examples of relative clauses, you can see that some of these contain commas and some do not. Can you add to these excerpts to make complete sentences of the examples? Try your luck, then compare your sentences with the following:

- The book that I forgot to bring contains my conference notes. (Which book contains my notes? The one I forgot to bring.)
- The lecture which Professor Grummby gave was hard to understand. (Which lecture was hard to understand? The one Professor Grummby gave.)
- The language, which she remembered verbatim, was from the codicil of the will. ("The language" has previously been identified, so the relative clause does not answer the question "which language?")

- The attorney, who had won the case, refused to discuss it with the press. ("The attorney" has previously been named or otherwise identified.)

- The plaintiff whose contract had been breached wanted to settle out of court. (Which plaintiff wanted to settle? The one whose contract had been breached.)

- The defendant to whom she had sent the letter was found guilty. (Which defendant was found guilty? The defendant to whom she had sent the letter.)

4. The distinction makes a difference:

Failure to understand the difference between restrictive relative clauses and non-restrictive relative clauses may cause you to write something you do not mean. In the following item, a newspaper journalist made that mistake because he did not know how to punctuate relative clauses. His news item read:

- Mary Smith, the mother of two who recently entered college, agreed that a college degree is necessary to get a good job.

As it is punctuated, this sentence *says* that Mary Smith's two children recently entered college. The author *meant* that Mary Smith had recently entered college, so he should have punctuated the sentence:

- Mary Smith, the mother of two, who recently entered college, agreed that a college degree is necessary to get a good job.

A single comma marks the difference in meaning.

That politicians are well aware of the importance of commas is shown by an anecdote *Time* magazine reported, which occurred as a Republican sub-committee on economic policy was drafting the party's position on increased taxes.* The first draft version stated that the party "opposes any attempts to increase taxes which would harm the recovery and reverse the trend to restoring control of the economy to individual Americans." (Restrictive clause, no comma; meaning: only those taxes that would harm recovery would be barred.) Party conservatives, however, were unwilling to bar only "harmful" taxes; they wanted the sentence to bar all taxes. So they insisted on adding a comma, and the final version stated that the party would "oppose any attempts to increase taxes, which would harm the recovery and reverse the trend to restoring control of the economy to individual Americans." The single comma, after "taxes" barred *all* taxes, not only "harmful" taxes.

Courts apply the same rule, under the rubric "Doctrine of the Last Antecedent." To see how it works, consider two regulations:

- Barred from interstate shipment are pears, apples, oranges, and lemons, which are unripe.

* August 27, 1984, at 14.

- Barred from interstate shipment are pears, apples, oranges, and lemons which are unripe.

Under the Last Antecedent Doctrine, the first sentence bars interstate shipment of all the listed fruits, if they are unripe. The second sentence bars from interstate shipment all pears, apples, and oranges, but permits shipment of lemons, unless they are unripe.

The Doctrine of the Last Antecedent has been cited and applied in a number of court opinions, for example in Davis v. Gibbs, 39 Wash.2d 481, 236 P.2d 545 (1951), in which the court said:

- Where no contrary intention appears in a statute, relative and qualifying words and phrases, both grammatically and legally, refer to the last antecedent.

"Contrary intention" would be indicated by a comma separating the qualifying phrase from the remainder of the sentence.

5.   That, who/whom, or which

a.   Use *that* in restrictive relative clauses only.

- The dog *that* I bought for my son barks constantly.
- The books *that* I left on the table are missing.
- The commission *that* promulgated the ordinance has convened.
- The argument *that* the plaintiff advances is fallacious.

Note: In written English, do not use *that* to refer to human beings, although in spoken, informal usage, *that* is sometimes used.*

- Written English: Anyone *who* wishes to comment may do so.
- Informal English: Anyone *that* wishes to comment may do so.

b.   Use *which* instead of *that* in restrictive relative clauses, if you prefer. (*Which* is somewhat more formal than *that*.)

- The erroneous information *which* my client received . . .
- The erroneous information *that* my client received . . .

c.   Use *which* and *who/whom* (not *that*) in non-restrictive relative clauses.

- The "establishment of religion" clause, *which* is a part of the first amendment . . .
- Senator Blank, *who* is the keynote speaker . . .

* Since most legal writing requires the use of formal English (and indeed legal usage tends to be conservative and some- what old-fashioned), the student is well-advised to avoid colloquial, casual usage in law school writing assignments.

Note: Groups of humans (corporations, courts, institutions, etc.) are usually referred to by *which* and a singular verb:

- Congress, *which is* in session . . .

- The committee, *which meets* in Room 10 . . .

- The Supreme Court, *which is* in session . . .

- The jury which decided the case . . .

d. In **restrictive relative clauses,** you may delete the pronouns *who, which,* and *that* when those pronouns function as objects in their own clauses.*

- The dog that I bought for my son barks constantly.

Substitute, if you wish, for succinctness:

- The dog I bought for my son barks constantly.

- The books which I placed on the table are missing.

Substitute, if you wish, for succinctness:

- The books I placed on the table are missing.

- The person whom I just met is your friend.

Substitute, if you wish, for succinctness:

- The person I just met is your friend.

However, if the restrictive pronoun functions as the subject in its own clause, do not omit it:

- The commission that promulgated the ordinance has convened.

- The person who just left was my attorney.

Do **NOT** substitute:

* The commission promulgated the ordinance has convened.

* The person just left was my attorney.

The exception to this rule is that when the verb is a form of "be," both the form of "be" and the relative pronoun may be omitted, for succinctness:

- The book which is on the table . . .

- The book on the table . . .

- The person who is responsible . . .

  The person responsible . . .

- The court that is sitting . . .

  The court sitting . . .

---

* You will need to use your "ear" for idiom and your good judgment to decide whether to delete or not. A good rule-of-thumb is: delete unless the result might confuse your readers.

e. How to decide whether to use *who* or *whom*

To answer this question, you can use a fairly simple formula. Think of every sentence as a **"surface structure"** that may contain more than one **"deep structure."** A sentence containing a relative clause is really two **"deep structure"** sentences, an **outer** and an **inner sentence.** Look at the following sentence:

- The attorney [who/whom] argued the case was the Public Defender.

This **surface structure** contains **two deep structure sentences:**

- **Outer Sentence:** The attorney was the Public Defender.
- **Inner Sentence:** [The attorney] argued the case.

Because *who,* in the **surface structure sentence** substitutes for the **subject** in the **deep structure Inner Sentence,** you need the subjective form, *who:*

- The attorney **who** argued the case was the Public Defender.

Now apply the same formula to the next sentence:

- The attorney [who/whom] the defendant requested was the Public Defender.

Here is the **deep structure** of that sentence:

- **Outer Sentence:** The attorney was the Public Defender.
- **Inner Sentence:** The defendant requested [the Public Defender].

If you were to substitute *he/him* or *she/her* for "the Public Defender" in the **deep structure Inner Sentence,** you would choose the **objective** form of these words (*him/her*). So you would also choose the objective form of the relative pronoun (whom):

- The attorney **whom** the defendant requested was the Public Defender.

The formula works just as well when a preposition is involved:

- The prisoner did not know [who/whom] he was talking to.

Deep Structure,

Outer Sentence: The prisoner did not know [something].

Inner Sentence: He [the prisoner] was talking to [her/him].

You can now see that you need the **objective** case of the relative pronoun (whom):

- The prisoner did not know **whom** he was talking to.

In written (and formal oral) usage, you will probably place the preposition (to) before the relative pronoun, re-casting the sentence as:

- The prisoner did not know **to whom** he was talking.

Note: To determine which **deep structure** is the **Inner Sentence,** look for the relative pronoun. The clause in the **surface structure** sentence that contains the relative pronoun (who/whom) is the **Inner**

Sentence of the **deep structure.** The word that the relative pronoun refers to is part of the **deep structure Outer Sentence.**

6. Where to place relative pronouns in sentences

This question is often raised in discussions about relative pronouns, and although the answer has more to do with syntax than grammar, it is included here to complete the relative pronoun discussion. Consider the following pairs of constructions:

- The room into which they were trying to break . . .

  The room they were trying to break into . . .

- The chair, the leg of which was broken . . .

  The chair, whose leg was broken . . .

- The person in whom the plaintiff had placed his trust . . .

  The person the plaintiff placed his trust in . . .

Neither the first nor the second construction in any of these pairs is superior to the other. The second member of each pair is more informal, and that consideration may guide your choice. But do not allow the fact that two constructions end with prepositions (into and in) deter you from using them. The "rule" that sentences should not end with prepositions no longer has force, if indeed it was ever valid. You have heard Winston Churchill's response to an aide who cautioned him against ending sentences with prepositions: "That is arrant nonsense up with which I shall not put!*

Caveat!

Whether you choose to place your prepositions in the middle of your sentence or at the end, be sure you do include them. A recent error, committed often by newspaper journalists, is the omission of the preposition altogether, perhaps because of a dilemma about where to put it (or the desire to save newsprint). Here are some examples from newspaper journalism: **

- This is the same location that hydrogen was found leaking. (Missing, the preposition *in.*)

- The refugee camps are now more livable. The number of refugees in them is the lowest level it's ever been. (Missing, in the first sentence, *in;* in the second sentence *at.*)

- That is another item the President tried to do patch-up work last week. (Missing, the preposition *on.*)

* On the other hand, do not write sentences like one a little boy reportedly asked his father at bedtime: "What did you bring that book I don't like being read to out of up for?" Though his question was quite clear, the five prepositions ending it may be somewhat excessive!

** For a discussion of the incorrect deletion of prepositions in legal writing see, below, pages 69–70.

Try your hand at re-casting these sentences to make them grammatically correct. Then check the following possible revisions:

- This is the same location in which hydrogen was found leaking.
- This is the same location (that) hydrogen was found leaking in.
- The refugee camps are now more comfortable to live in.
- The refugee camps are now more bearable.
- The number of refugees in them is at the lowest level ever.
- The number of refugees in them is the lowest it's ever been.
- That is another item on which the President tried to do patch-up work last week.
- That is another item the President tried to do patch-up work on last week.

III. Case and Number

A. Personal Pronouns

1. Identification

The personal pronouns are *I/me, you, he/him, she/her,* and *they/them.*

2. Function

Their case depends upon their function in the sentence.

Perhaps when were young we said things like, "Her and me went to the movies." Our elementary school teachers then persuaded us to say instead, "She and I went to the movies." In fact, we were so well persuaded that we may still use the subjective form of pronouns even when they are the objects of the verb or preposition. The result is ungrammatical constructions like:

- * Give Mary and I the briefs.
- * Between you and I, the reasoning is faulty.
- * For they who want to study, the library remains open.

You will see that these constructions are ungrammatical if you rewrite the sentences so that the pronoun comes immediately after the verb or preposition:

- Give me and Mary the briefs.
- Between me and you, the reasoning is faulty.
- The library remains open for them who wish to study.*

---

* *Them* is the objective form because it is the object of the preposition *for; who* is the subjective form because it is the subject of its own clause. These subject/object distinctions of personal and relative pronouns may in time be eliminated, but current good usage still requires they be made, especially in writing. The use of *those* avoids the problem in this location and is a more felicitous choice.

Once you have tested the case of the pronoun in your rewrite, you can redraft the sentence into its original structure.

3. After than or as

The personal pronoun takes the subjective or objective form depending upon whether it is the subject or object of the verb (in its own clause) either stated or implied. Thus:

- John admires Joe more than me.
- (John admires Joe more than John admires me.)
- John admires Joe more than I.
- (John admires Joe more than I do.)
- College students socialize more than law students; law students study more than they (do).
- Phil is younger than Jack but taller than he (is).

4. The -self pronouns: These are used only as reflexive or intensive pronouns. Do not use them as substitutes for *I* or *me*.

* John and myself were studying.

(*Myself* is an intensive pronoun; substitute *I*.)

* The question was addressed to myself.

(*Myself* is a reflexive pronoun; substitute *me*.)

The following two sentences indicate the correct use of intensive and reflexive pronouns:

- I can do it myself.   (intensive pronoun)
- I injured myself yesterday.   (reflexive pronoun)

B. Referent Pronouns

1. Reference to entities: Refer to a committee, a court, a corporation, an institution, or any other entity or body, as *it*:

- The Court based *its* reaffirmation of the federal right of interstate travel upon the Commerce Clause.
- May a city limit *its* population by zoning laws?
- Congress is empowered by legislation to protect *its* constitutional right to travel.
- The jury arrived at *its* decision quickly.
- The Dumkin & Dumkin Company argued that *its* liability was limited to 20% for the accident.

2. Reference according to number: Refer to singular nouns by singular pronouns, and to plural nouns by plural pronouns:

- Every physician is expected to comply with practices customary in *his* or *her* community.

- If a law school graduate fails to pass the bar examination *she* or *he* may retake it.

- If parties are involved in a dispute in state courts, *they* are subject to state rules.

a.   To avoid using either *he* or *she* (or some combination of these) to refer to a singular noun, you can recast the sentence to omit the personal pronoun:

- Every physician is expected to comply with practices current in the community the physician practices in.

- A law school graduate who fails to pass the bar examination may retake it.

- A party involved in a dispute in a state court is subject to state rules.

b.   Or you can recast the sentence, placing the subject in the plural when what you are saying applies to the group being discussed:

- Physicians are expected to comply with practices current in their community.

- Law school graduates who fail to pass the bar examination may retake it.

- Parties involved in disputes in state courts are subject to state rules.

Note: Writers who should know better often draft silly comments to avoid being accused of "sexist language." For example, a member of a university search committee recently said:

- When a candidate becomes President of this university, *they'll* have to deal with the problem of the state Sunshine Law. (Emphasis added.)

Rewrite that sentence to avoid the masculine pronoun *he* and also to avoid the implication of a joint presidency. Below are two possible re-writes:

- A candidate who becomes President of this university will have to deal with the problems of the state Sunshine Law.

- Any candidate who becomes President of this university must deal with the problems of the state Sunshine Law.

C. Count and Non-count Nouns

1. How to tell the difference

There are several ways to distinguish between count and non-count nouns. **First,** count nouns have plurals. For example, *cats, dogs, persons, books, chairs, houses, clouds,* and *mosquitoes* are among the many count nouns in the English language. Non-count nouns have no plurals. You would not say * *wealths,* * *informations,* * *happinesses,* or * *flours,* for these words are all non-count nouns.

Second, you can divide count nouns into units and count the units. You can say "one cat, two cats, three cats," and so on. But you cannot divide non-count nouns into units. Among the English non-count nouns are *information, salt, laziness, affluence,* and *flour.* If you are a native speaker of English, you would not say, for example, "one information, two informations, three informations." Although native English speakers seldom have difficulty distinguishing between count and non-count nouns, those who learn English as a second language often do.*

Third, you can identify count nouns by placing the indefinite article (*a/ an*) in front of their singular form. You cannot do that with non-count nouns. Count nouns not only *can* have the article (*a/an*) in front of them in the singular, but they *must* have an article, either the indefinite article (*a/an*) or the definite article (*the*). To illustrate:

Not: *Umbrella is handy in a tropical climate.

But: • An umbrella is handy in a tropical climate.

Note: *Item is missing from the list.

But: • The item is missing from the list.

Note: Of course, the articles are interchangeable before count nouns, and may be omitted before plural count nouns.

As you have seen by the examples, non-count nouns tend to be intangible; count nouns tend to be tangible. Contrast, for example, *father, church, lake,* and *feather* (count nouns) with *hope, desire, joy,* and *sympathy* (non-count nouns). Those non-count nouns that do denote tangible things often name bulky materials (like *dirt, butter, salt,* or *rice*).

Some nouns are tricky, in that they can occur either as count or non-count nouns. Some of these are *freedom, democracy, sin, fire, exercise,* and *depression.* For example, you can say:

• Freedom is precious, (or) our freedoms are precious.

• Exercise is good for you, (or) do one new exercise each day.

• Democracy is a form of government, (or) the U.S. is a democracy.

---

* That is because languages differ in what they consider count and non-count nouns. Even British and American English differ on some words, for example, *hospital,* which is a count noun in American and a non-count noun in British English.

2. Why you need to know the difference

One reason you need to know the difference between count and non-count nouns is that you use different modifiers to refer to the two groups.

With count nouns use:	With non-count nouns use:
many	much
few, fewer	little, less
number	amount

For example, it is *many joys* but *much happiness, few lakes* but *little water,* a *number of dollars* but an *amount of money, fewer opportunities* but *less chance.*

Note: *More* and *some* can be used with either count or non-count nouns.

It is interesting that in English, non-count nouns frequently become count nouns, but count nouns seldom become non-count. For example, in the lists above, we could have added *behavior* as both a non-count noun, and a count noun. Originally a non-count noun, *behavior,* especially in the language of psychologists, is now used as a non-count noun in statements like "the behaviors of ordinary persons." Most of us would still say, "the behavior of ordinary persons." The count noun *peas,* now the plural of *pea,* was a non-count noun, spelled *pease,* in Middle English (between 1100 and 1500).

D. Latin and Greek Terms

1.   English plurals are now acceptable substitutes for the Latin plurals of some Latin nouns. The list includes the following words and it may expand as the public becomes less and less familiar with Latin.

Singular	Plural
• curriculum	• curricula or curriculums
• medium	• media, mediums
• addendum	• addenda, addendums
• stadium	• stadiums (seldom, stadia)

2.   But lawyers use Latin in their profession more than other people, and you should know and use those Latin plurals that are still considered correct. Here are some Latin nouns for which Latin plurals are still properly used:

Singular	Plural
• criterion	• criteria
• datum	• data
• stratum	• strata
• alumnus	• alumni (male)
• alumna	• alumnae (female)
• dictum	• dicta

Note: Do not use the Latin plural form with a singular verb.

Avoid, for example	Write instead
* The criteria is . . .	● The criteria are . . .
* The data shows . . .	● The data show . . .
* The alumni contributes . . .	● The alumni contribute . . .
* The dicta indicates . . .	● The dicta indicate . . .

3. For some reason, Greek plurals are less puzzling to modern writers than Latin plurals, perhaps because many Greek plurals end like English plurals, with an *s*.

Some common Greek-derived words:

Singular	Plural
crisis	crises
hypothesis	hypotheses
analysis	analyses
synthesis	syntheses
antithesis	antitheses
thesis	theses
symbiosis	symbioses
paralysis	paralyses

IV. Sentence Structure

A. How to Avoid Sentence Fragments

A sentence fragment results when you place a capital letter at the beginning and a period at the end of a group of words that are not a grammatical sentence. Legal professionals do not make this error often, but when they do, their writing suffers a cosmetic blemish that is hard to overcome. The two main kinds of sentence fragments are

1. Dependent clauses used as sentences:

  * Whereas, the defense attorney asked for acquittal.

To avoid the sentence fragment, attach the dependent clause to the independent clause that it follows:

  ● The prosecutor asked that the accused be given a life sentence, whereas the defense attorney asked for acquittal.

Note: If you remember that a clause introduced by a subordinator is a dependent clause, and it cannot stand alone as a sentence, you will avoid this kind of sentence fragment.

2. Groups of words lacking a finite verb:

  * The defense attorney's motion for a directed verdict pending.

---

* Throughout, ungrammatical locutions are preceded by asterisks. However, *data* as a singular noun has gained general acceptance because of wide and current use by many educated speakers, particularly in spoken English.

To avoid this sentence fragment, add a finite verb:

- The defense attorney's motion for a directed verdict is pending.

  * The employee consenting to waive the defects.

To avoid this sentence fragment, attach it to a clause containing a finite verb:

- In consenting to waive the defects, the employee has assumed the risk.

Or redraft, using a finite verb:

- The employee consented to waive the defects.

B. How to Avoid Run-on Sentences

Run-on sentences are sentence fragments in reverse; instead of half a sentence, the run-on sentence is two sentences, incorrectly joined to make one:

- The victim of the attack was blind he could not see the threatening gestures of his attackers.

You can correct a run-on sentence in several ways:

(1) Divide it into two sentences.

- The victim of the attack was blind. He could not see the threatening gestures of his attackers.

(2) Divide it into two independent clauses. You may add either a coordinating conjunction or a conjunctive adverb—or neither.

- The victim of the attack was blind, so he could not see the threatening gestures of his attackers. (coordinating conjunction)

- The victim of the attack was blind; therefore he could not see the threatening gestures of his attackers. (conjunctive adverb)

- The victim of the attack was blind; he could not see the threatening gestures of his attackers. (no connecting word)

Note: You may, if you wish, use a coordinating conjunction preceded by a semi-colon.

(3) Divide it into independent clauses joined by a colon (indicating to your readers that the second clause will explain or amplify the first).

Note: These three choices are stylistic, not grammatical, and depend upon what relationship you wish to indicate between the clauses. Chapter Three, § II, will further discuss relationships between ideas.

C. What to Do About Dangling Participles

Standard English requires that when a participial clause has no subject, its implied subject is the subject of the following independent clause. Participles dangle when the implied subject in the dependent clause is not the same as

the stated subject in the independent clause. The sentences that follow
contain no dangling participles:

1. Being sick in bed, I missed class.

   (I was sick in bed.)

2. Opening the jar, I took a pickle.

   (I opened the jar.)

3. Followed by my dog, I left the house.

   (I was followed by my dog.)

But in the next three sentences the implied subject in the dependent
clause is not the same as the subject of the independent clause:

1. * Becoming senile, the daughter committed her mother.

   (Was the daughter becoming senile?)

2. * After identifying the remains, the body was buried.

   (Who identified the remains?)

3. * Being filthy and roach-infested, the plaintiff refused to rent the
   apartment.

   (Was the plaintiff filthy and roach-infested?)

To eliminate dangling participles, just add a subject to the dependent
clause; or re-word the sentence without the dependent participial clause:

1. Because her mother had become senile, the daughter had her
   committed.

2. After a relative identified the remains, the body was buried.

3. Because the apartment was filthy and roach-infested, the plaintiff
   refused to rent it.

In legal writing, dangling participles may be confusing.* Consider the
following sentences in which the missing subject of the first clause should be
"the son." As written, sentence (1) says that the spouse may be convicted of
murder; and sentence (2) says that "the share of his mother's estate"
committed the murder. Sentence (3) clarifies the writer's intent:

1. * If convicted of murder, the son's spouse would inherit his share of
   the mother's estate.

2. * If convicted of murder, the son's share of his mother's estate would
   go to his spouse.

3. * If the son is convicted of murder, his spouse would inherit his share
   of the mother's estate.

Note: A few words that were formerly participles have become prepositions
or adverbs, and are not therefore considered dangling. A common word in

---

* The following blooper, amusing rather than confusing, recently appeared in the local newspaper: "In pleading guilty, the state agreed to drop 65 other felony charges against [the defendant]."

this group is *considering.* Some others are *conceding, barring,* and *regarding.*
Thus the following constructions do not "dangle":

- Considering his lack of education, his progress has been amazing.
- Conceding the contrary argument to be valid, his point is still well-taken.
- Barring untoward events, the meeting will be held.
- Regarding your letter, the problem you discuss is being corrected.

D. Eliminate Redundancies.

1. The unnecessary *that:*

Too many legal writers add an extra *that* to their sentences.

Consider the following examples:

- * The Court ruled in the earlier case that because quantity, price, and conditions were all stated that a valid offer resulted.
- * It has been argued that because some students panic in a single final examination that several tests should be given.

In these sentences, **the second *that* is redundant; delete it** so that
the sentences read:

- The Court ruled in the earlier case that because quantity, price, and conditions were all stated there was a valid offer.
- It has been argued that because some students panic in a single examination several tests should be given.

Note: On the other hand, the same writers may omit *that* when it is necessary
for clarity. See pages 71–72.

2. The *would have . . . would have* error

The following sentences are ungrammatical:

- * If the defendant would have used his rear-view mirror, he could have avoided the accident.
- * If the attorney would have prevailed, he would have modified the judge's instructions.

The rule is that in conditional sentences, like those cited, you use the
locution *had . . . would (or could) have.* So change the sentences to read:

- If the defendant had used his rear-view mirror, he could have avoided the accident.
- If the attorney had prevailed, he would have modified the judge's instructions.

3. The extra *is*

The following examples are not misprints; they were taken from legal writing, and they are ungrammatical:

    * The fact is is that . . .

    * The problem is is that . . .

These errors are probably the result of analogy to a common noun-construction *what it is,* which does require a second *is:*

- What it is is a series of proposals.

The noun phrase *what it is* can be replaced by a noun or pronoun (for example, *the proposal* or *it*). The entire phrase acts as a subject in the sentence, and you need to add the verb *is.*

But *the fact* and *the problem* constitute the noun subjects in the other two illustrations, so you should add only the verb *is* to complete the subject-verb construction. The correct construction would then be:

- The fact is that . . .
- The problem is that . . .

4. The extra modifier

This kind of redundancy is not grammatical, but it should be included in the list. It is the adding of an unnecessary, and often misleading, modifier to a statement. See if you can recognize it in the following sentences:

- The defendant acted wilfully by allowing such immoral acts to continue.
- Judges should not tip the scales of justice improperly.
- We must protect citizens from the arbitrary harassment of police.

The excess modifiers in these sentences are *such, improperly,* and *arbitrary.* In none of the statements are those words necessary, and their inclusion may cause misunderstanding. Try your skill at deleting the excess modifiers in the following sentences:

- The burglars were able to accomplish their crime because of the insufficient number of inadequately trained guards.
- The grading of my paper displays a too-capricious procedure.
- The inebriated passenger failed to exercise due care by playfully grabbing the steering wheel while the car was in motion.

E. Avoid Incorrect Deletions.

1. The necessary preposition

Perhaps to rebut the accusation that their writing is wordy, lawyers sometimes omit necessary prepositions. The following appeared in legal writing:

* The defense has considered which newspaper the advertisement should appear.
* The Senate is the forum which he should make his case.
* The controversy abounds the press.
* The students browse the library.

All of these sentences need a preposition. In the first two, add one at the end of the sentence or in the middle. The only reason for choosing the middle of the sentence is that you usually prefer to save the end of the sentence for your most compelling points. Corrected, the sentences would read:

* The defense has considered in which newspaper the advertisement should appear, **or**
* The defense considered which newspaper the advertisement should appear in.
* The Senate is the forum in which he should make his case, **or**
* The Senate is the forum which he should make his case in.*

In the second two sentences, you do not have to make a choice. Just add the preposition:

* The controversy abounds in the press.
* The students browse in the library.

2. The required verb

The grammatical rule states that a verb can be deleted from a sentence only when the identical verb appears elsewhere in the same sentence. In the next two sentences the bracketed verbs were correctly deleted, for they were identical to the verbs that were present:

* I enjoy corporate law practice and probably always will [*enjoy* it].
* John has been on the city attorney's staff, and so has Mary [*been* on the city attorney's staff].

But, in the next two sentences, you should not delete the second verb, because it is not identical to the verb that is present:

* I have and always will believe in the jury system.
* He has and continues to proclaim his innocence.

In the first sentence the missing verb is *believed,* not *believe.* And in the second sentence the missing verb is *proclaimed,* and the verb that is present is *proclaim.* What can you do to remedy the situation? To be correct grammatically you would need to include the deleted verb, but that would make the sentences somewhat longer:

---

* Note that you can delete the pronoun *which* from this sentence. For a discussion of this point, see p. 57, above. See also *caveat,* at page 59, regarding missing prepositions.

- I have always believed and always will believe in the jury system.

- He has proclaimed and continues to proclaim his innocence.

If you don't like these last two sentences, English grammar provides an alternative that may be more to your liking. It's called the "all-time-present," and you recognize it in sentences like:

- She believes in justice for all.

- He insists on punctuality.

In these two sentences, the present tense verb (*believes, insists*) indicates action that occurred in the past and will continue into the future, as well as existing in the present. You can think of innumerable such statements ("I love television," "I walk two miles daily," and many others). So you can substitute for the two verbs in the cited sentences above, one verb expressing the all-time-present, and your statement will differ only slightly in meaning from that expressed by two verbs:

- I believe in the jury system.

- He proclaims his innocence.

3. The clarifying *that*

On page 68, under the heading "Eliminate Redundancies," "the unnecessary *that* " was discussed. But not all *that's* are created equal, and those now to be discussed are not redundant, and may be necessary to aid your reader to understand what you mean. You may find that you have to re-read the next three sentences because the clarifying *that* is missing:

- The judge held the flowerpot could constitute a deadly weapon.

- The defendant could reasonably have foreseen the cutting of the boat line would result in the boat's sinking.

- The court found a statute that was not colorblind was unconstitutional.

The problem in each sentence is that because the transitive verbs *hold, foresee,* and *find* take noun objects, the reader assumes that *flowerpot, cutting,* and *statute* are the objects of the verb (and not, as is the case, the subjects of their own dependent clauses). So initially, the reader understands the sentence to mean:

The judge held the flowerpot . . .

The defendant could reasonably have foreseen the cutting . . .

The court found a statute that was not colorblind . . .

If you, the writer, include the deleted *that,* however, you put the reader on notice that the object of the verb will be the entire clause that follows, not just the nearest noun:

- The judge held that the flowerpot could constitute a deadly weapon.

- The defendant could reasonably have foreseen that the cutting of the boat line would result in the boat's sinking.

- The court found that a statute that was not colorblind was unconstitutional.

Succinctness is desirable, but not when it is achieved at the cost of time and effort to the reader. When you are using the same kind of construction with a verb that could not possibly take as an object the noun that follows it, you will not confuse your reader, so you can either retain or omit the *that:*

- The juror did not think [that] the witness was telling the truth.

- City officials believe [that] the proposed development should be permitted.

- The district attorney stated [that] the persons indicted were in custody.

Because you can neither *think a witness, believe a development,* nor *state a person,* you have created no ambiguity by omitting *that.*

Chapter Three
Legal Writing Style

The grammatical skills reviewed in the last chapter provide the basis for effective writing, but they constitute only the first step. To write effectively, you must communicate effectively. Remember the discussion between the March Hare, the Mad Hatter, and Alice:

"Take some more tea," the March Hare said to Alice, very earnestly.

"I've had nothing yet," Alice replied in an offended tone: "so I can't take more."

"You mean you can't take less," said the Hatter: "It's very easy to take *more* than nothing."

* * *

"You should say what you mean," the March Hare went on."

"I do," Alice hastily replied, "at least I mean what I say—that's the same thing, you know."

"Not the same thing a bit!" said the Hatter. "Why, you might just as well say that 'I see what I eat' is the same as 'I eat what I see.'!" *

Communication skills are even more vital for lawyers than for people like Alice, for language is the primary tool of the legal profession, and lawyers are held to a higher standard of its use than other people.

But most entering law students tend to minimize the importance of legal writing. For one thing, they have been writing all of their academic lives and they tend to feel competent in that skill, while they view the courses that teach "the law" with appropriate awe, for these courses are new and strange.

However, the sense of competence in writing that most students feel may be unwarranted, for many students have majored as undergraduates in disciplines requiring little writing—disciplines like engineering and accounting. Other students have written substantial amounts of expository writing, but writing of a kind different from what they will be doing in law school. Until now they have been rewarded with A's for imaginative, emotional, discursive writing; now they will need to write logically, persuasively, factually, concisely.

To make the transition to effective legal writing even more difficult, law students are often assigned casebook reading containing court opinions that are badly written. Some of the opinions are old, written in a style and language no longer appropriate. Even some of the more recent opinions they read are not models of effective writing. They may contain verbiage, jargon, Latinisms, and other characteristics for which the legal profession is often

* From Lewis Carroll, *Alice's Adventures in Wonderland*, stanza 8.

justly criticized. The opinions assigned for reading are selected not for their linguistic excellence but for their legal significance, and new law students tend to mimic the bad writing rather than the good.

As law students you will learn that in legal writing, unlike much other writing, your personalities should remain in the background. Creativity and discursiveness, which perhaps earned you kudos as undergraduates, should give way to clarity and logical analysis. "Style" should not be visible; matter should dominate manner.

The story of the appearance of Caesar and Cicero before the Roman Senate is apropos. When Cicero, a brilliant orator, finished his speech urging the Romans to attack the invading Gauls, the senators applauded enthusiastically, declaring it eloquent. But after Caesar spoke, they rose to their feet and cried, "Let us fight the Gauls!" Legal writing, like Caesar's speech, should call forth action, not praise.

The material in this chapter should help you move your readers to action; the three sections will help you write clearly, effectively, and with propriety. These divisions sometimes overlap, but together they constitute the ABC's of good legal writing: accuracy, brevity, and clarity.

I. Writing It Clearly

A. Use Periodic Sentences Cautiously; Vary Your Sentence Structure.

A periodic sentence in English is structurally somewhat similar to a typical German sentence, which, as Mark Twain facetiously remarked, "goes on for several pages before it comes up at the end with the verb in its mouth."

Not all periodic sentences are bad. They are effective as long as they are not misused. Periodic sentences provide structural variety to your writing, and, strategically used, they induce your reader to continue reading in order to reach the important idea you have cleverly placed at the end. But long, involved periodic sentences on dull topics confuse more than they enlighten.

Periodic sentences are one of the three types of sentence structure found in English, stylistically speaking. The other two types are **loose** and **balanced**. You probably learned about these three types of sentence structure when you were in junior high school, but you may welcome a quick review.

In a **loose** sentence, the subject and predicate are close together; the subject tells what or who the sentence is about, and the predicate tells what the subject did. The typical sentence order of a loose sentence is subject-verb-object. (The predicate is composed of the verb and object, or if the verb has no object, only the verb.) In loose sentences, subject and predicate are close together, with no interrupting language separating them. The following sentences are loose in structure, although their grammatical structure is, respectively, simple, compound, and complex:

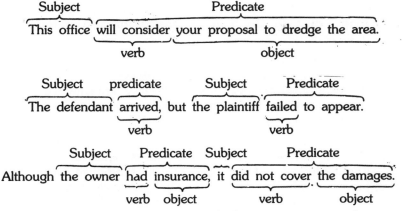

In lengthy or complicated sentences, the loose sentence provides stopping points along the way, at which the reader understands what the writer means thus far. In such sentences, loose sentence structure is a favor to your readers.

Unlike loose sentences, **periodic** sentences provide no stopping places. Because periodic sentences contain 'interrupters,' that is, clauses separating the subject from its predicate, or introductory clauses even before the subject of the sentence is stated, the reader must read the entire sentence before learning what it is about. Here is a periodic sentence:

> • On a dark night, when the moon was invisible and the stars were heavily shrouded in clouds, when only muffled earth sounds interrupted the stillness that surrounded me as I walked through the deep woods alone, deep in thought and unaware of any human presence, **suddenly a raucous cry split the silence.**

In the sentence above, the subject (a raucous cry), the verb (split), and the object (the silence) are delayed until the end. But the subject-matter of the sentence was probably sufficiently interesting to keep you reading. Unfortunately, the subject-matter of legal writing is usually neither exciting nor suspenseful. But legal writers seem to love the periodic sentence; certainly many of them overuse it. Consider, as a horrendous example, the following excerpt from § 25 of the Judiciary Act of 1789:

> • **A final judgment or decree in any suit,** in the highest court of law or equity of a State in which a decision in the suit could be had, where is drawn in question the validity of a treaty or statute of, or an authority exercised under the United States, and the decision is against their validity; or where is drawn in question the validity of a statute of, or an authority exercised under any State, on the ground of their being repugnant to the constitution, treaties or laws of the United States, and the decision is in favor of such validity, or where is drawn in question the construction of any clause of the constitution, or of a treaty, or statute of, or commission held under the United States, and the decision is against the title, right, privilege or exemption specially set up or claimed by either party, under such clause of the said Constitution, treaty, statute or

commission, **may be reexamined and reversed or affirmed in the Supreme Court of the United States upon a writ of error.** (Emphasis added.)

In this sentence, the subject (a final judgment or decree) appears in line one. But you had to read 15 lines further before you reached the verb (may be re-examined) and the remainder of the predicate. In between are dumped qualifying clauses. Neither interest nor suspense motivates you to read the sentence to the end, only the dogged determination (or the need) to understand the material.

Contrast the current version of this earliest antecedent: 28 U.S.C. § 1257. The drafters of 28 U.S.C. § 1257 have substituted **loose** sentence structure for the **periodic** structure of the earlier draft and added the qualifiers in a list at the end. Note how much clearer the current version is:

> • Final judgments or decrees rendered by the highest court of a State in which a decision could be had may be reviewed by the Supreme Court as follows:
>
> (1) By appeal, where is drawn in question the validity of a treaty or statute of the United States and the decision is against its validity.
>
> (2) By appeal, where is drawn in question the validity of a statute of any state on the ground of its being repugnant to the Constitution, treaties or laws of the United States, and the decision is in favor of its validity.
>
> (3) By writ of certiorari, where the validity of a treaty or statute of the United States is drawn in question on the ground of its being repugnant to the Constitution, treaties or laws of the United States, or where any title, right, privilege or immunity is specially set up or claimed under the Constitution, treaties or statutes of, or commission held or authority exercised under, the United States.

If you use periodic sentence structure in long, complicated sentences, you may confuse yourself as well as your readers. In the following sentence, from a student memo, when the writer reaches the end of his sentence, she uses the referent 'it' to refer to a subject that she has forgotten to set down. Here is the sentence:

> • In Peairs v. Florida Publishing Company, where the court held the newspaper publisher liable for injuries resulting from a pedestrian tripping over a wire loop left on a public parking lot by a newsboy, if the publisher was aware of the conduct of the newsboys and failed to take proper action to remedy the situation, even though the newsboys and carriers were called independent contractors, if the publisher meddled or interfered it was deemed an agent-principal relationship; accordingly we can establish a similar relationship in the instant case.

This sentence calls to mind a dinner-table rule enforced by my mother: Never talk with your mouth full. Here the writer, her mouth full of qualifying clauses, is making an almost-unintelligible statement because she is trying to say five things at once:

(1) The *Peairs* court held that an agent-principal relationship existed between the defendant Florida Publishing Company and its newsboy-employee, despite the publisher's designation of its newsboy as an independent contractor.

(2) The agent-principal relationship existed because the publisher had the right to interfere in the activities of its newsboys.

(3) As "principal," the employer has the duty to remedy a dangerous situation that the newsboy as "agent" caused.

(4) Therefore the newspaper publisher is liable for the injuries of a pedestrian who tripped over a wire loop that a newsboy-employee left on a public parking lot.

(5) A similar relationship exists in the instant case.

Put these sentences together, and you will have a paragraph that is longer than the single sentence from the student memo. But the message is also clearer. You may combine the five sentences into three longer ones and retain clarity; but you should avoid the periodic structure that caused the problem in the first place. Here is a possible re-write in loose sentence structure.

     • The *Peairs* court held that the Florida Publishing Company, a newspaper publisher, was liable for the injuries of a pedestrian who tripped over a wire loop left on a public parking lot by a newsboy, despite the publisher's claim that newsboys were "independent contractors." The court reasoned that the relationship between the publisher and the newsboys was that of agent and principal because the publisher had the right to interfere in its newsboys' actions. Therefore the publishing company as principal should have taken appropriate action to remedy the dangerous situation of which it was aware and which was caused by the newsboy as agent. A similar principal-agent relationship exists in the instant case.

Finally, here is another periodic sentence, this one from a court opinion, which shows that the opinion-drafter can lose his way in the maze of clauses if he uses periodic structure for a sentence replete with parenthetical insertions. Only a brave reader would attempt to unravel it:

The perjury charged in the indictment is in substance that in a certain cause theretofore pending in the Circuit Court of the _____ Judicial Circuit for _____ County, wherein the State of _____ was plaintiff and one Riley D _____ was defendant, in which the said Riley D was charged with unlawful intercourse with an unmarried female person of previous chaste character, who was at the time of such intercourse under the age of eighteen years, in which such cause the defendant herein, Raiford B., was sworn in due form of law as a witness to tell the truth, the whole truth, and nothing but the truth touching the matters in issue in said cause, **the said Raiford B. did wilfully, knowingly, falsely, and corruptly during the progress of said trial testify as follows:** [Emphasis added]

With this example of a periodic sentence, I rest my case. Use periodic sentences for variety in sentence structure, and to create suspense or expectation, but for complicated ideas, choose loose or balanced sentence structure.

Balanced sentences give your writing grace and polish, and may make it memorable. In the balanced sentence, the parallel structure and repetition of sentence patterns underline the similarity or contrast of the ideas presented. The most easily recalled passages of literature contain balanced sentences. Here is a passage from *Ecclesiastes*:

> • To everything there is a season, and a time to every purpose under the heaven:
>
> A time to be born, and a time to die; a time to plant, and a time to pluck up what is planted;
>
> A time to kill, and a time to heal; a time to break down, and a time to build up;
>
> A time to weep, and a time to laugh; a time to mourn, and a time to dance . . .

Benjamin Franklin's *Poor Richard* gave lawyers a drubbing—in balanced sentences that are still quoted:

> • A countryman between two lawyers is like a fish between two cats.
>
> • God works wonders now and then; Behold, a lawyer and an honest man!
>
> • A good lawyer, a bad neighbor.
>
> • Here comes the orator, with his flood of words and his drop of reason!

Contrast the statements of Benjamin Franklin and John Hancock during the drafting of the Declaration of Independence. Franklin's balanced construction has made his comment a household saying; Hancock's observation is recalled only by historians:

> • Hancock: "We must be unanimous; there must be no pulling different ways; we must all hang together."
>
> • Franklin: "Yes, we must all hang together or we will all hang separately."

Winston Churchill knew the power of the balanced sentence. Contrast his and Sir Anthony Eden's statements during World War II:

> • Eden: "We shall not let go until we have done the job, and we welcome all those who will give us a hand to finish it."
>
> • Churchill: "Give us the tools and we will finish the job."

Finally, in *The Nature of the Judicial Process* (1921) p. 129, Judge Cardozo used a balanced sentence to make an important point that he wanted to be remembered:

> Judges have the power . . . though not the right, to ignore the mandate of a statute, and render judgment in despite of it. They have the

power, though not the right, to travel beyond the walls of the interstices, the bounds set to judicial innovation by precedent and custom. None the less, by that abuse of power, they violate the law.

Note that in the last sentence, Judge Cardozo used periodic structure to make his point effectively. By the use of inversion in that short sentence, he placed his most important idea last, emphasizing it by its position. More will be said later in this chapter (pages 95–97) about placement for emphasis.

B.　Use Connectors Carefully.

1.　Language as connectors

As important as your ideas themselves are the words you use to connect and relate them. If your readers do not understand your point, you might as well have omitted it. Some connectors are **conjunctions** (like *but, for, and, or* . . .); others are **adverbs** (like *hence, therefore, however, since, although* . . .); sometimes **numbers** are connectors, sometimes a **word repeated** and preceded by **'the'** or **'this.'** Sometimes connectors are not words at all, but **punctuation marks.**

Although you will seldom need to consult a list to select transition language, here are some of the words most commonly used to express the following relationships:

- Temporal relationships: then, meanwhile, next, before, later, in a few days, until, then, when, after, following . . .
- Spatial relationships: above, below, nearby, beyond, opposite, adjacent to, adjoining, far from . . .
- Addition: furthermore, moreover, besides, also, again, in addition to, further . . .
- Causal relationships: because, since, consequently, so that, in order to, for that reason . . .
- Logical relationships: nevertheless, however, therefore, hence, thus, despite, but . . .
- Comparison and contrast: similarly, likewise, in a like manner, yet, but, on the contrary, notwithstanding . . .

Another way to provide transition is to repeat a word or phrase used in the previous sentence or paragraph. The repetition of "theories" in the following excerpt is an illustration.

- Several **theories** regarding the intent of the equal protection clause are discussed in this section of the paper. Differences in these **theories,** their weaknesses and strengths, and a proposal for alternative theories to avoid the unfavorable results of these theories will also be discussed.

(This device should be used sparingly, for it can cause repetitiousness.) All of this may seem elementary, and indeed it is, but too often, connectors are absent in legal writing. In fact, the better you know your subject, the more apt you are to omit connectors, probably because your mind inserts them even when you have not written them down.   Here is a paragraph from the thesis of an L.L.M. student who knew his subject very well—too well, in fact, to communicate it clearly:

> • Taxpayers and Congress play games with tax laws.   Congress enacts a tax law disallowing deductions for certain activities.   Taxpayers' lawyers find loopholes in the law so as to provide deductions for their clients.   Congress promulgates an amendment to the law to close the loophole.   The depreciation deduction allowed under Sections 167 and 168 permitted taxpayers to include borrowed amounts in determining the adjusted basis of property.   When taxpayers reduced their tax liability by depreciation deductions through heavily mortgaged property, tax shelters resulted.   Congress enacted Section 465 in 1976 to close the loophole.

The same paragraph, with connectors in boldface, is longer, but also clearer:

> • Taxpayers and Congress play games with tax laws.   **First,** Congress enacts a tax law disallowing deductions for certain activities.   **Then** taxpayers' lawyers find loopholes in the law so as to provide deductions for their clients.   **Next,** Congress promulgates an amendment to the law to close **the loopholes.   And so it continues.   For example,** the depreciation deduction allowed under Sections 167 and 168 permitted taxpayers to include borrowed amounts in determining the adjusted basis of property.   **This depreciation** resulted from depreciation deductions through heavily mortgaged property.   **Therefore,** in 1976, Congress enacted Section 465 in order to close **that loophole.**

Here is another actual excerpt from a law student's analysis of a case in which a workman sued the manufacturer of a machine in which he injured his hand:

> • The plaintiff worked in a factory.   He injured his hand while operating machinery provided by the defendant.   The plaintiff sustained a crushed hand.   The court stated that the plaintiff did not act out of choice.   The court reasoned that the plaintiff's occupation required that he do so.   The court reasoned that it was possible that plaintiff had been ordered to use machinery in the way in which he did in the course of his employment.   The court said that liability for an injury belongs to the party who is in the best position to eliminate dangers, in this case, the manufacturer.

Besides the absence of connectors, you probably noticed the monotonous repetition of one kind of sentence structure in the excerpt above: Subject–Verb–Object.   Variety of sentence construction is important to good legal writing.   You will notice that sentence variety, as well as connectors, improve the re-write:

> • The plaintiff, a factory worker, crushed his hand in a machine he was operating **and** brought suit against its manufacturer.   The court found that the plaintiff was not responsible for his injury **because** his occupation required that he operate **the machine.   Thus** he did not act

out of choice and may **even** have been ordered to use **the machine** in the way in which he did. In finding for the plaintiff, the court **also** stated that liability for injury belonged to the party best able to eliminate the danger, in this case the manufacturer.

Between paragraphs, transition is even more important than between sentences within a paragraph, for the reader expects that all sentences in a paragraph are somehow connected and transition merely shows him how. But the new paragraph signals either a new topic or a new direction for the previous topic. In the following excerpt, the repetition of "decision" tells the reader to expect a new direction for the previous topic:

- In its **decision** in *Smith v. Bagwell,* the Florida Supreme Court described punitive damages as recompense to the sufferer as well as punishment to the offender and an example to the community. It described compensatory damages as those which arise from actual and indirect pecuniary loss, mental suffering, medical expenses, and bodily pain and suffering.

- The court, in **this decision,** seemed to confuse the principle of compensatory damages—the means of compensating the victim for injury to his person—with the principle of punitive damages—punishment for the offender and a deterrent to the community.

The first draft of any writing is apt to lack transition, particularly when the writer knows his subject so thoroughly that he is unaware that transition language is missing. The problem is compounded when, as is often true in legal writing, the subject is complex. So as you read your first draft, add guideposts so that your reader can follow you to your destination.

2. Commas as connectors

The omission of the final comma in a series is now common. But I would include that comma in legal writing because its absence may cause problems. For example, in the sentence, "All of my assets are to be divided equally among my children: Mary, Joan, Edward and Mark," how many divisions did the testator intend? Should the assets be divided three ways, with Edward and Mark sharing a third? If the testator had added a final comma before *and,* there would have been no ambiguity.

The absence of the final comma in the following sentence creates an absurdity:

- The director of nursing explained that the clinic had been closed because of the dilapidated condition of the building, lack of facilities and vermin.

The absence of the final comma in the next sentence raises a question about meaning:

- Professor X enjoyed fishing in the Gulf of Mexico, traveling, the study of Egyptian art and history.

The addition of one comma would have clarified the following probate document language:

- The undersigned, _____, has received full payment of the claim filed in this proceeding against the above estate on _____, 19___
  . . .

It is not clear whether the *claim* was filed at the stated date or payment was *received* then. Add a comma, and you know that the claim was filed at that date:

- The undersigned, has received full payment of the claim, filed in this proceeding against the above estate on _____, 19___ . . .

To state that *payment* was received on the stated date, move the "date" phrase:

- The undersigned, _____, has received full payment on _____, 19___, of the claim filed in this proceeding against the above estate
  . . .

Commas that are misplaced may be as damaging as commas that are omitted. See, for example, the thirteenth amendmemt to the Constitution, which states:

- Neither slavery nor involuntary servitude, except as punishment for crime whereof the party shall have been duly convicted, shall exist within the United States, or any place subject to their jurisdiction.

A literal reading of this amendment would lead to the conclusion that both slavery and involuntary servitude can exist in the United States as punishment for the conviction of crime. The drafters intended no such meaning, yet the amendment has been uncritically copied into the constitutions of some state governments, perpetuating the error in the placement of the comma. Correctly placed, the commas would provide the intended meaning:

- Neither slavery, nor involuntary servitude except as punishment for crime whereof the party shall have been duly convicted, shall exist within the United States, or any place subject to their jurisdiction.*

3. Appropriate language to indicate causality

In the following sentences, **and** is a poor choice:

(1) If the landlord is guilty **and** violates the rule, his conduct constitutes constructive eviction.

Re–Write:

- If the landlord is guilty **because** he violated the rule, his conduct constitutes constructive eviction.

(2) If the defendant can prove that the statute was vaguely written **and** did not give adequate notice, the federal statute would override it.

---

* For more on the use of commas, see pages 45–47, above.

Re–Write:

- If the defendant can prove the state statute was vaguely written in that it did not give adequate notice, the federal statute would override it.

4. Replace vague connecting words with specific words.

(1) **After** studying hard, we found the final examination easy.

Re–Write:

Because we studied hard, we found the final examination easy.

(2) **Having** committed a heinous crime, the defendant received the maximum sentence.

Re–Write:

Because he committed a heinous crime, the defendant received the maximum sentence.

(3) Try **and** do your best.

Re–Write:

Try **to** do your best.

C. Say It Affirmatively.

1. Negative statements lack force.

They merely deny, so they are less forceful than affirmative statements. Therefore, when possible, state your ideas affirmatively. Compare the following pairs:

- He did not carry out his responsibility.

  He failed to carry out his responsibility.

- He did not fulfill his duty.

  He failed in his duty.

- He did not carry out the contract.

  He breached the contract.

2. Negative statements can be confusing.

Here is one from the Model Penal Code § 5.01(2):

- Without **negativing** the sufficiency of other conduct, the following, if strongly corroborative of the actor's criminal purpose, **shall not be held insufficient** as a matter of law. (Emphasis added.)

With the three negatives removed, the statement is clearer:

- Although other conduct may also suffice, the following conduct, if it strongly corroborates the actor's criminal purpose, shall be held sufficient as a matter of law.

Here are two sentences from different court opinions. Count the negatives and you can see why the sentences are almost unintelligible:

• Whether the case of an intrusion by a stranger who **does not have** title, on a peaceable possession, is **not one** to meet the exigencies of which the courts will recognize a still further qualification or explanation of the rule requiring the plaintiff to recover only on the strength of his own title, is a question which **has not** as yet been decided by this court.

• This rule should **not** be construed so as to entitle a person to recover for damage in a case where the proof shows that the defendant could **not** by the exercise of due care have prevented the injury, or where the defendant's negligence was **not** a legal cause of the result complained of by the plaintiff. [Emphasis added.] *

Try to unscramble the above sentences by deleting some negatives. Then check the possible re-writes below to see whether your understanding of what each means is similar to the author's:

(1) This court has not yet decided whether the case of an intrusion by a stranger who lacks title, on a peaceable possession, meets the exigencies required under the rule that a plaintiff can recover only on the strength of his own title.

(2) Under this rule plaintiff is entitled to recover for damages only when it is proved that the defendant, by exercising due care, could have prevented plaintiff's injury, or when defendant's negligence was a legal cause of the results plaintiff complains of.**

Unfortunately, you will find many opinions that contain confusing negative constructions. These tend to bewilder those law students who come from disciplines relatively free of that kind of writing. One way to make the sentence comprehensible is to substitute one affirmative for every two negatives in the sentence. (This strategy seems to work most of the time, but it is not guaranteed.) Another device is to change "not . . . unless" language to "only . . . when."

Rule-of-Thumb: In your own writing, delete as many negatives as you can from each sentence you have written, when you have used more than one negative.

3. Negative statements can be ambiguous.

Each of the following statements have at least two opposite meanings:

• Florida's educational problem is not being able to attract and hold its teachers.

Possible meanings:

(1) Florida's educational problem is that it is unable to attract and hold its teachers.

* Sentences like these recall George Orwell's remark that the statement "To my mind it is a not unjustifiable assumption," merely means "I think." (in "Politics and the English Language").

** In these re-writes, the verbs were also changed from passive to active voice in order to clarify the meaning.

(2) Attracting and holding its teachers is not Florida's educational problem.

- I have not been able to accumulate a sizable bank account due to the size of my salary.

Possible meanings:

(1) I have not been able to accumulate a sizable bank account, and my failure to do so is the size of my salary.

(2) I have been able to accumulate a sizable bank account despite the size of my salary.

4. Don't use *all* with negatives.

Another confusing combination is *all* **plus the negative.** For example, when you say "All cats are gray," you are dealing with totality. Not so when you add the negative. When you say "All cats are not gray," you are actually saying that *some* cats are. Your assertion is now synonymous with "Not all cats are gray." To assert totality, you must say, "No cats are gray." That sentence is the opposite of "All cats are gray."

The writer of a recent bulletin board notice was unaware of this problem. The notice read:

- On Tuesday, June 8 and Wednesday, June 9, all regularly scheduled classes will not meet.

What the notice *said* was that some regularly scheduled classes *would* meet. How should the notice have been worded?

However, as with all "rules," this one has some exceptions. The negative statement is useful when you want to convey **lukewarm enthusiasm**—or even **intentional ambiguity.** For example, when he was questioned about a former government official who was under indictment, President Reagan said, "Mr. _____ is not a dishonest man."

A law colleague tells me he responds reluctantly to requests of undeserving students for a recommendation, by writing, "I cannot recommend him too highly." The ambiguous negative is useful to damn with faint praise, to endorse with a degree of doubt. The professor of legal writing who says, "This is not bad writing," does not necessarily mean it is *good* writing. A 1975 court, in permitting the removal of a kidney from an incompetent man, used the negative to express its reasoning that, ". . . the transplant is not without benefit to him." *

Perhaps the final word on the use of negative constructions should be this: Someone once defined a lady as a woman who never insulted anyone without intending to do so. Similarly, never use the ambiguous negative without intending ambiguity.

* In re Guardianship of Pescinski, 67 Wis. 2d 4, 226 N.W.2d 180.

D. Use Expletives Sparingly.

Everyone knows the lay meaning of *expletive.* (You learned when you were five years old that expletives were words not to use, at least in your mother's presence). Although grammatical expletives are quite different, you are still advised to use them sparingly in legal writing. Grammatical expletives are words that are necessary to fill a slot that English syntax requires be filled. In the following two sentences, *there* and *it* are expletives:

- There is no reason to delay.
- It is easy to draft pleadings.

In these sentences, *there* and *it* contain no meaning. They are used merely to fill the necessary subject slot at the beginning of the sentences. In the sentences, the expletive construction does not impair the meaning. But often in legal writing the substitution of an expletive for the real subject prevents the reader from knowing who or what the real subject is. These sentences were taken from students' writing:

(1) There is a cause of action because the passenger suffered from the reckless conduct of the driver.

(2) There is the possibility that intoxication would be a defense if intent and knowledge are necessary elements of the crime.

(3) It was indicated in *Zell* that there is almost universal acceptance of extrinsic parol evidence.

(4) There is a strong suspicion that a crime occurred, due to the appearance of the room.

Missing from these sentences is an answer to the question, "who?" (or "what?"). *Who* had a cause of action? *Who* believed that intoxication might be a defense—and for whom? *What* indicated? And *who* suspected?

The way to eliminate those expletive constructions that may obscure your writing is to tell the reader *who* did *what* to *whom*. When you do that, you are usually putting a person or group of persons in the subject slot. A re-write of the four sentences above provides that information:

(1) The passenger has a cause of action against the driver because of the driver's reckless conduct.

(2) The accused person might plead intoxication as a defense if intent and knowledge are elements of the crime.

(3) The *Zell* opinion indicates that courts almost universally accept extrinsic parol evidence.*

(4) Police detectives strongly suspect that a crime occurred, due to the appearance of the room.

Even when you are not using expletives, you need to guard against failing to tell your reader "who did it." Law students tend to make actions, rules, etc.,

---

* In this sentence, passive voice verbs were changed to active. More on that sub- ject follows in this chapter, at pages 100–103.

the subject of their sentences, not persons, courts and other groups of individuals. I call the following "whodunit" constructions. They came from law students' papers:

(1) In *Garratt v. Dailey,* the question of intent in terms of subjective desire was resolved.

(2) The conceded volitional act was mentioned by Justice Hill.

(3) The moving of the chair was an act reflecting intent to cause the fall.

(4) The primary issue in this case was Brian's intent. His version that no intent existed was accepted by the court.

A state supreme court judge complained to me that this kind of construction conceals "a secret actor." In the sentences above, not only the actor, but the receiver of the action is unclear. I returned the students' papers with the following questions about the sentences:

(1) In *Garratt v. Dailey,* the court found that Brian (intended/did not intend) to DO WHAT TO WHOM?

(2) Justice Hill said that WHO CONCEDED THAT HE DID WHAT TO WHOM?

(3) When WHO? moved the chair, he intended to DO WHAT TO WHOM?

(4) The primary issue was whether Brian intended TO DO WHAT TO WHOM? The court accepted Brian's version of the facts: that Brian did not intend TO DO WHAT TO WHOM?

Legal disputes almost always represent disagreement among parties. Courts decide these disputes by applying legal rules to the particular actions of those parties. If you omit the parties from your discussion of legal problems, you are omitting the key factors.

But, as usual, there are exceptions to the rule that you should take care to say WHO did WHAT to WHOM. Experts use expletives to advantage when they want to leave the actor out. For example, consider the statement by William Kunstler, who was representing the son of Marlon Brando, who had shot and killed Brando's daughter's boyfriend. Kunstler reportedly said of the killing, "There has been a tragic shooting here."

E. Put Modifiers Where They Belong.

Modifiers belong next to the words they modify. If you fail to follow this rule, you may suffer serious consequences. For example, one hospital asked patients being admitted to sign the following consent form:

- I hereby authorize the Physician or Physicians in charge to administer such treatment and the surgeon to have administered such anesthetic as found necessary to perform this operation which is advisable in the treatment of this patient.

In this case, a patient sued after the surgeon removed her reproductive organs during surgery for a simple appendectomy. No attempt had been made by the surgeon to enlarge the scope of the operation. The court held against the hospital, stating that the consent form the patient signed was so ambiguous as to be almost worthless. The reason: the modifying clause, introduced by *which*. Because that clause followed the word *operation,* the court construed it to mean that the *operation* was advisable, though the hospital intended it to mean that the patient consented to the *anesthetic* and *treatment* that were advisable.

Courts have been asked to construe modifying language so often that they have given it a legal name: the **Doctrine of the Last Antecedent.** Under this doctrine, courts presume that drafters place modifying words and phrases next to what they intend to modify. For example, a court construed the language "an *ad valorem* tax on a leasehold interest or governmental property that is measured by income or volume of transaction," to mean that the governmental property was measured, although the drafter intended to say that the *ad valorem* tax was measured. Placing the clause beginning with *that* next to the wrong word caused him to lose the lawsuit.

In another case, a court held that only observance of a safety rule was required by a statute, when the court construed the following language, ". . . where injury is caused by the willful refusal of the employee to use a safety appliance or observe a safety rule required by statute." The drafter had intended to say that both were required by statute, but careless drafting lost his case.

In this latter example, placing a comma after the word *rule* would have avoided the problem. The language would then read, ". . . where injury is caused by the willful refusal of the employee to use a safety appliance or observe a safety rule, required by statute." For the Doctrine of the Last Antecedent states that where no contrary intention is indicated, referential language intended to apply to all antecedents, not only the closest, should be separated from the antecedent language by a comma.* The comma after *rule* would signify, under both the rules of grammar and the Doctrine, that use of a safety appliance *and* observation of a safety rule were required by the statute.

Law students misplace modifiers, sometimes with unintended humor. The following appeared on assigned papers:

- The proposed site was deemed unsafe due to contamination by a leading university scientist.

- Plaintiff was a passenger in a motorbus raped by the chauffeur.

- The robber entered the cafe and threatened the cashier standing at the register with a small-caliber handgun.

- Available in the administrative offices is a list of law students broken down by sex.

* The Doctrine of the Last Antecedent is discussed also in Chapter Two, at pages 55 and 56.

Can you correct the problems in the above sentences by rearranging them so that the modifiers are placed where they belong?

Sometimes the misplaced modifier is a one-word adverb. The writers of the following sentences misplaced the adverbs *properly, probably,* and *merely.* Can you correct their errors?

- Since no one was injured by the delay, the doctrine of laches was not properly invoked. (The writer meant that the court was correct in not applying the doctrine.)

- The plaintiff was probably killed by the defendant's negligence.

- He only died last week.

Even casebook authors sometimes carelessly err in the placement of modifiers, especially in using the small adverb *only.* The following sentences are from an evidence casebook:

- Rule 608(b) only limits extrinsic evidence from coming into the trial if a party's sole purpose . . . is to attack the witness.

- Courts at common law only relaxed the identity of parties requirement in civil cases.

- Rule 106, however, is only applicable to written statements.

Placing *only* where it belongs results in the following sentences:

- Rule 608(b) limits extrinsic evidence from coming into the trial only if a party's sole purpose . . . is to attack the witness.

- Courts at common law relaxed the identity of parties requirement only in civil cases.*

- Rule 106, however, is applicable only to written statements.

Before you make the point that little harm is done by misplacement of modifiers in the listed sentences, consider that sometimes meaning changes substantially, according to where you place a modifier, even a single-word modifier like *clearly, only,* or *probably.* Note the difference in meaning of the sentences below when these words are moved around:

- The material is clearly not obscene.

  The material is not clearly obscene.

- The company only sells textbooks to law schools.

  The company sells only textbooks to law schools.

  The company sells textbooks only to law schools.

- The appellant was probably severely injured because of the appellee's negligence.

  The appellant was severely injured probably because of the appellee's negligence.

* The phrase "identity-of-parties requirement" should be hyphenated. See the discussion of the use of hyphens at pages 50–52.

Because you can never be sure that your misplacement of a modifier in a legal document will not come back to haunt you, it is best to place them correctly.

F. Avoid Elegant Variation and Utraquistic Subterfuge.

1. Elegant variation

Grammarian H.M. Fowler gave the name *elegant variation* to the use of different names for the same referent. For example, if in your discussion of a house, you referred to it also as a dwelling, a residence, and a place of habitation, you were using elegant variation. Students tell me that they intentionally employ different names for the same thing because sometime in the past an English teacher told them that the practice avoided monotony. The avoidance of monotony may be of prime importance in much writing, but not in legal writing, where clarity is of prime importance, and the reader may well assume that different names refer to different things.

Here are some examples of possible confusion that elegant variation may cause. The following sentence is a student's statement of a 16th century legal rule for possession:

- For the **hunter** to have possession of the **beast,** the **pursuer** would have to **kill** the **animal** and leave it where the **beast** was **slain.** (Emphasis added.)

In this sentence, the hunter is also called the pursuer, the beast is also called the animal, and the act is described as both killed and slain. Confusion results: How many persons must do what to how many animals (or beasts) for the rule to apply?

2. Utraquistic subterfuge

Linguists Ogden and Richards gave this exotic name to the calling of several things by the same name. (H.M. Fowler called it *legerdemain with two senses,* when the same name was given to two things.) Whatever the name, the result is confusion for the reader, who reasonably expects the same word to mean the same thing each time it is used.

Illustrations of utraquistic subterfuge follow:

- A defendant is not *responsible* [for his act] if at the time of his unlawful conduct his mental or emotional processes or behavior controls were impaired to such an extent that he cannot be held *responsible* for his act. (Emphasis added.)

This sentence was part of a proposed jury instruction. The reader assumes that "responsible" means the same in both parts of the sentence. But this is not so: the first "responsible" means "able to discharge one's obligations"; the second "responsible" means "accountable for one's actions." Fortunately, this instruction confused no juries, for drafters of the Model Penal Code rejected it.

Another example:

- My client has a *cause* of action against the defendant because the *cause* of my client's injuries was defendant's conduct.

In this sentence, the word "cause" has two meanings, not one, as the reader would expect. A re-write might be:

- My client can maintain an *action* against the defendant because the defendant's conduct *caused* my client's injuries.

Finally, this:

- This law is unfair to the poor. For them *murder* may be punishable by execution, but the wealthy get away with *murder* in their business dealings all the time.

Here the writer hopes to strengthen his argument by using the word "murder" first literally, then figuratively. Some attorneys exploit the possibilities inherent in the multiple meanings of words. For example, the attorney for a physician charged with procuring an abortion for a patient, claimed that his client was protected from liability by the Statute of Frauds, which states that no one should be held for the debt, default or "miscarriage of another" without written evidence.* Awareness of the possible employment of 'legerdemain with two senses' prepares you to expose the practice and defend against it.

G. Avoid Adjective Buildup.

At least as confusing as the habits described above is that of adjective buildup, the placing of numerous adjectives in front of a noun. This unfortunate habit is evident in some legal casebooks, and even in court opinions, and too many law students eagerly adopt it. Here is an example from a casebook:

- Does the requirement that a federal district court spend time on a property claim which would, at best, be a **state small claims court matter** if **state-action-conferred federal jurisdiction** were not implicated, comport with Rostow's suggestion that the Supreme Court should "avoid wasting its ammunition in petty quarrels"? (Emphasis added.)

In the above sentence, a string of adjectives precedes two nouns, and the combination of adjective buildup and periodic sentence destroy its meaning.** Rewritten to avoid both problems, the meaning of the sentence emerges:

- Federal district courts are required to spend time on property claims that would otherwise be matters for state small claims courts if state action had not conferred jurisdiction upon the federal courts; does Rostow's suggestion that the Supreme Court should "avoid wasting its ammunition in petty quarrels" comport with this requirement?

Here is a sentence from a law student's paper; one can see that she is imitating what she considers "good" writing:

* Cited in Chafee, "The Disorderly Conduct of Words," 41 *Col.L.Rev.* 381, 387 (1941).

** Periodic sentences are discussed earlier in this chapter, at pages 74–79.

- In *Gibbons v. Ogden,* the Supreme Court upheld the **commerce Supremacy Clause interstate transportation regulation doctrine.**

Try re-writing the sentence by untangling the adjective buildup. You may get something like this:

- In *Gibbons v. Ogden,* the Supreme Court upheld the Supremacy Clause doctrine that regulates transportation in interstate commerce.

But, like all rules, this one can sometimes be broken. Consider the following opinion of a state supreme court, which adds humor without impairing clarity by the use of adjective buildup:

- We need not take a public poll to know that the most feared of all vehicles on the highways of this State [is] the old, overloaded, no-brakes, slick-tired, one-headlight, no-taillights, uninsured log truck.

That sentence illustrates the effective and intentional use of adjective buildup. But usually, as seen in the other examples, it is not effective—and is probably unintentional. How does adjective buildup come about? Suppose you want to write about lawyers—not all lawyers, only trial lawyers. To discuss their professional association, you add that word and the phrase becomes

- trial lawyers' association

The association has an executive committee, so you add that language, and you get

- trial lawyers' association executive committee

The executive committee is going to form an agenda for the trial lawyers' annual meeting, so now you have

- trial lawyers' association executive committee annual planning agenda meeting

The executive committee plans to set up the agenda on Tuesday, April 6, so you add that information. Finally you add the predicate to your sentence, and you have created a periodic sentence containing adjective build-up:

- The trial lawyers' association executive committee annual planning agenda Tuesday, April 6, meeting will take place in the Empire Hotel.

Of course, you can add more information and make your sentence even harder to understand, but you get the idea. Adjective buildup forces the reader to unwind the sentence by putting the multiple adjectives into clauses and phrases. But don't place this burden on *your* readers. The reason for explaining how adjective buildup comes about is to show you how to unravel adjective buildup so that you can understand sentences you are almost certain to come across in your law school studies.

H. Don't Shift Your Point of View.

Whatever you write, you make an unstated promise to your readers not to shift your point of view unless you let them know about it. If you change the subject or object of your sentence without notifying your readers, you are shifting your viewpoint, and that constitutes bad (and confusing) writing. Here is one illustration, from the office of an attorney (I have inserted the unanswered questions):

- Although zoning ordinances should furnish owners of historic properties some relief from the financial burden of maintaining their property for public benefit, decline in market value [of what?] and diminished expectations [whose? about what?] are not sufficient injuries [who received? who caused?] to constitute a taking of property [who took?] without just compensation [to whom?]

Put into the sentence guideposts which clearly point out to your reader the subjects and objects of the clauses, and your readers' questions (inserted above) are answered:

- Zoning ordinances should furnish owners of historic properties some relief from the financial burden of maintaining their property for public benefit. However, the injury to the landowners of a decline in the market value of their property or their diminished expectation of income from the property is not sufficient for the court to find that the state has taken private property without compensation to the property owners.

Here is another actual example, again with questions inserted:

- In order to collect exemplary damages [who collects?], the conduct causing the injury [whose conduct?] must be wanton, malicious, or grossly negligent as to show heedless or willful disregard for the rights and safety of others.

Here is a re-write, with the necessary guideposts added:

- In order for the victim of an injury to collect exemplary damages, the conduct of the person who caused the injury must have been so wanton, malicious, or grossly negligent as to show heedless or willful disregard for the rights and safety of others.

And here is an example from a student's examination answer:

- Defendant is guilty of driving recklessly, and with no opportunity to avoid the accident, the collision occurred.

Who had "no opportunity to avoid the accident"? Because he fails to insert the new subject (plaintiff), the writer is guilty of shifting his viewpoint without notifying the reader.

One **Rule-of-Thumb** repeated throughout this book is: Say **who did what to whom** in each sentence. Another way to state this is to say that you should take your readers by the hand and guide them through your writing. If you do so, you will not make unannounced viewpoint shifts.

II. Writing It Effectively

A. Use Sentence Structure for Emphasis.

For your legal writing to be effective, you must not only make your ideas clear but persuade your reader to your viewpoint. You can help accomplish both aims by **variety in sentence structure** and **appropriate placement of the sentence parts.**

1. Emphasis by type of structure

Somewhere in your academic past, you may have learned about grammatical sentence structure, but to refresh your memory, here is a short review. Grammatically, sentences are either **simple, compound,** or **complex.** The simple sentence is the least complicated and usually the shortest. It is composed of a single subject-predicate unit. The following are all simple sentences:

- I know John.
- Democracy lives!
- Our neighbors and their friends are active in politics.
- Mary spends her time studying and thus has little time for socializing.

Compound sentences are merely two or more simple sentences joined by a coordinating conjunction like *and, but, for,* and *so* or by a semi-colon either with or without a conjunctive adverb like *however, moreover,* or *nevertheless.* When you want to make several points of equal importance or join ideas that are closely connected, you will probably choose compound sentences to do so. The following are some compound sentences:

- I have known John for some time, but I do not know his brother.
- Democracy lives, and it will survive its present threats.
- Our neighbors and their friends are active in politics; they urge us to get involved.
- Mary spends her time studying; therefore she has little time to socialize.

Complex sentences contain at least one **main clause** and one **subordinate clause.** The main clause could stand by itself as a simple sentence and is therefore sometimes called the "independent" clause; the subordinate clause, often introduced by an adverb (like *when, while, because,* or *since*), cannot stand alone and is therefore sometimes called the "dependent" clause. Use complex sentences when you want to stress an important idea and subordinate a less important one. The following are some complex sentences:

- Because John is ethical and considerate, [subordinate clause] he is well liked. [main clause]
- Although Joe has retired from practice, [subordinate clause] he is still politically active. [main clause]

- After the trial ends but before sentencing the defendant, [subordinate clause] the court will consider mitigating circumstances. [main clause]

You can see the difference by comparing the compound and complex sentences below:

- Marbury's formal commission for the judgeship was signed, but it was not delivered. (The **compound** sentence indicates that both parts of the sentence are of equal importance.)

- Although Marbury's formal commission for the judgeship was signed, it was not delivered. (The **complex** sentence indicates that the main clause is the important one.)

Sentence variety also helps keep your readers alert and interested in your subject.

But inexperienced writers sometimes argue that short, simple sentences make writing clearer. Not necessarily. The next paragraph was written by a first-semester law student. The short simple sentences give the reader no guidance about the writer's intended emphasis:

- Abel's conduct seems to be negligent. The rules of torts defining negligence are applicable. We must examine Abel's conduct to decide his negligence. He threw a small airplane at Baker. The act of throwing the airplane is not disputable. He placed Baker at an unreasonable risk. He had the duty to avoid unreasonable risk to the other spectators. The damage suffered was a condition *sine qua non* of the act in question.

Contrast the following newspaper item about the docking of the aircraft carrier *Saratoga* after the end of the Persian Gulf hostilities:

- Thousands of people crowd the dock; they are a happy crowd, some of whom arrived as early as 3:00AM for the noon arrival of the *Saratoga*, to welcome the sailors back from the war. The dominant colors are red, white, and blue, in the people's clothes, the signs they are carrying, and the flags they are waving. Each person hopes to get the attention of that special sailor. But besides the messages and colors, there is another, deeper, statement: "We love America!"

(In this paragraph, the first sentence is **compound**; the second, and third are **simple**; and the **fourth** is complex. The variety makes the writing effective. Note that the **simple** final sentence embedded in the fourth **complex** sentence adds force. You can use this technique to improve your writing.)

2. Emphasis by placement of ideas

Be aware, too, that you can subtly alter the effect of your sentence by where you place the idea you want to emphasize. The end of each sentence should contain the most important idea because your reader will expect to find it there. Read the two sentences below. Although both report the same facts, the first is pessimistic in tone, the second optimistic. That is because the first ends with the bad news and the second with the good news:

> • Utility department crews are working around the clock to remove ice from downed wires and to restore service, although widespread blackouts are still present throughout the city, and hundreds of residents remain without lights or heat.

> • Although widespread blackouts are still present throughout the city and hundreds of residents remain without lights or heat, utility department crews are working around the clock to remove ice from downed wires and to restore service.

In the following three sentences, you can decide what idea is the most important by where it appears in each sentence:

(Most important point: the federal statute would override the state statute.) If the defendant can prove that the state statute did not give adequate notice because it was vaguely written, the federal statute would override it.

(Most important point: the state statute may be vaguely written.) The federal statute would override the state statute if the defendant can prove that the state statute did not give adequate notice because it was vaguely written.

(Most important point: the state statute might not have given adequate notice.) The federal statute would override the state statute if the defendant can prove that, because the state statute was vaguely written, it did not give adequate notice.

Note: because of the unconscious assumption of your readers that the most important ideas will be at the end of your sentences and the next most important at the beginning, you should put your **qualifiers, amplifiers,** and **ho-hum** language into the middle of your sentences. Some of these words are

Qualifiers:	on the other hand, however, in the alternative, nevertheless, on the contrary, for the most part . . .
Amplifiers:	in addition, for example, furthermore, specifically, moreover . . .
Ho-hum Words:	that is to say, in fact, as a matter of fact, indeed, in effect, effectively, certainly . . .

In the following paragraph, the student is not really conveying the point she wants to make: that a tire the defendant sold the plaintiff's father was not defective. Her point does not come across very clearly because of the poor placement of the ideas in her sentences:

> • Certainly the defendant owed a duty to the plaintiff to sell him a tire which would withstand normal wear and tear. However, defendant's breach of duty was not established by the plaintiff. Here the evidence indicates the tire was not defective because a blow-out was possible due to the condition of the road.

Can you re-arrange the language to make the point more effectively? The following re-write does the job by placing the important point at the end of each sentence and moving the ho-hum word (*certainly*) and the qualifier (*however*) from the beginning to the middle of the sentences:

> • The defendant certainly owed a duty to sell the plaintiff a tire which would withstand normal wear and tear in ordinary road conditions. Because the evidence indicates, however, that the tire may have blown out due to abnormal road conditions, the plaintiff has failed to prove that the defendant breached his duty by selling the plaintiff a defective tire.*

B. Make Lists; Use Parallel Structure.

Legal writing doesn't have to be murky, though too often it is. Murky writing becomes clear when you itemize your points, making lists in parallel form. The following definition (from a federal court opinion) is unnecessarily obscure:

> • To be liable for plagiarism it is not necessary to exactly duplicate another's literary work, it being sufficient if unfair use of such work is made by lifting of a substantial portion thereof, but even an exact counterpart of another's work does not constitute plagiarism if such counterpart was arrived at independently.

Re-written, as a list, the ideas are more clear. All three verbs were made parallel by being put into the third person singular:

> • A writer is liable for plagiarism if he or she unfairly **reproduces** a substantial portion of another writer's literary work and **passes** it off as his or her own product; but if the writer independently **arrives** at the counterpart, even an exact counterpart is not plagiarism.**

Lists untangle complex ideas. Here is a definition of negligence, from a formbook. It is made clear by the list form:

> • Negligence includes (1) the duty to use reasonable care, that is, to conform to a certain standard of conduct so that others are not subjected to unreasonable risk by your behavior; (2) the failure to conform to that standard, either by doing something you ought not do or by failing to do something you ought to do; (3) injury resulting to another because of your failure to conform to the standard set in (2), i.e., a causal connection between your conduct and the injury the other person suffers; and (4) loss or damages to another person's interests as a result of the injury.

Notice how the drafter of the negligence rule used parallel structure, introducing each clause by a noun (*duty, failure, injury, causal connection,* and *loss or damages*).

---

* **Caveat!** When words that are usually placed in the middle of the sentence are important to your point, put them in the attention-getting positions—at the end or beginning.

** This re-write also illustrates two other writing rules: (1) Put a person in the subject slot; (2) put the most important idea at the end of the sentence. You can avoid the use of *he* or *she* by making the subject plural (*writers are liable,* etc.).

But the drafter of the following excerpt (from a law office handout) forgot to use parallel structure:

> • A valid banker's acceptance contains the following: (1) a time draft; (2) signature of an officer of a bank; (3) when and where the acceptance is payable; (4) statement of the underlying transaction; and (5) "accepted" written across the face of the instrument.

The drafter of that handout violated two rules of parallel structure:

(1) The word that introduces the list must "fit" all the items on the list.

(2) The grammatical structure of all the items must be alike.

The re-write (below) follows the two-part rule. The introductory words (*time draft*) fit all list items, and each item begins with the *-ing* form of a verb (the present participle):

> • In order to be valid, a banker's acceptance must be a time draft (1) **containing** the signature of an officer of the bank; (2) **stating** when and where acceptance is payable; (3) **referring** to the underlying transaction; and (4) **bearing** the word *acceptance* on its face.

Finally, compare the following two examination answers comparing the holdings of two courts. The first answer does not clearly show the significance of the two different holdings, partly because the student failed to state his ideas parallelly. The second answer, framed in parallel language, is longer, but clearer.

> • In *Clark,* the court held that the first finder of loose logs had a right superior to that of the subsequent finder, and in *South Staffordshire,* under similar facts, the court ruled for the landowner because the found article was attached to his land, thus giving him a superior right to it.

> • Whether the found article was loose or attached to the land was the significant factor in *Clark* and *South Staffordshire.* In *Clark,* the court held that the first finder of logs floating in a bay was the rightful owner against a subsequent finder; but in *South Stafford-shire,* because the found rings were embedded in mud at the bottom of a pool, the court held that the landowner of the pool had a superior right over the subsequent finder.

C. Economize!

"Copious Dryden wanted, or forgot/The last and greatest art, the art to blot." (Alexander Pope, "Epilogue to the Satires")

On the other hand, it was said of Milton's writing, "Fewer words would not have served; more would have been superfluous." As legal writers, imitate Milton, not Dryden. But this advice is hard to take. Benjamin Franklin said that lawyers "say little in much," and that criticism too often applies today. Wordiness is to the writer what obesity is to the jogger. You can avoid wordiness if you (1) don't pontificate; (2) do use concrete language; and (3) do use active verbs.

1. Don't pontificate.

Lawyers are not the only writers who pontificate. Here is a sentence about acupuncture, written by a medical administrator:

> • If this is another potential modality that can have a positive outcome in the treatment of addiction, it would certainly be something we'd like to add to the continuum of services offered.

(Probable translation: If it works, we'll use it.) *

And the following paragraph is from an engineering journal article:

> • The behavior of individuals within a building during a fire situation has often been one of the critical determining factors relative to the eventual outcome of the fire incident. We will consider the individual relative to his physical, psychological, cultural, and time constraints during a fire occurrence within a building. The behavioral dynamics of the individual will usually be predicated and initiated by the many variables which are considered in the individual's perception of the threat created by the fire situation. Psychologically and physiologically, the human individual is not able to adjust to adaptable tolerance levels for the products of a fire occurrence . . . . **

As nearly as I can make out, the author of this gobbledegook is saying that individuals respond differently to fires, depending on whether they believe their safety is threatened. The piece is a blueprint for what to avoid. Notice that the author

(1) Never uses one word when he can use two. A fire is "a fire situation," "a fire incident," and "a fire occurrence."

(2) Never uses a simple word when he can use a fancy word. "Behavior" becomes "behavioral dynamics." "Decided" becomes "predicated and initiated," and "of" becomes "relative to."

(3) Engages in redundance whenever possible, as in "eventual outcome," for "outcome," "determining factors," for "factors," and "human individual," for "individual"—or "human," and "adjust to adaptable tolerance levels," for "adapt to."

(4) Uses passive verbs if he can, instead of active verbs: "will be predicated and initiated," and "which are considered."

(5) Throws in adjective build-up for good measure: What are "physical, psychological, cultural and time constraints"?

After reading this excerpt, you will agree that a good Rule-of-Thumb for legal writing is: **Write like a person, not a personage.*****

---

* Quoted in *ETC.*, Volume 46, Number Four, Winter 1989, p. 321.

** *Chemical and Engineering News*, August 19, 1974, p. 44. (The paragraph was cited as an example of bad writing.)

*** An early court decision must have tended to dissuade wordiness. The decision reads in pertinent part, "[Because the plaintiff stretched a normal 16–page pleading to 120 pages] the Warden . . . shall cut a hole in the . . . replication . . . and put [the plaintiff's] head through the hole . . . and lead [him] round about Westminster

2. Use concrete language.

One way to "say it" clearly is to use concrete language instead of abstract language like that in the excerpt above. Lawyers are often criticized for their use of abstract language. Someone wrote that the legal version of the Lord's Prayer would begin:

> "The Lord is my external-internal integrative mechanism . . . He positions me in a nondecisional stance. He maximizes my adjustment."

Abstract language refers to general and vague concepts. It utilizes jargon. It is ponderous, roundabout. Concrete language is particular, not general; it refers to actual, specific things. It is therefore plain, not abstruse. Contrast the statements of Benjamin Franklin and of Warren Burger, on the same subject:

- It is a false assumption that every graduate of a law school is, by virtue of that fact, qualified for ultimate confrontation in the courtroom. (Burger)

- Lawyers, preachers, and tomtit eggs: there's more of them hatched than come to perfection. (Franklin)

The first quotation makes its point adequately, but the second makes it emphatically—even though most of us have no idea what "tomtit eggs" really are!

A legal scholar used abstract language to criticize wordy judicial opinions. He wrote

- Superfluous words may debilitate a legal opinion into nugacity.

(He meant, I think, "Don't hide your opinion under a bushel of words.")

More than ever today those who draft contracts and other legal documents should use concrete language. For courts have held that if persons who sign contracts do not understand their meaning, the contracts are voidable. Plain English laws have been adopted in some states, and more states are considering them. But plain English need not be Dick-and-Jane language. It is merely clear, direct statement conveying your meaning accurately.

3. Write with active verbs.

When you use active instead of passive verbs, your writing is clearer and briefer. Active verbs put the actor into the driver's seat and inform your reader who did what to whom. Passive verbs often result in agentless writing. You can't tell who the actor is in this sentence: "The firearm was attempted to be used." The double-passives ("was attempted" and "to be used") make it hard to decide. This kind of sentence sometimes results from the author's revision of a sentence that started out as something like "The defendant attempted to use the firearm." What happens, in the revision, is that the actor

Hall while the courts are sitting." Milward
v. Weiden, 21 Eng.Rep. 136 (1566).

disappears. "The committee arrived at the decision" becomes, "The decision was arrived at by the committee," and then "The decision was arrived at."

The following sentence was part of a student's answer to a writing problem. See if you can re-write it using active verbs:

- If the defendant's car is found to have been purchased for transportation to and from work, it will be found to be a necessity and the defendant's contract will not be voidable despite his minority.

When you change the passive verbs, your sentence will read:

- If the court finds that the defendant purchased his car to provide transportation to and from work, it will hold that the car is a necessity, and the defendant will not be able to void the contract, despite his minority.

The second sentence is longer, despite the active verbs, because the actor was put into it, making it clearer. Often, however, the passive verb makes the sentence longer:

- The committee decided (active verb)

  The decision was arrived at by the committee (passive verb)

- The court held (active verb)

  The holding was reached by the court (passive verb)

- The plaintiff argued (active verb)

  The argument was presented by the plaintiff (passive verb)

It is a strange fact that law students gravitate toward passive verbs almost as soon as they reach law school. Someone once spoofed this tendency by quoting one law student as saying to another, "When law school was begun by me, a love affair between Donna and myself was caused to take place."

Resist the tendency. When you edit your first draft, remove unnecessary passive verbs and your writing will improve. But, as always, there are exceptions. Do not shun passive verbs completely. Use them judiciously when:

(1) the object of the verb is more important than the subject.

- When President John Kennedy was assassinated, newspaper headlines proclaimed, "Kennedy Assassinated." (The object of the action was more important than the subject.)

(2) the subject is unknown.

- When traffic congestion of unknown cause is reported, the sentence might read, "Traffic was congested on Route One during rush hour yesterday."

(3) the actor/subject wishes to dissociate himself from the act:

- The yearly subscription rate will be slightly increased beginning July 1, 1993.

Use active verbs instead of adjectives and nouns for more forceful effect. Compare the following pairs:

- She made a decision   She decided
- I had knowledge of   I knew
- He made an examination of   He examined
- It had a tendency to   It tended to
- This is violative of   This violates
- It is wasteful of   It wastes
- She made a statement about   She stated
- They put emphasis on   They emphasized

The phrases on the left include a verb with almost no meaning (*made, had, is, put*) plus either an adjective or a noun. On the right, a meaningful verb is substituted, making the noun or adjective unnecessary. Look for phrases like those above in your own writing and edit them out. Try your skill on the following paragraph:

> • This paper presents an examination of the duty of a manufacturer of warning of possible risks of its product's use by consumers. The examination will be of two federal court decisions, Davis v. Wyeth Laboratories, Inc., and Reyes v. Wyeth Laboratories, Inc. These cases contain a description of the sustaining of injuries by consumers after the injection of drugs. The issue is whether there was a sufficient warning by the manufacturers of the plaintiffs as to the information about the danger of the drugs.

When you substitute the right verb for the verb-noun/adjective combination, your new paragraph will look something like this (the new verbs are in bold-face):

> • This paper **examines** whether the manufacturer has a duty **to warn** consumers of possible risks they may **incur** when they **use** its product. Two federal court decisions **will provide** examples. In both cases, consumers **sustained** injuries after they **were injected** with the manufacturers' drugs. The issue was whether the manufacturer sufficiently **informed** the consumers that the injected drugs were dangerous.

Notice that this paragraph is both clearer and more succinct than its predecessor. A RULE OF THUMB: **When you can say the same thing in fewer words, do so.**

The paragraph below, from the same paper, is a real re-write challenge. It contains several faults: (1) the use of expletives; (2) the failure to say **who** did **what** to **whom**; (3) the overuse of passive verbs; and (4) weak verb/ adjective or noun combinations. Can you tackle the job? Here is the original paragraph:

> The court found there was a failure to meet the burden of providing a warning of the dangers involved when taking defendant's drug. The product was not of ordinary usage, so there was a duty to warn of its dangers. The court concluded that there is an absolute duty to warn that there are risks involved in the use of the product.

And here is a possible re-write:

> The court found that the **manufacturer failed** in its duty **to warn** the **consumers** that the **drug** might **be** dangerous. Since **consumers did** not ordinarily **use the drug, the manufacturer** had the **duty to warn them** of its dangers. **The court concluded** that the **manufacturer must warn consumers** that **they are** at risk when **they use** the **drug.**

D. Don't Use Vague Referents.

A comic strip shows a little boy holding up a cookie box so that his sister can see it and saying that if she can guess what kind of cookie is in the box, he will give it to her. Delighted, she correctly guesses, "chocolate chip," and he says, "Right!" and gives her the empty box, thus illustrating the intentional use of the vague referent "it." But, in legal writing, the unintentional use of vague referents can cause trouble—and litigation.

The small, unimportant-looking pronoun *it* along with its companions *this* and *which,* should refer to closely adjacent antecedent nouns. If their antecedents are too far away, if they refer to some nebulous concept not actually mentioned in the sentence, or if they have no antecedent at all, *it, this,* and *which* become **vague referents.** Vague referents cause confusion in all kinds of writing, but they are dangerous in legal writing, where precision is so important. These sentences were taken from law students' writing:

(1) Since defendants were playing a practical joke on the plaintiff, **it** shows intent on their part.

What shows intent? That is, what does the referent **"it"** refer to? The writer is aware that one of the elements of battery is "intent" and wants to say that defendants' playing a practical joke indicates their intention to carry out the battery. In his sentence structure, however, the noun phrase that "it" refers to is "practical joke," and practical jokes cannot possess intent. The sentence needs recasting:

- Defendants' playing a practical joke on the plaintiff showed their intent.

(2) If one wishes to be free of liability, **it** must be clearly stated.

The writer intends **"it"** to refer back to *wish*, but *wishes* here is a verb, not a noun, so the reference is unclear. The rewrite clarifies the meaning:

- In order to be free of liability, one must clearly disclaim it.

(3) The court held that since the petitioner believed he would be repaid, **this** was enough to prove a bona fide relationship.

Again, **"this"** refers back to a non-existent noun (*belief*). A re-write provides the noun and makes the vague referent unnecessary:

- The court held that the petitioner's belief that he would be repaid was enough to prove a bona fide relationship.

(4) The loss of sleep suffered by the plaintiff's daughter was caused by the accusations of the defendant, and **this** adds support to the plaintiff's claim of intentional infliction of emotional distress.

What adds support? **"This"** refers to nothing in particular. The sentence is grammatically improved by adding *fact* after "this," avoiding the vague referent but doing nothing to improve the clarity. In order to get rid of the vagueness, the idea of causality needs to be added:

- Because the accusations of the defendant caused the plaintiff's daughter loss of sleep, the daughter has a claim against the defendant for the intentional infliction of emotional distress.

In the re-write, it is clearly the daughter whose claim is validated by her loss of sleep. In the original sentence, the erroneous impression is that the mother's claim is based upon her daughter's sleeplessness. The claim of the daughter is given emphasis by placement, in the re-write, at the end of the sentence in the main clause, while the less important information is in a subordinate clause at the beginning of the sentence. If the accusations of the defendant were the most important information, the sentence positions would be reversed.

One more illustration; the vague referent **"which"** is the culprit:

(5) In the Senate debate there are a number of good reasons for the passage of the Equal Rights Amendment, **which** should be considered.

As the sentence is cast, the antecedent of **"which,"** is "Equal Rights Amendment." But the intended referent is "reasons." Recast, the sentence becomes clear:

- In the Senate debate about the Equal Rights Amendment, a number of good reasons for its passage should be considered.*

III. Writing It Properly

Called into the jury box of an English court at the start of a trial, a man asked to be excused, saying, "My wife is due to conceive today and I would like to be there."

The judge answered, "I think you have got that wrong. You may mean that your wife is about to be delivered of a baby. But whether I am right or you are right I certainly think you should be there." **

The English judge forgave the prospective juror for his mistake, but, as a lawyer, you had better use language properly. Words are your most important tool, and you need to use them well.

---

* For more on *which* as a vague referent, see the Doctrine of the Last Antecedent, at pages 55 and 56.

** Reported in "Glimpse," No. 42, December 1987, page 4.

A. Watch Out for Problem Words.

Some words cause more trouble than others. Four word-groups that may trip you up are (1) words with multiple meanings; (2) words with special legal meanings; (3) confusing pairs; and (4) vague, fad words.

1. Words with multiple meanings

These are words that have at least two meanings (sometimes opposite). Your writing should make clear which meaning you intend. Here are some of these words:

- **oversight:** can mean "unintentional error" or "intentional watchful supervision."

  The Brief was filed late due to an *oversight* on the attorney's part.

    (That is, the attorney made an error.)

  The Foreign Relations Committee has *oversight* over its subcommittee's proceedings.

    (That is, it has *authority* over its subcommittee's proceedings.)

- **effectively:** can mean either "well" or "actually."

  The responsibility was *effectively* discharged.

    (That is, it was carried out well or efficiently.)

  The responsibility was *effectively* discharged.

    (That is, it was actually carried out or was, in effect, carried out.)

- **sanction:** can mean "approval" or "penalty."

  The *sanction* of violence should never be government policy.

    (That is, government should never approve violence.)

  Official *sanctions* are being considered against Argentina.

    (That is, coercive measures are being considered.)

- **presently:** can mean "soon" or "right now."

  I will join the group *presently.*

    (That is, I will be there soon.)

  I am *presently* without an apartment.

    (That is, I am without one now.)

- **cite:** can mean "command," "point out," or "summon before a court of law."

  He was *cited* for his bravery.

    (That is, he was commended for bravery.)

  He was *cited* as a typical law student.

    (That is, he was pointed out as typical.)

  He was *cited* for a traffic violation.

    (That is, he was summoned before a law court.)

- **ultimately**: can mean "at the end" or "at the beginning."

  She *ultimately* reached her goal.

  (That is, she finally got there.)

  The two words are *ultimately* cognates.

  (That is, they had the same ancestor.)

- **may**: can indicate either *permission* or *possibility*.

  Students *may* adhere to the dress code.

  (That is, they are permitted to do so.)

  Students *may* adhere to the dress code.

  (That is, it is possible that they will.)

- **moot**: can pertain to a controversy that no long exists, because the issues have been settled or to a question that is unsettled, therefore debatable.

  The question is moot, the plaintiff having settled out of court.

  (That is, the question has been settled.)

  Whether the World Court is effective is a moot question.

  (That is, the question has not been settled.)

In the list above, the earliest meaning of each word appears first. Other words may soon be added to the list, for English usage constantly changes, with words coming into the language, leaving it, and gaining or losing meanings. Two possible candidates for future addition to the list above are *momentary* and *problematic*. Although dictionaries still list *momentary* as meaning "for a moment," journalists are beginning to use it to mean "in a moment." *Problematic* traditionally has meant "speculative"; it is now coming to mean "posing a problem."

2. Words with special legal meanings

The words on this list have an everyday meaning different from their legal meaning. Because your clients may be unaware of their legal meaning, you should be aware that they may not understand what you are saying.

- **cure**

The everyday meaning of this verb is "heal," as in, "Medicine *cures* illness." But the legal meaning may be "correct," as in "The court held that the trial proceedings *cured* defects in the pleadings."

- **constructive**

The layman understands this adjective to mean "helpful," as in, "The review of the performance contained *constructive* criticism." But the legal meaning is more likely "to be considered as," as in "constructive notice," "constructive admission," "constructive fraud," "constructive possession," and other legal terms.

- **facially**

This refers in common speech to a portion of the human anatomy, but the legal meaning may well be "that which appears on the face of the document, with no explanation." A "facial defect" is more likely to be an imperfection in a legal document than an anatomical defect, as in, "The statute is *facially* unconstitutional."

- **issue**

In everyday usage, this is a transitive verb (i.e., it must be followed by a noun-object) meaning "distribute." ("The Administration issued a policy-statement.") But in legal use it is sometimes an intransitive verb (i.e., it is not followed by a noun-object), meaning "come forth," as in, "The writ *issues*."

- **material**

The layman uses this word most frequently as a noun, meaning "substance," as in "The dress was made of flimsy *material*." To the lawyer, the word is more often an adjective meaning, "of the essence," as in, "The testimony of the eyewitness was *material*."

- **harmless**

The layman understands this word as meaning "not harmful." Law adds a second meaning, "blameless, not liable," as in "The defendant was held *harmless* for the bicycle accident caused by improper signing of bicycle paths."

- **lie**

The everyday meaning of this verb is "recline." In legal usage it adds the meaning "to be admissible," as in "an action lies in emotional distress."

3. Confusing pairs

In this category are words that people tend to use interchangeably although they have different meanings. Some of these word-pairs are confusing because they look alike; others are confusing because they are often misused:

- **affect/effect**

These two words are not interchangeable. The verb *affect* means "influence, change, or modify." You can *affect* decision-making with your vote. *Affect* also means "pretend" or "imitate"; you might *affect* interest in something that really doesn't interest you.

The verb *effect* means "bring about or accomplish"; for example, legislation is designed to *effect* an end. Because *to effect a change* (that is, to bring about a change) contains the idea of *affecting* something, *effect* and *affect* are often confused. But if you distinguish between the words, you may *effect* a change in usage that will *affect* your writing.

- **principal/principle**

These words receive heavy use in the legal profession. Be sure to distinguish between them. *Principles* are basic truths, rules or assumptions.

Your legal arguments will often be based upon legal rules, also called *doctrines* or *principles*. The word *principle* is never an adjective; it is always a noun.

The word *principal* can be either a noun or an adjective. As a noun it refers to the individual or party who is first in importance, rank, or degree. Schools employ principals and vice-principals. In contract law, reference is often made to the principal/agent relationship. The *principal* is one who empowers another (the *agent*) to act as his representative. The *principal* is one who has the prime obligation in a contract, or one who, in criminal law, commits a crime.

As an adjective *principal* means "chief, or first, or of highest rank", as in, The Constitution is the principal defense of our rights. You will also be referring to the *principal* (i.e., "main") argument for the prosecution or the defense.

• lie/lay

The discriminating writer maintains the distinction between these two words, which have become a shibboleth for educated usage. *Lay,* the word more often used, is properly a transitive verb, which means that it must be followed by a noun as object. Thus you *lay* a book on the table, *lay* down a law, and *lay* bricks to make a wall. In all these phrases *lay* means "put, place or set forth." (*Lay* has many other related meanings, for which consult your dictionary, but they all have in common some sort of placement, as in *lay a wager.*)

Lie is an intransitive verb; that is, it does not take an object-noun. You *lie* on the bed, or you *lie* down, *lie* meaning, in general usage, "recline." (The third meaning of *lie* is one that confuses no one: "tell an untruth.")

The problem with *lie* and *lay* is that the past tense of *lie* is identical with the present tense of *lay*. Although last night I *lay* on my bed, today I *lay* the books on my desk. The complete paradigm for each verb is:

lay	laid	laid
lie	lay	lain

• in/into

These prepositions are not interchangeable; *in* refers to a position, condition, or location, and *into* refers to a *change* of condition, indicating movement to another location. A person is sitting *in* a room, but when she leaves the room and enters another, she goes *into* another room. Both *in* and *into* have numerous other meanings (for which consult your dictionary), but the only confusion caused by the words is in this small but important distinction.

• bring/take

Although these words are not look-alikes, they are often mistakenly interchanged. They are distinguishable by the orientation of the speaker. Something is *brought* to the person speaking, or to his residence (when he is there), or to a place identified with him (when he is there). Thus you, as speaker, would tell someone to *bring* his class notes to you when he comes to your home or to *bring* them to your home tonight, when you are there. But if you are at the law school you would tell him to *take* the notes to your home or to *take* them to another place. The distinction is like that between *come* and *go*. (*Come* to me; *go* anywhere else.)

- **loan/lend**

A law school colleague asked me to include this pair, noting that she is really annoyed at their mis-use. Traditionally, *loan* was always a noun, never a verb. You could make someone a *loan*, but you could not *loan* money to her. Usage has changed that, and you have no doubt heard even educated speakers use *loan* as a verb. Meticulous users still retain the distinction, however, and I would recommend that you use *lend* as the verb and *loan* as the noun in your legal writing. (There is no point in irritating those who object to the more recent change in usage.)

- **imply/infer**

The distinction here is carefully observed in legal writing. The speaker/writer *implies;* the listener/reader *infers.* To *imply* is to intimate or to state indirectly; to *infer* is to draw a conclusion based on what someone has said or written.

- **foregoing/forgoing**

Notice the *e* in the first word. It indicates that the prefix (*fore*) means "before." Thus the *foregoing* is something that has gone before. The prefix *for* has nothing to do with what went before. It has the sense of *exhaustion* (as in *forspent*), "giving up completely" (as in *forsake* or *forswear* or *forgo*), or *prohibition* (as in *forbid*). "*Forgoing* the opportunity to obtain redress, the negligence victim declined to file suit."

- **credible/credulous**

Credible means "believable." (The witness was *credible.*) *Credulous* means "believing too readily, thus gullible." (The victim of the swindle was *credulous.*) These words are more often used in their negative forms: *incredible* meaning "unbelievable," *incredulous* meaning "disbelieving, skeptical."

- **eager/anxious**

Although these words are sometimes interchanged, they are not synonymous. You are *eager* for something to occur if you look forward to its occurrence; if you view the occurrence with fear or displeasure, you are *anxious* about it.

- **precedent/precedence**

A *precedent* is a judicial decision that may be used as a basis for decisions in similar subsequent cases. Pronounce it with first-syllable stress. *Precedent* may also mean "convention or custom." *Precedence,* pronounced either with first- or second-syllable stress, means "priority." The public right may have *precedence* over the right of an individual.

● **reason/rationalize**

As verbs, these words are not interchangeable. Courts *reason,* that is, they exercise their analytical powers to arrive at conclusions. Courts also sometimes *rationalize;* that is, they justify their decisions, or find excuses for them. Unless you are criticizing the opinion of the court, use the verb *reason.*

● **famous/notorious**

If you are **famous,** it is because you have done something to be proud of; If you are **notorious,** you have done something dishonorable. To be *notorious* is to be *infamous.* (That is the traditional distinction between the two words; *notoriety* is now being used to mean "fame," so the distinction will probably eventually disappear.)

● **tortuous/torturous**

The first of these adjectives has both literal and figurative meanings. It means "twisted or circuitous," its literal meaning as in "a tortuous path"; its figurative meaning as in "tortuous reasoning." The second member of the pair is the adjective form of the noun *torture.* It means "afflicted with or causing great physical or mental pain." Its meaning is only literal: "a torturous injury."

● **discrete/discreet**

The first adjective refers to individual, distinct parts. "The procedure requires a number of *discrete* steps." The second refers to a respect for reserve. "Attorneys must be *discreet* in their client-relationships."

● **farther/further**

Farther refers to literal distance, either temporal or spatial. "Cincinnati is farther from New York than from Louisville." *Further* is used in all other senses, especially to indicate degree or figurative space or time. "America goes *further* into debt every year." "Let me explain *further.*"

● **enormousness/enormity**

To refer to the size of something, use *enormousness.* The word *enormity* means "excessively wicked or outrageous." You might refer to the *enormity* of a crime, but the *enormousness* of an elephant.

● **reluctant/reticent**

Writers have recently begun to confuse these two adjectives, but they are not synonyms. The first means "hesitant or unwilling." The second means "characteristically silent or reserved." The witness may be *reluctant* to testify. Residents of Maine are reputed to be *reticent.*

● **economic/economical**

The first adjective is broader in meaning. It means "related to material wealth." The second means "thrifty" or "not wasteful." "*Economical* persons save money because *economic* disaster may strike."

- **historic/historical**

A *historic* event is one that is important in history. Anything concerned with history, whether it is important or not, is *historical.* *Historical* fiction often records *historic* events.

- **ingenious/ingenuous**

The first of these adjectives is derived from the noun *ingenuity,* which means "inventiveness or cleverness." The second means "lacking sophistication, frank, naive." Its noun form is *ingenuousness.*

- **unique/unusual**

Someday these two words will be synonymous. In fact, the second may disappear from the language. The reason is that *unique* (meaning "one of a kind") is often prefaced with *rather, very,* or *most.* Journalists and others who do this are unaware that *unique* is a Latin-derived word meaning "only" or "sole."

4. Vague and vogue words

Someone once said that the difference between the right word and the almost-right word is like the difference between lightning and the lightning bug. That may be overstating the point, but it is not an overstatement to say that if you are careful to choose words that carry a precise meaning, your writing will be much more accurate. The fact is, however, that it is easier to reach for a word that is widely used in numerous contexts instead of searching for a word that exactly expresses your meaning. The following words are too widely used to be useful:

- **where**

Where can mean *when, if, because, in which, that,* and perhaps other things as well. Henry Weihofen suggests that one should use *where* to express only place, as in "states where the rule is followed," but that "cases where the rule is followed," should be changed to "cases in which the rule is followed," or "cases that follow the rule." *

Whether you follow Weihofen's suggestion or not, you should consider substituting other words for *where* when doing so will express your idea more precisely:

> • False imprisonment occurs **where** one party acts in a manner intending to confine another within fixed boundaries. (Substitute when.)

> • **Where** a person's house is searched without a search warrant, he has a cause of action against the officer who conducted the search. (Substitute *if.*)

> • The defendant had reason to believe his life was in danger **where** the plaintiff had a knife. (Substitute *because.*)

* In *Legal Writing Style,* 2d edition, 1979, p. 40.

- The burglar read in the newspaper **where** another man had been arrested for the burglary. (Substitute *that.*)

(It is true that courts generally use *where* with all these meanings and more. But it is also true that court opinions are sometimes not models of clarity.)

- **as to**

This phrase is another favorite of lawyers, so often used by them that it has been called, "the lawyerly as to." Its overuse has resulted in its taking on so many meanings that it is hard to tell which one the writer has in mind. It may mean *for, about, of,*—or nothing at all, as in the phrase *as to whether.* Here are some examples:

- Suggestions **as to** improvement are welcome. (Substitute *for.*)

  We can only guess **as to** the reasons for the crime.
- (Substitute *about.*)

- There is no problem **as to** jurisdiction or **as to** whether to take this case. (Substitute *of* for the first *as to* and **omit** the second.)

- **address**

This verb is generally overused. Once used mainly in the context of directing a letter to its intended recipient, *address* has become a portmanteau word with at least the following meanings: "(1) direct, (2) call attention to, (3) attempt to answer, and (4) consider." In the following sentences it is used in these ways:

(1) She **addressed** the question to the Chairperson. (That is, she asked the Chairperson for an answer.)

(2) He **addressed** the matter of the safety measures the city had adopted. (That is, he called attention to the matter.)

(3) She **addressed** the problem of unemployment. (That is, she attempted to find a solution for it.)

(4) He **addressed** the liaison between the departments. (That is, he considered the liaison.)

- **establish**

This is another word that is well on its way to uselessness because it carries so many vague inferences. One student used it three times in a single sentence, with three different meanings:

- The court *established* (held, said) that the plaintiff did *establish* (provide) sufficient consideration for the offer by making the Dean's List as his uncle had *established* (required).

• pursue

The early case of Pierson v. Post exemplifies the original meaning of *pursue:* "follow in an effort to overtake." But the word has become a fad word and is now vaguely used in contexts like the following:

- The physician, *pursuing* anonymity . . . (seeking)
- The student *pursuing* law school (applying to)
- The late-dinner crowd *pursuing* a night out (enjoying)

What has happened to these words is now happening to others. The verb **affect,** for example, contains numerous meanings, including—but not limited to—"improve," "worsen," "ameliorate," and "retard." These meanings all carry the sense of "change," but more specific verbs can convey the kind of change you mean. Other currently popular and vague words are the verb/ adverb combinations *go to, look to,* and *look at,* which can mean almost anything, and therefore mean almost nothing. That's the trouble with vogue words; their meaning has been drained out of them by overkill.

Rule-of-Thumb: When you want to be precise, choose words that have specific meaning.

B. Avoid Legalese.

All professions have their own jargon. In a bureaucracy it is called *bureaucratese,* in education, *educese,* in law, *legalese.* But while bureaucrats and educators talk mostly to themselves, lawyers deal with the public. So if only to keep your clients happy, write so they can understand what you mean. And you have an additional incentive: recent legislation protects consumers from accountability for documents they sign but do not understand.

Legalese comes in at least three forms: **archaic language; joined synonyms;** and **throat-clearing.**

1. Archaic language

This is language that has survived through the centuries, much of it from as far back as the Middle Ages. If it has any modern meaning, the meaning is different now than it used to be. And much of it has altogether disappeared in English—except in legal documents. You have seen these words strewn lavishly throughout legal forms, words like *hereinbefore, hereinafter,* and *hereinabove; therefrom, thereunder,* and *thereof,* the *-eth* endings of Middle English third person verbs; and the triplets *said, same,* and *such.* You can replace some of these words with modern English. Others you can just discard, without loss of meaning. Here is an excerpt from a lease, containing typical legalese (emphasis added):

> • Tenant **hereby** further agrees to use **said** premises as a dwelling and for no other use, to pay the rent **herein** reserved when **same** is due, without any deduction **therefrom,** to pay all utility bills for **said** premises when and as the **same** shall become due, and not assign or sublet **said** premises or any portion **thereof**. . . . This lease, at the

option of the Landlord, shall **forthwith cease and terminate,** and **said** premises shall be surrendered to the Landlord, who **hereby** reserves the right to **forthwith** re-enter and re-possess **said** premises.

Here is the same paragraph minus the legalese:

> • The Tenant further agrees to use the premises as a dwelling, to pay the rent when it is due, and to pay all utility bills when they are due. The Tenant agrees not to assign or sublet the premises. The Landlord reserves the right to terminate the lease on demand, and to re-enter and to re-possess the premises.

Lawyers themselves sometimes do not know what legal archaisms mean. I have received letters from lawyers asking what statements like "Go hence without day," and "Affiant sayeth naught" mean.* The archaic "payment this day made" has been found ambiguous in court because it can mean either payment *was* made "this day" or payment *will* be made "this day."

The persistence of Latin and Anglo–French words in legal documents is another mindboggler—especially today, when almost nobody understands either language. You have looked up these words in your legal dictionaries, only to forget them at once, words like *laches, cestui que trust, gifts causa mortis, in pari materia,* and others too numerous to list. These are gradually disappearing from legal writing, and you can help the process along in your own writing.

2. Joined synonyms

In these compounds, usually joined by *and,* the first word means the same thing as the second word, or one word includes the other. In some of these compounds, the synonyms were coupled during the medieval period, as English lawyers began to abandon the use of French as the principal legal language. Others combine French and Latin (like 'cease' (French) and 'terminate' (Latin) in the quoted excerpt above. Many of these combinations still encumber legal writing; for example:

- acknowledge and confess
- breaking and entering
- deem and consider
- keep and maintain
- peace and quiet
- give, devise, and bequeath
- goods and chattels
- free and clear
- apparent and obvious

---

* The first means that the person appearing in court may leave and not have to return at a later date; the second means that the person filing an affidavit has nothing to add.

- within and around
- analyzed and evaluated

Rule-of-Thumb: When two words mean the same thing or one includes the other, omit one.

3. Throat-clearing

In oral interviews, as well as in their writing, politicians load their language with **throat-clearing,** the practice of saying one thing in several ways. You have heard them protesting on television that some fact or event has "in no way influenced, changed, or altered my decision." This reiteration, intended to reassure the listener about the speaker's sincerity, instead tends to bring it into question. Written throat-clearing evokes the same response. Remove phrases like those below from your writing, to make it more effective:

- the duty, responsibility, or obligation . . .
- in any manner, shape, or form . . .
- null and void and of no further force or effect . . .

In addition to cluttering your writing and making your argument less credible, needless repetition creates a seeming distinction where there is no actual difference in meaning.

Another kind of throat-clearing is what I call *the long windup,* introducing your remarks with numerous words when one or two would accomplish the same purpose. Here is a list; you might want to add to it:

For	Substitute
• The question as to whether	• Whether
• There is no doubt but that	• Doubtless
• He is a person who	• He
• In a reckless manner	• Recklessly
• This is a subject that	• This
• For the purpose of	• For
• In the same way as	• Like
• Until such time as	• Until
• During the time that	• While
• In the event that	• If

Here is a curable case of throat-clearing, from a law student's analysis of a hypothetical case:

> • An issue which has to be settled which pertains to the fact situation which deals with Abbott and Blair, who drove into a carwash to commit a theft is whether . . .

Your re-write would probably resemble the one below:

> • In the case of Abbott and Blair, who drove into a carwash to commit a theft, the issue is whether . . .

(Notice also that by putting the subject (*issue*) near to the verb (*is*), you make the sentence easier to read.)

If you don't "write with verbs," * you may find yourself in a long wind-up. Here is a short list of possibilities:

For	Substitute
• It is not necessary for you to	• You need not
• It has been held by most courts	• Most courts have held
• There are many points still to take into consideration	• Many points still need considering
• If the error was the result of	• If the error resulted from
• There are a few courts that have stated a rejection of	• A few courts have rejected

Finally, long wind-ups sometimes contain the over-used "the fact that," a phrase that you should edit out of your writing most of the time. Delete such combinations as:

- Due to the fact that
- It is a well-known fact that
- I should like to call your attention to the fact that
- It is a true fact that

That last item particularly annoys some persons, since it also involves *tautology*, needless repetition of the same sense in different words. Other tautologies are *new innovation, old antiques, four PM in the afternoon, erroneous misstatements, electrocuted to death,* and *he summed it all up in a final conclusion.*

C. Don't Make Impossible Comparisons.

You wouldn't compare apples and oranges, so avoid comparing incomparable things in your legal writing. The following statement compares New York *laws* to *Connecticut*—not to Connecticut *laws:* "The laws of New York, unlike Connecticut, provide for restitution as an alternative to prison for first offenders." To correct the problem, rewrite the sentence in either of two ways:

• The laws of New York, unlike those of Connecticut, provide for restitution as an alternative to prison for first offenders.

• New York law, unlike Connecticut law, provides for restitution as an alternative to prison for first offenders. (These sentences could also be crafted differently, of course, as long as the comparisons were correctly stated.)

Here are some more impossible comparisons, from law students' writing, followed by corrected re-writes:

---

* See more discussion of this subject at pages 100–103.

- Like the deadly weapon in *Bass,* the defendant in *Rogan* used his boot to assault his victim.

Like the Bass defendant, the Rogan defendant used his boot to assault his victim.

- Like the court in Amsted v. Rich, the decision here should be based on probable cause.

As in Amsted v. Rich, the decision here should be based on probable cause.

- Unlike inter vivos gifts, the donee does not acquire full title to property until the donor's death.

This donee, unlike the donee of an inter vivos gift, does not acquire full title to property until the donor's death.*

D.   Do Match Nouns and Verbs.

The mismatch of nouns and verbs, like other misalliances, can cause problems. Consider the following statement, from a student's paper:

- The *Brown* court followed the common law dislike for third party limitations in estates that would otherwise be freely alienable.

What the *Brown* court really did was *follow* the common law theory and *express* a dislike for certain limitations. The verb *follow* cannot have as an object the noun *dislike* (you can't *follow* a *dislike*).

Here are some other examples of mismatched nouns and verbs, along with rewrites correcting the condition:

- Statute § 460 states that deadly weapons obtained during the commission of a crime constitute burglary.

Because *deadly weapons* cannot possibly *constitute burglary,* the sentence needs re-writing. A possible re-write is:

- Statute § 460 states that the obtaining of deadly weapons during the commission of a crime constitutes burglary.

- The judge rebuked the language of the defense attorney.

But the verb *rebuke* requires a sentient being as its object. So rewrite the sentence so that the object of *rebuke* is a person:

- The judge rebuked the defense attorney for his language.

Will a Supreme Court decision cause rapes to "disappear"? That's what the next sentence seems to say:

- A U.S. Supreme Court decision that will allow publication of rape victims' names may mean the disappearance of rapes reported to the police.

---

* This sentence still suffers from confusion caused by two negatives. Can you re-write it to remove one?

On closer inspection, one finds that the writer intends only to predict that the number of rapes *reported* will decrease. A more exact statement would be:

> • A U.S. Supreme Court decision that will allow publication of rape victims' names may mean a reduction in the number of rapes reported to the police.

In the next sentence the noun/verb mismatch occurs because the verb "discriminate" requires a *human* noun as object.

> • The employer should not discriminate against an employee's religion.

The sentence needs recasting to supply one:

> • The employer should not discriminate against an employee because of his religion.

A noun/verb mismatch can also occur when one verb has *two* objects, but properly applies only to *one:*

> • U.C.C. section 2–207 affords advantages and drawbacks to industrial sellers.

The verb *affords* properly refers to *advantages,* but is improperly forced to apply to *drawbacks* as well. A more neutral verb would correct the statement:

> • U.C.C. section 2–207 has advantages and drawbacks for industrial sellers.

The same problem arises when two verbs have only one object, and the object is appropriate for only one of the verbs:

> • The evidence does not conclude but does support the fact that the information conveyed to the defendants was incorrect.

Evidence can *support* but not *conclude* facts. A simple change will solve the problem:

> The evidence is not conclusive but it does indicate that the information conveyed to the defendants was incorrect.

To avoid noun/verb mismatches, read over what you have written and ask yourself, "Does the verb I have chosen really fit its subject? Is the object I have selected really the appropriate object for the verb?"

E. Use Metaphors—But Carefully.

Metaphors, skillfully used, will illuminate your writing and may make it memorable. Recall Winston Churchill, using a work metaphor, as he asked the United States to supply arms, not men, in World War II: "Give us the tools and we will finish the job." (History records that we also sent men.)

But stale, mixed, or mangled metaphors will damage your writing. Your legal opponent may have thrown out the baby with the bathwater and sent a fox to guard the chicken coop, but find some other way to say it. Those metaphors are so stale that they have lost their vigor. Worse still is the stale metaphor that is also mixed.

Here are some that have done their authors no credit:

 • State department spokesman: We are not going to play this game with all our cards face up on the deck. (Combination of poker and ship metaphors.)

 • Political campaign speech: It's a new ball-game, and we're playing with a full deck. (Combination of cards and sports metaphors.)

 • On voting: If we all unite, we will be a force that will be heard. (How do you "hear" a "force"?)

 • On taxation: We need to bridge the battle and erase the financial gap. (But one "wages" battles and "bridges" gaps.)

 • On an opponent's record: His record speaks louder than any smoke screen. (Does a smoke screen "speak"?)

Mangled metaphors are no less comic, although they contain not two images but only one, mangled. There is the well-known statement in the concurring opinion in Griswold v. Connecticut: "The Due Process Clause of the Fourteenth Amendment stands on its own bottom." Other mangled metaphors their authors would like to be forgotten:

 • The proof of the pie is in the pudding. (Administrator at a Florida college, who was attempting a stale metaphor, "The proof of the pudding is in the eating," but mangled it)

 • The dents don't make a bit of difference. You can't see them unless you use a fine tooth comb. (A wellknown judge on a television program)

 • We've run so far down the road with entitlements that we're running up the wall and into the ground. (A U.S. senator)

 • We are creating a monster that's bound to backfire. (A city official criticizing annexation plans)

Metaphors tend to sneak into your writing when you are not watching. But get rid of the wrong kind.

Rule of Thumb: Never use trite metaphors, and be sure those you do use do their job.

F. Choose the Right Word.

As someone once commented, there's a lot of difference between your saying to a friend, "You look like the breath of spring," and "You look like the end of a long hard winter."

All of us sometimes grasp for the right word and grab the wrong one. For example, there's the law student who received a coveted committee assignment and wrote the chairperson a grateful letter, which began, "I have received your letter appointing me to the _____ committee and am looking forward to the assignation."

Judges are not immune from embarrassing locutions like the one above. From caselaw comes this interesting statement:

Navy physicians advised the plaintiff that they could not perform a vasectomy on the plaintiff; however, they advised his wife to have a tubal litigation.

Another judge wrote, "In an immediate sense, this [judgment] will add to the court's already damaged prestige." And a lawyer in a divorce action talked about a marriage being consummated, when he meant *culminated.*

The obvious advice is: when in doubt, check your dictionary, then your legal dictionary before you write your final draft.

Chapter Four

Reasoning . . . Legally

"Good sense is mankind's most equitably divided endowment. For everyone thinks that he is so abundantly provided with it that even those most difficult to please in other ways do not usually desire more than they have of this."

These words were written by the 17th century philosopher Rene Descartes, at the beginning of his *Discourse on Method,* Part One.* They are still true. Most of us, no matter how modest we may be about our accomplishments, pride ourselves on our "good sense." And the legal system is founded on that belief. The test of liability for tortious actions is whether a reasonable person (i.e. one of good sense) would act similarly in similar circumstances.

Therefore legal reasoning would appear to be just a matter of commonsense, of logical thinking, like that of any man-on-the-street, and no first semester law student would find it difficult. But legal reasoning is neither so simple as it would seem, nor so difficult as some law students believe. For legal reasoning does not rely merely on commonsense. It is based on precedent, what the law now is, with respect to a particular issue. Once you know what the law is, you can compare the facts of the case you are analyzing with the facts of cases on which the law has already spoken, and *then,* in deciding whether the law applies to the issue at hand, you can use the good sense Descartes attributed to all persons.

For the basic process of legal reasoning involves comparing cases to decide whether the law governing those cases is also applicable to your facts. That is, legal reasoning is reasoning by example, reasoning from case to case. This is what judges do; this is what you as law students will do in your memo- and brief-writing, and in final examinations.

I. Placing Facts Into Fact Categories

To compare cases, you will have to compare fact categories, not individual facts. What follows is an exercise to show how that is done, using simple fact statements. To place individual facts into one fact category, make a statement broad enough to include all of the facts, but no broader than necessary. (I call this process placing facts under "umbrellas.") Now make a general statement about (A) and (B) below so as to place them into a single fact category:

*Translation by Lawrence Lafleur.
Bobbs–Merrill Publishers, 1956.

(A) Employee A, who works for X company, is often late arriving at work.

(B) Employee B, who works for X company, is often late in returning from lunch.

A. First Category

The trick is to make your new category broad enough to encompass both facts, but not so broad as to make possible the inclusion of other facts. Your "umbrella" should just cover both statements of fact, without leaving room for others to enter. The two choices below were favored by my students:

(1) Employees A and B, who work for X company, often work fewer hours than they are paid to work.

(2) Employees A and B, who work for X company, are often tardy in beginning or returning to work.

The second choice is better than the first because it is narrower in scope. You can probably think of other facts that could be included under the umbrella of statement (1). How about the person who loafs on the job, although he arrives on time? How about the person who ducks out to do an errand during his time of employment? Both of these facts, and others you can no doubt mention, would fit under the umbrella of statement (1).

B. Second Category

Add fact (C) below to (A) and (B) and frame another fact category to cover all three statements:

(C) Employee C, who works for X company, often stays on coffee break longer than company rules permit.

Students were divided in their choice of a second category that would cover all of the facts thus far: (A), (B), and (C). Here were their suggestions:

(1) Employees A, B, and C, who work for X company, are often tardy for work.

(2) Employees A, B, and C, who work for X company, often work fewer hours than they are paid for.

(3) Employees A, B, and C, who work for X company, often cheat their employer.

Which of these three statements do you prefer? I would choose statement (2) for the following reasons: The word *tardy,* in (1), so often carries the meaning of late arrival that it seems less accurate than either of the others. On the other hand, statement (3) has two flaws: it is broader than need be for the purpose of providing that umbrella that just covers the three facts provided, and it contains a subjective conclusion in the word *cheat.* That word is slanted so that it becomes a *growl* word. Words that are slanted so as to convey disapproval on the part of the drafter are *growl* words; words slanted to convey approval are *purr* words. Both should be avoided, except for persuasiveness in carefully considered contexts.

C. Third Category

Add Fact (D), below, to (A), (B), and (C); then frame another fact category to cover all four:

(D) Employee D, who works for X company, often refuses to wear a protective mask when doing dangerous work in which such equipment is mandatory.

Obviously, this new fact differs considerably from the others. It seems, at first glance, not to fit into a single category with the three previous facts. But, as you know, facts that appear quite different on their face may be subsumed under the same umbrella if care is taken in stating the fact category. How is being late comparable to refusing to wear protective equipment? Students point out that both involve disobeying company rules. They chose the following for their third category:

- Employees A, B, C, and D all disobey company rules.

Now that you have placed all of the employees into the same fact category (i.e., under the same umbrella), consider the following problem:

> You are the attorney for Employee D, who has been fired from his job at X company for refusing to wear protective equipment while doing dangerous work. You will need, in defending your client, to distinguish his "rule-breaking" from the kind of rules that Employees A, B, and C have broken that resulted in their being fired.

To be successful, you will need to restate the fact category in which Employees A, B, and C are placed. My students decided on the following restatement:

- Employees A, B, and C, by disobeying company rules, waste company time and cost the company money in lost productivity.
- Employee D, by disobeying company rules, does not waste company time and does not cost the company money in lost productivity.

Now suppose you are the attorney for X company, which wants to include Employee D under the same umbrella as Employees A, B, and C. How would you do so? My students point out that you can properly include Employee D in the first statement above because his behavior could well cost the company considerable money due to his refusal to wear protective equipment, not only in lost productivity but in the expense of employee compensation, the cost of training another employee to do his job, and so on. So you would include all of the employees in the same category by making the following statement:

- Employees A, B, C, and D, who work for X company, may cause X company substantial financial loss by disobeying company rules.

II. Using Fact Categories in Legal Analysis

In your early semesters at law school, your professors emphasize that you are learning to "think like a lawyer." Learning to reason from precedent is part of that process. Learning to think in terms of fact categories instead of individual facts is another part. Once you have placed individual facts into fact categories, you can analyze and compare them more skillfully.

The following exercise exemplifies that process:

 • Your client, Jane Smith, wants to bring an action for unjust dismissal against her employer, the district manager of a theater chain.

She tells you the following story: She had worked for one year at a local theater as assistant manager, in training to become a manager at either that theater or another theater in the chain. Seven months ago, the manager under whom she served was transferred and a new manager arrived. He soon began to make suggestive remarks to Jane Smith and made it clear he wanted to have sex with her, but she was able to resist him successfully at work. However, at an office party two months ago, he became so aggressive that she left and drove to her apartment. He appeared at her door about an hour later and said he wanted to apologize. When she admitted him to her apartment, he sexually assaulted her.

She did not report his act to the police, but she did write to the district manager notifying him of the local manager's actions, and she says the district manager called her to say he would "take care of the matter." What he did was to transfer the new manager and fire her. She says she was never told that her work was unsatisfactory.

The district manager said, however, that Jane Smith was fired for unsatisfactory performance on the job. He said that her record indicated the following "black marks": She had been late for work six times, and once she did not come in at all and failed to call ahead to notify the manager. Her work record, prepared by a supervisor, stated that she was uninterested in doing a good job and seemed merely to be "putting in the required time."

Regarding her letter accusing the new manager of sexual assault and harassment, the district manager asked the manager about that, and the manager admitted that he and Jane Smith had had sex, but insisted she was a willing participant.

You have found the following case that was recently adjudicated in your jurisdiction:

 • The employees of XYZ Company have never been unionized, but some of them want to have the company recognize a certain union as the official bargaining agent for the employees. John Doe, a truck driver, who had worked for XYZ Company for four years, was active in the movement and was vice president of the union that was attempting to organize XYZ's employees. John Doe had twice met with the president of XYZ and had urged him to permit the union to be formed. John Doe says that the president was hostile, and he provided written proof that the president refused to hold an election to decide whether a majority of XYZ's employees wanted to unionize.

John Doe was fired six months ago. The president of XYZ says Doe was fired for incompetence on the job, not for union activities. Doe's record, written by his supervisor, indicates that he sometimes wasted work time exhorting other employees to join in the union activities. He had been involved in two accidents while driving the company truck (only one of which was held to have been his fault). He had been late for work four times, and once he quit work four hours early. His immediate supervisor reported that Doe was sometimes irascible and hard to get along with.

After being fired, John Doe sued XYZ Company to get his job back, alleging he had been improperly fired for union activities.

HELD, John Doe was improperly fired for union activities, and should be reinstated with back pay.

You can best compare your client's case with that of the already-decided case you have found by putting facts into fact categories and then drawing a chart to show the similarities (SIMS), dissimilarities (DISSIMS), and missing information (GAPS) in the two cases. The fact categories will also be fact similarities (SIMS). If the *crucial* (key) facts of your client's case are similar enough to the key facts of Doe's case, you can predict that your client, Jane Smith, will prevail in her suit against the theater company. If the key facts differ substantially, you can predict that Smith will fail in her suit. If there are a large number of GAPS, you will have to search for a more relevant case.

The following chart of SIMS, DISSIMS, and GAPS was prepared by law students.

III. Chart of SIMS, DISSIMS, and GAPS

SIMS:

   • Both Doe and Smith are former employees who have been fired.

   • Both Doe and Smith claim illegal firing (Doe for union activities, Smith for reporting sexual harassment and assault).

   • Both Doe's and Smith's employers state they were fired for incompetence.

   • Both work records, written by supervisors, indicate unsatisfactory performance on the job.

   • Both work records indicate employees' problems with supervisors.

• Both have a "writing." Doe has written proof that his company president refused to allow employees to meet to discuss unionizing. Smith has a copy of the letter she sent the district manager reporting the new manager's conduct.

DISSIMS:

• Doe had worked for XYZ Company for a considerably longer time: four years as against Smith's one year.

• Doe engaged in outside activity, but Smith "blew the whistle" on her supervisor.

• Doe's and Smith's complaints about their superiors differ considerably. Doe complained that his superior refused to act; Smith complains that her superior acted offensively.

GAPS:

• Doe's union activities were presumably well-known among the employees of XYZ Company. Did employees of the theater know of the harassment that Smith has complained about? (We should interview the other employees of the theater; perhaps they have been sexually harassed, or can corroborate Smith's claims.)

• Was the manager who wrote that Smith was incompetent the new manager or the former manager who was transferred? (Interview the former manager as to Smith's performance under his supervision.)

• What time period did the allegations about Doe's incompetence cover?

These SIMS, DISSIMS, and GAPS may not exhaust the possibilities, but you can see their helpfulness. They provide a way of looking at two or more cases as comparable entities rather than as collections of unrelated facts.

IV. Writing a Case Analysis

Now that you have constructed a chart integrating the two hypothetical cases, you can draft an analysis of them. The analysis, by comparing and contrasting the cases, will enable you to predict the outcome of Jane's case. Your analysis should be brief, clear, and tightly reasoned.*

Below is one student's analysis of the John Doe/Jane Smith cases:

• Jane Smith is less likely than John Doe to succeed in her claim of discrimination by the theater chain manager. Although both Smith and Doe were fired after engaging in action that their employers probably felt harmful to the company, Doe brought better evidence that his firing was connected to that activity. He was a longtime employee of the company (four years) who had engaged openly in the effort to unionize the

---

* In law school and beyond you will prepare case analyses and syntheses of actual cases and apply them to hypothetical fact situations. In law school examinations, you will also be expected to apply the rules, holdings, and reasoning of actual cases to hypothetical fact situations.

employees, an effort that the president had strongly resisted. He had written proof that the president was opposed to holding an election to determine whether a majority of the workers wished to unionize.

Smith had held her job for only one year, and her complaint against the company involved no ongoing activity on her part, but a one-time act on the part of another employee against her. She has no proof that the employee assaulted her except for her own word. The district supervisor can decide whether to believe her or whether to take the word of the new manager whom she has accused. The only "writing" that she has to offer is her own letter to the supervisor, not any writing by the manager or the district manager that would connect her firing to the accusation she made.

The black marks on Smith's record also seem more serious. During a four-year period, Doe had been late for work four times, while in one year Smith had been late six times. Furthermore, the incident she complains of occurred away from her employment, whereas the incidents Doe complained of occurred during the hours of work and on the business property. It is likely that the connection between Doe's activities and his being fired were more obvious to other employees than the connection between the incident Smith alleges and her firing.

Unless evidence is forthcoming to strengthen Smith's case, she will probably fail to win against her employer in her suit alleging discriminatory firing.

In her analysis the student excluded Smith from the umbrella covering the facts of the John Doe case, because she concluded that the distinctions outweighed the similarities of the two cases, so that Doe's case would not serve as precedent for Smith's.

Additional Facts Adduced in Smith's Case:

Now suppose that Smith has brought forth additional evidence. Another woman employee had prepared a written statement that the same manager whom Smith accuses, had cornered her in the office of the theater as she was leaving the premises. The other woman said that only the arrival of a male usher prevented an assault from occurring. The male usher involved corroborates that story.

Regarding the six times her record indicates that she was late, Jane Smith has a written statement from another employee on the same shift who asserts that Smith was usually only one or two minutes late, except on two occasions when Smith's car broke down en route to work.

As an exercise in case analysis, write another analysis including the new facts. Then read the following analysis by another student:

• Both John Doe and Jane Smith have brought forth substantial evidence to bolster their claims that their employers have fired them unjustly, discriminating against them for activities unconnected with their employment. Although John Doe was discriminated against for ongoing activities to organize a union at his workplace, and Jane Smith seems to have been fired only because she accused a superior of sexual assault away from the workplace, the cases have strong similarities.

Both employees were fired following their involvement in a situation their employer opposed. Doe's employer opposed the union; Smith's employer apparently disliked having to fire Smith's supervisor for his action and therefore chose to terminate Smith's employment to avoid having to do so. Neither employee seems to have substantial "black marks" during employment. Although Doe was employed for a longer period of time, he was involved in only one accident during the four years of driving a company truck, and had been late only four times. Smith's lateness, substantiated by another employee, usually involved only a minute or two; thus the six occasions recorded are not significant infractions.

Finally, both Doe and Smith provide corroboration for the discriminating behavior of their employers. Doe openly worked on behalf of the union activities and provided writing showing the company president refused to hold an election that might have permitted a union shop. Although Smith has only her own letter to the district manager, with no written response from him regarding her accusations, another female employee can corroborate that the same manager Smith has accused also attempted to assault her.

Given the similarity of the facts in the two cases, it seems likely that Smith will prevail if she brings suit against the theater district manager for discrimination in her firing.

Note the effective analytical techniques used by the students who drafted the analyses you have just read:

(1) Neither analysis contains "wasted" words. Both are terse, precise, factual. Neither contains presumptions or conjecture, and the reasoning is logical and persuasive.

(2) Stylistically, the analyses differ. The first answer states the drafter's **conclusion** first, followed by her explanations for arriving at her conclusion. That kind of reasoning is **deductive**. The second analysis begins with the drafter's reasons for reaching his conclusion, which is delayed until the end of the analysis. That is known as **inductive** reasoning.*

(3) The analyses differ in their method of persuasion. Although both drafters state at the outset that the two cases are essentially alike, the first analysis counterposes the strength of Doe's evidence against the relative weakness of Smith's evidence. The drafter of the second analysis carefully provides details to show that the dissimilarities of the two cases are relatively minor compared to their similarities.

---

* Deduction and induction are discussed at pages 231–236.

(4) Both drafters persuade the reader through their use of sentence structure and syntax. Both use complex sentences.* They then emphasize their point by placing it at the end of the sentence in the main clause.** Compare the two sentences below, one sentence from each analysis.

(from the first analysis)   Although both Smith and Doe were fired after engaging in action that their employers probably felt harmful to the company, Doe can bring better evidence that his firing was connected to that activity.

(from the second analysis)   Although John Doe was discriminated against for ongoing activities to organize a union at his workplace, and Jane Smith seems to have been fired only because she accused a superior of sexual assault away from the workplace, the cases have strong similarities.

V. Analogizing

The kind of reasoning just described is sometimes called *analogizing.* Analogizing involves comparing and contrasting the essential features of two or more cases. You will be analogizing cases throughout law school and in your legal practice because of the importance of the legal doctrine of precedent (*stare decisis*), which rests on the presumption that justice requires that persons in similar circumstances be treated similarly under the law.

In coming to decisions on the matter before them, judges apply the doctrine of precedent. Their reliance on precedent helps to avoid judicial opinions that otherwise might be based on whim or sentimentalism. The use of precedent also assures society that all persons will be treated equally under the law and allows members of society to plan their behavior knowing that they will be held to previously announced legal rules.

Courts rely on precedent by comparing the case at hand to earlier decided cases. They will do so when:

(1) the instant case is analogous in significant respects to the precedent case, and

(2) the opinion of the precedent case is either binding upon the instant case or is persuasive regarding it.

A case is considered analogous to a precedent case if its key facts, issue, and the rule of law to be applied are similar. However, even if a case is analogous to a precedent case, a court is required to follow the earlier court's decision only if that decision is binding upon it. Analogous decisions of superior courts in each judicial system are binding upon inferior courts in the

---

* Complex sentences are discussed at pages 94–95.   ** Placement for emphasis is discussed at pages 95 to 97.

same system. Analogous decisions of the highest state court are binding on
trial courts of the same state. Analogous decisions of the United States
Supreme Court are binding on all courts.

A court *may* follow any court decisions that are persuasive. Higher
courts in a jurisdiction may consider persuasive the opinions of lower court
decisions in the same jurisdicion and rely on those decisions, although the
decisions are not binding upon the higher courts. Analogous decisions of a
court in one judicial system may be adopted as persuasive by a court in
another system although those decisions are not usually binding.* Dictum
may be persuasive when it appears in the opinion of a higher court of the
same jurisdiction, although it is never binding. Dicta in decisions of the
United States Supreme Court are often accorded great weight by lower courts.

Once a court determines that conditions are correct for analogizing the
case at hand to an earlier case, it will probably follow the four-step analysis
below, which you will also use as you apply case law to hypothetical fact
situations in law school and to actual law cases in practice:

(1) Compare and contrast the key facts and the issues raised in the
earlier cases with the facts and the issues raised in your case.

(2) If the key facts and issues are similar, extract from the earlier cases
the legal principle(s) upon which those cases were decided.

(3) Apply those principles to your case.

(4) Arrive at a conclusion based upon (3).

These four steps may seem mechanical, but the results of analogizing are
far from cut-and-dried because the decision of whether facts are similar or
different is a subjective one. Only if the facts of your case are "on all fours"
can you assume that a court will find your case exactly like the previous one.
Hardly ever are facts of one case exactly like those of another; that situation is
about as rare as a final examination question containing exactly the facts of a
case studied in your casebook! Similarity is a matter of degree: other
relationships between cases may be expressed as "applicable," "analogous,"
"dissimilar," or "inapposite."

Because opinion-forming is a subjective process, courts may variously
interpret prior decisions. What an earlier case really *means* can thus be
determined only in subsequent court opinions. An illustration of this assertion
is the ancient case that established the "insanity defense," which provides that
insanity is a total defense to behavior that would otherwise be criminal. More
than 400 years ago, the court in *Beverley's Case* ** held that no felony or
murder could be committed without felonious intent and that a person
deprived of reason could not possess such intent. Later courts might well

---

* The legal doctrines of *res judicata* and
"full faith and credit" are exceptions. Stat-
sky and Wernet, *Case Analysis and Fun-
damentals of Legal Writing* (1977), have a
comprehensive treatment of analogization
(281–322).

** 76 Eng.Rep. 1118. 1121 (K.B.).
See G. Block, "The Semantics of Insani-
ty," *Oklahoma Law Review*, Volume 36,
Number 3, Summer 1983, at page 561.

have interpreted this rule to require a determination about whether the accused person did or did not have the requisite intent. Instead, later courts asked what degree of incapacity would excuse the accused person from criminal conduct. As a result of that interpretation, today a person is not guilty of a crime he committed with specific intent to do so if his mental capacity is judged to preclude his ability to form general intent. Had courts interpreted the legal principle in *Beverley's Case* differently, the modern insanity defense would not exist in its present form.

The case of *Laird v. State,* which follows, illustrates the subjective quality of judicial analogizing. Note how, in the majority opinion, earlier cases are used to justify the decision, while the same cases are cited in the dissent as justification for a different conclusion. The paragraphs of the majority decision are numbered for easy reference.

A. The *Laird* Case as Illustration

LAIRD v. STATE
Supreme Court of Florida, 1977.
342 So.2d 962.

SUNDBERG, JUSTICE.

(1) This is an appeal from a judgment entered in the Circuit Court of the Seventeenth Judicial Circuit, in and for Broward County. We have jurisdiction under Article V, Section 3(b)(1), Florida Constitution.

(2) Appellants John Laird and Lorraine Coffey were charged by information with one count of possession of cannabis in excess of five grams and one count of possessing paraphernalia. After pleading not guilty, appellants filed a motion to dismiss the information on the grounds that Section 893.13(1)(e), Florida Statutes, and related portions of Chapter 893, proscribing possession of marijuana, are unconstitutional as violative of the right to privacy. Appellants urged that the statutory provision, by including the private, noncommercial possession and/or use of marijuana in a private home, did not bear a substantial relationship to a proper governmental purpose.

(3) After denial of their motion to dismiss, appellants moved to withdraw their pleas of not guilty and enter pleas of *nolo contendere* to the possession count, while reserving the right to appeal the denial of the motion to dismiss. Appellant Laird admitted having the marijuana in his apartment on the day in question, and appellant Coffey admitted being present at the apartment. The trial court accepted appellants' pleas, withheld adjudication, and placed Laird and Coffey on two and one-half years' probation. The State entered a *nolle prosequi* as to the paraphernalia possession charge.

(4) Notice of appeal to the District Court of Appeal, Fourth District, was timely filed, but on appellants' motion, the cause was transferred to this Court by order of the District Court dated February 4, 1976.

(5) Appellants see this case—which raises the narrow issue of whether the State can prohibit private possession of marijuana in the home—as a clash

between a basic constitutional right to privacy and the State's police power. It is urged upon us that appellants enjoy the constitutional right to smoke marijuana in the privacy of Laird's domicile. The reasoning of cases such as Griswold v. Connecticut, 381 U.S. 479, 85 S.Ct. 1678, 14 L.Ed.2d 510 (1965), and Eisenstadt v. Baird, 405 U.S. 438, 92 S.Ct. 1029, 31 L.Ed.2d 349 (1972), is said to be applicable to the instant controversy. Appellants argue that a decision of the Supreme Court of Alaska, Ravin v. State, 537 P.2d 494 (Alaska 1975), provides persuasive authority for the position which they advance.

(**6**) For the reasons discussed herein we are unable to accept appellants' contention. We reject the notion that smoking marijuana at home is the type of conduct protected by the constitutional right to privacy and, on this record, affirm the trial court.

(**7**) In *Griswold v. Connecticut,* supra, the United States Supreme Court determined that a Connecticut statute which made the use of contraceptives a criminal offense was invalid as an unconstitutional invasion of the right to privacy of married persons. Mr. Justice Douglas, writing for the majority, found "that specific guarantees in the Bill of Rights have penumbras, formed by emanations from those guarantees that help give them life and substance." 381 U.S. at 484, 85 S.Ct. at 1681. The marital relationship was held to lie "within the zone of privacy created by several fundamental guarantees." Id. at 485, 85 S.Ct. at 1682. Justice Douglas placed heavy emphasis upon the marital relationship of the *Griswold* parties:

> "We deal with a right of privacy older than the Bill of Rights—older than our political parties, older than our school systems. Marriage is a coming together for better or for worse, hopefully enduring, and intimate to the degree of being sacred." Id. at 486, 85 S.Ct. at 1682.

(**8**) *Griswold's* protection of the privacy of the marital relationship was extended to certain intimate aspects of the lives of single persons as well in Eisenstadt v. Baird, supra, and Roe v. Wade, 410 U.S. 113, 93 S.Ct. 705, 35 L.Ed.2d 147 (1973). *Eisenstadt* invalidated a Massachusetts statute which made it a crime to sell, lend, or give away any contraceptive drug, medicine, instrument, or article. The statute permitted physicians to administer or prescribe contraceptive drugs or articles for married persons and allowed pharmacists to fill prescriptions for such items for married persons. The Court determined that the Massachusetts law could be upheld neither as a deterrent to fornication nor as a health measure nor as a prohibition on contraception. The third justification was dismissed on privacy grounds:

> If under *Griswold* the distribution of contraceptives to married persons cannot be prohibited, a ban on distribution to unmarried persons would be equally impermissible. It is true that in *Griswold* the right of privacy in question inhered in the marital relationship. Yet the marital couple is not an independent entity with a mind and heart of its own, but an association of two individuals each with a separate intellectual and emotional makeup. If the right of privacy means anything, it is the right of the *individual,* married or single, to be free from unwarranted govern-

mental intrusion into matters so fundamentally affecting a person as the decision whether to bear or beget a child. . . . 405 U.S. at 453, 92 S.Ct. at 1038.

(9) In *Roe v. Wade,* supra, an unmarried pregnant woman who wished to undergo an abortion sought a declaratory judgment that the Texas criminal abortion statutes, which proscribed all abortions except those procured or attempted by medical advice for the purpose of saving the life of the mother, were unconstitutional. The Supreme Court held, inter alia, that the right to privacy encompasses a woman's decision whether or not to terminate her pregnancy, but that a woman's right to an abortion is not absolute and may to some extent be limited by the State's interest in safeguarding her health, in maintaining proper medical standards, and protecting potential human life. After listing some decisions in which the Court or individual justices had discerned the existence of the constitutional right to privacy, Mr. Justice Blackmun, writing for the majority, declared:

". . . These decisions make it clear that only personal rights that can be deemed 'fundamental' or 'implicit in the concept of ordered liberty,' Palko v. Connecticut, 302 U.S. 319, 325, 58 S.Ct. 149, 82 L.Ed. 288 (1937), are included in this guarantee of personal privacy. They also make it clear that the right has some extension to activities relating to marriage [citation omitted]; procreation [citation omitted]; contraception [citation omitted]; family relationships [citation omitted]; and child rearing and education [citations omitted]." 410 U.S. at 152–153, 93 S.Ct. at 726.

This statement of the scope of the constitutional right to privacy remains the definitive statement of the law in this area.

(10) Appellants argue that another United States Supreme Court decision, Stanley v. Georgia, 394 U.S. 557, 89 S.Ct. 1243, 22 L.Ed.2d 542 (1969), controls the instant controversy. In *Stanley,* the Court reversed a conviction for possession of obscene matter in violation of a Georgia statute. The appellant in *Stanley* merely owned certain allegedly obscene films for showing in his own home; these films were seized from his residence incident to a search undertaken to find evidence of bookmaking activities. It is true that, in reversing the defendant's conviction, the Court found the right to privacy to exist in a context outside of the intimate personal relationships at issue in *Griswold, Eisenstadt,* and *Roe v. Wade,* supra. But in so doing the Court, speaking through Justice Marshall, laid special emphasis on Stanley's First Amendment rights:

". . . [Appellant] is asserting the right to read or observe what he pleases—the right to satisfy his intellectual and emotional needs in the privacy of his own home. He is asserting the right to be free from state inquiry into the contents of his library. Georgia contends that appellant does not have these rights, that there are certain types of materials that the individual may not read or even possess. Georgia justifies this assertion by arguing that the films in the present case are obscene. But we think that mere categorization of these films as 'obscene' is insufficient justification for such a drastic invasion of personal liberties guaranteed by the First and Fourteenth Amendments. Whatever may be the justifications for other statutes regulating obscenity, we do not think they reach into the privacy of one's own home. If the First Amendment means anything, it means that a State has no business telling a man, sitting alone in his own house, what books he may read or what films he may watch. Our whole constitutional heritage rebels at the thought of giving government the power to control men's minds." 394 U.S. at 565, 89 S.Ct. at 1248.

And in a footnote concerning contraband articles, the Court carefully limited its holding:

"What we have said in no way infringes upon the power of the State or Federal Government to make possession of other items, such as narcotics, firearms, or stolen goods, a crime. Our holding in the present case turns upon the Georgia statute's infringement of fundamental liberties protected by the First and Fourteenth Amendments. No First Amendment rights are involved in most statutes making mere possession criminal." 394 U.S. at 567, n. 11, 89 S.Ct. at 1249.

(11) In two recent cases the United States Supreme Court has declined to extend further the scope of the constitutional right to privacy. The Court recently affirmed the constitutionality of Virginia's anti-sodomy statute even as applied to two consenting adult male homosexuals. Doe v. Commonwealth's Attorney, 425 U.S. 901, 96 S.Ct. 1489, 47 L.Ed.2d 751 (1976), aff'g, 403 F.Supp. 1199 (E.D.Va.1975). In Paul v. Davis, 424 U.S. 693, 96 S.Ct. 1155, 47 L.Ed.2d 405 (1976), respondent's name and photograph were included in a flier of "active shoplifters," after he had been arrested on a shoplifting charge in Louisville, Kentucky. After that charge had been dismissed, Davis brought an action against petitioner police chiefs, who had distributed the flier to area merchants, alleging that petitioners' action under color of law deprived him of his constitutional rights. The Supreme Court, in denying Davis relief held, inter alia, that his contention that the defamatory flier deprived him of his constitutional right to privacy was meritless. Mr. Justice Rehnquist, writing for the majority, suggested:

". . . [O]ur other [1] 'right of privacy' cases, while defying categorical description, deal generally with substantive aspects of the Fourteenth Amendment. In Roe the Court pointed out that the personal rights found in this guarantee of personal privacy must be limited to those which are 'fundamental' or 'implicit in the concept of ordered liberty' as described in Palko v. Connecticut, 301 U.S. 319, 325, 58 S.Ct. 149, 82 L.Ed. 288 (1937). The activities detailed as being within this definition were ones very different from that for which respondent claims constitutional protection—matters relating to marriage, procreation, contracep-

1. The Court had just distinguished Roe v. Wade, supra; Terry v. Ohio, 392 U.S. 1, 88 S.Ct. 1868, 20 L.Ed.2d 889 (1968); and Katz v. United States, 389 U.S. 347, 88 S.Ct. 507, 19 L.Ed.2d 576 (1967).

tion, family relationships, and child rearing and education. In these areas it has been held that there are limitations on the States' power to substantively regulate conduct." 424 U.S. at 713, 96 S.Ct. at 1166.

Thus, as indicated ante pp. 963–964, Justice Blackmun's articulation in *Roe v. Wade* of the limited scope of the right to privacy remains the current state of the law.

(12) The foregoing discussion should suggest the inappositeness of the leading Supreme Court cases on the right to privacy and the case we decide today. Here we do not face the intimacies of the marital relationship or of procreation. There is no clear First Amendment issue posed by the question of whether appellant may legally smoke marijuana in his own home. Thus, we are not persuaded by the Alaska Supreme Court's resolution of this issue in *Ravin v. State,* supra. We note further that the *Ravin* court in part based its decision on state constitutional provisions which have no analogue in Florida.[2] 537 P.2d at 500–504.

(13) Appellant has presented to this Court a sampling of scientific authority to the effect that marijuana poses no significant public health problem. The State, recognizing the limitations of the procedural posture in which this cause reaches us, has made no effort to counter this material. In a proper case appellate courts may take judicial notice of such expert opinions, and, as noted by appellants, scientific authority on the subject of marijuana's harmfulness has been discussed in several such decisions. See, e.g., *Ravin,* supra; State v. Kantner, 53 Haw. 327, 493 P.2d 306 (1972); People v. Sinclair, 387 Mich. 91, 194 N.W.2d 878 (1972).

(14) This Court is ill-suited to make such a *de novo* judgment in a case, such as this one, which comes to us on a denial of a motion to dismiss. The record before us is simply inadequate to support a determination of whether the health hazards of smoking marijuana justify its proscription to the general public. None of the parties really argued whether the legislature lacks a "rational basis" for its decision to ban private possession of cannabis.[3] (Since we have determined that there is no fundamental right to smoke marijuana, the test becomes whether there is a "rational basis" for outlawing such an activity as opposed to a "compelling state interest" in the subject matter of the legislation.)[4] Thus in affirming the trial court, we do not foreclose the possibility of making such a determination on a properly-developed record

2. Art. I, § 22, Alas. Const., reads:

"The right of the people to privacy is recognized and shall not be infringed. The legislature shall implement this section."

See also Justice Boochever's concurring opinion in *Ravin,* supra, at 513–516.

3. "Left to another day is the question of regulation or prohibition of marijuana possession or sale in public and the issue of

denial of equal protection, as more harmful recreational drugs [alcohol and tobacco] are not similarly prohibited." Brief of Appellant, pp. 7–8.

4. For a critical discussion of this two-tier model, see Massachusetts Bd. of Retirement v. Murgia, —— U.S. ——, 96 S.Ct. 2562, 2568, 2573, 49 L.Ed.2d 520 (Marshall, J., dissenting).

wherein both sides have had an opportunity to present evidence of competing expert authorities before an impartial tribunal.

The judgments are affirmed.

ENGLAND, HATCHETT and DREW (Retired), JJ., concur.

OVERTON, C.J., and BOYD, J., concur in result only.

ADKINS, J., dissenting with an opinion.

ADKINS, JUSTICE, dissenting.

I respectfully dissent.

A constitutional right to privacy has been clearly established by the United States Supreme Court in Griswold v. Connecticut, 381 U.S. 479, 85 S.Ct. 1678, 14 L.Ed.2d 510 (1965); Eisenstadt v. Baird, 405 U.S. 438, 92 S.Ct. 1029, 31 L.Ed.2d 349 (1972); Roe v. Wade, 410 U.S. 113, 93 S.Ct. 705, 35 L.Ed.2d 147 (1973), and Stanley v. Georgia, 394 U.S. 557, 89 S.Ct. 1243, 22 L.Ed.2d 542 (1969). In *Stanley v. Georgia,* supra, this right was one basis on which the court allowed private possession of materials which the State could properly prohibit an individual from selling. The basis of the regulation considered by the court in *Stanley* was the exercise of the State's police power to protect the public morals and public decency. The court held that, although exercising the police power to these ends was proper, such power could not be validly extended to punishing private possession of obscene materials. The First Amendment rights of the individual were a second basis for the decision in *Stanley;* however, allowing regulation of these rights in public while condemning such regulation in private indicates that the right to privacy was the paramount justification for the decision.

No other constitutional rights were coupled with the right to privacy in the other cases cited above. They are clearly applicable to this case since they establish the individual's right to privacy with regard to birth control and abortion, which directly affect the individual's control over his or her bodily functions.

Brown v. Board of Education, 347 U.S. 483, 74 S.Ct. 686, 98 L.Ed. 873 (1954), establishes that the court may determine and take judicial notice of the facts which form the basis for legislation. The scientific information provided by appellant and discussed in Ravin v. State, 537 P.2d 494 (Alaska 1975); State v. Kantner, 53 Haw. 327, 493 P.2d 306 (1972); and People v. Sinclair, 387 Mich. 91, 194 N.W.2d 878 (1972), shows that the existence of the alleged harmful effects of marijuana have not been scientifically proven. It is questionable whether marijuana causes physical or moral damage, while the harmful effects of legal recreational drugs—alcohol and tobacco—have been well documented.

As in *Stanley,* however, the private possession of an object may be acceptable while the sale or use in public of the same object may not. The right to privacy is the only fundamental right which can reasonably be seen as infringed by the marijuana laws. No justification is shown for invalidating the statutes as they relate to sale. The regulation of this substance other than in the home is clearly a proper exercise of the State's police power.

B. The Analogizing Process

Note how the process of analogizing was carried out in *Laird*. In the following analysis, the left-hand margin numbers correspond to the numbered sections of the *Laird* decision.

Sections (1) to (4):

In the majority opinion, Justice Sundberg reviewed in these preliminary paragraphs the legal process by which the *Laird* case reached the Florida Supreme Court.

Section (5):

Justice Sundberg announced here that the "narrow issue" to be decided by this court is whether the State can constitutionally prohibit private possession of marijuana in the home. He noted that appellants see the case as opposing countervailing rights of the parties: the constitutional right to privacy versus the state's police power. Justice Sundberg noted that appellants urged, as precedent, cases like *Griswold v. Connecticut* and *Eisenstadt v. Baird* (both United States Supreme Court decisions) and, as persuasive, the Alaska case of *Ravin v. State*.

Section (6):

Here, at the outset, the majority announced its decision: The trial court decision is affirmed on the ground that the constitutional right to privacy does not protect the smoking of marijuana in the privacy of a home.

Section (7):

Beginning with this Section, and continuing through Section 12, the *Laird* Court reasoned from precedent to explain the basis for its decision. It did so mainly by distinguishing the cases adduced by the appellants, then by analogizing three additional United States Supreme Court cases (in Sections 9 and 11).

The *Laird* Court first distinguished the facts of *Griswold v. Connecticut* from the facts of the instant case. The Court noted that the majority opinion of *Griswold* emphasized the marital relationship of the involved parties. The *Griswold* Court held that it was the marital relationship that was protected by the "zone of privacy" emanating from the guarantees of the Bill of Rights. Therefore, said the *Laird* Court, the *Griswold* holding does not establish precedent for the *Laird* case, which does not deal with the marital relationship.

Section (8):

Here the *Laird* Court distinguished *Eisenstadt* using the same reasoning. It pointed out that, in invalidating a Massachusetts statute making it a crime to dispense contraceptives, the United States Supreme Court merely extended to single persons the zone of privacy enjoyed by married persons in similar relationships. It quoted *Eisenstadt*, which noted that unmarried persons, like married persons, had the right to be free from governmental intrusion into fundamental relationships. Unlike sexual relationships, the *Laird* Court implied, the smoking of marijuana was not a protected fundamental right.

Section (9):

Here the Court adopted the scope of the right to privacy enunciated in *Roe v. Wade*, another United States Supreme Court case. That right, said the *Roe* opinion, extends to marital activities, procreation, family relationships, child rearing, and education. This limitation, said the *Laird* Court, "remains the definitive statement of law in this area."

Section (10):

The *Laird* Court then disposed of appellants' argument that the United States Supreme Court decision of *Stanley v. Georgia*, which reversed a conviction for possession of obscene matter, controls this controversy. The Court distinguished *Stanley*, on the ground that, while *Stanley* extended the right to privacy beyond the intimate personal relationships set by *Roe*, its emphasis was on First Amendment rights. However, the Laird Court noted that in a footnote the *Stanley* Court stated that its decision in this case did not infringe "upon the power of the State or Federal Government to make possession of other items . . . a crime."

Section (11):

Here, the *Laird* Court reinforced its reasoning by listing cases in which the United States Supreme Court had declined to extend the scope of the privacy right. In *Doe v. Commonwealth's Attorney*, the Court had affirmed the constitutionality of Virginia's anti-sodomy statute. And in *Paul v. Davis*, the Court had held, *inter alia*, that the petitioner's contention was meritless, when he argued that the flier "defaming" him deprived him of his constitutional right to privacy.

Section (12):

Here the Court summed up its analysis by stating that the leading Supreme Court cases dealing with the right to privacy were inapposite to the case decided here, in that in this case the subject of intimacies of the marital relationship or of procreation were absent, and no clear First Amendment issue was involved.

Section (13):

The *Laird* majority now dispensed briefly with the appellant's "sampling of scientific authority" that marijuana use is not a significant health problem. "In a proper case," said the *Laird* Court, judicial notice may be taken of such expert opinions.

Section (14):

The dismissal of the evidence as to marijuana use continues here, the *Laird* Court stating that at any rate it has determined that no fundamental right to smoke marijuana exists in the Constitution, but that it does not foreclose the possibility of deciding later whether there is a "rational basis" for outlawing such activity.

Now Compare Justice Adkins' Dissent.

The *Laird* dissent clearly illustrates how reasonable minds can come to different conclusions under the doctrine of precedent, even when the precedent cases analogized are almost identical.

To begin, Justice Adkins adduced the same cases that the majority mentioned: *Griswold, Eisenstadt, Roe,* and *Stanley.* But whereas the majority distinguished these cases, the dissent analogized them. Justice Adkins began with *Stanley,* the United States Supreme case which extended the right to privacy to the private possession of obscene materials. This was the decision that proved most vexing to the majority, which resorted to distinguishing *Stanley* because its major emphasis was on First Amendment rights. The dissent, on the contrary, noted that the First Amendment rights of the individual were only "a second basis" for the *Stanley* decision, the right to privacy, being "the paramount justification."

The dissent added, without amplification, that in the other three cases, the right to privacy clearly extends to the control of the individual "over his or her bodily functions." These are the "fundamental rights" the dissent analogized to the smoking of marijuana within the privacy of the home.

What the majority put off for another time, the dissent considered important to the *Laird* case: the right of the Court to determine and take notice of facts forming the basis for legislation. The dissent noted that this right was expressed in *Brown v. Board of Education,* a case unmentioned in the majority decision, which minimized the factual data the appellant provided for consideration. The dissent added that in *Ravin* (and other cases) scientific information showed that harmful effects of marijuana were unproved. Thus, implied the dissent, regulation of the private use of marijuana without similar regulation of other legal recreational drugs,* was unjustified, although the regulation of marijuana "other than in the home" is a proper exercise of the State's police power.

As is clear in the *Laird* decision, reasoning from precedent can result in opposite conclusions. You will use this process throughout your legal career, so learn it well.

VI. Synthesizing

The analogizing process that the *Laird* Court carried out is one stage in the process of synthesizing cases, which you as law students and as practicing attorneys will be doing. To predict the outcome of the controversy you are dealing with, you will need to synthesize precedential opinions before you can

---

* Note that the dissent thus placed alcohol and tobacco in the same "fact category" as marijuana.

decide whether the precedent(s) they establish are applicable to your case. Are the decisions of the precedent cases consistent with each other? If so, do those decisions establish a rule that will control your case? The answers to these questions will decide your use of the precedent cases.

You have already briefed the following three cases: *Transatlantic Financing Corporation* (1966), *American Trading and Production Corporation* (1972), and *Northern Corporation* (1974). (See Chapter One.) Assuming that all three cases constitute precedent for a controversy that confronts you, you will need to synthesize them so that you can make a prediction as to the success of your case.

Your synthesis will include a comparison of the key facts, legal theories, issues, holdings, reasoning, and legal rules of the precedent cases. In your synthesis you will analogize and distinguish the cases, much as the *Laird* opinions did (above).

A. To Write a Case Synthesis:

(1) Write an opening statement discussing the common features of the cases.

(2) Discuss the cases, individually and with reference to each other. Begin with the key (operative) facts of each case; then, by referring to your case briefs, note how the cases resemble each other and how they differ (that is, analogize and distinguish the cases). In your analysis, discuss the causes of action, the issues raised, the reasoning of the courts, the court holdings, and the resulting rules (formulated, applied, expanded, narrowed, or overturned).

(3) Arrive at some conclusion(s) as a result of your analysis. For example, what legal rule(s) have been modified, abandoned, formulated, or rejected in these opinions? What legal trend(s) do the opinions indicate? What can be predicted regarding the adjudication of future disputes, in view of these opinions?

B. The Synthesizing Process

To aid you in synthesizing the above three cases, you should consider preparing a chart (based on your case briefs). My students have told me that such a chart (like that shown on page 145) is helpful in synthesizing a number of cases, for in the chart you can place immediately adjacent to each other all component parts of your briefs. You can then compare and contrast multiple cases with ease.

The following case synthesis was written by a student after constructing the Synthesis Chart on page 145.

C. Sample Case Synthesis

(of the three cases briefed at pages 18–19, 25–27, and 36–39.)

The application of the doctrines of impossibility and its offshoot, commercial impracticability, is demonstrated in the opinions of two federal circuit courts and a state supreme court. The cases are *Transatlantic Financing Corporation* (1966), *American Trading and Production Corporation* (1972), and *Northern Corporation* (1974). The first two cases involve contracts to ship oil from the United States to the Mideast. In each of those cases the carrier was forced, through no fault of its own, to take an alternative, longer route instead of its customary route via the Suez Canal, in order to deliver its cargo. In the third case, *Northern* sought damages incurred while attempting to perform an impossible contract.

In *Transatlantic,* the carrier owner requested relief for its additional delivery costs (about 15%) over the contract price. The District Court dismissed the *Transatlantic* libel suit against the United States for costs incurred by the ship's diversion from the normal sea route due to the closing of the Suez Canal, and the United States Court of Appeals affirmed.

In *American Trading,* the carrier requested relief in additional compensation for delivery costs incurred by its transportation of cargo to India via the Cape of Good Hope due to the Suez Canal closing. The United States District Court for the Southern District of New York dismissed its claim, and this court affirmed.

The third case, *Northern Corporation,* involved a contract to procure and haul rock. The contractor, through no fault of its own, was unable to complete its contract to haul rock and sought relief in payment for additional expenses incurred in attempting to do so, less revenue received. *Northern* sought recovery for its costs incurred in attempting to complete the contract, and *Chugach* cross-claimed to recover damages for delay in performance. The case was tried in superior court, which denied both parties' claims for damages and attorneys' fees. This court, considering the parties' appeals and cross-appeals, held that *Northern* was entitled to recover reasonable costs it incurred while attempting to perform a contract that was impossible to perform. The court refused to consider *Chugach's* cross-claim.

In *Transatlantic,* the court rejected the carrier's argument that the doctrine of deviation implied as a term of contract a voyage by the usual and customary route, so that when it was forced to take an alternative route, the contract became legally impossible to perform. The court listed three requirements necessary for the doctrine of impossibility to apply, only the first of which was present in *Transatlantic:* (1) a contingency; (2) allocation of the contingency by agreement or custom; and (3) occurrence of the contingency, rendering performance commercially impracticable. The court held that the risk of the contingency had not been allocated to the charterer and might more properly be allocated to the carrier, who might have purchased insurance to cover the contingency. Finally, the court rejected the carrier's argument that, by delivering the oil, it had conferred an in *quantum meruit* benefit for which it deserved payment. The court said that no in *quantum meruit* benefit is conferred when a carrier has collected its contract payment and seeks only additional compensation.

The court also rejected the application of the commercial impracticability doctrine to *Transatlantic,* since neither its crew nor cargo were harmed by the longer voyage. The court added that to justify relief under the impracticability doctrine there must be more variation than was present between the expected and the actual cost of contract performance. The *Transatlantic* court did not specify how much variation in cost was necessary to trigger the impracticability doctrine, but cited in a footnote an English case in which even twice the cost was insufficient for the doctrine to apply.

The *American Trading and Production Corporation* court also held that the carrier's contract to deliver oil to the Mideast was not rendered legally impossible despite the contract specification of transit through the Suez Canal, for the specification stated that the Suez Canal was the "expected" not the "required" route. Therefore, the court rejected the claim that the carrier conferred upon the charterer an in *quantum meruit* benefit, when it took an alternate, more costly, route. The court also rejected the carrier's argument that the doctrine of impracticability applied; the court noted that the requirements of "extreme and unreasonable difficulty, expense, injury or loss" were absent. In *American Trading,* the additional cost to the carrier was about one-third over the contract price, and this amount was held insufficient to trigger the doctrine of commercial impracticability. Nor was the additional length of the carrier's voyage (twice the expected distance) sufficient to constitute commercial impracticability.

However, in *Northern Corporation,* a state court did apply the doctrine of commercial impracticability when the contractor suffered the loss of two employees' lives and two trucks in his effort to haul gravel as specified in his contract, upon the demand of the other party to fulfill the contract. In applying the doctrine of commercial impracticability, the court said that a party is discharged from contract obligations if the costs of performance are so disproportionate to those contemplated by the contracting parties as to make performance "totally impractical in a commercial sense." In *Northern,* the "extreme and unreasonable difficulty," which is missing from *Transatlantic* and *American Trading,* was present. *Northern* also differs from the other two cases in that attempted performance was demanded by one party despite unreasonable and excessive losses to the other party.

In the three cases discussed, courts have defined the scope of the doctrines of legal impossibility and commercial impracticability. The *Transatlantic* court stated three criteria for legal impossibility: (1) a contingency not allocated to either party, (2) the occurrence of which (3) makes the contract performance commercially impracticable. This formula is consistently applied in the three cases. The facts of *Transatlantic* and *American Trading* failed to meet all criteria, courts in both cases noting that the variation between the carriers' contract price and the actual delivery cost was not great enough to constitute commercial impracticability.

The difference in *Northern,* where the contractor succeeded in his suit, were (1) the court found that the contractor's losses were excessive and unreasonable enough to trigger the commercial impracticability doctrine, and (2) the contractor suffered these losses attempting to perform the contract that the other party insisted upon despite losses to the contractor's property in his previous efforts.   Thus, *Northern's* losses satisfied the "excessive" requirement, and the demands by the other party satisfied the "unreasonable" requirement for commercial impracticability.

Based upon the holdings in these three cases, the application of the commercial impracticability doctrine results in the same damage awards as application of the legal impossibility doctrine.   For commercial impracticability to succeed, the plaintiff must suffer both excessive costs and physical harm in attempt to perform the contract.   Because commercial impracticability requires only two criteria, plaintiffs whose losses meet these criteria would be well advised to rely upon that legal theory instead of the doctrine of legal impossibility.

VII.   Applying Syntheses to Hypothetical Problems

In your law school legal writing classes you will probably be assigned two or more court opinions to synthesize.   Then you will be given a hypothetical problem about which you must make a prediction, based upon your synthesis. Later, in your legal writing course, you will be required to find precedent cases by your own research, then apply them to a hypothetical problem.

The chart on page 145 was used to prepare the synthesis of the three cases discussed above (*Transatlantic Financing Corporation, American Trading and Production Corporation,* and *Northern Corporation*).   A chart like this is useful when you prepare a synthesis that you will then use for your hypothetical problem.   You can brief the hypothetical problem, add it to the chart, and see at a glance the relationships between it and the precedent cases.

To test your ability to apply synthesized cases to a hypothetical problem, apply the relevant data from the synthesis of *Transatlantic Finance Corporation, American Trading and Production Corporation,* and *Northern Corporation* to the following hypothetical problem.   Analogize and distinguish.   Then, if you can, predict the likelihood of success for your client, Produce Packing House, in a suit against Frost Brothers.

Hypothetical Problem

Produce Packing House (PPH), a firm which prepares large volumes of fresh fruit for shipment in carload lots, contracted with Frost Brothers (Frost), a company which installs ice-making equipment, to install and maintain in the PPH plant ice-making equipment to prepare ice needed in PPH's operation.

In return, PPH agreed to purchase the total ice-making capacity of Frost's equipment from October 1 to June 30, each year, paying $8.00 a ton for the ice. Both parties signed a written contract to this effect on June 29, 1981.

Deficiencies in the equipment developed soon after it was installed, and PPH complained to Frost that it was not supplying the amount of ice needed. Frost attempted to remedy the situation, installing additional equipment, but these efforts were unsuccessful, according to the Chancellor, whose finding is binding upon the Court.

On March 26, 1982, PPH rescinded its contract, under the theory of impossibility of performance, alleging that Frost had assured PPH that its machinery would furnish all the ice needed by PPH, and the machinery was not capable of filling these needs. Frost contends that it should be reimbursed for the expenses it incurred in installing the equipment in the PPH plant, as well as for loss of contract.*

Directions:

Assume that *Transatlantic Financing Corporation, American Trading and Production Corporation,* and *Northern Corporation,* analogized above, (see synthesis chart, below), are opinions binding on this jurisdiction. In a written synthesis, apply the relevant facts of these three opinions to the above hypothetical problem, analogizing and distinguishing them as appropriate. Then, if you can, predict the likelihood of success for your client, PPH, in a suit against Frost.

---

* This hypothetical problem is an adaptation of Crown Ice Machine Leasing Co. v. Sam Senter Farms, Inc., 174 So.2d 614 (Fla. App.1965). You might want to read the opinion to see whether your prediction is accurate.

Synthesis Chart

	Transatlantic Financing Corp.	American Trading and Production Corp.	Northern Corp. v. Chugach El. Ass'n
Facts	Contract for shipment of oil to Mideast via alternative route, intended route being unavailable through no fault of either party.	Contract for shipment of oil to Mideast via alternative route, intended route being unavailable through no fault of either party.	Contract to procure and haul rock. Appellant paid additional costs in futile effort to fulfill contract, on demand of appellee.
Relief Requested	Payment for additional expenses incurred.	Payment for additional expenses incurred.	Payment for additional expenses incurred, less revenue already received.
Legal Theories	Breach of contract, under Doctrine of Deviation (Usual and customary route is implied.) Doctrine of impossibility (A thing is legally impossible when it can be done only at excessive cost.) *Quantum meruit* (When contract becomes a nullity, recovery for amount deserved is proper remedy.)	(1) In *quantum meruit* benefit conferred upon appellee for performance, since contract was legally impossible to perform through no fault of either party. (2) Commercial impracticability, which excused appellant from performance. (3) Contract (Liberties Clause) provides expressly for compensation in these circumstances.	(Appellant) (1) Breach of implied and express warranties entitles appellant to damages. (2) (Alternatively) contract impossibility justifies award of costs in attempting performance. (3) Increased costs to appellant constitutes compensable change under the changes clause of the contract. (Appellee) (1) Breach of contract: liquidated damages for delays in contract performance and for costs and attorneys' fees.
Issues	(1) Does the doctrine of deviation imply as a term of this contract a voyage by the usual and customary route? (2) Under doctrine of impossibility, did closing of Suez Canal render charter operator's performance legally impossible? (3) If so, did charter-operator confer in *quantum meruit* benefit upon charterer when he delivered cargo by an alternate, more costly route?	(1) Was contract legally impossible to perform, so as to confer benefit upon appellee for performance, payable in *quantum meruit*? (2) Was performance by appellant excused due to commercial impracticability? (3) Does Liberties Clause of contract expressly require compensation under these circumstances?	(1) Is appellant entitled to damages for breach of alleged express and implied warranties contained in the original contract? (2) (Alternatively) was the contract as modified impossible of performance? (3) If so, is appellant entitled to reasonable costs incurred in attempting to perform it? (4) Is appellee entitled to liquidated damages for delays in performance of the contract and for costs and attorneys' fees?
Holdings	(1) No. (2) No. (3) No.	(1) No. (2) No. (3) No.	(1) No. (2) Yes. (3) Yes. (4) Not applicable.
Reasoning	(1) Doctrine of deviation does not apply, for the Suez Canal route was not a condition of the contract. (2) Only one of the three conditions necessary for the doctrine of impossibility was present: unforeseen contingency. (3) In *quantum meruit* doctrine applies only when contract is a nullity; here charter-operator seeks relief only for additional expenses incurred in performance.	(1) Performance of contract did not require route through Suez Canal; thus no in *quantum meruit* liability. (2) No extreme or unreasonable difficulty proved by appellant; thus no excuse due to commercial impracticability. (3) Liberties Clause inapplicable since appellant did reach designated port.	(1) Contract was legally impossible to perform since conditions necessary to performance were not present. (2) If, on remand, appellee is found to have insisted on performance, when it knew or should have known of impossibility, appellant is entitled to costs incurred in attempting performance.

[D7290]

Chapter Five

Preparing an Inter-office Memo

This chapter will show you how you will be using your legal reasoning and writing skills in one of the first assignments you are likely to receive as a law clerk or new associate, drafting a memorandum of law.

I.   What Is a Memorandum of Law?

A memorandum of law is a written explanation, based on research and analysis, of the drafter's opinion regarding a legal problem. There are two kinds of legal memoranda: external memoranda and internal memoranda (usually called "inter-office memos").

With regard to the second kind of memorandum, the inter-office memo, in law practice you will usually be commissioned by a senior member of your law firm to draft an inter-office memo, which the senior member intends to use to advise a client about whether to bring suit or to decide how to proceed in a client's case once suit is brought. Usually you will be asked to consider only one or two issues when you prepare the memo.

Because it will be used to determine what course to take in a legal dispute involving a client, your inter-office memo should be thorough and unbiased. Both the strengths and weaknesses of the client's case must be explored objectively so that you can make an informed prediction as to the success of the case.

By contrast, an external memorandum of law is usually written to influence the decision of someone outside your firm so as to benefit your client. In the external memorandum of law you will stress the strengths of your client's case and attempt to minimize its weaknesses. External memoranda of law are, in that respect, similar to appellate briefs. They are advocative, attempting to persuade the reader to adopt the viewpoint and conclusions of the drafter. Law schools teach students, in their legal writing classes, the techniques necessary to write both kinds of memos and appellate briefs.

In this book, which concentrates on legal writing and analysis, the research component necessary in drafting a legal memo will be omitted. You will learn how to find the law as part of your legal writing courses. Here you can concentrate on the legal analysis and the drafting of the memo, without the need of doing the preliminary research. You will be given a fact situation, provided with a few authorities (case law and statutes), and will write a short (3 to 5 page) memo on one or two issues. Having successfully accomplished this assignment, you will need only to learn how to find the law in order to write a competent full-scale inter-office memorandum.

II. The Heading of the Inter-office Memorandum

The particular form of your inter-office memo, commissioned by your senior colleague, will, of course, be decided by your law firm. But in the heading, the following parts are usual: (1) the title, (2) the name of the person to whom the memo is addressed, (3) your name, (4) a brief statement of the subject-matter of the memo, (5) the client's name, (6) the office file-number, and (7) the date. In writing your short memo, you should follow this form, to familiarize yourself with it.

III. Format of the Body of the Inter-office Memo

Like the heading, the body of the inter-office memo will vary according to the custom of your law firm. However, the following parts are almost always included:

BRIEF STATEMENT OF FACTS

QUESTIONS PRESENTED

    ISSUE I:

    ISSUE II:

    ISSUE III:

SHORT ANSWERS:

    ISSUE I:

    ISSUE II:

    ISSUE III:

DISCUSSION

CONCLUSION

IV. How to Handle the Short–Memo Assignment

A. Brief Statement of Facts

In this section you will briefly state the key facts of the case your supervisor has assigned, excluding facts that are not relevant to the issues you are to analyze.

B. Questions Presented

These are the issues raised in the case (or assigned to you to analyze). If your senior in the law firm has asked you to draft the memo, that person has probably also formulated for you the issues you are to consider. In the memo assignment provided below as an exercise, you should attempt to formulate the issues for yourself before checking to see whether they are essentially the same as those stated. (Issue-finding is challenging and extremely important to legal analysis, so you should practice framing issues as often as possible.)

C. Discussion

I give students who are writing their first short memo the following outline to use in writing the discussion section. The outline helps to insure that you will include in your discussion all the necessary points and exclude irrelevant points. Be sure, however, to write the discussion in essay form; do not merely submit a fleshed-out outline as your discussion. In your discussion each issue should be analyzed separately, and the cases/statutes, etc., used to decide each issue should also be considered separately. Another important point: be sure to come to some tentative conclusion regarding each issue before moving to the next issue. It is also helpful, when there are several cases involved in your discussion, to come to some preliminary conclusion after discussing each case. Your final conclusion is, of course, the subject of the last section of the memo.

Suggested Outline for Drafting the Memo Discussion Section:

I. First issue

    A. First Case

        1. Brief facts, holding, reasoning, rule

        2. Apply to *your* case.

            a. Analogize.

            b. Distinguish.

            c. Conclude tentatively re first issue, first case.

    B. Second Case

        1. Brief facts, holding, reasoning, rule

        2. Apply to *your* case.

            a. Analogize.

            b. Distinguish.

            c. Conclude tentatively re first and second cases, this issue.

II. Second (third and subsequent) issue; follow format of first issue.

    A. First case: repeat as in I.A. above, but do not repeat precedent case facts that have already been stated.

    B. Second case: repeat as in I.B. above, but do not repeat precedent case facts that have already been stated.

D. Conclusion

This represents your best judgment based upon all your legal analysis. It includes a prediction as to the outcome of the case and your recommendation to your senior partner about how it should be handled, if this is pertinent. What you should not do in the conclusion is re-hash any of the analysis that resulted in your final conclusion. That should be provided only in the discussion section.

V. Preparing Your First Memo

Your legal writing professor has given you the following hypothetical fact situation to use in preparing your first memo assignment:

- Joe Poor was a freshman at Prestige Law School. At the beginning of Joe's first semester, the dean told the assembled freshmen, "Look at the person on your right and the person on your left. Next semester, one of you will be missing.

These words terrified Joe. At Prestige Law School, students paid for a whole year in advance and received no refund if they left after one semester. Joe had worked for two years to earn the money to attend law school, and he was determined to succeed there. During the semester he studied hard, briefed all of the cases in his casebooks, volunteered in class, joined a study group, and prepared course outlines.

Two weeks before finals Joe received a letter from his uncle, Phil Rich. The letter said, in part:

> I hear that you are attending Prestige Law School. I want you to be a credit to me and to the family name; if you make the Dean's List I will give you a new sports car.

During the two weeks preceding final exams, Joe and all the other freshmen studied extra-hard. Joe barely ate or slept, spending all his time studying. When his grades arrived, he found he had made the Dean's List, and he went to visit Uncle Phil to tell him the good news and to remind him of his promise. At dinner, however, Joe could not resist disagreeing with Uncle Phil about politics, and his uncle flew into a rage and now wants to avoid giving Joe the car.

Phil Rich has consulted your law firm to find out whether he can legally refuse to give Joe the car. Your senior partner has asked you to research two court opinions and to write a memo to help him in answering Rich's question. The two cases are *Dorman v. Publix–Saenger–Sparks Theatres, Inc.,* and *Chester v. State.*

A. Dorman v. Publix–Saenger–Sparks Theatres, Inc.

DORMAN et al. v. PUBLIX–SAENGER–SPARKS THEATRES, Inc.

Supreme Court of Florida, Division A.
Dec. 7, 1938.

Error to Circuit Court, Alachua County; H.L. Sebring, Judge.

Suit by Mrs. R.E. Dorman, joined by Robert E. Dorman, her husband and next friend, against the Publix–Saenger–Sparks Theatres, Inc., to recover "bank night" prize. To review a judgment for defendant after demurrer was sustained to the declaration, plaintiff brings writ of error.

Reversed and remanded with directions.

* * *

BUFORD, Justice.

In this case plaintiff in error sued defendant in error filing a declaration in three counts. The first count of the declaration alleged:

"That the defendant, at the time of the institution of this suit and at the times hereinafter referred to, conducted and operated in the City of Gainesville, Florida, among others, two certain motion picture theatres commonly known respectively as the Florida Theatre and the Lyric Theatre; that at the times hereinafter referred to and for upwards of ten months next prior to the institution of this suit, the defendant, in connection with said motion picture theatres, conducted a scheme or plan of advertisement therefor commonly known as Bank Night; that by said scheme or plan the defendant proposed and advertised to the public in said City of Gainesville that on Tuesday night of each week the defendant would pay a certain sum of money on the succeeding Tuesday night to that person who attended said Florida Theatre or Lyric Theatre, or who was sufficiently near either of said theatres on the outside thereof to claim the said sum, by making the presence of such person known to the officers or agents of either said Florida Theatre or Lyric Theatre from within either of said theatres, from the lobby of either of said theatres, or from a point on the outside of either of said theatres, within a reasonable time on the night of the drawing after the name of the person entitled thereto was announced by or on behalf of the defendant from the stage of either of said theatres, the lobby of either of said theatres, or in front of each of said theatres, and that the name of the person to whom the said sum of money would be paid would be determined by having some blindfolded person chosen by or on behalf of the defendant draw from a cylinder on the stage of the Florida Theatre one of the numbers designated on the pieces of paper contained in said cylinder, and that the pieces of paper contained in said cylinder would disclose the respective numbers assigned by or on behalf of the defendant at the time of registering to such persons as had registered their names in books provided by the defendant for that purpose, and for the permission to make which registration the defendant made no charge whatsoever; that the sum which the defendant proposed and advertised as aforesaid the defendant would pay under the scheme or plan aforesaid on Tuesday, September 28, 1937, was the sum of $500.00; that on Tuesday, September 28, 1937, the plaintiff, pursuant to and in reliance upon the defendant's aforesaid plan or scheme, was present outside said Lyric Theatre and nearby thereto at the time the defendant caused to be determined under the plan or scheme aforesaid the name of the person entitled to receive said sum of $500.00, and at that time the plaintiff was one of those who had prior thereto, in conformity with the defendant's said plan or scheme, registered in one of the defendant's registration books provided for the purpose aforesaid. That on Tuesday night, September 28, 1937, pursuant to and in conformity with defendant's said plan or scheme aforesaid, the defendant caused to be drawn on the stage of the Florida Theatre from the cylinder aforesaid, one of the pieces of paper containing the numbers of the registrants aforesaid, and that the number so drawn was the number which the defendant had assigned to the plaintiff at the time of the plaintiff's registration, and that the defendant then and there caused to be announced from the stage of said Florida Theatre that the plaintiff was entitled to the said sum of $500.00; that the plaintiff, at the time and place last referred to, within a reasonable time from plaintiff's name being announced by or on behalf of the defendant from the stage of the said Florida Theatre as the name of the person entitled to said sum of $500.00, did from the nearby proximity of said Lyric Theatre and from the lobby thereof make the presence of the plaintiff known and claim said sum of $500.00, to the employees of the defendant at the box office of said Lyric Theatre and the lobby of said Lyric Theatre, and did keep and perform each and every act and thing required of the plaintiff by the terms of the defendant's aforesaid plan or scheme, to entitle the plaintiff to receive from the defendant the said sum of $500.00, nevertheless, the defendant, in violation of its said proposal and undertaking, did then and there refuse, and at all times thereafter has continued to refuse, to pay to the plaintiff said sum of $500.00, or any portion thereof."

There are no material differences between the first count and the second and third counts. The same cause of action is alleged in slightly different language, but the basic facts are alleged alike in all counts.

Demurrer was filed stating a number of grounds and the demurrer was sustained without indication by the court upon what ground or grounds it was sustained.

The plaintiff refusing to plead further, judgment was had on demurrer sustained to the declaration and writ of error was sued out.

The first three questions submitted by defendant in error in its brief are as follows:

"Did the published proposal or advertisement to give away a sum of money under the plan of bank night alleged in the declaration constitute or result in an offer to enter into a binding legal contract which could become effective by one merely attending the drawing and not purchasing a ticket of admission?

"Did not the proposal and advertisement to give away a sum of money under the plan of bank night alleged in the declaration constitute a mere published notice of voluntary intention to make a gift as distinguished from an offer to contract?

"Does presence at or near a place in anticipation of receiving a gift or gratuity constitute a consideration or convert a mere published intention to make a gift at such place into a contract or create legal responsibility for refusal to make a gift?"

Aside from the questions above stated, the demurrer presented the question of whether or not the allegations of the declaration on the face thereof showed that the transaction described in the declaration and constituting the cause of action constituted a lottery. It, therefore, becomes necessary for us in determining the merits of the demurrer to determine whether or not the plaintiff is barred from recovery because the transaction constituting the basis of the cause of action was a lottery.

The first question to be determined is whether the offer of the Theatre Company is one to make a gift upon condition or one for a binding contract upon acceptance and performance of the terms of the offer.

In Williston on Contracts, Vol. 1, Sec. 112, p. 232 (1920 Ed.) it is said:

"If a benevolent man says to a tramp,—'if you go around the corner to the clothing shop there, you may purchase an overcoat on my credit', no reasonable person would understand that the short walk was requested as the consideration for the promise, but that in the event of the tramp going to the shop the promisor would make him a gift. Yet the walk to the shop is in its nature capable of being consideration. It is a legal detriment to the tramp to make the walk, and the only reason why the walk is not consideration is because on a reasonable construction, it must be held that the walk was not requested as the price of the promise, but was merely a condition of a gratuitous promise. It is often difficult to determine whether words of condition in a promise indicate a request for consideration or state a mere condition in a gratutious promise. An aid, though not a conclusive test in determining which construction of the promise is more reasonable is an inquiry whether the happening of the condition will be a benefit to the promisor. If so, it is a fair inference that the happening was requested as a consideration. On the other hand, if, as in the case of the tramp stated above, the happening of the condition will be not only of no benefit to the promisor but is obviously merely for the purpose of enabling the promisee to receive a gift, the happening of the event on which the promise is conditional though brought about by the promisee in reliance on the promise will not properly be construed as consideration."

Applying the test set out by Williston we find that if the attendance by the public (of which plaintiff in error was one) or the registration of the public was a benefit to the promisor, it is a fair inference that the attendance and registration were requested as a consideration. And it is axiomatic in the law of contracts that a benefit flowing to the Theatre Company from a third party is sufficient consideration irrespective of whether there is a benefit flowing from the promisee. Page on Contracts, Vol. 1, Section 531 (1919 Ed.). It is not necessary that the registration or presence of plaintiff in error alone should supply this benefit.

In 13 C.J., Contracts, Section 150, p. 318, it is said:

"In the matter of a benefit, a mere expectation or hope, or a contingent benefit, is sufficient, as, for example, the expectation of advantage or profit from the thing promised."

Thus, it is immaterial whether or not the presence of the participants in "bank night" actually increased defendant in error's box office receipts. The hope or expectation that it would was sufficient. Under this rule we are of the opinion that the registration and attendance of the public were a benefit to the Theatre Company.

Since the requested acts (registration and attendance at the theatre) resulted in a benefit to the Theatre Company, and were done on the faith of the promise to pay, such acts must be regarded as having been requested as the consideration for a valid and binding contract rather than as mere conditions to a promise to make a gift.

The next question presented is whether or not the registration and attendance of the plaintiff in error is sufficient consideration to support a contract, a breach of which would subject the promisor to liability for damages.

The consideration required to support a simple contract need not be money or anything having monetary value, but may consist of either a benefit to the promisor or a detriment to the promisee. Williston on Contracts, Vol. 1, Sec. 102 (1921 Ed.); [et al.]

"It is not necessary that a benefit should accrue to the person making the promise; it is sufficient that something valuable flows from the person to whom it is made, or that he suffers some prejudice or inconvenience, and that the promise is the inducement to the transaction. Indeed, there is a consideration if the promisee, in return for the promise, does anything legal which he is not bound to do, or refrains from doing anything which he has a right to do, whether there is any actual loss or detriment to him or actual benefit to the promisor or not." 13 C.J., Contracts, Sec. 150, pp. 315, 316. [et al.]

It stands admitted on the record that at the time of this particular drawing, Mrs. Dorman, the plaintiff in error, "pursuant to and in reliance upon the defendant's aforesaid plan and scheme, was present outside said Lyric Theatre and near thereto" and that plaintiff in error "was one of those who had prior thereto, in conformity with the defendant's said plan or scheme, registered in one of the defendant's registration books, provided for the purpose aforesaid." Both of these acts involved the doing by Mrs. Dorman at defendant's request of something which she not only was under no obligation to do, but had a right not to do. Therefore, such acts come well within the accepted definition of "legal detriment" and were in themselves ample consideration for defendant's agreement to pay, regardless of whether they were of any pecuniary value. See Earle v. Angell, 157 Mass. 294, 32 N.E. 164, which held that attendance at the funeral of promisor pursuant to the latter's request and agreement to pay the promisee $500 if he would do so was sufficient consideration to support the agreement, and that having performed, the promisee could recover the $500 in an action against the promisor's estate.

In its brief the defendant in error has cited a number of cases involving the elements of consideration holding that mere attendance at the theatre would not be a sufficient consideration to constitute a lottery. Then defendant in error contends that these elements do not furnish a consideration in any case, whether a penalty is involved or whether civil rights are involved. This contention is not well founded.

In Simmons v. Randforce Amusement Corporation, 162 Misc. 491, 293 N.Y.S. 745, decided by the Municipal Court of the City of New York, the plaintiff sought to recover $250 by reason of being the holder of the winning number drawn by defendant on one of its "bank nights". It was held that the act of a person in signing his name in a book and attending the night of the draw, at the request of the theatre, was "adequate consideration" for promise of a prize by the theatre to its patrons and others. The plaintiff was allowed to recover from the theatre on its refusal to pay for breach of contract.

In Commonwealth v. James Wall, Mass., 3 N.E.2d 28, it is said [page 29]:

"One may give away his money by chance, and if the winner pays no price, there is no lottery. 'Price' in this connection means something of value and not the formal or technical consideration which would be sufficient to support a contract. Yellow–Stone Kit v. State, 88 Ala. 196, 7 So. 338, 7 L.R.A. 599, 16 Am.St.Rep. 38; Hull v. Ruggles, 56 N.Y. 424, 427; Chancy Park Land Co. v. Hart, 104 Iowa 592, 595, 73 N.W. 1059. * * *

"There was error, however, in instructing the jury in substance that any technical and non-valuable consideration 'whether registration of the name or anything else' would be a sufficient price."

In Lee v. City of Miami, 121 Fla. 93, 163 So. 486, 101 A.L.R. 1115, this Court, in a majority opinion, held:

"1. At common law, lotteries were illegal only when they became public nuisances.

" 'Lottery' is a scheme for distribution of prizes by lot or chance. It is game of hazard in which small sums are ventured for chance of obtaining larger value either in money or other articles. 'Lottery' exists where pecuniary consideration is paid and it is determined by lot or chance, according to some scheme held out to public, what and how much he who pays money is to have for it. 'Lottery' is scheme by which result is reached by some action or means taken, and in which result man's choice or will has no part, and in which human reason, foresight, sagacity, or design do not enable man to know or determine result until same has been accomplished.

"2. Constitutional prohibition against lotteries was intended to suppress schemes for distribution of prizes by lot or chance which infected entire community or country and not merely individuals therein, and any gambling device reaching such proportions is 'lottery' within constitutional prohibition (Const. art. 3, § 23).

"3. While Legislature cannot legalize gambling device which amounts to lottery, it can regulate and prohibit any and all other forms of gambling (Const. art. 3, § 23).

"4. Statute licensing and regulating coin-operated devices, including automatic coin-operating vending and amusement machines with premium features, coin-operated skill machines and premium trade machines, *held* not violative of constitutional prohibition against lotteries, since machines enumerated in statute were not 'lotteries' per se (Acts 1935, c. 17257; Const. art. 3, § 23)."

The writer did not concur in that opinion, but running through all the definitions which were applied to "lottery", either in the majority opinion or in the dissenting opinion, there was to be found the requirement that to constitute a lottery there must be a hazard of something tangible of value paid or agreed to be paid by the player in consideration for the privilege of participating in the game or scheme in which there was a chance to win a much larger amount. A lottery has been defined as a sort of gaming contract by which for a valuable consideration one may by favor of the lot obtain a prize of value superior to the amount or value of that which he risks. See American Encyclopedia. In Commonwealth v. Wall, Mass., 3 N.E.2d 28, the Supreme Judicial Court of Massachusetts had under consideration judgment of conviction of one charged with the offense of being concerned in setting up a lottery for money, and it was shown that the alleged lottery complained of was the operation by a moving picture theatre of what is known as "Bank Night". There the Court said [page 29]:

"We agree with the defendant that the essence of a lottery is a chance for a prize for a price. * * * "One may give away his money by chance, and if the winner pays no price, there is no lottery. 'Price' in this connection means something of value and not the formal or technical consideration which would be sufficient to support a contract. * * * On the other hand, a game does not cease to be a lottery because some, or even many of the players are admitted to play free, so long as others continue to pay for their chances. * * * So here the test is not whether it was possible to win without paying for admission to the theatre. The test is whether that group who did pay for admission were paying in part for the chance of a prize. The jury could disregard all evidence introduced by the defendant favorable to him. They could take a realistic view of the situation. They were not obliged to believe that all the ingenious devices designed to legalize this particular game of chance were fully effective in practical operation. An important feature of the plan was the necessity that the person whose number was drawn should appear at once and claim the deposit. The time allowed for appearance was entirely within the control of the defendant. No definite time seems to have been fixed. A participant inside the theatre would have the advantage of immediate presence in a place of comfort. He could hear the number and the name read. He could identify himself at once. A participant outside the theatre must wait in discomfort in the hope that if his name should be drawn within he would be notified and would hear the call soon enough to crowd through toward the front of the theatre within such time as might be allowed. The object of the defendant was to fill the theatre, not the lobby or the sidewalk. We think the jury could find that the unusual crowds which completely filled the theatre on 'Bank Night' paid to come in partly because they had, or reasonably believed they had, a better chance to win the prize than if they had stayed outside, that they paid their money in part for that better chance, and that the scheme in actual operation was a lottery. There was no error in denying the defendant's motion for a directed verdict.

"Our conclusions of law as to 'Bank Night' are not in conflict with those reached by the Supreme Court of New Hampshire in State v. Eames [87 N.H. 477], 183 A. 590. The difference between the cases is that the New Hampshire court on agreed facts held that 'free participation is a reality.' We think the jury in this case could find that it was not a full and complete reality on as favorable a basis as paid participation. * * * "

In State v. Eames, 87 N.H. 477, 183 A. 590, much the same question was presented. In that case, however, the statute defining lottery was the controlling factor. The enunciation by the court, however, is persuasive. There the court said [page 592]:

"The problem presented by 'Bank Night' and similar schemes is to determine whether it is an evasion of the statute or an avoidance of it, and this question is essentially one of fact. In answering this question, we do not propose to close our eyes to reality. The test by which to determine the answer to this question is not to inquire into the theoretical possibilities of the scheme, but to examine it in actual practical operation. If, as the state contends in its brief, although this contention does not appear to be borne out by the agreed facts, 'the great majority of people pay for such privilege,' then it is an evasion and as such is not to be countenanced. As we understand the actual situation of this case, however, free participation is a reality. If this is so, then, regardless of the motive which induced the defendant to give such free participation, the scheme is not within the ban of the statute. Violation is shown only when, regardless of the subtlety of the device employed, the state can prove that, as a matter of fact, the scheme in actual operation results in the payment, in the great majority of cases, of something of value for the opportunity to participate."

In Central States Theatre Corporation v. Patz et al., D.C., 11 F.Supp. 566, District Judge Dewey said [page 568]:

"It seems to me that under this situation the plaintiff corporation is conducting a lottery. The elements necessary to constitute a lottery are: First, a prize; second, a chance; and third, a consideration. The plaintiff corporation admits the first two elements are present, but denies that there is any consideration paid by any one on the prize itself. I am unable to agree with this. While the registration book may be open to the public generally, it is within the foyer of the theater, and very few people would be presumptuous enough to enter the theater, register and not buy a ticket for the entertainment. The very purpose of the registration book being within the foyer of the theater is to induce people to enter the theater. Also that part of a scheme which permits a person to participate in the result of the drawing, if any, by not being inside of the theater, but on the outside, is a subterfuge, as the drawing is at 9 o'clock at night and the percentage of people who would stand outside and wait for the drawing at that time must be comparatively few. The question whether or not there is a paid consideration for the opportunity to win a prize necessary to constitute a lottery is a question of fact which must be determined from the facts and reasonable deductions and inferences to be drawn therefrom in each case. There can be no question that if a person wants to give a prize in appreciation of patronage, he should have the right to do so.

"In this case there was an admission charge to the theater, and the question of fact, it seems to me, is whether or not from this admission charge the scheme and plan was to deduct a certain percentage and use this fractional fee to pay or offset the loss which might be occasioned by the $150 prize. If that was the intention, I can see no reason why it would not be a lottery. Here there was a carefully planned scheme to appeal to the cupidity of the public and the spirit of gambling and speculation, carrying with it the attendant detrimental results which were intended to be prohibited by the statutes making gambling and lottery offenses, and at least the scheme is unfair and contrary to public policy.

"Taking it by its four corners, which the plaintiff insists the court should do in determining the issues of the case, it is very apparent that the increase in the attendance is from those persons who are interested in the drawing and not in the picture, and that they have paid their entrance fee primarily in the hope of being successful on the wheel of fortune. It may be that this number is small in comparison to the whole, but, if it is a lottery as to a few, or a lottery comparatively small in its consideration, it is a lottery nevertheless."

So it appears by the weight of authority in this country that the scheme known as "Bank Night" may be conducted as a lottery or it may be conducted in such manner that it is not a lottery.

On the face of the declaration it is not made to appear that it is a lottery because allegations necessary to show that the plan or scheme referred to when put into operation constituted a lottery are lacking. See State v. Eames, supra.

It will be observed that the statement has often been made that whether or not the plan or scheme as carried out by those operating Bank Night constitutes a lottery is a jury question. This is true in the sense in which the statement is applied. But whether or not the operation of such a scheme or plan constitutes a lottery under a given state of facts is a question of law. Stated in another way, we may say that whether or not the perpetration of certain stated acts under certain stated conditions constitutes the conducting of a lottery is a question of law for the courts to determine, while whether or not the alleged acts were perpetrated under the alleged conditions is a matter of fact which may be determined by a jury or in chancery by the chancellor.

When this cause goes back to the lower court and additional pleadings are filed, the question of whether or not the transaction complained of constitutes a lottery may be further presented or, upon the trial, if there should be a trial, it may develop that the transactions constituted a lottery and that the plaintiff is thereby barred from recovery.

We only hold here that the declaration on its face states a cause of action and does not allege sufficient facts to affirmatively show that the involved transaction constituted a lottery.

For the reasons stated, the judgment is reversed and the cause remanded with directions that it be returned to the rolls and further proceedings be had in accordance with law and practice.

So ordered.

* * *

B.　Chester v. State

William K. CHESTER, Appellant, v. The STATE of Florida et al., Appellees.

District Court of Appeal of Florida.
First District.

June 17, 1965.

Interpleader action by state to procure an adjudication as to the person or persons entitled to a reward which had been offered by the state for information relating to a crime. The Circuit Court, Leon County, W. May Walker, J., held that an attorney was not entitled to any part of the reward, and the attorney appealed. The District Court of Appeal, Wigginton, J., held that where all information revealed to the state by the attorney for an accused client was already known to the state and the attorney merely performed his duty for his accused client in arranging for the client to testify for the state in prosecution of the client's confederates for murder, the attorney was not entitled to the reward.

Decree affirmed.

* * *

WIGGINTON, Judge.

Appellant has appealed a final decree rendered by the Circuit Court of Leon County, In Chancery, which denied him any share of the reward offered by the State of Florida for information leading to the arrest and conviction of the party or parties responsible for the disappearance of Judge C.E. Chillingworth. It is contended that the chancellor misconceived the legal effect of the evidence and applied thereto an incorrect principle of law in finding and holding that appellant was not entitled to all or a portion of the reward.

This interpleader action was instituted by the State of Florida, through its proper officials, for the purpose of seeking an adjudication as to the person or persons entitled to the above-mentioned reward of $100,000.00. All persons, including appellant, who were known to have or assert any claim to the reward, or any portion thereof, were joined as defendants in the action. The amount of reward was deposited in the court registry and the State of Florida was discharged from any further obligation or responsibility with respect to the subject matter of the cause. The various claimants filed their claims asserting entitlement to all or such part of the reward fund as the court may deem them entitled. Upon consideration of the evidence adduced during the trial the chancellor entered his decree finding that three of the claimants were entitled to receive the entire reward in the proportions fixed in the decree. It was further decreed that appellant Chester was not entitled to any part of the reward, and his claim was therefore disapproved and rejected.

On June 15, 1955, Honorable C.E. Chillingworth, a distinguished jurist of the State of Florida, together with his wife, mysteriously disappeared from their home in Palm Beach County. An extensive investigation surrounding their disappearance was instituted and carried forward by the law enforcement officers of Palm Beach County and the State of Florida. As a result of this investigation it became evident that Judge Chillingworth and his wife had been murdered, and that three men were primarily responsible for the crime, to wit: Joseph A. Peel, Jr., Floyd A. Holzapfel, and George David (Bobby) Lincoln. The evidence reveals that despite the complete information obtained by the law enforcement officials regarding the facts and circumstances surrounding the murder event, and the complicity of the three above-named men in the perpetration of the crime, the State nevertheless continued its investigation without charging or arresting any of the suspects awaiting the time when further evidence might be developed which would assure a successful prosecution and conviction.

The Florida legislature, in its regular 1957 biennial session, enacted a law which provides in pertinent part as follows:

"Section 1. A reward of one hundred thousand dollars ($100,000.00) is hereby established for information leading to the arrest and conviction of the party or parties, or any of them, responsible for the disappearance of Judge C.E. Chillingworth."

It was while the investigation of this case was in progress that appellant Chester, a duly licensed and practicing attorney of West Palm Beach, was employed to represent the interest of the above-mentioned Lincoln who was then incarcerated in the Federal Correctional Institution at Tallahassee. Appellant visited Lincoln at the latter's request in reference to the Chillingworth's disappearance and murder. On this occasion Lincoln made a full and complete disclosure to appellant of the facts and circumstances surrounding the murder of Judge and Mrs. Chillingworth, and of his participation in that crime. Lincoln further disclosed to appellant Holzapfel's and Peel's participation in the murder and thereupon requested appellant to take this information and do with it what he could for Lincoln's best interest. Appellant agreed to the request made of him by his client, and stated that he would contact the state attorney at West Palm Beach regarding the matter. It was agreed at that conference that if it were not inconsistent with his duty as a lawyer, appellant would claim the reward offered by the State in connection with the Chillingworth murder. Following the conference appellant promptly conferred with the state attorney on two or more occasions on behalf of his client Lincoln with the result that an agreement was reached whereby Lincoln would turn State's evidence and testify fully, fairly and truthfully on behalf of the State in the prosecution of Holzapfel and Peel for the murder of Judge and Mrs. Chillingworth, in exchange for immunity from prosecution for either of said crimes and also for the crime of having murdered a third person. Lincoln was subsequently transferred to Palm Beach County where he made a full and complete written disclosure of the facts surrounding the crime. Lincoln's testimony as an eyewitness was the final link of evidence needed by the State to assure the successful prosecution and conviction of Peel and Holzapfel for the Chillingworth murders. After the latter two suspects were arrested and Holzapfel learned of Lincoln's confession, Holzapfel likewise confessed his complicity in the crime and pleaded guilty to the indictment brought against him charging murder in the first degree. It was upon the testimony of both Lincoln and Holzapfel that Peel was subsequently tried and convicted of murder in the first degree, with the recommendation of mercy.

Based upon the foregoing evidence the trial court reached the following finding and conclusions, to wit:

> "It seems clear that the information furnished by claimant Chester, as reflected in Lincoln's confession and turning of state's evidence, was not furnished in response to the reward offer but furnished in response to his sacred and solemn duty to his client, Bobby Lincoln. Irrespective of the reward, it was the duty of claimant to 'use every endeavor in his power' in behalf of his client. Apparently, the information furnished by Chester was furnished in an effort to save Lincoln from evident doom. As a matter of law, the reward in nowise could have influenced, changed or altered the effort, duty or responsibility of Chester to his client and was, therefore, no inducement and no consideration for the information furnished by him. Moreover, the state has already paid in full and to the utmost extent for such information by granting Lincoln immunity against prosecution in three separate and distinct murder cases.

> "It follows, therefore, that Chester did nothing beyond the scope of his legal duty in the defense of his client Lincoln and is, therefore, not entitled to participate in the reward offered by the state for which he has made claim in this proceeding."

We have carefully considered the evidence and the authorities on which appellant relies to demonstrate reversible error. It is our conclusion that the chancellor neither misconceived the legal effect of the evidence nor applied to it an incorrect principle of law in reaching his conclusion that appellant was not entitled to share in the reward.

From our consideration of this case we conclude that it was not the information furnished by appellant to the state attorney regarding Lincoln's participation in and knowledge of the facts surrounding the disappearance of Judge Chillingworth which led to the arrest and conviction of the perpetrators of the crime. All facts related by appellant to the state attorney were already known to the law enforcement officers working on the case, including Lincoln's participation in the crime. It was the willingness of Lincoln to testify on behalf of the State in return for immunity from prosecution which enabled the State to successfully prosecute and convict Holzapfel and Peel. The only services of value rendered by appellant were to his client as a result of which his client received immunity from prosecution in return for his testimony. For these services appellant was or is presumed to have been compensated under his contract of employment with Lincoln. Appellant performed no services nor furnished any information beyond that performed and furnished in representing his client which could be said to have led to the arrest or conviction of those charged with the crime. A different situation would be presented if the evidence revealed that appellant, after gaining information concerning the crime from his client, used that information in discovering and developing other evidence or information which would have been of value to the law enforcement officers in securing the arrest and conviction of the criminals.

There is another cogent reason why appellant failed to demonstrate his entitlement to all or a part of the reward. The primary purpose which motivated the State of Florida in offering the reward in question was to induce those having knowledge of the crime to develop and then divulge that knowledge to the law enforcement authorities, thereby making available to them information not otherwise obtainable. As said by the Supreme Court of Alabama in Mosely v. Kennedy:

> "We think it clear that the reward allowed by the aforesaid section * * * is a reward to spur individual initiative and diligence, whether the individual acts in an official or private capacity. * * *"

It is clear from this record that the only knowledge of the Chillingworth crime possessed by appellant was divulged to the law enforcement officers in the discharge of his duty to his client, Lincoln, which duty he was ethically bound to discharge regardless of whether a reward had been offered by the State. It is equally clear that the availability of the reward provided by the statute had no effect on spurring the individual initiative and diligence of appellant in the premises. He owed his client all of the initiative and diligence which he possessed in rendering the legal services he was obligated to perform irrespective of whether the possibility existed for him to share in the reward. We are of the view that the conclusion reached by the chancellor was the correct one, and the decree should not be disturbed.

For the reasons above stated the decree appealed is affirmed.

* * *

C. How to Handle *Dorman* and *Chester*

As you read *Dorman,* you will realize that one of the questions (whether the theater was operating a lottery) is not at issue in the hypothetical fact situation. The *Dorman* case, however, is relevant to your facts. The *Dorman* court is helpful in that it clearly states how to decide whether a contract exists. The question, said the *Dorman* court, is whether the theater's offer was only to make a gift upon a condition or to create a "binding Contract" upon acceptance and performance of its terms.

Before framing the first issue, however, you will need to consult the second case you were given, *Chester v. State.* Perhaps, after carefully reading and briefing that case, you will revise your issue statement. In considering *Chester,* repeat the procedure you used for *Dorman,* and you will probably conclude that *Chester* does not deal with the first issue that *Dorman* and your case consider (whether Rich's promise constituted an offer to contract or a mere gratuitous promise). So you are ready to frame the issue in your case, using only the *Dorman* opinion.

1. How to state the issue

There are certain conventions that issue-statement requires:

(1) The complete issue-statement contains a rule of law plus the facts of your case.

(2) The issue must be answerable by "yes" or "no."

(3) The issue can be framed either as a direct question or an indirect question.

(4) The issue must be drafted as one sentence.

To explain the above requirements: (1) The reason that the complete issue-statement contains both the law and the facts of a case is obvious if you consider the issue-statement, "Are the accused guilty of burglary for breaking into a drive-in carwash at 9 P.M. on February 9, 1991?" Your immediate response would be, "Under what law?" Unless you are told what the law is in the jurisdiction where the act took place, you cannot answer the question.

(2) The reason for this requirement is clarity. If you were able to state an issue as an either/or question, the chance of ambiguity would substantially increase.

With regard to the last two requirements, (3) and (4), convention dictates this form. Convention also requires that when you frame the issue as a direct question, you end it with a question mark. On the contrary, it is inappropriate to use a question mark if you frame the issue as an indirect question (beginning with "whether"), although you will find a number of 19th century opinions that did just that. Courts now prefer that plain English rules of grammar be observed in legal writing, and these prohibit the use of question marks to follow indirect questions.

With these guidelines, you are ready to frame the first issue of your case. You can do so using either a direct question or an indirect question:

Issue I: Under contract law, is Phil Rich's promise to give Joe Poor a car an offer to make a binding contract, upon acceptance and performance of the terms?

or

Issue I: Whether under contract law Phil Rich's promise to give Joe Poor a car is an offer to make a binding contract, upon acceptance and performance of the terms.

Note that the first statement of the issue is a direct question, the second statement is an indirect question.

In order to frame the second issue, you will need to re-read both the *Dorman* and the *Chester* cases, for the question of whether the offeree supplied consideration to the offeror appears in both. In the *Dorman* case, as in your case, the second issue is reached only if the first issue is answered by "yes." As in *Dorman,* if your conclusion in the instant case is that Phil Rich made a mere gratuitous promise, based upon a condition, Phil Rich can legally avoid giving Joe Poor the car, and the second issue would be irrelevant. The second issue should therefore be stated as an "if so" issue. Below are two ways you can state the second issue:

Issue II: If so, under contract law, did Joe Poor provide consideration for Rich's offer by making the Dean's List?

Issue II: If so, whether under contract law, Joe Poor provided consideration for Rich's offer by making the Dean's List.

2. Writing the short answer

Leave this section of your memo for last. When you have finished drafting your Discussion and Conclusion sections, you will find it an easy matter to write short answers to the issues, although the answers might be hard to articulate now.

3. Writing the discussion section

Now draft the discussion section of your memo. After you have finished your rough draft, consult the following memo, which was written by a student like yourself.

D. One Student's Answer

INTEROFFICE MEMORANDUM OF LAW

TO: Senior Colleague
FROM: New Associate
Re: Rich's promise to his nephew

CLIENT: Phil Rich

FILE #:   891011

DATE: January 1, 1992

BRIEF STATEMENT OF FACTS:

Joe Poor, Phil Rich's nephew, began law school last semester. Two weeks before his final examinations, Phil Rich promised Poor a new sports car if Poor made the Dean's List. Poor did so, but Rich wants to know whether he can legally refuse to give Poor the car.

> ISSUE ONE: Whether under contract law Phil Rich's promise to his nephew Joe Poor was an offer for consideration, which upon acceptance and performance of the terms would become a binding contract.

> ISSUE TWO: If so, whether under contract law Joe Poor provided consideration for Rich's offer when he made the Dean's List.

SHORT ANSWERS:

> ISSUE ONE: Probably. Although the benefit to Rich is intangible, it probably meets the *Williston* test.

> ISSUE TWO: Probably not. It fails to meet the test for consideration stated in both *Dorman* and *Chester*.

DISCUSSION:

The issue of whether a promise was merely to give a gift based upon a condition or an offer for consideration was raised in *Dorman, et al., v. Publix–Saenger–Sparks Theatres, Inc.* In *Dorman,* the defendant-theater advertised a "bank night," in which the theater offered the chance to win a prize of $500 to persons who came to the theater, registered in a book, and received a numbered ticket. Ms. Dorman did so, held the winning ticket, and further complied with the terms of the offer by making her presence known and claiming the prize, but the theater refused to give her the prize.

After the trial court sustained the defendant's demurrer, Ms. Dorman appealed. The appellate court said that the first issue was whether the theater's advertisement of a prize to persons at or near the theater constituted an offer for consideration or a mere gift based upon a condition. The court applied the test in *Williston on Contracts:* If the theater would receive a benefit from the public's attendance and registration for the gift, the theater's offer would constitute one for consideration. The court also cited to *13 C.J. Contracts, Section 150,* for the rule that even if the theater received no actual benefit, but merely expected to benefit from the conditions of its promise, the promise constituted an offer to contract. Thus the court held that the *Publix–Saenger Theater* had made Ms. Dorman an offer to contract, not merely an offer of a gift.

The instant case resembles *Dorman* in that both the theater and Phil Rich made a promise they wished to avoid fulfilling. Just as the theater in *Dorman* expected to benefit from its promise by increased patronage, Rich expected to benefit from his promise to Joe Poor in that the prestige of Joe Poor's making the Dean's List would be "a credit" to Rich and to "the family name."

However, the benefit the theater in *Dorman* expected to receive was a tangible one—financial gain. The "credit" that Rich and the family name would receive from Poor's success was insubstantial, not countable in dollars and cents. Thus a court may consider Rich's offer to be more like the offer it cited as a test in *Williston,* in which a benevolent man requires a tramp to walk around the corner to a clothing shop in order to get a coat.

Rich's promise to Poor seems to be somewhere between the theater's offer and the benevolent man's request to the tramp. Because Rich apparently valued the prestige as a benefit to himself and to the family name, the hoped-for benefit, though intangible, is probably substantial enough that his promise will be considered an offer to contract, upon acceptance and performance by Poor.

The issue of whether there was an offer for consideration does not appear in the second precedent case, *Chester v. State,* because the offer is a part of the facts of *Chester.* But the second issue, whether the offeree provided consideration, appears in both *Dorman* and *Chester.* And for a contract to exist, the second issue must be answered affirmatively.

In discussing the second issue, the *Dorman* court defined consideration as something that is either a benefit to the promisor or a detriment to the promisee. Something of value must flow from the promisor to the promisee, or the promisee must suffer some "prejudice or inconvenience" as a result of being induced to fulfill the offer. In *Dorman,* the court said that the test was whether the theater's offer induced the promisee to do something she was not legally bound to do and had a right not to do, or to refrain from doing something she would otherwise have done.

The *Dorman* court reasoned that in being present outside the theater and complying with the other requirements of Bank Night, Ms. Dorman did something at the theater's request that she was under no legal obligation to do. Her presence at the theater was a legal detriment to her and constituted consideration, completing the contract between the theater and Dorman. (The *Dorman* court then considered the question of whether the theater was conducting a lottery, an issue that is not relevant here.)

Under the *Dorman* precedent, if Joe Poor, as a result of Rich's promise, did anything he was not legally bound to do and had a right not to do, or refrained from doing something he otherwise might have done, Joe provided consideration, creating a contract the breach of which would be actionable.

Joe Poor may have provided sufficient consideration for a contract by studying hard and doing all he could do to succeed in law school. But Joe's incentive for doing so is not as clear as was Ms. Dorman's. He went to law school with the intention of doing well, studied hard, and did all that was necessary to succeed academically even before receiving Rich's letter. True, he redoubled his efforts the last two weeks before examinations, but this is normal for law students, as indicated by the fact that all of his fellow students did likewise.

Thus, under the *Dorman* test, it is likely that a court would reason that Joe Poor had acted in response to his own inducement to succeed in law school rather than as a result of his uncle's promise, and that he had suffered no detriment as a result of being induced by the offer. If his conduct constituted a benefit to Rich, under the *Dorman* reasoning, there would be a contract. But because the "benefit" Rich received was intangible (in fact, the family "name" to be enhanced was *Poor* not *Rich*), the court would probably hold that the benefit was not sufficient to constitute consideration.

The same issue of consideration was examined in *Chester v. State.* Attorney Chester appealed a Circuit Court holding that he was not entitled to a reward offered by the state for information relating to a crime. Attorney Chester represented a client incarcerated in prison, whom the state knew to be one of three men primarily responsible for the crime. In his role as lawyer, Attorney Chester received from his client a full disclosure of the facts of the crime. Attorney Chester agreed to take the information to the state attorney and use it to his client's best interest and then to claim the reward the State was offering. The State granted the client, in exchange for the information Chester proffered, immunity from prosecution for that crime and for another crime.

In the *Chester* case, the appellate court affirmed the lower court decision, reasoning that, in proffering the information on behalf of his client, Chester did nothing beyond the scope of his legal duty to defend his client, and was therefore not entitled to the reward the State had offered. The only service that Chester rendered, said the court, was to his client, for which the client received immunity from prosecution. The court reasoned that Chester performed this service to his client under his contract of employment. He was ethically bound to render the best possible legal services to his client, regardless of whether the State offered a reward.

The Chester court thus applied the same test for consideration that the *Dorman* court used: whether as a result of the promise the offeree did something he was not legally bound to do or refrained from something he had a right to do. In deciding that Chester did nothing in response to the State's offer and therefore provided no consideration, the court found that no contract existed between the State and Attorney Chester. The court reasoned that the offer was "no inducement," and no consideration was provided to the State by Chester's actions on behalf of his client.

This reasoning seems applicable here. A court may find that in making the Dean's List, Joe Poor was induced by his own interests rather than by his uncle's offer. Joe had begun to study hard well before he received his uncle's offer, and even after the offer did nothing he would not otherwise have done had he not received the offer. If so, Joe Poor provided no consideration, and there was no contract between himself and Rich.

However, Rich's case is not as strong as that of the State in *Chester*. For Joe Poor, unlike Chester, was under no legal obligation to do well. His obligation to himself seems less demonstrable than Chester's to his client. If Joe Poor can prove that he increased his efforts to do well due to Rich's offer, the court may agree that he did something as a result of Rich's offer that he would not otherwise have done.

Because Joe probably cannot prove that he expended effort beyond what other freshmen were putting forth, the court will probably conclude that he did nothing beyond what many freshmen law students do. He, like the other freshmen, felt impelled by the Dean's words at orientation (one of three new students will fail), and not by the offer he received two weeks before final exams. Thus there was no contract between Rich and Poor.

CONCLUSION

Under the *Dorman* and *Chester* precedents, it appears that Phil Rich can avoid giving his nephew Joe Poor the car he had promised to give him. Although a court may decide that Rich's offer was for consideration, not for a gift upon a condition, it would probably conclude that Joe acted because of his own wish to succeed in law school not because of Rich's offer and no contract resulted.

E.   How the Student Organized the Memo Discussion Section

(1) The student began by dealing with the first issue. No introduction was necessary because the relevant material was presented in the **Brief Statement of Facts** and the **Issues.**

(2) The student first summarized the relevant facts of *Dorman,* including the way the matter reached the appellate court. Then came the rule that the appellate court used, the reasoning of the court, and its holding.

(3) Next the student compared *Dorman* to the instant case, first analogizing and then distinguishing *Dorman.*

(4) After this analysis, the student came to a conclusion about how the court would probably decide the instant case under *Dorman* with regard to the first issue. (Note that the conclusion was stated in terms of probability not certainty.)

(5) The memo writer next noted that the *Chester* case did not involve the first issue of the instant case. She then used transitional language to move to a discussion of the second issue.

(6) Regarding the second issue, the student discussed the *Dorman* precedent first. Because she had already provided the *Dorman* facts, they were omitted, except as needed in the analysis of the second issue. As to *Dorman,*

the discussion of the legal rule the *Dorman* court applied, its reasoning, and then its conclusion regarding the second issue were presented in that order.

(7) Next came the analysis of the second issue of the instant case under the *Dorman* precedent. The memo-writer first analogized the Rich case to *Dorman* and reached a temporary conclusion regarding the instant case. Then she distinguished Joe's actions from those of the plaintiff in *Dorman*, and concluded, regarding *Dorman*, that a court would probably come to an opposite holding in the instant case.

(8) Moving to the second issue as it was decided in *Chester*, the writer included a summary of the relevant facts of *Chester*, a discussion of how *Chester* reached the appellate court, the reasoning of the appellate court, the test it applied, and its holding in *Chester*. (This procedure mirrored the procedure followed in the discussion of the first issue.)

(9) Next, as she had done in *Dorman*, the student analogized the instant case to *Chester*, then distinguished it from *Chester*, and concluded that because the similarities outweighed the differences, Joe Poor would probably not be successful in proving that he provided consideration for Rich's promise. (Note again: probability, not certainty, as her conclusion. Remember that, in legal predictions as in life, nothing is certain.)

(10) Now comes the bottom line: no consideration, thus no contract. No contract, thus no liability for its breach. The Conclusion sums up this final prediction.

F. One Last Comment

As you have seen, memo-writing is neither mysterious nor difficult. To be successful, you need to thoroughly understand your case and the precedential cases, analyze objectively, and organize your analysis logically and methodically. No magic, just painstaking work.

* * *

The inter-office memo you have just learned to write is considered a "simple" memo, because it contains only two issues and is relatively short. In your law practice you will also write "complex" memos, so-called because they have three or more issues and are considerably longer (15 pages or more). The form of the complex memo differs from that of the simple memo only in that it contains more parts, perhaps including a Table of Contents, a Table of Authorities, and an Appendix that includes items like photographs and charts.

The appellate brief, discussed in the next chapter, is always complex, for it is written to be submitted to an appellate court. Brief-writing is usually taught during law students' second year, and is assigned as a legal research and writing course. The next chapter explains how to write effective appellate briefs.

Chapter Six

Writing the Appellate Brief *

I. What Is an Appellate Brief?

A former colleague once commented that an appellate brief is a document written by a disgruntled practitioner who should have been better prepared at trial. Put more politely, an appellate brief is a litigant's way to challenge the final decision of a lower court.

A party or litigant who is aggrieved by a trial court's judgment or order can usually appeal to a higher court, where a panel of judges will decide whether the trial court was correct. An appellate brief is the written document submitted to the reviewing court to inform it of the material facts, legal issues involved, and why the law as applied to the facts should bring about the result the party seeks.

A brief is distinguishable from an inter-office memorandum, which objectively analyzes the law and facts. The purpose of an appellate brief is to persuade the reviewing court to rule in your favor. Your audience is a panel of judges who must resolve a controversy. As an advocate for your client, your duty is to interpret and argue your client's position in the most favorable light. While being scrupulous and honest, you must nevertheless advance your client's cause.

Generally the appellant—the person bringing the appeal—is asking the appellate court to alter a lower court's ruling based on one or more of the following arguments:

1. The lower court's ruling relied on erroneous facts;

2. The lower court's ruling relied on erroneous conclusions of law; or

3. The lower court's ruling misapplied the law to the facts.

Since appellate courts are usually limited to a record of the lower court proceedings, the first argument is the most difficult and least often used. Working at best from a cold transcript of witness testimony, appellate courts are reluctant to make judgments concerning a witness's credibility or to elicit further testimony. Moreover, the trial court's view of the evidence comes to the appellate court clothed in a presumption of correctness. Still, the first argument may be used in instances where the lower court assumes a fact not

* This chapter was prepared by Leanne Pflaum and Michael Giordano, lecturers and Assistant Directors of Legal Writing at the University of Florida Law College. Ms. Pflaum and Mr. Giordano are experienced attorneys both at the trial and appellate level, who, in addition to their teaching duties, remain active as consultants to attorneys throughout the state of Florida. I am greatly indebted to them for their expertise and for this significant contribution.

in evidence, (meaning there is no record evidence to support a trial judge's findings), or where the lower court plainly overlooked or ignored a pertinent fact or facts.

In most cases an appellant seeks relief based on the second or third arguments, or a combination of these. Let us assume (for example) that the testimony at a motion hearing or trial conclusively established that your client was a front-seat passenger in an automobile in which the police found contraband. Assume further that one cannot be guilty of illegal possession of contraband without proof of (1) knowledge of the presence of the contraband; (2) knowledge of the illegal nature of the contraband; and (3) the ability to exercise present dominion, custody or control of the contraband. Finally, assume that the judge ruled on the record that your client's presence in the automobile, coupled with the fact that the contraband was in plain view, was a sufficient basis to find your client guilty of possession of contraband.

On appeal, you may not be able to challenge the factual findings that your client was present or that the contraband was in plain view or that police found the contraband in the automobile. However, you could argue that (1) no evidence established that your client knew the substance in the ashtray was illegal; (2) no evidence established that your client had the ability to exercise control of the contraband; and (3) the elements of the offense (possession) were not proven by the established facts. Mere presence, you would argue, is not sufficient to establish either knowledge of the illicit nature of the contraband or your client's ability to exercise dominion or control over a substance found in someone else's automobile.

Regardless of the theory you choose for requesting appellate relief, once the choice is made you must focus on the specific relief you want. An appellate court usually will only (1) affirm the lower court's ruling; (2) modify the lower court's ruling; or (3) reverse the lower court's ruling. If the appellate court reverses the lower court ruling it will usually remand the case to the lower court for further proceedings, or in some criminal cases simply discharge the defendant/appellant. The appellant usually asks the appellate court to reverse the lower court ruling. The appellee usually seeks to have the lower court ruling upheld. Occasionally, however, both appellant and appellee feel aggrieved by a lower court decision and each side asks the appellate court to modify that decision.

II. Types of Briefs

In most appellate proceedings there are three types of briefs: (1) an initial brief, (2) an answer brief, and (3) a reply brief. In a situation involving a cross-appeal, a cross reply brief may be filed.

All briefs must conform to technical requirements of the forum in which you are seeking redress. Make it a habit to review the applicable rules of appellate procedure before submitting any brief. Rules vary from court to court. The rules are occasionally amended, and must be checked. Failure to follow the rules will adversely affect your credibility. (Moreover, modern appellate rules are surprisingly short and simple.)

III. Choosing the Issues, i.e., The Question(s) Presented

As an appellant's counsel, the first step in preparing the brief is a *thorough* reading and re-reading of the record pleadings, and transcript(s) to select the issues in the case. These are the points which will be headings in your brief. While reviewing the record and transcripts you are, of course, looking for significant errors that may lead to reversal. Obviously one cannot spot such errors without keeping abreast of current case law. Other helpful sources for issue spotting are the documents, motions, and memoranda filed by the trial attorneys; any disputes at trial involving the admissibility of evidence, or jury instructions; arguments by counsel to the judge or jury; objections by counsel to evidence or arguments (such as inflammatory witness testimony); and court rulings during summary judgment proceedings or trial. Your job is to carefully review the entire record of the trial court proceedings, from initial complaint to final judgment, looking for unfair, irregular or erroneous rulings by the judge.

Finding and phrasing the issues is one of the most difficult tasks in brief writing and requires considerable thought and broad knowledge of the law. Discussion with colleagues or others can provide additional perspectives on your case. Attorneys who are criticized for constantly talking about their cases are often searching for insights they may have overlooked. Even an issue or point not argued extensively below may provide a basis to win an appeal. One appellate attorney handled a criminal case in which the defendant's trial attorneys had argued extensively that the police had conducted an illegal search of a vehicle. The officers had claimed that the vehicle was stopped because of faulty tail-lights. Although it was a minor point, the appellate attorney argued that although one tail-light was out, that type of car was equipped with four tail-lights, while the law required only two. Thus he argued that the officers' initial reason for stopping the defendant was improper, so it did not matter that the search after the stop was justified. The appellate court agreed and reversed the lower court's ruling upholding the motions to suppress and dismiss. See Wilhelm v. State, 515 So.2d 1343 (Fla. 2d DCA 1987).

When initially gathering possible issues don't be afraid to list all possible issues. Deciding which issues to include and which to omit is not a precise science. Obviously you must omit issues which, after further research, are found to be without merit. But arguments abound concerning whether to include all issues. On the one hand including marginal issues may take the appellate court's attention away from the more tenable issues in your arsenal. Further, if you list too many issues in your brief the appellate court may find it hard to believe that a learned trial judge would commit that many reversible errors. The writer's credibility might suffer as a result.

Also, it is always important to remember that appellate judges spend their working lives reading briefs—thousands of them, many poorly written and confusing—so it is a good rule-of-thumb to draft briefs that are as short and simple to read as possible.

If you do decide to include a secondary issue you are not especially enthusiastic about (remember the tail-light), be honest with the appellate court: Explain that the issue may be minor, but that you feel compelled to raise it. Also, think seriously about discussing any minor issues toward the end of your brief.

After narrowing your issues, look at what's left and examine your side's strengths and weaknesses *and* the strengths and weaknesses of the other side. Argue with yourself from your opponent's point of view. Don't be your own worst enemy by thinking only of your own arguments. Unless it is really an "easy appeal" you need to see the case from the other side so that you can respond when the opposition makes its presentation.

IV. Framing Issues and Order of Discussion

The purpose of the issue(s) or question(s) presented is to state the precise legal issue(s) of your case, in a non-argumentative manner. The language used to frame your issues and the order chosen to present the issues to the court requires some attention. A well-written question makes the court's job easier because it specifically notifies the court of the crucial legal issues and operative facts. Further, a properly worded question bolsters your credibility by informing the court that you as an appellate writer understand the possible scope of appellate review and are presenting a viable and meaningful question to the court.

Your task of persuading and informing the court in the question presented is made a bit more difficult by a few formal constraints. One constraint is that you must present your issue as an indirect question, beginning with *whether*. Frame your issues(s), in terms of trial court error, not on abstract issues of law. For example don't write, "Whether respondeat superior is applicable in a worker's compensation claim." Instead write, "Whether the trial court erred by applying the doctrine of respondeat superior in a worker's compensation claim."

Frame your issue from general to specific. That is, include the rule of law to be applied, and some pertinent facts of record. For example: "Whether the trial court erred in applying the doctrine of constructive possession against a passenger in an automobile owned by another in which police found contraband where the State presented no evidence that the passenger knew of the presence of the contraband." Careful wording is important. Let the court know "up front" that you understand the rules of appellate review and are presenting your appellate argument within the accepted rules.

Assume your appeal involves the federal employment discrimination laws (Title VII), and that your client is a female associate of a law firm who alleges she was denied partnership because she is a woman. Consider the following question presented:

WHETHER TITLE VII APPLIES TO LAW FIRMS

This question fails to tell the court what this case is all about. It introduces the legal principle, but only in an abstract way. That principle will not help the judge understand the case. You must inform the judge of the connection between the legal principle and these parties. Consider this question:

WHETHER TITLE VII PROHIBITS A LAW FIRM FROM DENYING PARTNERSHIP ON THE BASIS OF SEX.

This is better. This question informs the judge that these parties have a controversy over a denial of partnership, and the plaintiff alleges that the reason for the denial was her gender. This question succeeds in its function of informing the court. But what about persuasion? The question fails to preview the argument. It misses the opportunity to begin the persuasive process at the outset. Consider this alternative:

WHETHER TITLE VII PROHIBITS A LAW FIRM FROM DENYING PARTNERSHIP TO A FEMALE ASSOCIATE WITH AN OUTSTANDING SEVEN–YEAR WORK–RECORD.

This question prepares the court for your argument. The court now knows the area of law involved and has an idea of the points you will be discussing.

It is also important to determine which issue to put forth first. There are two main schools of thought. Many writers follow the concept of advancing the strongest issue first. This is generally the issue with the most compelling support. The thinking behind this concept is that since the courts are overworked, the court's enthusiasm for your argument will be strongest as it begins reading your brief. You must capture your reader's attention immediately and a positive first impression will lend credibility to weaker arguments later in your brief.

There is some merit to this argument; however, it should never be a hard and fast rule. Many writers advocate sticking to a chronological presentation of your issues. These writers argue that the absence of a flowing chronological narrative is just as deleterious to your goal on appeal as advancing a lesser question first because it may confuse your reader.* Discussing issues "out of order" can also lead to a lengthy, cumbersome and repetitious brief. Give your reader credit for being able to see the whole picture through a well-written chronology.

For example in the "tail-light" criminal case, the police stopped the accused before they searched his car. Police searched the car before making the arrest. By discussing the propriety of the stop before the propriety of the

---

* See also discussion elsewhere, pages 219–222, 242–244, and *passim.*

search and concomitant arrest, you not only provide the court with an easy-to-remember narrative, but avoid unnecessary repetition in your brief.

V. Sections of the Brief

Generally appellate briefs contain eight sections: (A) Title Page, (B) Table of Contents, (C) Table of Citations, (D) Questions or Issues Presented, (E) Statement of the Case and Facts, (F) Summary of the Argument, (G) Argument or Discussion Section, and (H) Conclusion. (Note: Some appellate courts have administrative rules governing the type of paper, color of brief covers, length, margins, nature of contents, applicable citation rules, and binding and form of briefs, etc.)

A. Cover or Title Page

The cover or title page appears on the front cover of your brief. Include the names and designations of the parties, the court hearing the case, the court which issued the verdict or ruling, the party whose brief this is, and the name and address of the attorney representing that party.

B. Table of Contents

The Table of Contents should contain page references for each section of the brief, including your argument headings in full and other tables of the brief. The headings in the argument should be typed in uppercase; the subheadings in upper and lowercase, indented, and either underlined or in bold. A Table of Contents should not be a cryptic referral to a page number. Your goal is to clarify, to guide your reader.

C. Table of Citations (Table of Authorities)

The Table of Citations or Table of Authorities is an alphabetical list of the cases, statutes and other authorities used in your brief, divided into categories and paginated. First list cases in alphabetical order, with citations. Then list constitutional and statutory provisions, and any administrative regulations. Other authorities may be listed under miscellaneous or other specific categories. In the Table of Authorities you should list the page or pages of the brief on which each citation appears. Be sure to use the uniform system of citation adopted in the jurisdiction encompassing the appellate court.

D. Questions (or Issues) Presented

The purpose of this section is to state the precise legal issues in your case, incorporating the key facts of the case, in order to tell the court what the appeal is about. The number of issues in the case will generally determine the number of questions presented.

E. Statement of the Case and Facts

The best appellate attorneys secretly believe that appeals are won or lost on the statement of the case and the facts, not in the actual legal argument. The theory is this: If, after reading an appellant's statement of the facts, the appellate court is persuaded that the appellant has suffered some unfair injury, the court will be inclined to reverse and will find a legal basis for doing so, since there are so many legal doctrines to choose from.

On the other hand, if the appellate court believes, after reading the briefs that the appellant is probably a scoundrel who is just trying to manipulate the system, the court will usually find some way to affirm. The single most important task in an appellate brief is to find the proper balance between portraying the facts in a light favorable to your client, and distorting the record. If you do cross the line into distortion, your opponent will usually point that out to the court, and you will lose your credibility and probably the appeal; but if you don't state the facts favorably, you won't win the heart and mind of the court and may lose for that reason.

In every appeal, with a few exceptions, the clerk of the lower court transmits a record of the proceedings to the appellate court. Usually, insuring that a proper, complete record has been transmitted is the obligation of the appellant. The record usually consists of all the pleadings, motions, and other documents filed in the lower court, that court's opinion, all exhibits and evidence introduced in the trial court and transcripts of testimony taken during the course of the court proceedings. The record constitutes the appellate court's sole "official" source of information about the lower court proceedings. Virtually all court rules require that each assertion of fact in a brief be cited to a specific page in the record. That is so not only when you recite a fact in the Statement of the Case and Facts, but also when you analyze the fact in the Argument section of the brief—even though the reader would be able to find the citation by a search through the Statement of the Case and Facts.

A shortened version of the record called an appendix (required in some state jurisdictions and most federal circuit courts, and optional in others) helps appellate judges focus on important documents or evidence which may be buried in a voluminous record. Only items already in the record on appeal may be included in an appendix—the appendix may not be used as a way of adding new items to the record on appeal. Even in those jurisdictions that do not require an appendix to be filed, appellate judges appreciate your submitting one with your brief. The appendix may be attached to the brief itself or be a separate labeled document. Check the rules in your jurisdiction regarding submission of an appendix. In addition to record excerpts, an appendix may include law review articles, out-of-state cases, and excerpts from treatises to which you have cited in your brief. Although the judges can find these things for themselves, they will appreciate your doing it for them.

The purpose of the Statement of the Case and Facts is to show the appellate court that it has jurisdiction over the case, to explain the procedural context in which the issues on appeal arose, and to provide the court with the factual background of the case. Include the type of case (i.e., contract, slip-and-fall, etc.), where litigated, and date and nature of the order appealed. Many times it is recommended, and in some jurisdictions required, that this section of your brief be divided into two parts (i.e., Statement of the Case and Statement of the Facts).

First, outline the procedural history of your case. The standard of review from a motion for summary judgment, for instance, generally differs from the standard of review of a jury verdict. Assist the appellate court with a clear, unencumbered procedural overview of the path your case took below and indicate the name of each party to the appeal, the party's position (Appellant, Appellee, etc.), the party's status in the court below (plaintiff, defendant, etc.).

Next, set forth an accurate statement of the facts of the dispute. This statement of facts can be crucial to your appeal. It too is often best accomplished in a chronological narrative, like a story. Your statement of facts must be accurate, i.e., contain only the facts of record, and be non-argumentative. However a good statement of facts must also be persuasive.

Be sure the appellate court has an adequate understanding of the background of the dispute, which facts support your arguments and conclusions, *and* which facts your opponent will surely proffer against you. You should present unfavorable facts before your opponent does; otherwise the court will consider that the unfavorable facts are more harmful than they really are. Include all facts you will need to refer to in your argument, and omit facts you will not refer to in your argument. Don't refer to facts outside the record. To the novice writer including *all* material facts is often the most difficult task. If the court believes you have altered or omitted pertinent facts, you will lose your most valuable asset—your credibility.

Besides being accurate, the statement of facts should be interesting and concise. Include only facts relevant to the issues on appeal. The court will appreciate a statement that is concise and to the point. Mere recitations of witness testimony make for boring reading. Capture your reader's mind at the outset.

Use plain English! Avoid colloquial expressions. Avoid legalese, police jargon and medicalese.* Where possible, humanize your story and your client by using names. Constant reference to Appellant, Respondent, and "real party in interest" makes for difficult reading. Don't distract your reader's attention from the matter at hand by forcing your reader to go back to the title page to see who's who. Don't argue in the Statement; save your argument for the argument or discussion section of your brief. For example, avoid saying: "It is obvious the court erred here . . ." or "The evidence is overwhelming that. . . ." You may, however, through juxtaposition of facts condition your reader for the argument you will be making later. For example, you may say: "The evidence showed the sky was blue. (R. 6). The court said the sky was green. (R. 6)." This juxtaposition properly allows the reader to draw the

* For more on these subjects, see pages 98–103 and 113–116.

conclusion that the lower court erred. Take care not to go too far. For example, you should *not* say: "The court held the sky is green (R. 6) even though the evidence clearly showed the sky is blue." (R. 6). This is argument and overt argument has no place in your statement of facts.

Tell your story in a clear and orderly fashion. The Statement tells a story and must begin by setting the stage. To be able to follow the tale, the court must first be told the context in which the tale is set. Until you say what type of case this is, the court will not be able to appreciate the significance of the details you have provided. Tell the story in logical order; don't leave gaps in the story or confuse the court by ignoring chronological order.*

Use subheadings to make lengthy statements more comprehensible. Sub-headings serve to simplify complex facts. Use them to provide transition and for emphasis.

Avoid long paragraphs and sentences. These can cause the court to lose track of the story line. A rule of thumb: If your paragraph is more than ¾ of a page long, it is probably too long.

Choose language whose denotation and connotation favors your client. If you want to stress what your client did, or what was done to her, use precise, action-packed words. For example: "Ms. Smith viciously stabbed Mr. Jones three times with a butcher knife." (R. 6). On the other hand, if you want to de-emphasize what your client did, use neutral language. For example: "The complaining witness was wounded in the incident." ** (R. 5).

Strategically use subordinate and main clauses for emphasis.***

Proofread your work. Errors distract your reader and may cause your ability in other areas to be questioned. Don't weaken your cause by taking your reader's mind off the intended message.

With respect to both your Statement of the Case and your Statement of the Facts, speak from a position of authority, by supporting each factual assertion with a reference to the appropriate page of the record, for example (R. 6). By accurately citing to the record, (1) you assist your reader in finding pertinent portions of the record (2) you bolster your credibility by accurately pointing out where both positive and negative facts can be found in the record; and (3) you follow the rules of appellate procedure. If your research has developed a cogent reason for the appellate court to reverse or modify the lower court ruling, say so, and accurately point out which part of the record on appeal supplies the factual basis which will allow the appellate court to "hang its hat" on your argument.

---

* This advice is equally pertinent in all legal writing. See, for example, in exam-writing, pages 245–247.

** Note, too, that this second illustrative sentence substitutes a passive verb for an active verb and also omits the doer of the action. See also, on this subject, pages 100–103.

*** For discussion of these, see pages 94–95.

F. Summary of the Argument

The summary is often the most difficult part of the brief to write, yet it is one of the most important sections. It should convey the heart of your argument and persuade the court to accept your view of the case. It should *not* be a mere repetition of the headings or issues listed in your table of contents. It should *not* be simply a series of conclusions. It *should* include your main conclusion and the facts and legal principles relevant to that conclusion. It *should* distill and logically present the main components of your argument. In short, your summary should be persuasive, complete, and to the point.

G. The Argument

The argument, complete with citations to facts of record and authorities in support, should cover each issue on appeal. Briefly, tell your reader what you are going to cover, explain the in's and out's case, and then make your point.

For example, tell the appellate court that the trial court erred by applying the doctrine of *respondeat superior* in an intentional tort case. Explain that legal authority presupposes that *respondeat superior* applies solely in negligence cases. Then set out the facts, issue(s) that arose from the facts, the rule(s) of law that should have been applied, the application of this rule to the facts, and the conclusion that should have been reached. Finally, point out that by misapplying a negligence doctrine in a case involving an intentional tort, the court erred and your client was harmed by the error.

1. Argument headings

Each section of your argument, broken down by issues, begins with a heading of one or more sentences in capital letters, single-spaced and indented. The purpose of the argument heading is to state the legal conclusion you want the court to reach on each issue and the reasons for that conclusion. The heading sets the stage for your argument and should be the most concise, distilled statement possible.

The heading should tell the court what the issue is, include the central facts or ideas you will use in your argument, state a legal conclusion and the reasons therefor, and be persuasive. Subheadings should be used where appropriate. Standing alone, the headings should tell your client's story and persuade the court to act in your client's favor.

Subheadings (lower- and upper-case, single-spaced, and either underlined or "bolded") are useful if the argument is complex or if you wish to stress a particular point. Some examples:

> I. THE NEED TO PROTECT THE CONSTITUTIONAL RIGHTS OF UNITED STATES CITIZENS, COMBINED WITH THE IMPLICIT INTENT OF CONGRESS AND THE ABSENCE OF CONFLICT BETWEEN TITLE VII AND MOST FOREIGN LAWS, MANDATES

THE APPLICATION OF TITLE VII TO UNITED STATES CITI-
ZENS EMPLOYED ABROAD BY UNITED STATES COMPANIES.

A. Acts of Congress intended to protect the constitutional rights of citizens mandate extraterritorial application.

B. By expressly excluding aliens employed abroad from coverage under Title VII, Congress has indicated the intent to otherwise apply Title VII extra-territorially to citizens, while providing a safeguard against possible conflicts with foreign laws.

II. AN INDIRECT SEX DISCRIMINATION CLAIM, BASED ON THE
PREFERENTIAL TREATMENT OF AN EMPLOYEE INVOLVED IN
A SEXUAL RELATIONSHIP WITH THE EMPLOYER, VIOLATES
THE PROHIBITION AGAINST SEX DISCRIMINATION UNDER
TITLE VII.

A. Title VII should be construed broadly as a remedial statute, as intended by Congress and recognized by the Supreme Court.

B. The EEOC Guidelines, recognized by the Supreme Court as guidance for defining sex discrimination, specifically recognize indirect sex discrimination as a violation of Title VII.

C. Public policy and changing attitudes toward sexual behavior in the workplace suggest a broad definition of "sex" under Title VII.

Argument headings help to organize your major points, but the argument itself must guide the reader by flowing logically from one point to the next.

2. The argument itself

The argument section is the "contention" section. It must illustrate how the facts of record, coupled with the applicable legal authorities, support your client's contention. As suggested previously, guide your reader's mind. Don't assume your reader will make all the logical connections needed to support your contention. Take your reader by the hand and walk through the problem.*

Use moderate language. Avoid being flippant, colloquial, and overly emotional. When attacking your opponent's arguments use common sense and avoid irritating your reader.** A thesaurus might help. Your opponent did not "lamely posture," his "reliance was merely misplaced." Your opponent's argument was not "incomprehensible," it was merely "difficult to follow." Your opponent's arguments are not "ludicrous," they are merely "questionable." While you may be advocating a position to redress a wrong,

---

* This writing strategy has been described earlier. See, for example, pages
79–83, and *passim.*

** For additional discussion, see pages
247–250.

remember that your reader is a court of law. Be respectful, yet positive and forthright.

a. Use of authority

By the time you begin to write your brief, you should have already completed your research. In addition to looking to codified laws such as statutes, regulations, etc., your research includes court decisions interpreting codified laws and addressing the common law. Common law is court-created law that recognizes, affirms, and enforces principles and rules of action deriving their authority solely from usages and customs of immemorial antiquity.

In the federal court system, United States Supreme Court decisions are controlling precedent, as are circuit and district court decisions from your jurisdiction. Circuit and district court decisions from other jurisdictions are persuasive authority, but are not controlling.* Don't say an issue has been "resolved" when your authority is a decision in another circuit. Instead, use persuasive language. If the other circuit is the only one that has considered the issue, introduce the case by saying something like: "In the only decision that has considered the issue of use of the confrontation clause at a criminal sentencing hearing, the Eighth Circuit Court of Appeals supported the view that. . . ."

If other circuits have considered the issue and arrived at a different conclusion, acknowledge the opposing view, but distinguish the cases by showing that the facts differ. In the state court system, United States Supreme Court decisions are again controlling precedent, as are decisions of higher level courts. Courts also generally follow their own decisions if these decisions do not conflict with those of higher level courts.

(1) Primary authority

In determining how much weight to give a particular argument, the reviewing court considers the source of legal authority. Primary authority is more persuasive than secondary authority. In briefs that discuss federal statutory issues, primary authority includes not only case law and statutes, but also federal regulations and legislative history. You may also discuss legislative history and then cite to a case that describes that history. It is more authoritative to cite directly to the source of the history, i.e., to the Congressional Record. If, however, you want to make the point that a particular court has interpreted the history to stand for a certain proposition, cite the case as well as the actual source of the history.

(2) Secondary authority

If you cannot find primary support for your view, secondary authority can be extremely helpful. Examples of secondary authority are: American Jurisprudence, Corpus Juris Secundum, ALR, Florida Jurisprudence, and law

---

* For earlier discussion of precedent, see page 121 and Chapter Four, passim.

review articles. A law review article may provide an excellent discussion of public policy and a creative argument. However, do not cite to a law review instead of to a case. Secondary authority should *never* be used in place of primary authority. If the law review article and the case stand for the same proposition, cite to the case.

b. Writing the argument

Before beginning to write outline your argument.* A strong outline sets forth each step in your reasoning process and demonstrates where each case or statute fits into your argument. It should provide a cohesive, cogent view of your case. If it doesn't, changing the order of the parts may make your argument stronger. If the parts of your outline do not comprise a cohesive whole, you need to do further analysis, further research, or both.

If you find it difficult to create an outline, start by organizing a portion of your argument. Choose one argument you will include in your brief. Find in your research notes all the facts and cases that relate to this one argument. Then decide how best to arrange them to advance the argument. Work from your argument heading to subheadings, and then to topic or thesis sentences, inserting the authorities you will use to support each point. Repeat this procedure with your other arguments, and then arrange the parts, creating an outline of your entire argument.

Divide your argument into sections developing separate claims for relief, based upon your argument headings, which will introduce each argument or contention. The legal arguments supporting each claim may then be introduced by subheadings if there is more than one argument or the argument is particularly complex. Within each section of the argument you should thoroughly analyze the legal points and facts relevant to your claim. To accomplish this, you must introduce the issue, explain the relevant law, work with the decision from the court below and the most persuasive authorities you can find, argue your facts and compare cases, rebut opposing argument, and conclude. A brief's persuasiveness arises from well-supported arguments, adequately reasoned and explained. The most successful brief is one which the court could adopt as its opinion in the case.

Organization of your analysis is very important. To make the structure of your argument clear, announce in your headings and subheadings the legal conclusions you want to prevail and your reasons for the court to adopt them. You can then organize the facts and authorities to carry the reader to that end. Begin each paragraph introducing a new topic with a topic sentence that refers to the proposition that paragraph is advancing rather than to the facts of a case. Your analysis should be guided by the opinion below, the type of legal argument you are making, and the degree of support that you have.

The structure of the argument is determined by the type of legal argument you are making and will vary according to the point you are making. Some

* See pages 214–217 for a discussion of outlining in thesis writing.

arguments will be fact oriented. If the rule of law is well-established and the sole issue is application of the rule to the facts, your discussion can hone in at once on the particular facts of the case. The opening paragraph will probably do so in some detail.

In contrast, some arguments are primarily legal questions about which precedent controls the case or how a statute should be interpreted. Here, your opening paragraph might well discuss with the law you think should control and your authority for so arguing. Other arguments are more policy-centered; at issue is the purpose of the rule and desirability of its end. In contrast to a fact-centered or legal argument, a policy-centered argument may treat the facts of the case somewhat briefly but discuss jurisdictional trends and secondary authorities at length.

(1) Analysis of factual issues

Begin your analysis of factual issues with your conclusion or thesis, the proposition you want to prove by analyzing precedent. Next, show how the legal principle(s) support your conclusion. To do this, you usually must explain the precedent case sufficiently so the judges can understand the key facts, issue, holding, rule and policy of that case.* Key facts are crucial because they must be examined to decide whether the legal rule applies. After explaining the precedent case, show why the judges should conclude that the key facts or policies in your case and the precedent case are sufficiently similar that the holding of the precedent case should apply to your case. Stress the reasoning in cases, not just the facts. Finally, restate your conclusion. The four elements of this formula: thesis, rule of law, analysis and conclusion form the easy to remember acronym TRAC. This formula should be employed throughout your brief. For example, your analysis in the tail-light case discussed previously could proceed as follows:

[First, tell the court what you will be proving. Start out with an assertion.]	The officers used the inoperable tail-light as a pretext to stop appellant's vehicle and to search it for evidence of violation of other laws.
[Second, explain the legal principles involved in the precedent case, making sure to mention the key facts the precedent court relied on in reaching its result.]	To make a valid investigatory stop of an automobile, the officer must have a "founded" or reasonable suspicion that the person has committed, is committing, or is about to commit a criminal offense. A mere or bare suspicion is never sufficient. Williams v. State, 454 So.2d 737, 738 (Fla. 2d DCA 1984). The officer's suspicion must be founded upon observed facts interpreted in light of the officer's knowledge, training, and practical experience. Id. at 739.

---

* For definitions of these terms, see pages 10–12.

[Third, persuade the court that these key facts correspond to key facts in your case and that the policies and rules expressed in the precedent case apply to your case.]

In the instant case, the trial court denied the appellant's motion to suppress the seized evidence because the court held that the evidence may have been properly seized pursuant to a valid stop for a traffic infraction, an inoperable tail-light. However, section 316.221, Florida Statutes (1985), provides in pertinent part: "(1) Every motor vehicle . . . shall be equipped with at least two tail-lamps mounted on the rear. . . ."

[Fourth, restate your conclusion.]

Officer Sloggett testified that appellant's vehicle had four tail-lights, only one of which was inoperable. Thus, appellant had not committed a traffic infraction. Appellant was stopped, as the officers readily admitted, for a field interrogation. The officers used the inoperable tail-light as a pretext to stop the appellant's vehicle and to search it for evidence of violation of other laws. The evidence was unlawfully seized and, accordingly, must be suppressed.

To distinguish authority slightly alter the above formula. Although still focusing on the key facts, legal principles, rules and policies of the precedent case, but instead of explaining how they apply to your case, show why they do not apply.* For example, in the tail-light case:

The state's reliance on Bascoy v. State, 424 So.2d 80 (Fla. 3d DCA 1982) and State v. Holmes, 256 So.2d 32 (Fla. 2d DCA 1971) is misplaced. Both *Bascoy* and *Holmes* involved situations in which the individuals stopped had committed offenses for which any citizen would have been arrested. The stops for traffic infractions in those cases were not pretexts.

Never ignore relevant cases against you. If you acknowledge your weaknesses and do your best to argue them, you at least clear the air and get the worst behind you. The judge who is otherwise disposed to decide the case your way may be able to strengthen your argument with his own research or analysis. If you ignore the weakness, you lose the benefit of the judge's analytical skills, the judge is left with a nagging doubt about the validity of your conclusion, and your credibility may also suffer.

(2) Analysis of legal issues

The TRAC analytical formula applies when the rule of law is settled, and the question is whether the rule applies to the facts of your case. Often, however, your issue on appeal is which rule of law the court should endorse. For example, there may be a split of authority over the meaning of a certain word in a statute. If your issue on appeal turns on how the court should interpret the word, you would not use the above formula, because the facts of

---

* Note how this procedure was accomplished by the judge who wrote the dissent in *Laird v. State*, above, pages 136–137.

the precedent cases are irrelevant to the meaning of the word. Instead you would analyze legislative history, policy arguments, legal principles, and holdings of cases that have interpreted the word.

3. Organizing the argument

Begin with your strongest issue—the one that has the most support (unless logic requires that you first deal with a weaker threshold issue as in a chronological presentation). Within your discussion of each issue, state your strongest argument first. Discuss case precedent and statutory interpretation before you discuss a general policy argument derived from a law review article since the former two carry more weight than the latter with a court deciding an issue. Anticipate your opponent's arguments and confront damaging precedent after you make and support your argument. Place your strongest words or points at the beginning and end of sentences, paragraphs, and discussion sections where they will have the most impact.* After you acknowledge contrary authority, and distinguish it (only as a last resort say a case is wrong), return to your own position to leave a strong impression of your position on your reader.

Judge James E. Lehan of the Second District Court of Appeal of Florida, has formulated a list of *do's* and *don't's* for the argument section of the appellate brief. Many of his comments are applicable to effective legal writing generally, and have been discussed elsewhere in this book. Those particularly relevant to brief-writing are included below:

DO:

1. Be accurate.

    a. Be sure your argument tracts your statement of facts.

    b. Be sure your cases stand for what you say and you say what the cases stand for.

    c. Check the accuracy of your citations.

2. Test your draft so that a reader less perceptive than yourself can understand it.

3. Quote from statutes, rules, and cases. But cut the quotations to short, pertinent segments, using dots to indicate omitted material.

4. Recognize what standard of review the appellate court will apply.

5. Provide in your brief the material that the judge would put into his written opinion if he accepts your position.

And we would add *DO:*

Have case citations refer to the page or pages from which a proposition is drawn. Likewise, statutory citations should refer to the specific subsection in question. All statutes should be cited to their official source; in

---

* For the application of this *caveat* elsewhere, see pages 95–97, 244, and 249.

federal statutes, the United States Code. When citing to a statute generally, cite to the most recent edition of the U.S.C., which is published every six years. When citing a specific statutory amendment, cite to the year the amendment was passed.

DON'T:

1. Don't string cite without good reason. Choose one, two or three cases that support your view.
2. Don't personally criticize the opposing lawyer or party.
3. Don't try to impress the court by using foreign words or legal jargon unnecessarily.

H. The Conclusion

The conclusion section of your brief should not be long, seldom more than a paragraph or two. However, a one- or two-paragraph conclusion that says why the court should adopt your view leaves the judge with your most persuasive thoughts. The conclusion should state precisely what remedy you want the appellate court to provide. Because appellate courts are limited in the type of relief they can provide, make sure your argument provides the authority to enable the appellate court to grant you the relief you request. Don't be afraid to summarize key facts and the authority you are relying on as a preface to requesting relief from the appellate court. The conclusion can help summarize what your reader has read in your brief so the reader will remember all the points of your argument section not just your final point.

The Appellee's Brief

Even though the appellee won in the court below, the appellee should file an answer brief to the appellant's brief. Often, the appellate court views the failure to file a brief as an acknowledgement of defeat.

The appellee's brief should respond to the appellant's contentions as well as point out to the court any other reasons why the court below was correct. The structure of the appellee's argument may vary from that used in the appellant's brief—the appellee should begin with the strongest argument even though this issue was not the first issue in the appellant's brief. As a general rule, put the appellee's view of the case first in every section of the brief including Questions Presented, Statement of Case and Facts, and Summary of the Argument.

The following pages contain a model appellant's brief and a model appellee's brief for you to use as an aid in writing your own briefs.

Judge Lehan Summarizes:

The key to effective advocacy is communication. A brief provides your best method of communicating with the court and gives you the best opportunity to win your case. Make the most of it by using good methods of communication and by avoiding pitfalls which are generally recognized as bad communication. Remember that you are communicating with an appellate judge, not writing a treatise on the law or a human interest story about the facts. Keep in mind that the judge very much wants and needs help and guidance from you. He does not want to be diverted from his task by obstacles and irrelevancies which interfere with your line of communication with him. Avoid the mistakes some lawyers unwittingly make by creating those obstacles. Good brief writing can be learned.

IN THE UNITED STATES COURT OF APPEALS FOR THE
ELEVENTH CIRCUIT

CASE NO. 88–4624

JACKSON INSURANCE COMPANY
OF AMERICA and ROBERT GRADY,

Appellants,

v.

ALAN HALL,

Appellee.

_____

_____

ON APPEAL FROM THE UNITED STATES DISTRICT COURT
FOR THE NORTHERN DISTRICT OF FLORIDA

_____

BRIEF FOR APPELLANTS

Attorney for Appellants
University of Florida
College of Law
Gainesville, FL 32611

ORAL ARGUMENT REQUESTED

TABLE OF CONTENTS

TABLE OF CITATIONS

OPINION BELOW

On March 20, 1990 the United States District for the Northern District of Florida entered an order on cross motions for summary judgment in favor of Appellee Alan Hall. The court's opinion is attached.

STATEMENT REGARDING JURISDICTION

The final judgment of the United States District Court for the Northern District of Florida was entered on March 20, 1990. The jurisdiction of this Court is invoked pursuant to 28 U.S.C. § 1291 (1990).

QUESTION PRESENTED

WHETHER THE TRIAL COURT ERRED IN RULING THAT THE DECEDENT'S STEPFATHER, WHO HAD NOT ADOPTED THE DECEDENT, SHOULD RECEIVE THE DECEDENT'S LIFE INSURANCE BENEFITS, AND THAT THE DECEDENT'S NATURAL FATHER, WHO WAS IDENTIFIED ALONG WITH THE DECEDENT'S MOTHER AS THE "BY LAW" BENEFICIARY OF HIS INSURANCE, WAS IMPROPERLY PAID THESE BENEFITS.

STATUTES INVOLVED

Title 38 U.S.C. § 765(9) (1990), Servicemen's Group Life Insurance, provides in relevant part:

§ 765 Definitions

* * *

(9) The term "parent" means a father of a legitimate child, mother of a legitimate child, father through adoption, mother through adoption, mother of an illegitimate child, and father of an illegitimate child but only if (a) he acknowledged paternity of the child in writing signed by him before the child's death; or (b) he has been judicially ordered to contribute to the child's support; or (c) he has been judicially decreed to be the father of such; or (d) proof of paternity is established by a certified copy of the public record of birth or church record of baptism showing that the claimant was the informant and was named as father of the child; or (e) proof of paternity is established from service department or other public records, such as school or welfare agencies, which show that with his knowledge the claimant was named as father of the child. . . .

Title 38 U.S.C. § 770(A) (1990), Servicemen's Group Life Insurance, provides in relevant part:

iii

§ 770   Beneficiaries; payment of insurance

(a) Any amount of insurance under this subchapter in force on any member or former member on the date of the insured's death shall be paid, upon the establishment of a valid claim therefor, to the person or persons surviving at the date of the insured's death, in the following order of precedence:

> First, to the beneficiary or beneficiaries as the member or former member may have designated by a writing received prior to death (1) in the uniformed services if insured under Servicemen's Group Life Insurance, or (2) in the administrative office established under section 766(b) of this title if separated or released from service, or if assigned to the Retired Reserve, and insured under Servicemen's Group Life Insurance, or if insured under Veterans' Group Life Insurance;

> Second, if there be no such beneficiary, to the widow or widower of such member or former member;

> Third, if none of the above, to the child or children of such member or former member and descendants of deceased children by representation;

> Fourth, if none of the above, to the parents of such member or former member or the survivor of them;

> Fifth, if none of the above, to the duly appointed executor or administrator of the estate of such member or former member;

> Sixth, if none of the above, to other next of kin of such member or former member entitled under the laws of domicile of such member or former member at the time of the insured's death.

STATEMENT OF THE CASE AND FACTS

This is a claim for $25,000.00 life insurance benefits under a decedent's servicemen's group life insurance policy issued through Appellant Jackson Insurance Company of America.

The decedent, Thomas Grady, was survived by his natural parents (Mary B. Hall and Robert Grady) and his stepfather, Appellee Alan Hall. At the time of his death, on June 2, 1988, the decedent was a sergeant in the United States Army in Marktbreit, Germany. (R. 34)

On October 22, 1987, the decedent executed Form VA29–8286, the "servicemen's group life insurance election", where he designated the beneficiaries to receive payment of his servicemen's group life insurance proceeds as "by law". (R. 40) As explained in paragraph 2 of this election, the "by law" designation will result in payment of insurance benefits pursuant to operation of law. The form provided as follows:

IMPORTANT—READ CAREFULLY

PROVISION OF THE LAW FOR PAYMENT OF INSURANCE

If you do not name a beneficiary to receive the proceeds of your insurance, it will be paid under the provisions of the law, to your survivor(s) in the following order:

    (1) Widow or widower; if none, it is payable to

    (2) Child or children in equal shares with the share of any deceased child distributed among the descendants of that child; if none, it is payable to

    (3) Parent(s) in equal shares; if none, it is payable to

    (4) A duly appointed executor or administrator of the insured's estate, and if none to

    (5) Other next of kin.

NOTE: If you want a specific person to receive your insurance, then you must name the person in Part 2, otherwise, it will be paid as provided above. (R. 40)

In the "instructions to member" section of this form which follows, the form advises

There are no restrictions on the beneficiaries you may name. In some family situations such as if you are a stepchild or stepparent or were abandoned by a parent or are separated from your wife, etc., you may by naming beneficiaries specifically include or exclude certain persons as you desire. (R. 40)

On the same date that the decedent made his "by law" designation on the servicemen's group life insurance election, he completed a "record of emergency data" (Defense Department Form 93) designating his mother, Mary Hall, and his stepfather, Alan Hall, as 50% co-beneficiaries of any unpaid pay and allowances and also for any death gratuity pay. (R. 41) The servicemen's unpaid pay allowances and death gratuity pay are totally separate and distinct from, and have no bearing upon, the servicemen's group life insurance. These benefits are handled by a branch of the service and are not administered in any way by Jackson. (R. 38)

Following the death of Thomas Grady, claims were made for the proceeds of his servicemen's group life insurance policy by his mother, Mary Hall, his stepfather, Alan Hall, and his natural father, Appellant Robert Grady. Based upon the decedent's "by law" designation in the insurance election, Jackson paid the proceeds of the policy to his natural parents, Mary Hall and Robert Grady, in equal shares.

Appellee Alan Hall, the decedent's stepfather, sued Appellants Jackson and Robert Grady seeking a declaration that he was entitled to half the proceeds of the servicemen's group life insurance policy benefits. He asserted that the decedent's identification of Alan Hall in the Defense Department Form 93 showed that the decedent's intent was to pay insurance benefits to the stepfather and natural mother, rather than to the natural parents in accordance with the "by law" designation.

Cross motions for summary judgment were filed by the parties. (R. 40, 42, 45, 46) The trial court granted summary judgment in favor of Alan Hall and this appeal followed. (R. 51, 52, 53, 54) Appellants request this Court to reverse the judgment below and remand with instructions to enter summary final judgment in favor of Appellants.

2

SUMMARY OF ARGUMENT

The servicemen's group life insurance election form and the Department of Defense Form 93 are separate and distinct documents which cannot be construed together because they relate to entirely separate and distinct types of benefits which are administered and paid by separate and distinct entities. The trial court erred in ruling that the beneficiary designation identified on the Defense Department Form 93 superseded the "by law" beneficiary designation on the servicemen's group life insurance election made by decedent. Contrary to the trial court's ruling, the fact that both documents were completed on the same date is evidence of intent for the distinct benefits to go the distinct beneficiaries rather than, as the court ruled, for all benefits to go the same beneficiaries.

ARGUMENT

THE TRIAL COURT ERRED IN RULING THAT THE DECEDENT'S STEPFATHER, WHO HAD NOT ADOPTED THE DECEDENT, SHOULD RECEIVE HIS LIFE INSURANCE BENEFITS AND THAT THE DECEDENT'S NATURAL FATHER, WHO WAS IDENTIFIED AS THE "BY LAW" BENEFICIARY OF HIS INSURANCE, WAS IMPROPERLY PAID THESE BENEFITS.

Decedent's "by law" beneficiaries were his natural parents. Absent legal adoption, the natural mother and father are the "by law" beneficiaries of insurance proceeds. See Prudential Insurance Company of America v. Ellwein, 435 F. Supp. 248, 250 (W.D.N.Y.1977). It is established in 38 U.S.C. § 765(9) "Servicemen's Group Life Insurance," that a stepparent who has not adopted a deceased serviceman is not a parent for purposes of determining the proper beneficiary of a servicemen's group life insurance policy pursuant to a "by law" designation and the requirements of 38 U.S.C. § 770. As the Ellwein court stated, "the term [parent] under section 765(9) is limited to the categories there defined and does not include a person who is a stepparent or a person in loco parentis." 435 F. Supp. at 253. See also, Prudential Insurance Company of America v. Johnson, 200 N.W.2d 115 (N.D.1972) ("We hold that the word 'parents', as used in the Servicemen's Group Life Insurance Act, does not include a stepfather who has not legally adopted the insured."); Hafley v. McCubbins, 590 S.W.2d 892 (Ky.App.1979). Because the decedent was never legally adopted by Hall, nor abandoned by his natural father, Robert Grady, the "by law" designation of beneficiaries mandated payment of the policy proceeds solely to the natural parents and to the exclusion of Hall.

It is well-settled law that the principles of judicial construction cannot be applied to vary the meaning of a clear and unambiguous contract. Rather, the intention of the parties must be determined solely by the explicit language of the agreement, despite whatever the actual intention might have been. In Foreman v. Continental Cas. Co., 770 F.2d 487, 488 (5th Cir. 1985), the court held that where the contractual language is unambiguous and subject to only one possible meaning, any evidence of the parties' actions or intentions is irrelevant. See also Reed v. Knollwood Park Cemetery, 441 F. Supp. 1144 (E.D.N.Y.1977).

The undisputed evidence establishes that the decedent's servicemen's group life insurance policy election designated his beneficiaries as "by law." This precludes examination of any extraneous documents which identify the stepfather, Hall, as a beneficiary of any other potential proceeds. In the case of J.C. Penney Co., Inc. v. Koff, 345 So.2d 732 (Fla. 4th DCA 1977), it was noted that courts are "barred from using evidence to create an ambiguity [or] to rewrite a contractual provision." Id. at 735. In the instant case, consideration of the Defense Department Form 93 improperly creates an ambiguity because it is inconsistent with the plain and unequivocal "by law" designation which was completed on the servicemen's group life insurance election form. The trial court's assumption that the decedent wanted all benefits to go to the stepfather is pure speculation and is contrary to another equally likely (but also speculative) scenario which is also supported by the record: the decedent was anticipating marriage at the time he made his "by law" election and was in fact engaged to be married. Based upon the explanation given on the servicemen's group life insurance election form, it is arguable that the decedent intended his prospective bride to be the intended beneficiary under the "by law" designation. Unfortunately, he was not yet married at the time of his death so the "by law" benefits passed to his natural parents in the absence of any alternative or contingent beneficiary designation on the form.

Contrary to settled law, the trial court improperly contravened the strong public policy against looking into the mind of the decedent at the time of contract in an attempt to ascertain the decedent's true intent. In the case of Prudential Insurance Company of America v. Parker, 840 F.2d 6 (7th Cir. 1988), the decedent was covered by a servicemen's group life insurance policy with both parents listed as beneficiaries. After the parents' divorce, the decedent completed two forms naming his father as sole beneficiary and mailed these forms to the father. Id. at 7. Upon death, however, the military had no record of this change and paid 50% of the policy proceeds to each parent. Evidence of the decedent's true intent was not considered and the statements on the policy designation form were followed literally because "it is so difficult to reconstruct a person's donative intentions after his death." Id. The court further stated that insurance statutes governing intent with respect to beneficiaries must be strictly construed and "apparently [38 U.S.C.] section 770 is in this tradition." Id. A strict construction of the decedent's beneficiary designation has only one result: the natural mother and father are each entitled to 50% of the proceeds, to the exclusion of Hall's claim.

The decedent's failure to specifically designate his stepfather as a beneficiary resulted in his natural parents becoming his "by law" beneficiaries. In the case of Prudential Insurance Company of America v. Johnson, 200 N.W.2d

115 (N.D.1972), the court also ruled upon a servicemen's group life insurance policy beneficiary discrepancy. The court stated that "the serviceman in this case had the right to designate his beneficiary. He could have named his mother, his stepfather, his natural father, or anyone else he saw fit to name. We cannot speculate on the reason for his failure to designate a beneficiary." Id. at 118. The same rationale applies in the instant case. The decedent knew that Robert Grady was his natural father and that he was never legally adopted by his stepfather, Alan Hall. The decedent was placed on clear and unambiguous notice of the effect of designating his beneficiaries as "by law" by the plain and unambiguous language on the servicemen's group life insurance election form.

The trial court erred in relying on the case of Prudential Insurance Company of America v. Smith, 762 F.2d 476 (5th Cir. 1985) because it is factually distinguishable. In that action, the decedent was divorced from his first wife and had married a second woman at the time of his death. Id. at 477. The servicemen's group life insurance policy designated the beneficiary as "by law." The first wife claimed that the divorce was invalid and therefore that she was the legal widow and entitled to policy proceeds. Id. at 478. Before ruling that the second wife was intended to be the decedent's beneficiary, the court consulted previously filed documents. Id. This is factually unlike the instant case because the court in Smith did not alter the "by law" designation, but merely reviewed other documents to determine who was the legal widow entitled to receive the "by law" benefits. The court's intention was simply to determine who was legal wife. By contrast, in the instant case, the court's research of other documents was not to determine who was a legal beneficiary (the natural father or the stepfather who never legally adopted decedent) but rather to attempt to ascertain decedent's intent. The judgment below should be reversed.

CONCLUSION

The clear and unambiguous documentation established that the decedent's natural parents, Mary Hall and Robert Grady, are his "by law" beneficiaries of the life insurance proceeds and were properly paid these benefits pursuant to this "by law" designation. It is respectfully requested that this Court reverse the summary judgment and order of the district court and remand this cause with directions to enter summary final judgment in favor of Appellants Robert Grady and Jackson Insurance Company of America.

Respectfully submitted,

_____

(Name of Attorney)
Attorney for Appellants

CERTIFICATE OF SERVICE

I CERTIFY that a true and correct copy of the foregoing was furnished to Attorney for Appellee by hand delivery this 30th day of October, 1989.

_____
Attorney for Appellants

IN THE UNITED STATES COURT OF APPEALS FOR THE
ELEVENTH CIRCUIT

CASE NO. 88-4624

JACKSON INSURANCE COMPANY
OF AMERICA and ROBERT GRADY,

Appellants,

v.

ALAN HALL,

Appellee.

_____

_____

ON APPEAL FROM THE UNITED STATES DISTRICT COURT
FOR THE NORTHERN DISTRICT OF FLORIDA

_____

BRIEF FOR APPELLEE

[Attorney for Appellee]
University of Florida
College of Law
Gainesville, FL 32611

TABLE OF CONTENTS

TABLE OF CITATIONS

OPINION BELOW

On March 20, 1990 the United States District Court for the Northern District of Florida entered an order on cross motions for summary judgment in favor of Plaintiff/Appellee Alan Hall. The court's opinion is attached.

STATEMENT REGARDING JURISDICTION

Appellee concurs with Appellants' jurisdictional statement.

QUESTION PRESENTED

WHETHER THE TRIAL COURT CORRECTLY HELD THAT WHEN A SERVICEMAN HAS UNMISTAKABLY INDICATED IN WRITING THAT HE CONSIDERS HIS STEPFATHER TO BE HIS PARENT, THAT DEFINITION OUGHT TO APPLY TO THE TERM "PARENT" IN A SIMULTANEOUSLY EXECUTED LIFE INSURANCE FORM.

STATEMENT OF THE CASE AND FACTS

While much of Appellants' recitation of the facts is correct, Appellants have subtly stressed certain facts and deemphasized others, which distorts the actual basis for the district court's ruling and necessitates this restatement:

In 1987 Thomas Grady was a sergeant serving in the United States Army in Germany. On October 22 of that year, he was presented by the military with two forms to fill out: (1) Form 8286, a life insurance form which contained a section in which the serviceman was to designate his insurance beneficiaries; and (2) a Defense Department "Emergency Data" form (also identified as "Form 93") which *also* requested the serviceman to designate his beneficiaries for purposes of certain other military death benefits.[1] (R.40) The life insurance form (Form 8286), instructed Sergeant Grady to either name his intended beneficiaries or else write the words "by law" on the form if he wanted to adopt the distribution scheme which is printed on the reverse side of the form, to wit: a distribution of benefits to the serviceman's widow, if any, and if none then to the serviceman's children, if any, and if none then to the serviceman's "parents". (R.40) Sergeant Grady wrote "by law" and thereby adopted the pre-arranged distribution formula. (R.41) At the same time Sergeant Grady filled out Form 8286, he filled out Form 93 (described as "this extremely important form"), wherein Sergeant Grady was asked the following information and provided the following answers (emphasis supplied):

	[*Questions*]	[*Answers*]
4.	Spouse and Name/Address:	SINGLE
5.	Children and Names/Relationship/DOB/Address:	NONE
6.	Father's Name/Address:	*ALAN HALL/101 MEADOWBROOK DR. TALLAHASSEE, FL 32074 (STEPFATHER)*
7.	Mother's Name/Address:	MARY B. (BATES) HALL/SEE ITEM # 6
8.	Do not notify due to ill health:	NONE
9.	*Beneficiary(ies) for DG if no surviving spouse or child/address/ percentage*	*MARY B. & ALAN R. HALL/ PARENTS/SEE ITEM # 6/50% EACH*
10.	*Beneficiary(ies) for unpaid pay and allowances/address/percentage*	*MARY B. AND ALAN R. HALL/PARENTS/SEE ITEM # 6/50% EACH*

---

1. Copies of the two forms were of course submitted to the court at trial, and the Record presumably includes an original and/or various copies of these forms. Some of the printed material on Form 93 is important to this appeal, yet is not legible on some copies; Appellee has therefore attached to this Brief an additional copy of Form 93.

As shown above, Sergeant Grady's answers to questions 6, 8 and 9 specifically identified his stepfather Alan Hall as his *parent,* and provided that Alan and Mary (as "parents") were to receive all of his death benefits. (R. 42) In addition, *only* Alan and Mary are named in the form, and only they are identified as persons to be notified if Sergeant Grady were to become a casualty (see the "Instructions to Service Member" on the form). (R. 41) Robert Grady is not identified anywhere on the form, as having any relationship to Sergeant Grady, or even as a "person" to be notified in the event of Sergeant Grady's death or illness. (R. 42)

Appellants' brief is thus slightly misleading in implying that Sergeant Grady merely designated "his stepfather" as a 50% co-beneficiary of non-life insurance death benefits. In fact, Sergeant Grady specifically identified Mary and Alan Hall as his parents, *the very term he adopted by reference on Form 8286.* (R. 39)

The dispute in this case arose from the fact that while Sergeant Grady's mother was married to Alan Hall, and although Sergeant Grady plainly considered Alan to be his father (hardly surprising since Sergeant Grady had lived with him since he had been four years old), Alan Hall had never formally adopted Sergeant Grady. (R. 26)

Sergeant Grady died in the service in June, 1988, unmarried and without children. (R. 22) Despite the claims against the life insurance benefits by Alan and Mary Hall, Appellant Jackson paid one-half of the life insurance benefits to Robert Grady, and Appellee Alan Hall filed suit in district court seeking the recovery of that money. (R. 1, 28) Cross motions for summary judgment were filed by Jackson and Alan Hall, and Hall's motion was granted by the trial court. (R. 40–46, 51–54) Jackson and Robert Grady then appealed. Appellee requests this Court to affirm the judgment below.

SUMMARY OF ARGUMENT

The trial court properly construed the decedent's handwritten "by law" designation of beneficiaries (which adopted-by-reference a distribution of benefits to his "parents"), in a manner consistent with the decedent's simultaneous written identification of Alan and Mary Hall as his parents. The trial court's construction of the "by law" designation in a manner consistent with the decedent's own definition of the critical term was not only sensible and just, it was specifically authorized by the controlling legal authority, the Fifth Circuit's decision in Prudential Insurance Co. of America v. Smith, 762 F.2d 476 (5th Cir. 1985), as well as applicable Florida law.

ARGUMENT

THE TRIAL COURT CORRECTLY GAVE EFFECT TO THE CLEAR
INTENT OF THE DECEDENT THAT THE TERM "PARENTS" IN HIS
LIFE INSURANCE BENEFICIARY SELECTION MEANT HIS MOTHER
AND STEPFATHER, THE PERSONS WHOM HE SPECIFICALLY
IDENTIFIED AS HIS PARENTS IN A CONTEMPORANEOUSLY EXE-
CUTED DOCUMENT.

As the trial judge remarked, one ought not to allow "formulaic technicali-
ties" to obscure what indisputably occurred in this case: Sergeant Grady was
handed two related forms by the United States Army, one to designate his
beneficiaries for purposes of life insurance benefits, and the other to designate
his beneficiaries for other military death benefits. On the first of these forms
he wrote the words "by law" to adopt a predetermined distribution scheme to
his "parents." On the second form he was specifically asked to identify his
mother and father, and he specifically identified them as Mary and Alan Hall.
Not only that: Sergeant Grady then proceeded to twice identify Mary and
Alan Hall as his *"parents,"* selecting that term himself and thus defining the
very term used in Form 8286! Sergeant Grady provided that information in
response to the instruction that

> This extremely important form is to be used by used by you to show
> the names and addresses of your spouse, children, parents and any
> other person(s) you would like notified if you become a casualty,
> and, to designate beneficiaries for certain benefits if you die.

Those were the "extremely important" instructions given to Sergeant
Grady, and in response thereto he specifically wrote that Alan R. Hall was his
father's name and that Alan and Mary Hall were his parents. To state the
dispositive facts in a slightly different manner, at the very same time that
Sergeant Grady wrote the words "by law" on one form, which meant that his
life insurance would be paid to his "parents," Sergeant Grady wrote on the
accompanying extremely important Emergency Data form that Alan Hall and
Mary Hall were his "parents and his designate[d] beneficiaries if [he] died."

Under these rather special circumstances, it would have been irresponsible
for the trial judge to have blinded himself to Sergeant Grady's Emergency
Data information and accept Jackson's formulaic argument that the term
"parent" *may only* be construed, in accordance with the statutory definition, to
mean Robert Grady, even though Sergeant Grady had at the very same time
expressly and unequivocally identified Mary and Alan Hall as his parents and
did not identify Robert Grady even as someone who ought to be notified in
the event of his death.

Appellants' brief is misleading if intended to imply that the instructions on
the life insurance form (8286) indicated that Sergeant Grady ought not to use
the "by law" designation for a stepfather. Actually, the form contained the

3

comment that persons with a stepchild or stepparent could by naming beneficiaries "specifically include or exclude certain persons," a thoroughly ambiguous comment which only begged the question in Sergeant Grady's case, namely whether his stepfather could also be a "parent." As the trial judge correctly noted at the summary judgment hearing, nowhere does the life insurance form explain that the adoption of the term "parent" would not authorize a distribution to his stepparent; moreover, it appears that Sergeant Grady did exactly what the form suggested—he proceeded to carefully name the beneficiaries he specifically wanted to include, and specifically avoided naming Robert Grady as his father or parent!

The Fifth Circuit decision in Prudential Insurance Co. v. Smith, 762 F.2d 476 (5th Cir. 1985), governs these very special circumstances, because Smith involved *the same* special circumstances. In that case, another Army sergeant stationed in Germany filled out the very same forms in the same manner, except that the term at issue was a wife/spouse rather than father/parent. Sergeant Smith wrote "by law" on Form 8286 and on the Emergency Form, executed at the same time, identified Irene Smith as his wife. Id. at 477. After his death, the sergeant's first wife claimed she was entitled to the insurance benefits because she was the sergeant's only lawful wife (just as Robert Grady claims in this case that he was entitled to the benefits because he is the sergeant's only lawful father). Id. As here, the trial court ruled that the spouse identified as such on the Emergency Data form was the spouse for purposes of the life insurance form, and as here the insurer appealed and contended that the trial court had erred by affording weight to the information contained on the Emergency Data form rather than simply applying the statutory definition. Id. at 477. The Fifth Circuit affirmed, however, based on the sergeant's written expression of intent on the Emergency Data form. Id. at 480. Just as the trial judge found in the instant case, the Fifth Circuit in Smith held that the sergeant had "unmistakably showed" who *he* defined as his intended beneficiary. The Fifth Circuit emphasized in Smith that the decedent's actual intent was the decisive issue, *not* the definitions contained in the statute. Id. at 479–80.[2]

The Fifth Circuit wrote in Smith that the sergeant's "by law" designation was intended to designate as beneficiary the spouse which the sergeant identified as his spouse (rather than the spouse as defined by law) and that such donative intent was unmistakable in view of the Emergency Data form identifying Irene as his "wife." Id. at 480. Based on that clear and contemporaneous donative intent, the court rejected Prudential's "strict statutory construction" arguments. Id. (As shown below, the Fifth Circuit's analysis is entirely consistent with the relevant rules of interpretation of both contracts and wills.)

Despite Appellants' efforts to distinguish Smith, no principled distinction can be drawn between Smith and the instant case: Appellants have argued that

---

2. Indeed, the Fifth Circuit noted that the statutory framework itself indicated that the serviceman's actual intent was paramount, since it specifically invited the serviceman to identify anyone as the beneficiary (and to change beneficiaries at will), noting that such designations were to govern over the "by law" distribution scheme. Id. at 480.

the difference is that Sergeant Smith had good reason to believe that Irene was his lawful wife as well as de facto "wife" (because he had no reason to question the validity of his divorce from his first wife), while Sergeant Grady had reasons to doubt that Alan Hall was his lawful father, and even indicated his doubts with the parenthetical qualification "(stepfather)" on Line 6. But that distinction misses the legal point entirely, which is that Sergeant Smith defined Irene as his spouse on the Emergency Data form, and Sergeant Grady defined Alan as his parent on the same form, and by these definitions disclosed their *intent* with respect to their beneficiaries in the event of death. If anything, Smith is a slightly more difficult case because the key term on the life insurance form was "widow" which (to a highly formulaic mind anyway) might be distinguishable from the term "spouse" on the accompanying Emergency Data form, while in the instant case Sergeant Grady used, in his own words, exactly the same term printed on Form 8286.[3] Thus, the only "distinction" which can be drawn between Smith and the present case is that here it would require even a greater suspension of judgment to conclude that when Sergeant Grady wrote "by law" on Form 8286 he might possibly have intended a distribution to a male parent named Robert Grady. Such a hypothesis is ludicrous in light of Sergeant Grady's answers on the Emergency Data form.

Though the Smith decision is plainly controlling in this case, Appellants have attempted to muddy the legal waters by citing other decisions which have little or no bearing on this case. Both Prudential Insurance Co. v. Ellwein, 435 F. Supp. 248 (W.D.N.Y.1977) and Hafley v. McCubbins, 590 S.W.2d 892 (Ky.App.1979) are completely irrelevant, being principally concerned with the state law meaning of "abandonment" (and in neither case was the court dealing with an insured who had provided clear written evidence whom he considered his parents or intended beneficiaries to be). Reed v. Knollwood Park Cemetery, 441 F. Supp. 1144 (E.D.N.Y.1977), is even farther afield, involving as it does New York State regulations of cemeteries and the interpretation of certificates of indebtedness under New York law. The same could be said for Appellants' reliance on Foreman v. Continental Cas. Co., 770 F.2d 487 (5th Cir. 1985) which involved the interpretation under Mississippi law of an insurance policy protecting a school board, holding that the particular policy did not cover rapes and beatings by school officials.

In Prudential Insurance Co. of America v. Johnson, 200 N.W.2d 115 (N.D.1972), a serviceman failed to make a designation on the life insurance form, and the court held that his natural father rather than his stepfather was

---

3. Sergeant Grady not only explicitly identified Alan and Mary Hall as his "parents" at lines 9 and 10 of the Emergency Data form—which is precisely the term used in the accompanying instructions to form 8286—but in answer to question 6 he specifically named Alan as his father with the parenthetical notation ("stepfather"), almost as if trying to forestall any possible argument that he was confused about terminology and thought his male parent could be anyone *other than* Alan. Thus Sergeant Grady made his intent unmistakable in three different ways, by identifying Alan and Mary as his "parents," identifying Alan as his "father", and identifying his male parent and stepfather all as the same person: Alan Hall.

entitled to insurance benefits, in the absence of any indication whatever by the decedent of his actual intent. As the court itself stated: "We cannot conclude that because the stepfather married the mother, the child automatically became his as an incidental attachment of the mother." Id. at 118. The court in Johnson thus held, in the absence of any evidence of intent, that a natural father was presumed to be the child's parent, notwithstanding the existence of a stepfather who was married to the decedent's mother. (Hardly the case here.) Likewise, in Prudential Insurance Co. of America v. Parker, 840 F.2d 6 (7th Cir.1988), the issue was whether a putative beneficiary was entitled to benefits when the serviceman had sent the supposed beneficiary a designation form which, however, had never been received by the military as required by 38 U.S.C. § 770. (The court refused to give effect to the designation under such circumstances.) Parker stands for the proposition that courts should not casually disregard the statutory limitations in 38 U.S.C. § 765 et seq., a proposition which the trial judge in this case recognized and which Appellee does not challenge.[4] The statutory definition of "parent" in § 765(9) ought to create a very strong presumption that a designation to a "parent" incorporates the statutory definition of that term (though the presumption would, of course, be far more persuasive if the form gave warning that stepchildren and stepparents are not "lawful" children and parents under the statute—a fact which very few servicemen would know, especially if the legality of their relationship had never been an issue before). Only in very special circumstances, as in Smith and the present case, should the presumption be rebutted by unmistakable evidence of decedent's own definitional intent. One must be mindful of Judge Cardozo's admonition (in a somewhat similar context, involving the presumption of validity which the law attaches to a first marriage in the event of a contest between two wives of a decedent), to beware of such statutory presumptions "gone mad." Matter of Findlay, 170 N.E. 471 (N.Y.1930) (quoted with approval in Dolan v. Celebrezze, 381 F.2d 231 (2d Cir.1967)).

The "presumption gone mad" admonition seems especially pertinent in this case, when one stands back and considers what actually transpired here: Sergeant Grady was informed that by writing the words "by law" on the insurance form he would be selecting a (likely) distribution to his "parents." Sergeant Grady was simultaneously handed an "extremely important" form and invited to identify who his parents were, which is exactly what he did! Even if one hypothesizes that Sergeant Grady was subjectively aware of the latent ambiguity in his use of the term "parents" (because of his atypical circumstances), such a concern would have immediately evaporated upon being handed a form in which he could specifically identify who he defined as

---

4. *Parker* makes sense because it would invite an administrative nightmare if claimants were recognized without the insured giving the military any evidence of such designation, especially when multiple claimants appeared. No such danger arises from *Smith,* however: The instant case and *Smith* only involve the issue of the insured's "definitional intent," not the issue of the genuineness of a designation.

his parents. Most people assume that the law is unreasonable and that since donative intent would appear to be the sole issue when identifying beneficiaries for death benefits, the law would not "veto" such unmistakable expressions of donative intent; under such circumstances not even a "Philadelphia lawyer" would have lingering concern that the law, in utter disregard for a plain identification, would blindly proceed to interpret the term "parent" to mean someone other than the person specifically identified as his "parent" on the Emergency Data form.

Jackson has also cited a minor Florida opinion, J.C. Penney Co., Inc. v. Koff, 345 So.2d 732 (Fla. 4th DCA 1977), for the proposition that courts ought not to use evidence to "create an ambiguity" or "rewrite a contract." Koff involved an attempt by a land purchaser to evade a signed purchase contract because of a subsequent zoning change, which attempt the court rejected because the contract did not authorize recision for that reason. Id. at 734. The decision is inoffensive and entirely irrelevant. Even granting the dubious assumption that Sergeant Grady entered into a "contract" with Jackson (rather than simply filling in a Defense Department form), the cardinal rule of contract law which applies in this case is that Sergeant Grady's actual intent must govern. That, indeed, is the principal goal of a court in construing a contract—to ascertain and effectuate the party's intent. See J & S Coin Operated Machines, Inc. v. Gottlieb, 362 So.2d 38 (Fla. 3d DCA 1978), and the dozens of other Florida decisions for the same proposition collected in 11 Fla.Jur.2d *Contracts,* § 107. A court is to ascertain and effectuate a party's intent not merely by looking at the face of the document, but also by looking at the surrounding circumstances (including related documents) which underlie the transaction. See, e.g., Tampa Federal Savings & Loan Assn. v. Aeon, 403 So.2d 1002 (Fla. 2d DCA 1981). The dispositive surrounding circumstance in this case, of course, is the fact that Sergeant Grady was specifically invited to define (in the Emergency Data form) the very term ("parent") which he had adopted by reference in the insurance form. Such a definition by a party to a contract is critical for it is the *best* indication of the party's intent. (See the dozens of Florida decisions standing for this proposition which are collected in 11 Fla.Jur.2d, *Contracts,* at § 113, n. 29 et seq., and §§ 122, 133). Moreover, where as here two documents are executed in a contemporaneous transaction, then the "contemporaneous instrument rule" applies. See Druhill Construction, Inc. v. RSH Constructors, Inc., 518 So.2d 951 (Fla. 1st DCA 1988); International Ship Repair v. General Portland, Inc., 469 So.2d 817 (Fla. 2d DCA 1985).

Of course it is notoriously easy for parties litigating a contract dispute to cite selected "rules" of contract interpretation for their respective positions. But it appears Appellants have rashly fired the first shot without inspecting their ammunition, for the trial judge's decision is actually bolstered by the cardinal rules of contract construction, namely that the court should be guided first and foremost by the contracting parties' actual intention, as to which there can be little doubt in the instant case in view of Sergeant Grady's own express definition of terms in a contemporaneous instrument.

This court may also be curious—as Judge Harris was below—whether Florida law governing the construction of wills provides useful guidance. It does: See generally, First Nat'l Bank v. Moffett, 479 So.2d 312 (Fla. 5th DCA 1985) (the intent of testator should prevail even if court must refer to "the testator's general plan"); In Re Estate of Rice, 406 So.2d 469 (Fla. 3d DCA 1981) (either patent or latent ambiguities may be resolved by referring to extrinsic evidence of the testator's actual intent); In Re Estate of Campbell, 288 So.2d 528 (Fla. 3d DCA 1974) (using a later codicil to construe the intent of testator in a prior will).

In Humana, Inc. v. Estate of Scheying, 483 So.2d 113 (Fla. 2d DCA 1986), the testatrix had left half her estate to a named hospital, which then changed ownership and its name. The trial court invalidated the devise, and the district court reversed:

> In construing a will, the primary consideration is ascertaining the intent of the testator. [citations omitted] Furthermore, the misnomer of a devisee will not cause the devise to fail where the identity of the devisee can be identified with certainty.

483 So.2d at 114. See also In Re Estate of Lenahan, 511 So.2d 365 (Fla. 1st DCA 1987) ("The intention of the testator is the polestar which guides all will construction proceedings . . . parol and other evidence is admissible to . . . explain latent ambiguities . . . *the intention of the testator must be gathered from the will itself, read in the light of the extrinsic evidence.*" Id. at 371) (emphasis supplied); Wilson v. First Florida Bank, 498 So.2d 1289 (Fla. 2d DCA 1986) (where a court read into a will a devise based on a letter to the intended beneficiary); West v. Francioni, 488 So.2d 571 (Fla. 3d DCA 1986) (where a testator did not explain his intent carefully, and the court stated: "The Court, while avoiding making a will for a man who did not succeed in making one for himself will nevertheless, if the general intention of the testator is clear, give effect to such intention" even if it meant disregarding the literal words he used, id. at 572–573); In Re Estate of Wood, 226 So.2d 46 (Fla. 2d DCA), cert. denied, 232 So.2d 181 (Fla.1969) (courts should liberally construe words of testator to honor an intended devise even if that required the court to disregard various other "rules and canons of interpretation"); In Re Estate of McGahee, 550 So.2d 83 (Fla. 1st DCA 1989) (authorizing the use of a letter to interpret a will).

Sergeant Grady's donative intent was apparent because he actually defined his terms in a contemporaneous instrument, and that donative intent was rightly honored by the district court. That decision should be affirmed.

8

CONCLUSION

For the reasons stated above, Appellee Alan Hall respectfully requests this Court to affirm the judgment of the district court.

Respectfully submitted,

_____

(Name of Attorney)
Attorney for Appellee

CERTIFICATE OF SERVICE

I CERTIFY that a true and correct copy of the foregoing was furnished to Attorney for Appellants by hand delivery this 25th day of November, 1989.

_____

Attorney for Appellee

Chapter Seven

How to Organize and Develop a Thesis

Thesis: A proposition maintained by argument; a research dissertation advancing a point of view, especially one required for an academic degree.

As a senior law student you will probably be assigned a legal research paper as a requirement for graduation. This "senior thesis" assignment causes many law students considerable anxiety, even though they have written numerous papers in law school: essay examinations, pleadings, memoranda, and appellate briefs. This assignment differs from those, however, because it requires the drafter to consider both the plan of attack and the organization of ideas.

To allay the fears of senior students as they begin to prepare their senior theses, I hold thesis seminars at the beginning of their senior year to answer students' questions about thesis preparation. The first and most common question is "How do I begin?" The answer is easy: Begin with an outline.

I. The Outline

A. Who Needs to Outline?

You do. If you ask the question, it is probably because you are reluctant to prepare an outline. But writers who hate to outline are most in need of doing so. The failure to organize your ideas before you begin to write your paper may cause you to outline after you finish writing—and having to reorganize your entire paper. For a thesis without the structure an outline provides is like Christmas tree ornaments without the tree. Without structure, a writer's bright ideas, like the Christmas tree ornaments, will end in a heap on the floor.

Samuel Johnson commented to his friend Boswell on the need to organize ideas, when he said of a mutual acquaintance: "He has a great deal of learning, but it never lies straight. There is never one idea by the side of another; 'tis all entangled." To avoid tangles, prepare an outline.

What else does an outline accomplish?

- It helps you avoid gaps and digressions.
- It shows you where transitions are needed.

- It tells you what you should include in the text and what you should footnote.
- It tells your reader what is coming and where.

B. What Should the Outline Contain?

This is the second question students ask as they think about writing a thesis. It is harder to answer, and it reminds me of a question a little boy asked his mother in a letter from camp: "Yesterday we went on an overnight hike in the woods and I lost my sweater. Where do you think I should look for it?"

Fortunately, more help is available for thesis writers than the mother could give her son. Following is an all-purpose outline that should be adaptable to almost any thesis topic. But because it is generalized, it is not completely suitable for any specific use. It is helpful only as a starting point. Adjust the outline to suit your particular topic, then continue to modify it as you develop your thesis. You should consider any outline you prepare as organic, not established. Always be sure to adjust the outline to fit your thesis, not your thesis to fit your initial outline.

Sample Outline

I. Introduction
   A. Why you chose this subject
   B. What you intend to do with this subject

II. History
   A. The genesis of your subject
   B. The changes that have occurred during its development
   C. Why it has developed into its present state

III. Status quo
   A. Its advantages
   B. Its defects
   C. Why it cannot (should not) continue

IV. Changes suggested (attempted) by others
   A. Advantages
   B. Defects

V. Your ideas for change
   A. Advantages
   B. Defects

VI. Conclusion
   A. Predictions
   B. Summary of ideas presented in paper

The above sample outline can be adapted to fit your thesis topic. Suppose, for example, that your topic is that the language of regulations and legislation is often confusing and could be improved by the use of plain English and suitable punctuation. You might use the divisions of the sample outline to prepare your initial outline, perhaps as follows:

Your Outline

   I. Introduction
   - A. Examples of avoidable litigation that occurred due to badly constructed statutes and regulations
   - B. Illustration of language and punctuation modification that would have prevented the litigation
   II. History of your topic
   - A. Discussion of the origin and development of the currently used language and punctuation in legal documents
   - B. Discussion of the historical reasons for resistance to changes in form
   III. Status quo
   - A. Illustration of current "new" style of drafting
   - B. Illustration of current "old" styles of drafting
   IV. Changes suggested (attempted) by others
   - A. Lawyers in the forefront of the plain English movement
   - B. States that have passed laws regarding plain English
   - C. Non-legal critics who have suggested changes
   V. Your ideas for change
   - A. How your suggestions differ from others
   - B. Advantages of your ideas
   - C. Possible disadvantages of your ideas
   VI. Redraft of a poorly crafted statute, applying your ideas to improve clarity

C. How to Use Your Research in Your Outline (and Adapt Your Outline to Your Research)

In the "olden days" (B.C.: before copiers), to do their research authors laboriously covered large numbers of index cards with voluminous notes, indicating at the top of each card where in their manuscript the notes on that particular card applied. They had to take care to copy verbatim whatever quotations they might need to use and to summarize all of the other ideas succinctly enough to fit on the index cards. Furthermore, the source of all material had to be meticulously noted so that it could be referred to if necessary for verification later. Thus both outlining and research were time-consuming, burdensome processes. Some writers still use this method, although it is the one most apt to cause error—and writer's cramp.

Writers who take advantage of photocopiers have an easier job. They may still prefer to use index cards, one to a source, with the source of the data indicated at the top of each card. Much less writing is necessary, however, because the materials consulted can be photocopied. Index card notations will refer to the photocopied materials and the labor of notetaking is therefore minimized.

The simplest method (and the one I recommend) is to apply your research directly to your outline, while at the same time adapting your outline to your research. Use a looseleaf notebook for your outline. Assign one page of the notebook to each heading and sub-heading of your outline. Then, as you do your research, label it with a few identifying phrases and put those phrases into your outline. At the same time, on the photocopied research material, indicate where in your outline it belongs. As you continue your research, you may find that the material belongs elsewhere in your outline or that your outline needs revision. If you decide, for example, that heading III is really better as heading VI, it is easy to switch the pages in the looseleaf notebook.

Another distinct advantage of this method is that, once you have placed all relevant material into each heading and subheading, you can put it into the proper order within its category and decide what transitional words or paragraphs are needed to make the ideas flow. When your outline is fully fleshed out, you will be able to add relevant material in order to fill any gaps, and to eliminate or assign to the footnotes any material that prevents a clear logical presentation of your ideas. When you have done all this, your paper will be all-but written. The first draft should be easy to write; after that, it will be just a matter of polishing.

For those of you who own computers, this advice sounds hopelessly archaic. Using a word processor to prepare your thesis will make your task easier and faster. With a word processor you can add or delete text where and when you like. The form and the language of your paper can be readily modified. Once you have become adept at preparing manuscripts on a word processor, you will probably use no other method.

II. Organization of the Thesis

The organization of your thesis as an entirety is hard to discuss because, unlike its paragraphs and sentences, the complete thesis cannot easily be set forth for dissection and criticism. However, there are some helpful guidelines for thesis organization. Professor Barbara Child compares the document drafter to an architect and construction engineer.* That metaphor is also appropriate for thesis writers. As the architect of your thesis you will want to

---

* In *Drafting Legal Documents,* 129 (1988).

construct it so that the divisions are logically arranged and the subdivisions are convenient for readers to find and to follow.

A. General Guidelines for Thesis Organization

1. All of the subdivisions of your thesis should refer directly back to your central topic, your main subject. All subdivisions should also relate clearly to one another.

2. Your finished thesis should contain no reiteration of ideas, no conclusions lacking complete analysis. The total should be the sum of the parts, not more or less.

3. All inappropriate information should be excluded. No matter how useful the subject may be in another context, resist the temptation to include it here.

B. Help for Your Readers

1. Make general assertions first.

In your thesis, ordinarily discuss general assertions before qualifications, important subjects before less significant ones, more widely held theories before idiosyncratic ones, and more conventional views before radical ones. What follows is a proposed constitutional amendment, which failed to follow the simple arrangement just suggested. It was turned down by the voters. (Perhaps they did not understand it).

> • No moneys derived from any fees, excises, or license taxes, levied by the state, relating to registration, operation, or use of vehicles upon the public highways except a vehicle-use tax imposed in lieu of a sales tax, and no moneys derived from any fees, excises, or license taxes, levied by the state, relating to fuels used for propelling such vehicles except pump taxes, shall be used for other than cost of administering such laws, statutory refunds and adjustments allowed therein, cost of construction, reconstruction, maintenance and rights-of-way, payment of highway obligations, the cost of traffic regulation, and the expense of enforcing state traffic and motor vehicle laws.*

The re-write below follows the suggested format and is clearer:

> • Certain sources of revenue will be used exclusively for the administration of these laws. The sources include all fees, excises, or license taxes which are levied by the state and relate to the registration or use of vehicles on public highways or to the fuels used in propelling these vehicles. The sources of revenue exclude pump taxes and vehicle-use taxes imposed in place of sales taxes. The costs of administration of these laws include the cost of refunds and adjustments that the laws allow, the cost of construction and maintenance of public highways and bridges,

---

* To be sure, this paragraph has other problems: it is one long periodic sentence, which needs breaking up, and it contains several ambiguous negatives. These defects are discussed in Chapter 3.

the cost of highway rights-of-way, the payment of highway obligations, the cost of traffic regulation, and the expense of enforcing state traffic and motor vehicle laws.

In the above re-write the author

(1) began with a broad statement,

(2) explained what the statement includes,

(3) explained what the statement excludes,

(4) listed the costs of administration.

2. Put your ideas into appropriate order.

a. Prefer chronological development.

The chronological arrangement of your ideas is usually the easiest for your reader to follow, so unless you have reason to adopt a different arrangement, take the advice given to Alice: "Begin at the beginning . . . and go on till you come to the end; then stop." *

Some legal writers ignore this good advice, and confusion results. Note the difference in the two excerpts below, both taken from the "Facts" section of memos. The first is confusing, the second easy to follow, because the second author developed his subject chronologically:

> • D.W. Indy now files a motion to suppress evidence that he refused to take a breathalyzer test in compliance with Florida's implied consent statute. D.W.I. was arrested on June 13, 1981, by Officer Gettum for driving under the influence of alcohol to the extent that his normal faculties were impaired. D.W.I. refused the breathalyzer test at the police station. He was read the *Miranda* rights and Florida Statute § 322.261, providing that a refusal to take the test would result in a three-month suspension of his driver's license. Officer Gettum says he also showed Indy the implied-consent statement on Indy's driver's license. Prior to trial, Indy filed a motion to suppress evidence of his refusal to take the breathalyzer test, claiming that Officer Gettum told him that he had the right to refuse to do so. Officer Gettum denies that he did so.

In the paragraph above, the writer discusses in sentence one the most recent event (D.W.I.'s filing of the motion to suppress evidence). But in the second sentence, the writer moves back in time to discuss the earliest event (D.W.I.'s arrest). Because he did not deal with the events in the order in which they happened, the writer is then forced, at the end of the paragraph, to repeat what he had said at the beginning. Repetition of this sort can be avoided by discussing events in their natural order, and you will place less of a burden on your reader to understand what you are describing. The writer did this in his re-write.

---

* In *Alice's Adventures in Wonderland*, (Turtle Soup), line 12. This advice is relevant to all writing and is discussed *passim*.

• On June 13, 1981, Officer Jones arrested D.W. Indy for driving while under the influence of alcohol to the extent that his normal faculties were impaired. When taken to the police station, D.W.I. was read his *Miranda* rights and Florida Statute § 322.261, providing that a refusal to take a breathalyzer test in compliance with Florida's implied consent statute would result in a three-month suspension of his driver's license. Officer Gettum says he also showed D.W.I. the implied-consent statement on his driver's license. D.W.I. claims, however, that Officer Gettum told him at the police station that he had the right to refuse to take the breathalyzer test. Officer Gettum denies this. D.W.I. now files a motion to suppress any evidence of his refusal to take the breathalyzer test.

Here are two more paragraphs, taken from the "Facts" sections of memos. Note how chronological development improves the second paragraph:

• K.R. owns a pawnshop in a high-crime area of El Dorado. When he arrived at his shop on October 8, 1981, he saw two teenaged girls hurriedly leaving. K.R.'s clerk said that a ring worth about $1,000 was missing from its usual place. On his car radio K.R. heard that a number of jewelry thefts had occurred in the neighborhood. This especially concerned K.R. because his insurance coverage had recently been cancelled. He pursued the girls, who were running down the street.

• While driving to his pawnshop, located in a high crime area of El Dorado, K.R. heard on his car radio that a number of jewelry thefts by teenaged girls had recently occurred in the neighborhood. This news especially concerned K.R. because his insurance had recently been cancelled. As K.R. arrived at his shop, he saw two teenaged girls hurriedly leaving his shop. K.R.'s clerk said that a ring worth about $1,000 was missing from its usual place. K.R. pursued the girls, who were running down the street.

If you use chronological development you will avoid the writing fault that is sometimes called *hysteron-proteron,* Greek for "the last before the first." Hysteron-proteron is often successfully used in poetry; for example, in Shelley's "I die, I faint, I fail," the order of the events must surely have been reversed.

In legal writing, the result is less felicitous. Hysteron-proteron results in wordiness and sometimes confusion. Here is an example from a student's paper. See if you can untangle it:

• In Jones v. Jones, involving a man and woman who had just been divorced, the man signed a note evidencing a loan from his wife, while they were still married. Then, after the divorce, by mutual consent, the former wife released the former husband from the debt. Since she was not repaid by her former husband, she took a bad debt deduction.

Your re-write may look something like this:

> • In Jones v. Jones, a man signed a note evidencing a loan from his wife. Then the couple were divorced and, by mutual consent, the man was released from his debt. The woman took a bad debt deduction because she had not been repaid by her former husband.

As a reader, you can recognize hysteron-proteron when you are disappointed in your expectation of what comes next in a discussion. In the following paragraph, for example, stop after the first sentence and consider what you expect to follow; then read on to find out whether your expectation is satisfied.

> • In some instances the Roman commander would delegate the authority to decide the death sentence. But in any case, the commander's *lictors* were probably the executioners. This authority would sometimes be granted to the military tribunes who were next in command to the commanders. Or the delegation of the punishment would be awarded to the *centurions*.

The first sentence promises that the author will next discuss the instances in which the Roman commander would delegate authority. Instead, he begins another idea in the second sentence, returning in the following sentences not to the *instances* of delegation, but to the groups who would administer it. (A couple of paragraphs later, the writer does get around, belatedly, to telling the reader what he promises to tell him here.)

Here is another paragraph from the same paper—and it contains the same problem:

> • Ancient Roman military success was based on the fact that those chosen to take part in military operations had something to fight for. The soldiers knew that the outcome of their battles would determine whether they had something to come home to. Since the Republican military establishment required, from the start, that all those in its ranks own some property and/or be citizens of Rome, the soldiers knew that battles would determine whether they kept their homeland of Rome free from external conquerors and internal subversives. They had property and positions to lose if their defense of Rome was weak.

The first sentence promises the reader he will learn what it was the Roman soldiers had to fight for. In the last sentence, the reader does learn. Why not rearrange the paragraph so that the information promised appears in sentence two? The result might look something like this:

> • Ancient Roman military success was based on the fact that those chosen to take part in military operations had something to fight for. All soldiers had either property or position to lose if their defense of Rome was weak, for the Republican military establishment required from the start that all those in its ranks own some property and/or be citizens of Rome. Thus the soldiers knew that whether they had something to come home to would be determined by the outcome of their battles.

When the sentences are placed in their proper order, one sentence can be omitted. This is often true when disorganized sentences are rearranged because unnecessary repetitions and *non sequiturs* are more apt to creep into illogically arranged paragraphs. The material omitted will often be found to belong somewhere else in the paper.

b. Use logical development.

Some discussions do not lend themselves to chronological development. Perhaps events do not occur in chronological sequence. Perhaps the points you need to make should be discussed in the order of their importance to your general thesis. Then you should choose logical development. As long as you discuss one point at a time, and as long as your discussion is thorough (but not repetitive), focussed (not discursive), your ideas will emerge clearly and cogently. In the following paragraphs, the first draft of a paper, the writer did not organize her ideas well, and the reader is hardput to understand just what she is getting at:

First Draft

• Much of the dispute about the purpose of the equal protection clause centers on whether it should be interpreted as prohibiting the consideration of race in governmental decision-making or whether the equal protection clause should be interpreted as imposing upon government an affirmative duty to remove the effects of past discrimination against minorities. The Supreme Court has struggled to resolve the conflict about whether illicit motive or disparate impact is the touchstone in constitutional violations, whether de jure or de facto segregation is condemned by the equal protection clause. This conflict is seen in the phenomenon of suburbia.

This paper will argue that the equal protection clause should be concerned with the substance of governmental decision-making as it affects minorities. Motivation is largely irrelevant as a constitutional basis for a violation of the equal protection clause if the effect is further subordination of victims of discrimination. As the white middle class has abandoned the cities, the tax base has decreased, and the familiar minority ghettos have burgeoned.

Placed in logical order, the writer's ideas become clearer:

Second Draft

• Much of the conflict about the purpose of the equal protection clause centers on whether it should be interpreted as prohibiting the consideration of race in governmental decision-making or whether the equal protection clause should be interpreted as imposing upon government an affirmative duty to remove the effects of past discrimination against minorities. This conflict is seen in the Supreme Court's struggle to resolve the question of whether illicit motive or disparate impact is the touchstone in constitutional violations, whether de jure or de facto segregation is condemned by the equal protection clause.

This paper will argue that, although color-blind decision-making is necessary, if the results of such decision-making nevertheless discriminate against minorities, the equal protection clause should be interpreted as prohibiting such results. In such cases, motivation is irrelevant. The phenomenon of suburbia illustrates de facto discrimination against minorities, occurring along with color-blind decision-making.

The writer has improved this second draft by logically developing her subject:

First, she has stated her topic: possible interpretations of the equal protection clause.

Second, she has narrowed the topic to the Supreme Court's effort to decide on a test for violation of the equal protection clause.

Third, she has further narrowed the topic: the impact of the problem upon minorities.

Finally, she has indicated her purpose: to argue for one interpretation of the role of the equal protection clause.

Note how the discussion leads from a broad, general statement of the topic to a narrowing of the topic by examples and qualifications. This kind of logical development helps the reader follow your reasoning and makes your argument persuasive.

But the second draft is not yet clear. It suffers from other writing flaws that have been discussed elsewhere in these pages. Some of the writing flaws that remain are:

- The use of noun phrases instead of verbs.
- Some elegant variation ("conflict/dispute"; "prohibit/condemn").
- The failure to say **who** did **what** to **whom.***

In her third draft, below, the writer has further improved her discussion by correcting these flaws. Compare the following draft with the second:

Third Draft

Much of the conflict about the purpose of the equal protection clause centers upon whether the clause merely prohibits the government from considering race as a factor in making decisions or requires government to remove the effects of past discrimination. This conflict is seen in the Supreme Court's struggle to decide which of two tests it should apply to decide whether the equal protection clause has been violated:

(1) Was an "illicit motive" the basis for decision?

(2) Did the decision adversely impact minorities?

---

* See Chapter Three for discussions of these problems.

This paper will argue that the second test is the appropriate one to apply to government decision-making. If a government decision causes a disparate impact upon minorities, the question of whether the decision was arrived at in a "color-blind" manner (that is, whether or not it was prompted by an illicit motive) is irrelevant. If the decision results in de facto segregation, the equal protection clause should prohibit it.

The phenomenon of suburbia illustrates de facto discrimination against minorities. . . . [This and subsequent paragraphs elaborate on this theme.]

C. The Paragraph

"Just as the sentence contains one idea in all its fullness, so the paragraph should embrace a distinct episode; and as sentences should follow one another in harmonious sequence, so the paragraphs must fit on to one another like the automatic couplings of railway carriages. . . ." (Winston Churchill)

1. Why paragraph?

Paragraphs break up your writing into units which, properly arranged, permit the orderly movement of ideas from the beginning of your manuscript to its conclusion. Paragraphing is therefore important in all writing, but even more important in legal writing, in which clear and logical reasoning is essential. The familiar paragraph indentation at intervals on each page of writing promises the reader that with each paragraph a new set of ideas is being introduced and developed. Conversely, large blocks of unindented print discourage even the most interested reader from making the effort to learn what the writer has to say.

So paragraphing is psychologically important to the reader. It is also important to the writer. The process forces him to develop fully the ideas he has introduced, since he knows that a paragraph of fewer than four to six sentences probably indicates incomplete idea development * and that a paragraph of more than half a page of print is not only a fearful bore to read but a combination of too many ideas. The four-to-six-sentence rule can (and should) be broken occasionally. One-or-two-sentence paragraphs, sparingly used, are effective for summation of arguments, interjection of contrasting ideas, transition devices, or emphasis. Here is an illustration:

> • Many university students first came into contact with the word "ripoff" when, in 1969, it appeared on posters placed around campus announcing a "Ripoff Rally," at which students were invited "to see how many ways you are getting ripped off." Included in the discussion at the rally were victims of injustice (black students) and the injustices them-

---

* In legal writing, in which sentences tend to be longer than in ordinary writing, the four-sentence minimum may sometimes be relaxed. Another criterion is the number of words: if your paragraphs have fewer than 50 or more than 250 words, you should check their content to see if you should combine or divide paragraphs.

selves (e.g., a proposed tuition hike). The context indicated that "ripped off" meant "cheated" or at least "treated with great unfairness." But to a large majority of university students in 1969, the word "ripoff" was clearly new and indefinable. Of the twenty students in my transformational grammar class, not one could provide a suitable definition.

One year later I asked students in my transformational grammar class to define "ripoff" again; all twenty students in that class could provide a working definition.*

Every paragraph should contain a central idea. In most paragraphs, that idea is expressed in one sentence, usually called a "topic sentence." The topic sentence often comes first in a paragraph, sometimes following an introductory or transitional sentence. Or it comes last, expressing in general the individual points made within the paragraph. Rarely, the central idea of a paragraph is left unstated, implicit in the ideas contained in the paragraph, as in the following example:

> • A factory survey of men all doing the same sort of work for the same length of time showed some were exhausted at day's end while others still seemed highly energetic. What made this difference? Analysts turned up one curious fact. The tired ones expected to do nothing but rest after work. The lively ones all had plans for the evening.

The unstated topic sentence in this newspaper account is, of course, that a person's after-work plans affect the amount of energy the person has at the end of the workday. Perhaps the idea is left unstated because it is open to attack. It is at least arguable that only those workers who knew they would have energy left at the end of the workday made plans for the evening.

2.　Paragraph development according to topic

Paragraphs can be developed by any of the following methods: definition; classification; process; illustration; cause and effect; comparison and contrast; induction; and deduction. Frequently, more than one method of development occurs in a single paragraph.

Many books on English composition imply that you should choose among the methods of paragraph development before writing each paragraph. This procedure would be stultifying and a waste of time, for you are no doubt using these methods quite intuitively as you write. However, after you have finished writing the first draft of your manuscript, if any paragraphs seem undeveloped, overdeveloped, or confusing, consider varying your methods of paragraph development as one means of improving your writing. Here they are:

a.　Definition

Definition explains what something is by saying what it includes and what it excludes. The item being defined is first put into a class of similar items and

---

* Block, "A Year of Ripoffs," *American Speech*, Vol. 45, Nos. 3–4, 1970, p. 210.

then is differentiated from those items. The following paragraph exemplifies the process of definition:

> Historically, larceny was a common law felony, while embezzlement and false pretenses were statutory innovations. Larceny, the trespassory taking and carrying away of another's personal property with the intent of depriving him permanently of it, is a crime against possession, not ownership. Thus, one commits larceny by stealing the ill-gotten gains of a thief, but not by taking property from its rightful possessor when the possessor parts with it voluntarily. Therefore, larceny, under its strict definition, did not include fraud or the abuse of trust by a servant or another entrusted with one's possessions.

In **sentence one** of the definition, larceny is called a "common law felony," and is distinguished from embezzlement and false pretenses, statutory crimes. In **sentence two,** larceny is defined more narrowly, as a crime against possession, not against ownership. **Sentence three** introduces, as part of the definition of larceny, an example of what constitutes larceny. Finally, **sentence four** defines larceny by stating what it does not include (fraud or the abuse of trust by a person entrusted with one's possessions).

You can use definition, not only to explain, but to persuade, by deciding what to include and what to exclude. For example, Model Penal Code sections 221.0 and 221.1 define burglary as the entering of a building or occupied structure with the purpose of committing a crime, unless the premises are open to the public at the time, or the actor is privileged to enter. Whether the facts of the case you are considering are covered by the definition may depend on the meaning of "occupied structure." Must the occupant be in general occupancy or only present when the burglary occurred? What does "license to enter" include? (Licensees have been defined by courts as persons using premises through the owner's "sufferance," or "permission," or as invitees who step beyond the limits of their invitation.) You can persuade your reader to your point of view by arguing for the inclusion or exclusion of one or more of these definitions.

b. Classification

Classification places items into categories, according to their similarities or their differences. In their opinions, courts sometimes expand and sometimes narrow classes—and occasionally even create new ones. In his dissent in *Roth v. Wisconsin State University,* Justice Thurgood Marshall argued for the expansion of basic liberties protected by the Fourteenth Amendment so as to include a right to work. That right, he argued, was "the very essence of the personal freedom and opportunity that it was the purpose of the Amendment to secure."

In *Griswold v. Connecticut,* Justice William O. Douglas, writing for the majority, used abstract language with considerable skill to create the presumption necessary to classify marital relationships under a "right to privacy." In words often repeated but less often analyzed, he wrote that "specific guarantees in the Bill of Rights have penumbras, formed by emanations from those guarantees that help give them life and substance." He then placed the marital relationship "within the zone of privacy created by several fundamental guarantees."

Expanding that "zone," the Court, in *Eisenstadt v. Baird,* extended the right to privacy to certain intimate aspects of unmarried individuals. In that decision, the Court held, among other things, that Massachusetts could not enforce a law intended to act as a prohibition of contraception. In its decision, the court skillfully expanded the *Griswold* right to privacy, which it had found to exist in marriage, to the intimate relationships of single individuals. Notice the reasoning the Court used to justify that expansion of the class:

> • If under *Griswold* the distribution of contraceptives to married persons cannot be prohibited, a ban on distribution to unmarried persons would be equally impermissible. It is true that in *Griswold* the right of privacy in question inhered in the marital relationship. Yet the marital couple is not an independent entity with a mind and heart of its own, but an association of two individuals each with a separate intellectual and emotional makeup. If the right of privacy means anything, it is the right of the *individual,* married or single, to be free from unwarranted governmental intrusion into matters so fundamentally affecting a person as the decision whether to bear or beget a child. . . . 405 U.S. 453, 92 S.Ct. 1038.

On the other hand, the *Roe v. Wade* Court seemed to narrow the same classification, holding that while the right to privacy encompassed a woman's decision to continue her pregnancy, that right was not absolute, being limited by the interest of the State in safeguarding her health, maintaining proper medical standards, and protecting potential human life. Justice Harry A. Blackmun, writing for the majority, said:

> • [O]nly personal rights that can be deemed "fundamental" or "implicit in the concept of ordered liberty," Palko v. Connecticut, 302 U.S. 319, 325, 58 S.Ct. 149, 82 L.Ed. 288 (1937), are included in this guarantee of personal privacy. They also make it clear that the right has some extension to activities relating to marriage [citation omitted]; procreation [citation omitted]; contraception [citation omitted]; family relationships [citation omitted]; and child rearing and education [citations omitted]. 410 U.S. 152, 153, 89 S.Ct. 1248.

The Florida Supreme Court, in *Laird v. State,* declined to expand the right to privacy to include the right to private possession of marijuana in the home.*

In arriving at that decision, the Florida court carefully distinguished the cases cited above, noting that the Supreme Court had declined to further extend the scope of the constitutional right to privacy in several other cases. The Florida court said that the Supreme Court had limited privacy rights to those fundamental of "implicit in the concept of ordered liberty":

* See at page 131.

. . . [O]ur other "right of privacy" cases, while defying categorical description, deal generally with substantive aspects of the Fourteenth Amendment. In *Roe* the Court pointed out that the personal rights found in this guarantee of personal privacy must be limited to those which are "fundamental" or "implicit in the concept of ordered liberty" as described in Palko v. Connecticut, 301 U.S. 319, 325, 58 S.Ct. 149, 82 L.Ed. 288 (1937). The activities detailed as being within this definition were ones very different from that for which respondent claims constitutional protection—matters relating to marriage, procreation, contraception, family relationships, and child rearing and education. In these areas it has been held that there are limitations on the States' power to substantively regulate conduct.

c. Process

Process involves orderly, step-by-step explanation. The ability to describe procedures and events in the proper order and without omissions is valuable in legal writing because of the importance of detail, accuracy, and completeness in legal matters. In the following excerpt the process to be followed in a lawsuit is described:

> The first step in a lawsuit is the decision to sue someone. In making this decision intelligently, the potential litigant must discover whether the grievance he has suffered is one for which the law furnishes relief, whether it is probable that he will win the lawsuit, and whether the time, effort, and expense of bringing the suit will be worth the gain if he does win. The second step is to determine in which court to bring the action, and the choice of court will depend not only upon the preference of the litigant but upon which court has jurisdiction both over the subject matter and over the person against whom the suit is being brought, and which court has proper venue.*

The "process" method of organization is valuable not only in law practice but also in getting through law school, where skill in reasoning clearly in a detailed and orderly manner is valued. Some writing critics maintain that those who cannot express distinctions clearly in language cannot think clearly either, and that as a result they behave inefficiently. One professor writes that sloppy thinking causes sloppy conduct:

> • To think, we must devise connected chains of predications, which, in turn, require fluency of language. Those who are fluent in no language just don't have the means for thinking about things. They may remember and recite whatever predications experience provides them, but they cannot manipulate them and derive new ones. Mostly, therefore, they will think and do those things that the world suggests they think and do.**

---

* These two steps are only the first in a long, complicated process.

** W. Mitchell, *Less Than Words Can Say* (1979), pages 157–158.

d. Illustration

The method of illustration in paragraph development is one in which concrete examples are used to explain an abstract concept or to persuade the reader of its validity. The following textbook definition of constructive possession uses several examples:

> • Constructive possession is the possession that the law annexes to the title, distinguishing constructive possession from in fact or in deed possession, achieved by actual occupancy. Courts have found constructive possession to exist in several situations, as when (1) an employer delivers property to his employee; (2) the owner delivers property to another for a transaction to be completed in his presence; (3) a bailee breaks bulk; (4) a wrongdoer obtains possession but not title to the property by lies; (5) a wrongdoer finds lost or mislaid property; or (6) property is delivered to a wrongdoer by mistake.*

Courts use illustration freely to provide analogies that justify their reasoning in arriving at decisions. You will use it too as you write appellate briefs in the attempt to persuade a court to adopt your view of a case. Here, an English court employs illustration to explain why it decided that a dock owner owed the plaintiff ship painter a duty of care to provide a safe stage for him to stand on while painting a ship:

> • [T]here may be the obligation of such a duty from one person to another although there is no contract between them with regard to such duty. Two drivers meeting have no contract with each other, but under certain circumstances they have a reciprocal duty towards each other. So two ships navigating the sea. So a railway company which has contracted with one person to carry another has no contract with the person carried but has a duty towards that person. So the owner or occupier of house or land who permits a person or persons to come to his house or land has no contract with such person or persons, but has a duty towards him or them. . . .**

Both the textbook author and the opinion writer used multiple examples to make a point. In some situations one striking example is often substituted. For example, in arguing that capital punishment is unfair, the point might be successfully made if one individual who would have been executed is subsequently found to have been innocent of the crime for which he had been convicted.

e. Cause and effect

You use this type of paragraph development whenever you raise a question of why something occurs and then provide the answer. If you persuade your audience that a causal relationship exists between the two

---

* LaFave and Scott, *Criminal Law*, West Publishing Co., 1972 (p. 622).

** Heaven v. Pender, 11 Q.B.D. 503, 1883. (Note that the court is also reasoning deductively. Deduction is discussed ahead, at 233f.)

occurrences, your argument will be convincing. In the following paragraph, the author advances a reason for the development of the *mens rea* doctrine in criminal law:

> • The concept of *mens rea* was not always part of common law. Anglo–Saxon law had held that intent was not a necessary element of crime. The act itself was considered rather than the intent behind it, and reparation was demanded of the actor for the consequences of his act. But beginning in the ninth century, this objective standard of criminal responsibility was increasingly rejected by the church. Concern for the eternal soul of the criminal and belief in the Augustinian doctrine of free will led the church to adopt instead a subjective standard of responsibility: if the actor intended freely to commit the crime, he should be punished not only in heaven but on earth. Thus was born the modern doctrine of *mens rea.**

f. Comparison and Contrast

In your legal writing as students, in your legal arguments as lawyers, and in your legal decisions as judges, you will often use comparison and contrast as you analogize and distinguish the facts of already-decided cases from the facts of your case. That is because courts "reason from precedent," deciding cases in accordance with rules laid down in earlier cases with the same facts.

Because the facts of your case probably do not exactly resemble the facts of the precedent cases, the court's decision about whether to apply the rule established by precedent will depend upon the number and weight of the positive resemblances compared with the number and weight of the negative resemblances (the similarities and dissimilarities between your facts and those of the cases that resulted in the rule). Of course, what is one lawyer's material and relevant fact may be another's immaterial and irrelevant red herring. You will need to persuade the court to accept your view.

As law students you will learn to analogize by comparison and contrast, by noting similarities and dissimilarities of cases. Often, as you learned in Chapter Four, what seem like dissimilarities in facts turn out to be, when you categorize them, actual similarities, and seeming similarities sometimes turn out to be dissimilarities. Your legal training and perceptiveness will enable you to tell the difference.

In applying comparison and contrast, the thesis writer (or the law student writing a final examination) will attempt, without bias, to reach the appropriate conclusion. The brief writer, on the other hand, is an advocate for a client. He therefore tries to show either that despite seeming similarities, the facts of his client's case can be distinguished from those of prior cases or that despite seeming differences the facts are similar enough to warrant the same decision. Here is the way one student used comparison and contrast in his brief for a

* Block, "The Semantic Delusion of the Insanity Defense," University of Oklahoma Law Review (1983).

defendant businessman being sued by a visitor to the premises who had been injured. The relevant facts in the instant case were:

> • A customer visiting a business was walking in the business parking lot and was hit and injured by the truck negligently operated by a driver employed by the owner of the business.

In a similar case, a superior court in the same jurisdiction had held the owner of a business liable for injuries to a pedestrian. The facts in that case were:

> • A pedestrian crossing a business parking lot was hit and injured by a truck negligently operated by a driver employed by the owner of the business.

These facts are facially similar. In the one aspect in which they differ, the relationship between businessman and visitor in the instant case seems even closer than in the prior case. Here the visitor was a customer; there a mere pedestrian crossing the premises. The brief writer, as he searched for distinguishing facts, found, however, that in the prior case construction in the parking lot created a hazardous condition, whereas in the instant case the premises were safe for visitors. Further research revealed that, in the prior case, the owner of the business knew that the parking lot was unsafe, yet failed to warn visitors of that fact. The brief writer was able, therefore, to distinguish the facts of his case from those of the earlier case, and to argue that the differences were material.

g. Induction

Induction is the process of forming a general conclusion (a generalization) by examining a number of particular examples. The process of induction is therefore essentially a search for the explanation of a pattern. At the close of your examination of the relevant particulars you will make an *inductive leap,* a shift from the listing of particular examples to a conclusion about the entire group, including those particulars that are not available for your inspection. In doing so, you make the assumption that the unavailable particulars exactly resemble the ones you have examined.

The conclusion you reach at the end of the inductive process is expressed as a probability, not a certainty. The more particulars you have to examine the more certain will be the generalization you can form from examining them. When you use induction, and when you examine how others use it, be careful to avoid two errors: **hasty generalization** and **faulty generalization.** If you decide on the basis of too limited a sampling, you are guilty of hasty generalization.* Because a certain lawyer lost a case yesterday, last month, and last year, you should not generalize that she is an ineffective advocate, for your sampling is too limited. If you conclude that all college students favor a strong military after interviewing only the students in R.O.T.C. classes, your sampling is faulty and so is your generalization.

* For further discussion, see page 237.

In an English negligence case, *Home Office v. Dorset Yacht Co., Ltd.,* the court explained how courts use induction as they reason from the holdings of individual cases to reach a legal rule that will govern future similar cases:

> The justification of the courts' role in giving the effect of law to the judges' conception of the public interest in the field of negligence is based upon the cumulative experience of the judiciary of the actual consequences of lack of care in particular instances. And the judicial development of the law of negligence rightly proceeds by seeking first to identify the relevant characteristics that are common to the kinds of conduct and relationship between the parties which are involved in the case for decision and the kinds of conduct and relationships which have been held in previous decisions of the courts to give rise to a duty of care.
>
> The method adopted at this stage of the process is analytical and inductive. It starts with an analysis of the characteristics of the conduct and relationship involved in each of the decided cases. But the analyst must know what he is looking for, and this involves his approaching his analysis with some general conception of conduct and relationships which ought to give rise to a duty of care. This analysis leads to a proposition which can be stated in the form:
>
> > In all the decisions that have been analysed a duty of care has been held to exist wherever the conduct and the relationship possessed each of the characteristics A,B,C,D, etc., and has not so far been found to exist when any of these characteristics were absent.*

As law students and as lawyers, you will use inductive reasoning to form a general conclusion from particular details. In your reading of case law you have seen inductive reasoning used by courts in their opinions. For example, in *Ploof v. Putnam,* an early decision, the court determined by inductive reasoning that the plaintiff was justified in entering the property of the defendant, because of the doctrine of necessity.

> • There are many cases in the books which hold that necessity . . . will justify entries upon land and interferences with personal property that would otherwise have been trespasses. . . .
>
> A traveller on a highway, who finds it obstructed from a sudden and temporary cause, may pass upon the adjoining land without becoming a trespasser, because of the necessity. . . .
>
> An entry upon land to save goods which are in danger of being lost or destroyed by water or fire is not a trespass. . . . [In one such case] the defendant went upon the plaintiff's beach for the purpose of saving and restoring to the lawful owner a boat which had been driven ashore and was in danger of being carried off by the sea; and it was held no trespass. . . .
>
> This doctrine of necessity applies with special force to the preservation of human life. One assaulted and in peril of his life may run through

---

* (1970) A.C. 1004 (H.L.)

the close of another to escape from his assailant. . . . One may sacrifice the personal property of another to save his life or the lives of his fellows. [In one case] the defendant was sued for taking and carrying away the plaintiff's casket and its contents. It appeared that the ferryman of Gravesend took forty-seven passengers into his barge to pass to London, among whom were the plaintiff and defendant; and the barge being upon the water a great tempest happened, and a strong wind, so that the barge and all the passengers were in danger of being lost if certain ponderous things were not cast out, and the defendant thereupon cast out the plaintiff's casket. It was resolved that in case of necessity, to save the lives of the passengers, it was lawful for the defendant, being a passenger, to cast the plaintiff's casket out of the barge; that if the ferryman surcharge the barge the owner shall have his remedy upon the surcharge against the ferryman, but that if there be no surcharge, and the danger accrue only by the act of God, as by tempest, without fault of the ferryman, everyone ought to bear his loss, to safeguard the life of a man.*

This somewhat lengthy excerpt shows how meticulously the *Ploof* court used precedent cases as particulars in order to reach a general rule that it then applied to the case at hand. Notice the number of particular cases cited. The court reasoned that: (1) In all of these previously decided cases, the doctrine of necessity applied to certain facts; (2) the facts of the case under consideration were sufficiently similar to the facts of the precedent cases to warrant the application of the doctrine of necessity to *these* facts.

h. Deduction

Deduction is the opposite of induction. In legal reasoning, the generalization reached by the process of induction after an examination of a number of particulars becomes the rule (doctrine, principle) governing subsequent similar cases (new particulars).

Perhaps the most famous example of deduction is the syllogism described by Aristotle in his system of formal logic:

- **Major premise:**   All men are mortal.

  Minor premise: Socrates is a man.

  Conclusion: Socrates is mortal.

In a syllogism, the major premise is a generally accepted truth; the minor premise identifies the item under consideration as being within the class described by the major premise; and the conclusion then follows that the minor premise is governed by the same reasoning that governs the major premise. In legal writing the major premise is a legal rule (doctrine, principle); the minor premise may be a case with similar facts that is under consideration; and the conclusion would be that the rule governs the new case.

* Ploof v. Putnam, 81 Vt. 471, 71 A. 188 (1908).

You will recall the *Home Office* opinion, an excerpt of which was quoted to explain the inductive reasoning process. You read there the court's conclusion:

> • In all the decisions that have been analysed a duty of care has been held to exist wherever the conduct and the relationship possessed each of the characteristics A,B,C,D, etc., and has not so far been found to exist when any of these characteristics were absent.

This conclusion, reached by inductive reasoning, is now the major premise of a syllogism, and in subsequent cases possessing the same characteristics, a duty of care will be held to exist. (And in *Home Office,* the court did indeed find that the government (Home Office) owed a duty of care to a boat owner for the actions of reformatory boys who escaped from a minimum security encampment.) So in the common law, the major premise is formed "from the cumulative experience of the judiciary" (in the words of Lord Diplock, the English jurist who wrote the *Home Office* opinion).

The cumulative experience of the judiciary governed the formation of a somewhat different major premise in an American case, in which a plaintiff suffered severe injury from the criminal acts of two work-release inmates of a nearby penitentiary, who assaulted her while employed by the defendant company. The court, in *Roberson v. Allied Foundry & Machinery Co.,* held that the company did not owe a duty of care to Mrs. Roberson to protect her from attack by the inmates. That holding was based upon a major premise derived from previous individual cases, and is stated as the "general rule" in the excerpt from the case:

> • Work release inmates are certified to the employer by the State Board of Corrections to be "non-dangerous." Also, employers are instructed by the Board to treat work release employees in the same manner as other employees and to apply the same policies with them as with other employees. Except with regard to a few restrictions imposed by the Board on employers and work release employees, those employees stand in the same relationship with their employers as non-inmate employees. We cannot justify a finding of a special relationship in this case on the bare fact that work release employees are state inmates.

There is no authority in Alabama addressing the specific question at hand. However, our decision seems to be in keeping with recent decisions in Alabama, following the general rule that one has no duty to protect another from criminal attack by a third party. See *Berdeaux v. City National Bank* (bank owes no duty to protect customer from injury during armed robbery); *Gaskin v. Republic Steel Corporation,* (employer owes no duty to protect employee from attack by third party on employee's premises); *Parham v. Taylor,* (employer owes no duty to protect employee from criminal acts of third parties on employer's premises). [Citations omitted.]

We are sympathetic with Mrs. Roberson and understand that she has suffered severe injury. We cannot agree, however, that she should be compensated by rewriting the law of torts. Finding no authority or justification for the premise that a special relationship exists between Allied and its work release employees sufficient to impose a duty on Allied to supervise these employees outside the scope of their employment, we hold that no such duty exists in this case. The trial court's decision granting summary judgment to Allied was therefore not in error, and is, thus, affirmed.

In legal writing the syllogism can expose faulty reasoning. Consider, for example, the following paragraph, from an appellate brief:

> • Contracts in Florida between physicians and patients have been held legally enforceable wherein the physician agreed to withhold the use of artificial methods to postpone a patient's death, when the patient was suffering from an incurable and painful illness. Dr. X, a Florida physician, contracted with his patient, a Florida resident, to withhold, at his patient's request, artificial methods to maintain life. The patient, terminally ill, told the physician not to use artificial methods to prolong his life, and the physician complied with the patient's request. Since the physician was fulfilling the terms of a legally enforceable contract, he can not be held liable for malpractice.

To discover the fallacy in the syllogism, look at the major premise, in the first sentence of the paragraph. Unless the major premise contains an accepted legal principle, the entire syllogism will be invalid. The statement does not reveal whether the legal principle stated in the first sentence is valid in Florida, since we do not know whether all Florida courts, a majority or only some Florida courts have adopted the principle. Furthermore, the individual described in the minor premise may not be a member of the class described in the major premise, for the facts do not indicate that his illness was "painful," nor do they state that he resides in a jurisdiction covered by the major premise.

The syllogism can also be used to expose specious logic. Suppose, for example, that a powerful group of individuals in your city wishes to raze an old neighborhood so as to construct a shopping center, which you oppose. The argument this group advances is that the old buildings in the neighborhood, though not unattractive, present a hazard, old buildings often being decrepit and rodent-infested. You can discredit this argument by showing that the underlying syllogism is based upon specious logic:

> • **Major premise:**　All old buildings are decrepit and rodent-infested.
>
> **Minor premise:**　These buildings are old.
>
> **Conclusion:**　These buildings are decrepit and rodent-infested.

You could point out the fallacy of the major premise and build your opposing argument on the following syllogism:

> • **Major premise:**　Unless old buildings are decrepit or rodent-infested they should be preserved if they are beautiful or of historical interest.

Minor premise: These old buildings are not decrepit or rodent-infested, and they are beautiful and historically interesting.

Conclusion: These old buildings should be preserved.

If the minor premise can occur outside the boundaries of the major premise, the syllogism is also fallacious:

- **Major premise:**   Attorneys are skilled in syllogistic reasoning.

  Minor premise: Jane Doe is skilled in syllogistic reasoning.

  Conclusion: Jane Doe is an attorney.

Even if the major premise is a generally-accepted truth, the syllogism is faulty because persons other than attorneys may be skilled in syllogistic reasoning, and Jane Doe may be one of those persons.

Specious reasoning is most easily hidden in the **enthymeme,** a syllogism stated in a reduced form, with one step missing (usually the major premise). The comment, "He must be a panhandler: he's dirty and he's loitering on the street corner," is an enthymeme, the unstated major premise of which is fallacious: All dirty people who loiter on street corners are panhandlers. Here is an enthymeme-containing excerpt from a political speech:

- During his years in the state legislature, Representative Quagmire has often spoken out in favor of federal handouts, even though he himself has profited from the free enterprise system which is about to be undermined by federal handouts. Communists in Russia and China also favor handouts and oppose the free enterprise system upon which this nation was founded. Let's replace Quagmire with John Dogood, a man of strong ideals and get the communists out of state government.*

This paragraph is loaded with enthymemes that are invalid because they contain fallacious major premises. Some of these are:

- People who have profited from the free enterprise system should not speak out in favor of federal handouts.
- Federal handouts are incompatible with free enterprise.
- People with "strong ideals" oppose federal handouts.
- Handouts are bad because communists in Russia and China favor them.
- All persons who favor federal handouts are communists.

III.   Avoiding Logical Fallacies

Beginning with Aristotle, philosophers have classified and discussed the various kinds of logical fallacies. An author whose name is seldom included in the list is Max Shulman, whose marvelous tale, "Love is a Fallacy," should

---

* The use of slanted language, as used in this paragraph, is discussed in Chapter Eight, page 250.

be on *every* law student's reading list.* Not only is it good for a laugh (a rare-enough commodity in the serious pursuit of legal education), but it describes the perils of fallacious reasoning as well as many philosophical treatises do.

"Love is a Fallacy" is about a clever, logical, supercilious law student who has met a beauteous coed he considers suitable for his companionship in *every* respect, *except intellectually.* He therefore takes on the task of teaching her logic so that she will become a superior intellectual being, worthy of himself.

Read the story to find out how it ends; suffice it to say that along the way the author defines and illustrates the logical fallacies most of us sometimes engage in.

Some of the most common of these logical fallacies are defined and illustrated below:

1. The *Post Hoc* fallacy (short for *post hoc propter hoc,* Latin for "after this, therefore on account of this") is fallacious reasoning suggesting that because one action or event follows another action or event, the second is caused by the first. You've heard people complain, "Every time I make plans to go to the beach, it rains." (Therefore to prevent rain, don't make plans to go to the beach.) If dogs reason, they probably employ the *Post Hoc* fallacy. As you walk past, they bark furiously at you from their yard, and as you continue down the street, they probably get a measure of satisfaction from the belief that they were the cause of your moving on.

2. *Dicto Simpliciter* involves the application of a general rule to cases that are actually exceptions to the rule. For example, "Smoking does not cause cancer. My Uncle Charlie smoked two packs a day, and he lived to be 90." "My Webster's Dictionary does not list the word 'inumbrate.' Therefore you should not use it in your brief." ("My" Webster's may be a *circa* 1900 edition!)

3. *Hasty Generalization,* the converse fallacy, involves jumping to a conclusion without adequate sampling; e.g. "Professor Brown frequently forgets to call roll; college professors certainly are absent-minded." (The conclusion may be correct, but it cannot be deduced without much broader and more representative sampling.)

4. *Non Sequitur* (literally, "it does not follow") consists of a conclusion that does not logically follow from its supposed proof. In fact, the "proof" may have no relationship to the "conclusion" that depends upon it. Consider the statement: "No nation can survive without an all-powerful leader, for without a captain with complete power, a ship would flounder." (Is a ship analogous to a nation?)

5. In the *Ad Hominem* fallacy, a person is attacked for inappropriate reasons. When Al Smith was a candidate for president, opponents attacked

* "Love is a Fallacy" is one of the stories
found in *The Many Loves of Dobie Gillis,*
Aeonian Press, Inc., 1976, page 39.

him because of his religion, not because of his experience, ideology, or actions. Political detractors made fun of President Ford's supposed physical clumsiness, hoping thereby to imply mental ineptness as well. More recently, a vegetarian food bar at an airport was closed because some complained that the manager "looked like a hippie."

6. Closely allied to the *Ad Hominem* attack is a fallacy called "poisoning the well," the question "When did you stop beating your wife?" being the classic example. By basing his question upon the presumed guilt of his adversary the speaker puts him in the untenable position of acknowledging guilt no matter how he answers the question. Unethical attorneys have been known to use such questions in order to trap a witness into making incriminating statements.

7. The "rhetorical question" also becomes a logical fallacy when it is used as an indirect attack. "Is our do-nothing President ever going to take a firm stand on inflation?" is an example. As in "poisoning the well," the rhetorical question is a form of question begging: it fails to prove the presumption on which it rests.

8. Another form of question begging is the use of circular reasoning: "What is a sentence?" "A sentence begins with a capital letter, ends with a period and expresses a complete idea." "How do you know whether the idea expressed is complete?" "Because it begins with a capital letter and ends with a period." The problem with circular reasoning it that it seems to provide an answer but actually does not.

9. The *either/or* fallacy results, say linguists, from the structure of the English language, which seems to suggest polar choices by setting up dichotomies like "right/wrong," "good/bad," and "black/white," instead of considering various possibilities between the opposites. This condition may be utilized deceptively by a lawyer who poses his solution as the only one of two possibilities.

A foreign student enrolled at this university told me he had been misled by the *either/or* character of English. In order to obtain a scholarship, he had to answer the following question: "Have you, at any time, ever plotted to overthrow the United States government or engaged in any subversive activity against it?" The unfortunate fellow thought he had to decide between the two alternatives, and after much soul-searching, he chose one. (Needless to say, he did not get the scholarship.)

10. *Argumentum ad Populum* ("Appeal to the Masses") is a device used by demagogues and other unscrupulous individuals. They appeal to the prejudices of the masses instead of discussing the issues at hand. They may appeal to racial or religious bias, patriotism, or to their listeners' sense of superiority or inferiority—whatever appeal can be expected to cause immediate, unthinking, emotional reaction. During one political campaign, a conservative newcomer to politics characterized the incumbent, who was known as a liberal, as a man who believed in Pragmatism and whose sister was a well-known Thespian. These revelations were reportedly made to rural voters who

were suspicious of "isms," and who may have confused "Thespian" with "Lesbian." At any rate, the incumbent was ousted from his position.

11. In the *Tu Quoque* fallacy ("You do it yourself"), the argument made is that if one person or one group has the right to do something, all other similar persons or groups should also be given that right. This argument is fallacious if (1) the groups are not identical, (2) the situations are not similar, or (3) the "right" should not be held by the first party. For example, university students sometimes argue that because the university administration and faculty can choose curricula and appoint deans and professors, students should also have that right. But the groups are not identical in character because university students are transients and faculty and administrators are relatively permanent. If this distinction makes a difference, the argument is fallacious.

12. The *Fallacy of Misplaced Authority* rests upon the premise that credentials in one area are transferable to another area. Thus the expert in one field becomes automatically expert in another field. So film stars are quoted as pundits on politics, best-selling novelists become authorities on child care, and sports celebrities are quoted on breakfast cereal boxes as nutritionists.

Fallacious also are the opinions of a bona fide authority, who does have credentials in the field under discussion, but whose objectivity is in question. The president of an oil company can hardly be expected to discuss without bias the taxation of oil companies' excess profits, nor can a food scientist who is also a paid consultant to a hamburger chain be expected to offer unbiased testimony on the subject of the nutrition of fast foods.

Chapter Eight

How to Do Your Best in Final Examinations

You are fortunate to be attending law school today. You were probably not greeted at orientation with the ominous warning: "Look at the person on your left. Look at the person on your right. Next semester one of you will be gone."

Most law schools no longer fail a large number of freshmen students. Still, the prospect of that first battery of final examinations looms ahead, and most freshmen approach these examinations with considerable trepidation. And with reason. Law students know that everything (or almost everything) depends on their performance in final examinations.

The end of the first semester is approaching. As a new law student, you have done everything right. You have fully prepared for class, capably answered the professor's questions, and even volunteered comments on your own. Nevertheless an inadequate performance on the final examination can do you in.*

This chapter should help you answer those essay questions competently. You will learn how to present your knowledge so the professor will know *that* you know and *what* you know. Confidence in your ability to write well will allow you a degree of ease and relaxation during the examination.

I. Preparing for the Final Examination

Final exam preparation must start on the first day of class.

(1) Carefully read (and re-read) the assigned material, underlining or highlighting important points. Put a question mark in the margin next to a point you do not understand, and when the point is discussed in class ask about it (or discuss it with your professor after class).

(2) In your class notes, use several colors of ink. For your own thoughts use one color. For other students' comments, use a second color. And for the professor's comments use a third color ink. (Do not make the mistake of assuming that when a professor nods as a student is commenting, the professor necessarily agrees with the student. Professors often nod just to encourage student participation.)

---

* But do all of these things. Not only do some professors give credit for class performance, but you will learn the material better if you participate fully.

240

(3) Before class, write case briefs of the assigned cases in your casebook. In class, correct your case briefs, as necessary. (For the corrections, use the color of ink you reserve for your professor's remarks.)

With preparation like the above, you surely would have received an "A" as an undergraduate. But not, alas, in law school. That is why students find law school a humbling process. You are now competing with the "crème de la crème." Gathered in your law school classes are the students who made the "A's" as undergraduates, and they are all determined to study hard and do well.

Furthermore, the quantity of material to be learned—though massive—is finite, so these highly motivated students will learn it. Finally, most law schools grade examinations "on the curve." All these factors make the competition formidable.

To succeed in law school, you must not only know the subject matter but be able to communicate that knowledge within a stipulated time (that is never sufficient). Moreover, this ability may earn you only a "C+." The students who get the "A's" write examinations that are not only clear, but succinct and well-organized, and have proper emphasis and focus. An essay answer that begins in left field and winds circuitously back to home base, no matter how salient the ideas presented, will not merit an "A." So you may know more about the law than your friend, put it all down on your examination paper, and still receive a "C+" while she gets an "A."

The key word is *practice*. To write well, write; there is no shortcut. Once you have learned the techniques of organization, case analysis, and case synthesis, perfect these by doing as much writing as you can before the final examination arrives. Write outlines of your course material: in standard English, in complete sentences, and in your own words. Don't take the easy route of quoting huge chunks from your casebook. Force yourself to learn and use appropriate legal language.

From your casebook, select cases to analogize and synthesize. Write essay answers to questions your professor or your casebook author has asked. In addition, use the materials at the end of this chapter. There you will find essay-type questions that can be answered by applying the legal rules that precede each set of questions. The questions are similar to final-exam essay questions, and they cover a range of first-year subjects. A sample answer written by a first-year student follows each question. You can check your answer against the answer provided. To expand your answer, add your casebook materials to the given legal rules. This will help you review the course materials as you practice your writing.

II. Taking the Final Examination

The fateful day arrives. You have, by studying and writing answers to practice essay problems, avoided exam-panic that can be so extreme that it prevents adequate performance. Now that the examination lies before you, what is the first thing to do? The obvious answer is also the wrong answer. Do not begin to write immediately, assuming that your ideas will fall into order. Instead, quickly read the entire examination, orienting yourself to the job at hand and deciding how much time to spend on each question. Often the professor has done the latter for you, either by suggesting a time limit for each question or by allotting a specific weight for each question. If he has given no indication of the value of each question, assume that they are all of equal weight and allot equal time to each.

Having done so, don't borrow time from a subsequent question in order to finish answering *this* question. When the time has expired for the question you are answering, leave some space so that you can return to it later, then jot down briefly the points you must still cover, and go on to the next question. If you have time at the end of the exam period, you can finish writing your answer; if not, your professor will at least know by your jottings that you could have done so had there been time.*

As you assess the questions, you may find the first one very difficult. A subsequent question might seem easier to deal with. Especially if they are both of roughly the same weight, don't waste valuable time wrestling with the difficult question. No one says you must answer the questions in order. Go on to the first equally weighted question that seems more manageable. "Warming up" is part of the game. Once you have warmed up on a less difficult question, you will probably find the previously intractable one easier to manage. Furthermore, in the midst of answering another question, you may suddenly receive an insight that will help you answer a previous question. If you do, stop long enough to write down that insight, lest it disappear as suddenly as it arrived.

Once you select the question you will answer first, read it again, slowly, underlining all of the language that seems significant.** Look carefully at the final directions so that you will be sure to comply with them. Then list on your scratch pad the **major issues** that must be resolved before the question can be answered. Leave room between **major issues** for **subissues, legal doctrines,** and **analysis.** Arrange the issues in the order in which you will discuss them.

Several arrangements are possible. Perhaps the most natural is **chronological,** as in a hypothetical problem like the following, in which a single individual is beset by a series of difficulties. The words in boldface are those you would have underlined as you read the problem:

> A, an **adult, rented a boat** from a **small business** at the side of a lake, and was happily fishing when a **heavy tropical rainstorm** occurred. As A hurriedly began to row toward shore, one of the two oars

---

* Sometimes a professor writes an examination that no one in the class can complete in the time given. If you indicate how you would have completed your answer had you had time, you are better off than the students who merely leave the space blank.

** From the underlined language you can extract the key facts. For the definition and discussion of key facts, see Chapters I and II.

broke, slowing his progress substantially. He finally reached land, soaked and shivering, pulled the boat onto the beach and dashed toward a house, **owned by H,** which was **unoccupied and unlocked.** As he went inside to get out of the rain, the floor boards, which were **rotten,** gave way, and A **fell and twisted his ankle.**

A remained in the house, in pain, until the rain subsided, then he managed to row back to the **rental shop. Entering the shop,** A fell on a **broken step** and **banged his head.** The **shopowner,** B, sympathized with A about his fall and A told him that his ankle was very painful. B thereupon told A that he had had **much experience with broken ankles,** and that A's ankle was clearly broken and should be splinted and strapped. Luckily, said B, he had some ace bandage for sale, so A bought the bandage, and B **strapped and splinted A's ankle.**

Several days later, since the ankle continued to be painful and turned blue, A consulted a physician who found that A had a **sprained ankle, worsened by B's ministrations,** a mild **concussion,** resulting **from having struck his head,** and **bronchial pneumonia,** probably from **exposure** to the **rain and cold weather.** Discuss A's possible claims against H and B.

Probably the most effective way to deal with A's several claims is **chronologically.*** At issue, first, is A's status with regard to H, and H's consequent rights and duties vis-a-vis A. The answer to these questions will depend on the key language that you have underlined in your reading. After you have thoroughly discussed A versus H and reached a conclusion, you will move on to A versus B.

In some fact situations, on the other hand, one issue is the **threshold** issue—that issue, a decision about which will obviate any further discussion. When this is the case, you should discuss the threshold issue first. One state Supreme Court decided a threshold issue in a case involving two children who were struck by an automobile while walking home from school. One child was killed and the other severely and permanently injured. The children's father brought an action against (among others) the used car dealer who had sold the automobile, alleging that at the time it left the dealer's control it was defective and not reasonably safe for driving and operation. Two issues arose in the appeal: first, whether as a matter of law, strict liability extends to the seller of a used car and, second, whether a bystander who has been struck by a defective, unreasonably dangerous car may sue under a theory of strict liability.

The court first considered the issue of whether the dealer could be held strictly liable, noting that because this issue was answered in the negative, the second issue need not be considered. The first issue, then, was the **threshold issue,** because its disposition made consideration of the second issue unnecessary.

* For more on this subject, see pages 219–222.

When you are writing your answer to an examination question, however, you do not have the luxury of deleting the other issues even if the answer to the first issue would normally dispose of them. Instead, you should point out that because the court might decide differently, you will now discuss the other issues.

A third method of organization can best be used when a single plaintiff brings a number of actions based on one occurrence. **The action most likely to succeed** should probably be discussed first, then the others, in order of diminishing likelihood of success. Similarly, if one victim has possible claims against a number of individuals, the individual against whom the victim has the strongest claim should be dealt with first. Other factors being equal, priority should be given to the claim against the individual with the "deepest pocket."

Another procedure is to use reverse order, dispensing first (briefly) with the claims least likely to succeed, and so labeling them. For example, when you are discussing a claim of battery, and the only element in question is the intent of the defendant, you might briefly discuss why and how all of the other elements are not in question and then explore fully the issue of intent.

Whatever your decision about the order of the major issues, you will use the space you have left under each one to list **subissues, legal principles,** and **precedents** that you must apply to come to a conclusion about the major issues. If enacted laws apply, show whether they govern the facts of your case.* If cases provide precedent, show that the facts of your case resemble (or differ from) the facts of the precedential cases. It is unlikely that your case will precisely fit either under legal principles or common law precedent. Your job will be to decide whether the hypothetical problem you have been given fits closely enough for the principles and common law precedent to apply. That will require an educated guess about whether the differences between your facts and the precedent are material enough to prevent the application of the legal doctrine governing the precedent or whether the differences in the facts are not material enough to remove your case from the application of the rule.**

Beginning law students tend to think that their conclusions should always be unequivocal: a firm "yes" or "no." In fact, professors seldom present in final examinations hypothetical problems that require such conclusions. So a cautious "perhaps" may turn out to be the proper response—or "probably yes" or "probably no." Whatever your final conclusion, it will be less important than the thoroughness of your analysis.

What you have jotted down on your scratch pad should not have taken you more than one-fifth of the time you have allotted to the question you are answering. If your efforts have been effective, the result of your jottings will

* Enacted laws include constitutions and charters, statutes and ordinances, and court rules that govern procedures to be followed in litigation.

** This is the process of analogizing and distinguishing, discussed in Chapters Four, Five, and Six.

resemble the results of the well-known formula for examination-taking, called IRAC. More law students can repeat the formula than can successfully use it, so I have described how the formula works before naming it. IRAC stands for "issue," "rule," "analysis," and "conclusion." You should check your outline against these steps.

- Have you included all relevant issues and none that are irrelevant?
- Have you arranged them in the best order for discussion?
- Have you utilized all applicable legal authority ("rules")?
- Is your analysis of that authority, as it applies to your facts, complete and objective?
- Have you satisfactorily analogized and distinguished your facts and those of the cases which are most similar to yours?
- Does your conclusion follow logically from these steps?

If so, your answer should be logical, well-structured, and complete.

Consider the following hypothetical fact situation:

A, a college professor, carrying his briefcase in his rear bicycle basket, was bicycling carefully along the bike path parallel to B's house. A loudly barking dog leaning out of a passing car startled A causing him to veer and hit the curb, catapulting A into B's flower garden, bending A's bicycle frame and ruining B's flowers. B observed the incident from his front window, and while A went back to pick up his eyeglasses from the bike path where they had fallen, B snatched A's briefcase. Carrying the briefcase toward his house, B yelled, "When you pay for the damage, you'll get this back." A dashed after B and grabbed back his briefcase so roughly that B fell down, angry but unhurt. A left, carrying his briefcase and dragging his bent bicycle. Discuss possible tort actions of B against A and A against B.

Using a chronological approach, you may decide that the first issue to be resolved is whether B has a cause of action in trespass against A for A's first entry onto B's property. The applicable rule is that a non-volitional entry upon property is no trespass unless the entry is preceded by negligence. A's entry can be characterized as non-volitional by reference to the given facts. You will probably recall similar cases in your casebook that may provide precedent and indicate how the legal rule was interpreted by the courts.

Now you must decide whether to continue with the claims of B against A or to switch to the possible claims of A against B, thus maintaining the chronological approach. Either procedure is acceptable, as long as you are consistent in your development and clearly indicate your procedure.

When you begin to discuss the conduct of A as he grabbed his briefcase from B, you may decide to state the rule that reasonable force necessary to recover possession of chattel after wrongful taking is permissible after fresh pursuit. You should then follow immediately with the issues of whether the degree of force used to retrieve his briefcase was reasonable and whether A's pursuit will be considered "fresh." Reversal of the order of issue and rule will not change the sequence of the other steps, analysis and conclusion.

The IRAC formula may be modified to suit your purpose. You may choose, for example, to begin with the conclusion. If you do, you will be using the deductive method of reasoning.* Be sure, when you use deduction, that you then explain your analysis. You may choose to reverse the issue and rule in an entire question or in part of the question. If you do, the formula you use will be RIAC. And in questions in which the legal rule is supplied, you will extract the issues from the fact situation and apply the rule.

Although you can thus re-arrange the IRAC formula to suit your needs in each situation, be sure to clothe IRAC in appropriate attire. That is, the IRAC skeleton should not be apparent, for IRAC is a structure on which to build, not a final product. Without complete documentation, adequate development, and clear transition, the IRAC formula will be ineffective.

III. Some Do's and Don't's for Better Exam-Writing

Over the years I have read numerous essay examinations written on various topics. When I began to read these exams, I assumed that the writing problems would be as varied as the subject matter. Surprisingly, that is not so. Students' writing, regardless of the subject, contains certain definable and correctable defects. These are discussed below, divided into two categories, problems of content and problems of style. The categories sometimes overlap, and some of the problems are discussed also elsewhere in this book. But they are important enough to collect them and repeat them here.

A. Suggestions Regarding Content:

(1) Be sure you answer the question you were asked. That statement seems too obvious to make, but many of the examination answers I have read contain well-considered answers to a question the professor did not ask. Perhaps the student was careless in his reading of the question; perhaps he was nervous, but the professor is sure to assign another reason: the student could not answer the question asked. The solution: be sure, just before you begin to write, to take one more look at the question.

(2) Begin your answer where the question leaves you. Your answer should not start somewhere else and meander back to the subject under scrutiny later (in *medias res,* as the Greek epics did). Your professor expects a precise answer to appear up front. and will be unwilling to search for an answer hidden deep in the material. No mid-stream answers; begin at the beginning.

---

* For discussion of deduction, see pages 233–236.

(3) Ordinarily, begin your answer with a general statement responding directly to the question asked, indicate how you will break down your answer, and then do so. Keep in mind always the relationship of the points you are making to the question that was asked, and show that relationship in your writing, omitting digression and irrelevancies.

(4) Base your discussion on legal grounds. As a legal professional, the basis for your arguments is the law. The layman is entitled to approach a fact situation intuitively, emotionally, morally, ethically. You must deal with what recourse a party has under the law, what the law *can* do, not what it *ought* to do. (However, if you are asked what the law *should* do, give your most cogent advice.)

(5) Complete your analysis. Do not state the law and fail to relate it to the instant facts. Do not state the law and the facts and fail to analyze and conclude after applying the appropriate law to your facts. Do not state a conclusion without showing how you reached it. (This last flaw in reasoning is called "conclusory" or "conclusionary" reasoning and is almost always severely penalized.) The IRAC formula is useful in checking to be sure your analysis is complete.

(6) Adopt the requested role. If your professor asks you to take the role of an associate advising a law partner about a client's chance of success in a law suit, be objective, not partisan, in your analysis. Avoid polemic and rhetorical flourishes. Even if you have been asked to assume the role of the attorney for a client, don't imitate Perry Mason addressing a jury. Don't jump in on one side of the dispute and argue it heatedly. If your client's case has some weaknesses, acknowledge them and then try to show that they are offset by strengths elsewhere. Your professor is hoping for light, not heat, on the subject.

Above all, do not make your case by omitting, twisting, exaggerating, or otherwise manipulating the facts to your advantage. Don't forget that your professor wrote those facts and will not take kindly to your changing them. You may, however, presume facts that are missing, but necessary to your analysis. Just clearly label these as presumptions.

(7) Don't be misled by the "obvious" question. Your professor is too clever to write simplistic legal problems on your final examination. (If the questions are easy, how can she discriminate among the answers?) The more obvious a question appears to you, the more you should suspect that you may be missing something. If you cannot find anything complex about the question, write the obvious answer, but leave room in case the light should dawn as you are answering a subsequent question.

(8) Just answer the question. Don't teach law or editorialize. Avoid comments like the following:

- The case of *Palsgraf v. Long Island Railroad Co.* is the landmark American case on the question of duty in torts. (Teaching the law)

- It is an unfortunate fact that the *McCall* rule, when applied to this case, bodes ill for the defendant. (Editorializing)

(9) Usually, be a "putter-inner." This rule is not invariable. Some professors prefer succinctness and selectivity. But one professor tells me that the difference between the "B" and the "D" students in his classes is that the former are "putter-inners" and the latter are "leaver-outers." He means that not only must the analysis be complete, but that all possible issues must be explored, even those that may be unlikely or farfetched. If your professor fits this description, include all possible issues and arguments.

B. Suggestions Regarding Style

(1) Keep your own personality out of your writing. Write with ideas instead. Therefore avoid the first person approach, as in "I think," "I believe," "I would suggest." Worst of all is "I feel," an expression anathema to many law professors, who expect a cerebral rather than a visceral response to their examination questions. Almost as annoying is the folksy "we" approach, as in "we must consider carefully," or "we will next discuss."

Instead of the first person use third person, as in "the defendant is probably liable" (not "I think the defendant is liable"). The effect of your writing will be less biased, the writing more succinct with the third person approach. Some examples follow:

This	Not This
The facts indicate	I have found that the facts indicate
The courts concur	In my research, I find that courts concur
The next issue	Let us consider the next issue
The evidence suggests	It is my opinion, based on the evidence

(2) Don't strike a pose. To achieve style, affect none. Call attention to what you are saying, not how you are saying it. Write like a person, not a personage. Explain even complicated ideas clearly, succinctly, and with appropriate legal language. The affectation of elegance and the appearance of profundity will not enhance good ideas nor mask their absence.

(3) Say it precisely and say it once. Writing is unlike speeches, in which you are advised to say what you are going to say, say it, then say what you have said. In written material, the reader can look back if he wants reiteration. If you are using language like "In other words," or "Again," or "That is," you are probably being repetitive.

(4) Don't try for either superiority or humility. Certain language creates the appearance of pompousness and arrogance; for example, "without question," or "it is evident that," or "obviously." (If you were a professor, would you like your test question to be described as "obvious"?) Avoid, also, self-deprecating comments like "I may not have discussed this fully," or "More could probably be said," or even "(sp.?)" after words you think may be misspelled. A good maxim is: Don't assert your superiority; your professor may not agree. Don't advertise your shortcomings; your professor may not notice them.

(5) Properly emphasize. Don't deal with all issues as if they were equal. Knowing which to highlight and which to subordinate and how much space to give each may make a difference in your grade.

(6) Make persons (plaintiffs, courts, companies) the subjects of your analysis. Compare the following statements:

- In the present case, a plea bargain was negotiated with a sentence of two years. However, after demanding and receiving a jury trial, the sentence received was ten years.

- Although the defendant could have negotiated a sentence of two years if he had agreed to plea-bargaining, he insisted on a jury trial and received a sentence of ten years.

  In the second statement, the writer has said **who, what,** and **whom.** One way to do this is to use active verbs, which help you put persons into the subject slots.

(7) Don't begin by saying what is *not* possible. Don't raise arguments only to deny their validity. Avoid starts like the following:

- The plaintiff might claim emotional distress, but that action would fail.

- Given the present circumstances, both *Mink* and *O'Brien* are weak precedential authority. Using *Mink* and *O'Brien* will only point to other theories that might apply.

(8) Generally, do not restate the facts of the hypothetical problem you are supposed to address. The professor knows what she asked; don't paraphrase it and give it back to her. She will not take kindly to the waste of her time and your space.

(9) Generally, do not state the law in the abstract before applying it to the question. Go to the heart of the matter at once. The skill your professor is trying to measure is whether you can apply the law to the given facts, analyze thoroughly, and conclude. One professor recently complained that many students learn the law in their first year of law school, but do not learn how to apply it until much later—and sometimes not at all. Don't let this criticism apply to you.

(10) Avoid hyperbole. It weakens your argument. For example, one student wrote, "That was a bald, unmitigated lie." That kind of bombast does your argument no good. The student might better

have written, "That was not true." Hyperbole is intended to make your writing more forceful, but it has the opposite effect. It dulls your reader's sensibilities and discredits your assertions. And it is unprofessional.

(11) Avoid slanted language. Like hyperbole, slanted language tends to weaken your credibility. The words to avoid are those that are sometimes called "purr" and "growl" words, and they tend to diminish the effect of your good reasoning. As in an inter-office memorandum, the language should have the appearance of objectivity. Avoid sentences like the following:

- The uproarious screams of the unruly gang terrified the poor plaintiff, who was gravely injured as she escaped.

(12) Don't make jokes.

It's strange but true that some students write comments they think are funny in their examinations. Perhaps they do so out of nervousness or tension. Whatever the reason, be aware that what may seem funny to you in your stressful situation will probably seem distinctly un-funny to the professor as he grades your paper in his study, intent only on assessing your understanding of the subject matter.

(13) Use past tenses for discussing decided case, present tense for stating rules derived from them:

The *Surocco* court **held** for the defendant, who **had ordered** the plaintiff's house blown up to stop a fire. The court **said** that a house on fire **is** a nuisance, which **is** lawful to abate.

(14) Spell correctly. Avoid the "I've told you and told you" criticism. Some professors place considerable weight on correct spelling and may penalize students who spell words incorrectly. I can recall one professor who marked every misspelling of *judgment* on a student's paper with red ink. Unfortunately for the student, he had used that word more than ten times on his test papers, and by the tenth time the professor had marked it, she bore down so heavily with her ballpoint pen that it looked as if she had broken the point. That is why I have dubbed the criticism the "I've told you and told you" criticism. To the professor it seemed as if she had told the student over and over about that one misspelled word. Though the student had made only one spelling error, to the professor it seemed like ten.

C. Suggestions Regarding Organization

(1) Use a separate paragraph for each issue. The first sentence of each paragraph is usually the topic sentence. Deal with subordinate issues immediately following the main issues from which they arise.

(2) Place arguments in their most effective order, with those most likely to succeed up front. Or dispense with less cogent arguments first, but briefly, and so label them.

(3) Write in paragraphs of about four to six sentences. Fewer sentences indicate incomplete development of ideas. More sentences than six probably indicate the inclusion of unrelated ideas—or redundance. Proper paragraphing makes your writing appear well organized.

(4) Separate and clearly label pro and contra arguments, e.g., liabilities and defenses to liabilities.

(5) If space is no problem, leave some room after each answer for possible later inspiration. In allocating time, leave a few minutes at the end for editing.

(6) Finally, bear in mind the theory of the Greek Anaxagoras, teacher of Socrates, about the origin of the universe: "All things were in chaos when mind arose and created order." Socrates, hearing this, reasoned that man, thinking for himself, could bring similar order to human affairs. Your job is to bring order to the mass of unorganized data presented in your essay examinations—and awaiting you in your legal practice.

IV. Problems for Exam–writing Practice

The suggestions for exam-writing you have just read should help you write more effective examination answers. But more important than reading *how* to write well is to write, write, write. Therefore the following materials will provide for you hands-on writing practice of the kind you will be doing in those final exams. The problems provided range from simple to moderately complex, but you will need to use the same analytical skills to answer them all. They differ only in complexity, not in kind, and as you improve you will be able to handle the most complicated examination questions as easily as simple ones.

The legal areas the problems cover are those you study during the first year of law school: criminal, tort, property, and contract law. The legal rules you need to apply in order to answer the problems are stated at the beginning of each set. One caveat: the rules that are given are not necessarily the law in your jurisdiction, nor are the rules exhaustive. They are provided so that you can by-pass legal research and concentrate on improving your legal analysis and writing.

After each problem is a sample answer written by a first-year law student. It is not a model answer, but it does contain competent legal analysis, applied to the problem. The sample answers are guides, not blueprints. Your answer will not be a carbon copy of the sample answer; in fact, your answer may be better.

After you have answered a few of the exam-questions, begin to time yourself as you write answers. Students responding to similar problems in a classroom setting required about 40 minutes to answer the more complex problems. Shorter questions should take about 25 or 30 minutes to answer. If you take longer than the suggested times, you need to keep practicing your analysis and writing. As you write more and more, you will find you write more quickly. If, on the other hand, you are finishing your answers more quickly than suggested, check to make sure your analysis is thorough. The ability to answer exam-questions quickly and thoroughly is a valuable attribute in law school.

Writing answers to the problems in this book is only a beginning. Check your casebooks for questions that require essay-type answers. When your professor suggests additional reading and analysis of legal problems, don't just think about how you would answer them, force yourself to write down answers. It is painful to force yourself to organize your thoughts and get them on paper, but (as used to be said in another context) "no pain, no gain."

Finally, your law library may contain old essay examinations your professors have put on file. Tackle those questions. Students sometimes complain to me that the questions do not include sample answers! But more valuable than sample answers is the clue you obtain to your professor's examination style as you read and try to answer those exam-questions.

Writing Problems

General Directions: Using only the given legal rules, write answers to the legal problems that follow. You need no additional rules to answer the problems, although you can add to the given rules additional rules you have learned in class. You may not need to use all of the rules in order to answer every question.

Writing Problems and Sample Answers

Set I

Legal Rule

Burglary: Breaking and entering into the dwelling of another in the nighttime with the intent of committing larceny.

Definitions

1. "Dwelling": Someone must live therein or have lived there and intend to return.

2. "Nighttime": Between an hour after sunset and an hour before sunrise.

3. "Breaking": Force, however slight, must be used in entering, and the entry be without the consent of the occupant. Some part of the body must enter, or an implement which is then used to effect the crime.

4. "Larceny": The taking and carrying away, with the intent to steal, of the personal property of another.

Problem I

The E.Z. Marks had bought a new home. They moved all their possessions into it, but left the premises at 6 P.M. to stay overnight at a motel because their electricity had not yet been connected. Atilla Z. Hun entered the house through an open window. He carried out silver and china, leaving through the back door, which he had unlocked from the inside. Is Hun guilty of burglary?

Answer to Problem I

A.Z. Hun's conduct fulfills one of the elements of burglary: by taking silver and china from the Marks' house with the intent to steal, he has committed larceny. The intent to steal can probably be imputed to Hun since he entered without the consent of the owners and through an open window.

Three questions remain, however. The first is whether Hun's action occurred at night. Since the facts indicate that the Marks ceased moving their possessions into the house because of darkness, Hun probably entered the house after dark, and thus an hour or more after sunset, satisfying the definition of "nighttime." Even if that requirement is satisfied, however, there is a second question of whether Hun's entry was into a dwelling. The rule states that in order to be a dwelling, someone must live there. Since the Marks had not yet moved in, the house may not qualify under this definition. The court must decide whether a house, prepared for next-day occupancy, qualifies as a dwelling.

The third issue is whether Hun's action meets the definition of "breaking." Since his entry was through an open window, it does not, for some force must be used to achieve the entry, and Hun used no force. The unlocking of the door might meet the definition of "force, however slight," but Hun unlocked the door to leave, not to enter.

Hun will therefore probably not be found guilty of burglary, since his behavior fails to satisfy at least one of the required elements.

Problem II

At 10 P.M., while Ben Zene was at the movies, Ken Twin climbed the high fence surrounding Zene's house and entered the porch through the unlocked porch door. He then loaded all of the porch furniture onto the back of his pickup truck. Although the living room windows which opened onto the porch were locked, Ken was able to maneuver one open by using a long wire. He climbed through that window, intending to take items from the house, but, hearing a noise, decided to leave hurriedly instead. Discuss.

Answer to Problem II

Ken Twin is probably guilty of burglary for his first act of removing the porch furniture and putting it into his truck. He had the requisite intent to commit larceny, and his entry through the unlocked porch door will probably constitute "force, however slight." Whether the porch will be considered a dwelling under the given rules is a second issue. If it is so defined, Twin has committed burglary even before he entered Zene's house itself.

Twin is also guilty of burglary for his second act, entry into Zene's house. (1) He had, as he entered, the intent to commit larceny; (2) he used force (the wire) in gaining entry; and (3) he entered without the occupant's consent. The actual absence of the owner does not change his occupant status, nor the status of his home as a dwelling. Twin's change of mind about the burglary does not nullify the "intent" requirement; the intent must only be present at the time of the entry.

Problem III

At 2 A.M., M.I. Tired, intoxicated and seeing a house that appeared empty, broke a window, climbed through it into the house, and went to sleep on the livingroom rug. The house is unoccupied, since its owner, Fig Nuton, is away on reserve military service. When M.I. awakens four hours later, he notices—with the first rays of daylight—Nuton's valuable coin collection and decides to take it. He leaves with the coins through the back door. Has M.I. Tired committed burglary?

Answer to Problem III

M.I.'s conduct satisfies some of the elements of burglary. He has committed larceny after breaking and entering a dwelling. The absence of the owner does not change the status of the house as a dwelling, if the owner intends to return, and the facts indicate that he does. M.I.'s breaking of the window satisfies the breaking requirement, and the owner has not consented to the entry. The nighttime requirement is satisfied despite the actual occurrence of the larceny during the daytime, since M.I. entered at night, and intent on entry is relevant under the rule.

However, the "intent" requirement for burglary is absent here. M.I. broke into Nuton's house only to sleep, not to commit larceny. The requirement of intent is not met when he later changed his mind. The jury may, however, infer intent from M.I.'s behavior, disbelieving M.I.'s claim that he did not intend to take the coin collection at the moment he entered the house. If so, M.I. will probably be found guilty of burglary.

Problem IV

Ima Thief worked as a cleaning woman for the D. Zasters. They regularly provided her with a key by which she could enter to clean during their absence. She had secretly taken that key to the L. Icit Key Company and had a duplicate key made.

Since she knew that the Zasters were away on vacation, Ima entered the house with her duplicate key, broke the lock on a wall safe, and exited with the contents. The time at which this occurred is uncertain. Ima says that the incident occurred at 3 P.M., but a neighbor of the Zasters says she saw Ima in the yard of the Zaster house at 9 P.M., although she did not see Ima entering or leaving the Zaster house. Is Ima guilty of burglary?

Answer to Problem IV

Ima Thief's conduct fulfilled some of the elements of burglary:

She intended her act, and she committed larceny. The Zasters' house, though empty at the time, was a dwelling according to the legal definition, and Ima's entry was without the consent of the Zasters.

The crucial issues to be determined are (1) whether entry by a duplicate key, achieved illegally, constitutes a "breaking" and (2) whether the jury will believe Ima's statement that the incident occurred at 3 P.M.

Entry by an illegally-gained key will almost certainly constitute "breaking," the slight force being Ima's using the key to open the lock and pushing the door (or pulling it) open. With regard to the second issue, the jury will have to decide whether the neighbor really saw Ima in the Zasters' yard at 9 P.M. If the jury believes the neighbor, it may well conclude that the incident occurred at night and not, as Ima asserts, at 3 P.M. The jury will then probably find Ima guilty of burglary.

Writing Problems and Sample Answers

Set II

Legal Rules

I. Because there is a duty to conduct oneself with the care for others that a reasonable person would take, negligent conduct is that which imposes an unreasonable risk upon others.

II. A causal link must exist between a negligent act and the harm suffered by the victim of it (the act is the cause-in-fact, "but for" which no harm would have occurred).

III. If customary practice is dangerous, conforming to that practice may not prevent one's conduct from being negligent.

IV. If a person contributes proximately to his own injuries, he is barred from recovery (contributory negligence); if a person, voluntarily, with knowledge of the hazard, places himself in a position of danger, he assumes the risk and is barred from recovery (assumption of risk).

V. If a person fails to exercise a "last clear chance" to prevent injury to another, he is liable despite contributory negligence by the other person.

VI. Violation of a state statute constitutes negligence per se.

Problem I

Spectators at college football games held in Rah–Rah Stadium customarily use their programs to make small paper airplanes which they sail through the air toward the playing field. Abel attended the Paluka U. versus Rah–Rah U. game, and after a Rah–Rah touchdown he and other fans hurled these airplanes, with some vigor, downward through the air. At that moment Baker stood up, turned around, and waved to friends in the stands above. Abel's airplane struck Baker's eye, causing considerable damage to the cornea and necessitating surgery.

Discuss Baker's claims and his chance for success against Abel.

Answer to Problem I

Baker (B) may have a cause of action in negligence against Abel (A) because the tossing of paper airplanes in a crowded football stadium may be considered to impose unreasonable risk upon other persons. If so, the argument that A was engaging in a customary activity along with others will not succeed. Courts have held that, even when the custom, dangerous activity may be considered negligent.

B would not have suffered harm except for A's act; thus there is a causal link between B's injury and A's tossing of the airplane. A may argue, however, that B assumed the risk of injury from flying paper planes when he attended the football game. Unless A was an out-of-town visitor who did not know of the Rah–Rah custom, this argument may succeed.

A may have another argument under the theory of contributory negligence. "But for" B's standing up and looking up into the stands, the airplane may have struck him on the back of his head, without harm. The question, then, is whether B's act contributed to his injury when, aware of the airplanes floating through the air all around him, he stood up and looked upward. If so, B will be barred from recovering.

B's chance for success in his claim will depend on (1) whether A's conduct in tossing paper airplanes violated the duty of care for others, (2) and if so, whether B assumed the risk of injury by attending the game, (3) or whether B negligently contributed to the accident by looking back and upwards while airplanes were being tossed. The court may well find that B's contributory acts bar him from recovering from A's behavior.

Problem II

I. Ken Duit drove his car to his eye doctor's office for an eye examination. The doctor put drops in Ken's eyes, blurring Ken's vision, and suggested that Ken wait for two hours before driving home in order for his eyes to return to normal. After half an hour Ken grew bored and decided to leave, although his vision was still somewhat blurred. As he drove along slowly and carefully, he came to a section of the road where construction was taking place and crews of workers were working, having parked their trucks in the bicycle path along the side of the road.

At this time I. Mae Student was bicycling home from classes. Seeing the construction trucks parked on the bicycle path and the crews at work next to them on the edge of the roadway, she decided she would be safer biking on the left side of the road facing oncoming cars than on the right side of the road in the stream of traffic. (A state statute requires that bicyclists either use bicycle paths or ride in the stream of automobile traffic.)

Ken, driving as far as possible to his right in order to leave plenty of room for oncoming vehicles on his left, failed to see Mae and hit her bicycle, causing injuries to Mae. Discuss Mae's negligence claim against Ken.

Answer to Problem II

Ken has the duty to conduct himself with the care that a reasonable person would have for others. In driving with blurred vision despite his doctor's advice, Ken fails in this duty. If his action is the cause-in-fact of Mae's injury Ken will be liable for negligence, according to the given legal rules.

In addition, although the facts do not say so, a state statute may prohibit persons from driving with impaired vision. If so, Ken is in violation of it and therefore negligent per se.

However, Mae's negligence claim may fail because the "but for" link between Ken's behavior and Mae's injury is not established. Mae's own actions may have contributed to her injury. By bicycling on the left side of the road she was, in fact, negligent per se because she was in violation of a state statute. However, Mae can defend against that charge by arguing that it was necessary for her own safety to ignore the statute. In this case, with trucks parked on the bikeway, Mae may have been within her rights to choose what seemed to be a safer alternative.

Her choice may bar her from recovery, however. By riding her bicycle facing traffic, Mae placed herself in a position of danger. She thus "assumed the risk" and contributed toward the harm that she received. She could have instead dismounted from the bicycle and walked it along in whatever paths were provided for pedestrians. If, in so doing, she had been forced to use the roadway and had been struck by Ken, her claim against him would have been much stronger, for vehicle drivers should expect pedestrians to walk on the left and drivers have a duty of care to avoid hitting them.

As it is, Mae's likelihood of success is small. Even if Ken is held negligent for driving with blurred vision, Mae will probably be barred from recovery because of assumption of risk and contributory negligence.

Problem III

Rae C. Driver is driving south in a 35-mile-an-hour zone at 35 miles an hour. The traffic light at the intersection is red as she approaches it, but it suddenly turns green and she continues through it without slowing down. Meanwhile, D.E. Termind is approaching the same intersection, driving east at 35 miles an hour. He sees Rae coming toward him at his left, but the traffic light is still yellow, so he continues through, because it is legal to continue through a yellow traffic light. He assumes Rae will apply her brakes because the light is still red in her direction. D.E.'s assumption is wrong, and Rae's car hits his. Discuss liability.

Answer to Problem III

Both parties are liable for negligence. By not slowing down as she approached a red traffic signal, Rae C. Driver imposed an unreasonable risk upon others. Her conduct was the cause-in-fact of the harm that she and D.E. Termind suffered; "but for" her negligence, the collision would not have occurred.

On the other hand, "but for" D.E. Termind's attempt to beat Driver's approaching car by proceeding through the intersection, the collision would not have occurred. D.E. Termind's conduct may therefore be considered to be the cause-in-fact of the accident.

His conduct will also be considered negligent because of the "last clear chance" rule. Seeing Driver approaching, he had the final opportunity to slow down and stop on the yellow light, thus averting the collision. Even if Termind is not held negligent for failing to take advantage of the last clear chance to avoid the accident, he will probably be barred from recovery because of contributory negligence or assumption of risk. His behavior contributed to the accident, and he chose to assume the risk of crossing the intersection in front of an oncoming car.

Writing Problems and Sample Answers

Set III

Legal Rules

I. A person is liable to another for battery if he acts intending to cause a harmful or offensive contact with another, or the apprehension of such contact, and harmful or offensive contact results.

    A. If a person intends a harmful or offensive contact with another, or intends to cause apprehension of a harmful or offensive contact with another, and harmful or offensive contact with a third person results instead, the one causing the harm or offense is liable to the third person.

    B. In order for a person to be harmed or offended, he need not himself be touched; anything so closely connected with his body as to be customarily regarded as part of his person is considered to be part of himself.

II. A person is liable to another for assault if he acts intending to cause a harmful or offensive contact or apprehension of an imminent contact to another person and he thereby causes the other person to be apprehensive of an imminent contact.

    A. Assault lies even though the person gives the other person the opportunity to avoid the result by obeying a command, unless the first person is privileged to enforce the command.

    B. Mere words do not constitute assault.

III. A person is not liable for otherwise actionable conduct in assault or battery if the receiver of the conduct has consented to it or if public interest in the conduct is great enough to justify the harm caused or threatened to the receiver.

    A.   Anyone subjected to assault or battery has the privilege of using reasonable force to protect himself, but exceeding this privilege will make him the aggressor.

    B.   Consent to conduct is terminated if the person to whom the consent was given exceeds the bounds of the consent.

Problem I

Alfred and Betty are friends who enjoy practical jokes and often play them on each other. Without any ill will and entirely as a joke, Alfred hangs a bucketful of cornmeal over a closed door in such a way that when Betty opens the door the cornmeal will fall on her. The trick works; Betty is covered with cornmeal. Being a good sport Betty laughs at first. Later, however, she develops an eye infection from the cornmeal and requires extensive medical treatment. Betty is now considering legal action. What likelihood has she of success?

Answer to Problem I

Betty (B) may have a cause of action against Alfred (A) in battery. A intended to place the cornmeal so that it would fall on B. The resulting contact may well be considered enough to constitute the "offensive contact" required for battery. That A did not intend to cause the eye infection that occurred does not reduce his liability for his action, since he did intend the conduct that resulted in the eye infection. The question is whether A intended an offensive or harmful contact. The facts state that A had no "ill will" and intended his prank "entirely as a joke." Without the intent to cause offense or harm, there can be no battery.

Also crucial in deciding A's liability for battery is whether B had consented to his conduct. If B's consent to their practical joking relationship is held to constitute her implicit consent to his cornmeal prank, A will not be held liable for battery, even if he did intend an offensive contact, unless the bounds of B's consent are judged to have been exceeded in this case.

A may argue that B, by her initial reaction of laughter following the incident, signified that she did not consider the bounds of her consent to have been exceeded. However, B's interest in pursuing a claim against A indicates that, at least after her initial laughter, she did consider her consent to their practical joking relationship to have been exceeded by A's conduct in this incident.

B's delay in taking action will not preclude her recovery of damages. There is no requirement that the victim of harmful or offensive conduct bring suit without delay. If the court is convinced that A intended an offensive or harmful contact that was not impliedly consented to by B, or if it believes A's conduct exceeded the bounds of B's consent, B will succeed in her action against A for battery.

Problem II

A. Player is playing tennis with a friend, B. Tsim, a much better player. A does not like to lose, and as the game progresses he becomes more and more irritable. Finally when B wins the set, A runs to the net brandishing his racquet and yells, "Duck, or I'll hit this ball right into your face!" He then hits the ball wildly. B ducks. A intended to miss B even if B did not duck, and the ball does not come close to B. However it does strike C. Knott, who is behind a bush out of A's vision, searching for a lost ball. C suffers a concussion. What is A liable for, if anything?

Answer to Problem II

Both B and C may bring suit against A. A is liable to B for assault. A drove the tennis ball toward B intending to cause B apprehension of an imminent offensive or harmful contact. Although A provided B with an option by which B could escape harm, A is still liable, for A is not privileged to enforce his command ("Duck!"). Since B did duck, he clearly expected that otherwise the ball was likely to hit him, and feared injury as a result. Although mere words do not constitute assault, the words here were reinforced by conduct that is actionable.

Although A may argue that he was only joking and thus lacked the requisite intent to offend or harm B, the context indicates that this is not true. The further argument by A that B's consent to play tennis encompassed consent to A's final action will probably fail because A's conduct exceeds the bounds of what is normal in a game of tennis.

C has no claim against A in assault, for he did not see the tennis ball that A hit wildly toward C and therefore did not suffer apprehension of imminent contact. C does have a claim against A in battery although A did not intend to strike C with the ball and in fact was not even aware of C's presence behind the bush.

All of the elements requisite for C's claim of battery are present. A intended by his act to cause apprehension of imminent contact. That this apprehension occurred in B, not C, does not remove A's liability. A's liability extends to C, the injured third person. As to the argument that A struck C only by mistake, that fact does not eliminate A's liability to C. When intent to commit battery is present, and an unintended victim receives the action, the doer of the act is liable to that person just as if he were the intended victim. C therefore has a cause of action in battery against A.

In order to answer the next set of problems, you will need to add the following legal rules to those you have been using. Remember that all rules do not necessarily apply to all the problems.

Legal Rules

IV. If a person intends to confine another within fixed boundaries or if his action results in such a confinement and if the other person is conscious of or harmed by the confinement, the first person is liable for false imprisonment:

   A. If the person confining another person does not intend to do so, and

   B. If the confinement is transitory or otherwise harmless, the first person is not liable.

V. A person is privileged to retake property that another person has wrongfully taken from him, after first asking the taker to return it. If the first person is mistaken in his belief that the property was taken, the privilege is nullified.

VI. A person who recklessly or intentionally causes severe emotional distress to another is subject to liability for that distress and, if bodily harm results to the second person, is liable for that harm as well.

   A. In order for language to be reckless it must be so outrageous as to exceed the bounds of decency.

   B. A person is liable to a third person for emotional distress for conduct described in V (above) if that person is a member of the immediate family of the person at whom the conduct was directed, whether or not the third person suffers bodily harm, and to any other person present who suffers bodily harm from the conduct of the actor.

Problem III

While shopping at a grocery store, Ms. K. Smart (K) saw a five-pound bag of sugar with one price sticker placed over another. The top sticker read "$3.00," but K peeled it off and found another reading "$2.50." When she attempted to pay for the sugar at the checkout counter, the Checker (C) noticed that the top sticker had been removed and said to K, "What a cheat! What a gyp! It's cheats like you that make food prices go up!" K had already placed $2.50 on the counter, and, very upset at C's words, she picked up the sugar and headed for the door.

The store manager (M), hearing the checker's words, assumed that K had not paid for the sugar, and he stopped in front of K as she was about to leave the store. K pushed M to one side in order to get to the door, saying, "Get out of my way, you Jerk!" M attempted to take the sugar out of K's hand, but instead knocked her pocketbook to the floor, causing it to open and the contents to spill out. M then stepped aside, and K picked up her belongings and left the store, carrying the sugar. What liability, if any arises from this incident?

Answer to Problem III

K has no claim in assault against C because "mere words" do not suffice for an action in assault. As to a claim of intentional infliction of emotional distress by K against C, two elements of the tort are present: (1) C's words were uttered intentionally and (2) for the purpose of causing K distress. However, mere insults are not enough to activate this tort and C's words, though unfair and unkind, fall within the description of mere insults. To be actionable, the language would have to be describable as "outrageous" by a reasonable person.

M, in attempting to bar K's exit, may be liable for false imprisonment. His act seems intended to keep K inside the store. She was aware of her confinement, as evidenced by her pushing M aside in order to depart. However, the fact that she was able to push him out of her way will probably nullify her claim of false confinement.

With regard to K's liability to M in battery, this action will also probably fail. Although K's words were accompanied by an action offensive to M (pushing him) she is privileged to free herself from her confinement, and her effort to do so does not seem excessive.

M's conduct, in trying to grab the sugar from K, is unprivileged, whether he was reacting to K's shove or attempting to regain possession of merchandise he believed had not been paid for. He is privileged to use reasonable force in protecting himself against K's shove, but his grabbing of the sugar was not in self-protection, but an attempt to regain possession of the sugar. His effort in this respect is not privileged, for (1) he must request that K give him the sugar before trying to re-take it, and (2) the privilege to regain possession is nullified because he is mistaken in his belief that K has not paid for it. (Even if K owes an additional 50 cents for the sugar, the first reason nullifies any privilege of M.)

Whether M is liable for battery against K for knocking her pocketbook to the floor will depend upon whether his offensive intent was directed at some item closely related to K's person. If he had intended contact with K's pocketbook, he would be probably liable for battery, because a woman's pocketbook is so closely associated with her body as to be considered a part of her person. But although M's offensive contact was with K's pocketbook, he intended contact with the sugar. Unless the bag of sugar is considered so closely associated with K that an intended offensive contact with it is equivalent to an intended offensive contact with K herself, M will not be liable for battery.

The likelihood is therefore that none of the behavior described in the fact situation is actionable in torts: neither C's conduct toward K, nor K's conduct toward M, nor M's conduct toward K.

Problem IV

Two 12–year–old boys, Cain (C) and Abel (A), are playing a game of throwing stones at each other on the sidewalk in front of their house. A stone thrown by A hits C on the head, causing C considerable pain. In retaliation, C hurls a stone at A, which misses A and knocks off the hat of a pedestrian (P) who is walking past.

Thinking that A had thrown the stone, P angrily grabs A and shakes him, saying, "I'm going to knock your block off." A kicks and hits P until P frees A and leaves, threatening to have A arrested. Discuss tort liability.

Answer to Problem IV

Regarding A's liability to C: C was harmed by a stone that A threw at him intentionally. In order to satisfy the requirements of battery, A must have intended to cause the harmful or offensive contact. The element of assault may be present if C saw the stone approaching and was apprehensive of imminent, offensive contact.

However, A will probably not be held liable to C because C has consented to A's conduct by agreeing to play the game—and in fact was also engaging in throwing stones. C's consent will eliminate liability for an act for which A would otherwise be liable.

Regarding C's liability to P: C is liable to P for battery because C acted intending to cause a harmful or offensive contact (throwing the stone) and did so when the stone struck P's hat. The hat that was knocked from P's head is so closely connected with P that it will probably be considered part of P's person. If P saw the stone before it reached him, C may also be liable to P in assault, for placing P in apprehension of an imminent contact. However, since P did not know who had thrown the stone, he may not have seen it before he was struck, removing C's assault liability.

If A was placed in reasonable apprehension of imminent physical harm by P's threat, accompanied by P's act of shaking A, P is liable for assault. Whether P actually intended to "knock [A's] block off" is not relevant if A was apprehensive that P would do so. Even if P did not harm A by shaking him, if A was offended by that act, P is liable to A for battery since P's behavior was intentional and without privilege.

P may also be liable to A for false imprisonment. By holding his arm, P briefly prevented A from getting away. A was aware that he was confined, as indicated by his struggle to free himself. However, P may argue that he did not intend to confine A, only to retaliate for A's supposed act of striking P's hat with a stone. Since A's confinement was only transitory and since A was not harmed by it, P's defense against the charge of false imprisonment may succeed.

Finally, regarding A's kicking and hitting of P: Since A acted in order to escape from P, who had mistakenly confined A, A will probably not be held liable to P for battery. One is permitted to defend himself against another unless one's reaction is excessive, which it does not seem to have been in this case.

Writing Problems and Sample Answers

Set IV

All of the rules below may not be applicable to each problem, and the usual caution applies: the rules are not complete and should not be relied upon in answering problems other than those posed here.

Legal Rules

(Possession of Personal Property) *

I. Possession of property consists of physical possession plus the intent to possess and exclude others from possession.

II. Possession is a basic property interest carrying certain rights such as:

    A. the right to continue peaceful possession against everyone except those who have a better right;

    B. the right to recover possession when the property is wrongfully taken.

III. The finder of property has certain rights:

    A. the finder of lost property on the land of another acquires title against all but the true owner, especially when the finder is not a trespasser;

    B. the finder of "treasure trove"—coins or money secreted by an unknown owner—has the same rights as the finder of lost property;

    C. the finder of abandoned property (property voluntarily relinquished by its owner) is entitled to possession and title of the property;

    D. the finder of misplaced property, however, does not obtain title, but the owner of the property on which it was found is considered to be the holder of the goods for the true owner.

Problem I

One A. Hunter was engaged, with his hounds, in the hot pursuit of a fox in a wild, unpossessed area. N. Termeddler, happening upon the scene and seeing that the fox was tiring, killed the fox and carried it away. A. Hunter sued for the value of the fox and received a judgment in his favor; N. Termeddler now appeals. You are a judge in the court of appeals; write an opinion for the court.**

* From C.H. Smith and R.E. Boyer, *Survey of the Law of Property*, 2nd Ed., 1971, pp. 456–457.

** These facts are adapted from a famous early legal decision which you may wish to read. See Pierson v. Post, 3 Caines 175 (Supreme Court of N.Y., 1805).

Answer to Problem I

Wild animals living in their natural state are owned by no one. Therefore a person who (1) has the intent to possess the animal and exclude others from possession and (2) gains physical possession of the animal is the rightful owner.

A. Hunter (A) intended to possess the fox and was engaged in the effort to capture it. However he had not yet mortally wounded the fox, nor had he brought it under certain control in any other way. Mere pursuit of a wild animal, although accompanied by the intent to capture it, does not convey the right of possession.

N. Termeddler's (N's) interception of A's pursuit of the fox and his subsequent gaining of physical possession of the animal satisfied the two requirements of possession: intent to possess exclusively and physical possession. N's conduct may have been unkind and discourteous, but A has no legal remedy available to him. Therefore the judgment of the court in awarding ownership of the fox to A was erroneous and should be reversed. This court finds in favor of the plaintiff, N. Termeddler.

Problem II

Four boys were playing, as was their custom, in a vacant lot. One of the boys found what looked like a large ball of used twine that had been re-wound for later use and then either lost or thrown away. The boys played with the ball of twine for some time, throwing it from one to the other until it finally began to unravel, revealing that the center was composed of old paper currency in the amount of $10,000. The boy who found the ball now claims the money. Is his claim likely to be upheld by a court?

Answer to Problem II

The boy's entitlement to the money inside the ball of twine depends first of all upon whether the twine had been lost, abandoned, or misplaced. If the ball of twine had been abandoned, the finder has title superior to that of any other person. If the twine had been lost or is classified as treasure trove, the finder has rights superior to all but the right of the true owner. If the twine is classified as misplaced, the lot owner may hold it for its true owner.

In this fact situation the true owner of the twine is making no claim for it and is, in fact, unknown. The twine may well be considered to be lost property. Then the only claim to the money other than that of the finder would be that of the owner of the vacant lot, if the boys were trespassers upon the lot when they found the twine. Since they were in the habit of playing on the lot, they will probably not be considered trespassers. If they are not trespassers, the boy who found the twine may be held to be the rightful owner.

The question now becomes whether the boy who found the twine can be said to have found the money enclosed within the ball of twine. It is arguable that he did not, but that the money was not found until it was revealed by the unravelling twine. If so, then all the boys, by their tossing the ball of twine back and forth, participated in "finding" the money and all will be considered co-finders and entitled to a pro rata share of the money.

If the true owner of the money should appear and demand the money back, his claim will prevail unless the boys were able to prove that the ball of twine had been abandoned by the true owner.

Problem III

A maid in a motel, while cleaning the room of a departed guest, found a bundle of dollars, secured by a rubber band, between the mattress and box springs of the bed. She took the money to the motel owner and gave it to him for keeping until the original owner claimed it. She made the provision, however, that should the original owner not claim the money within a year, she would return for it. The motel owner attempted to locate the owner of the bills, but did not succeed. At the end of the year, the maid returned and demanded that the money be turned over to her. Does she have the right to it?

Answer to Problem III

The maid's right to the money, if she has the right, is only against all others except the rightful owner. The question of whether she has even that right depends upon whether the money is considered to have been lost, abandoned, or misplaced.

In this situation, the final category seems to be the appropriate one. The money was probably not abandoned, since it was carefully secured by a rubber band and placed in a spot from which the owner probably intended to remove it. For the same reason, it is likely not to be classified as lost. The owner probably knew where it was; he merely forgot to retrieve it when he left the motel.

If the money was misplaced by the owner, the owner of the property where the money was left is entitled to retain possession of it, as against the right of the maid, for two reasons: (1) the original owner may still remember where he left the money and return to claim it; and (2) the duty of the maid is to turn over to her employer any property left in the rooms and found in the course of her employment.

The maid therefore has no legal right to enforce her provision that the money be turned over to her by the motel owner at the expiration of a year unless the original owner was found. The motel owner will continue to hold the money for the true owner.

Writing Problems and Sample Answers

Set V

The following set of problems deals with contracts. The same caveats apply here as to the previous problems. The rules provided are not necessarily in effect in your jurisdiction and are certainly not complete. They should be used only in the problems provided here. All of the rules are not applicable to every problem, but you will need no other rules to deal with the problems. Allow about one hour to read and answer each question.

Legal Rules

    I. Parties are free to make whatever contracts they please as long as the contracts involve no fraud or illegality.

    II. Minors (persons under 21) and mentally incompetent persons have no legal capacity to incur contractual duties.

        A. Thus contracts minors enter into are voidable by them.

        B. But contracts minors enter into for the necessities of life are not voidable.

        C. If a minor represents himself as an adult and thereby receives and retains benefits from a contract, he cannot void the contract by pleading his minority.

    III. The mental illness or defect of one party to a contract makes the contract voidable by that party or his successor in interest, unless the party's mental disability has not affected the making of the contract.

    IV. Courts will not permit the enforcement of shockingly unfair (unconscionable) contracts.

Problem I *

A, a public school teacher for more than 40 years, became mentally ill at age 60 and took a one-year leave of absence from her teaching. Her psychiatrist subsequently diagnosed her illness as involutional psychosis, complicated by cerebral arteriosclerosis.

Some years before her illness, she had elected Option One of the Teachers Retirement System in which she was enrolled, this option allotting small periodic money payments to her after her retirement, with her husband as beneficiary of the unexhausted reserve after her death. However, when her leave of absence expired at the end of the year, and while she was still under psychiatric treatment, A executed an application of retirement revoking her previous assignment of her husband as beneficiary and requested instead the maximum payment of benefits during her lifetime, with nothing payable after death. At the same time she borrowed $8760, the maximum cash withdrawal possible, from the retirement system.

Three days before she changed her retirement option she had written the Retirement Board a lucid letter stating her intention to retire and requesting the answers to eight specific questions about the various alternatives available to her. The chief clerk of the Board testified that he responded to A's

---

* These facts are similar to those of a famous case, Ortelere v. Teachers Retirement Bd., 25 N.Y.2d 196, 303 N.Y.S.2d 362, 250 N.E.2d 460 (1969). You may wish to read the actual decision.

questions both in writing, and orally when she appeared before him. She did not receive the written statement, however, until after she had changed her retirement plan during her personal visit. Two months after retiring, A died.

A and her husband, B, had been married happily for 38 years at the time of her death. After she took leave of absence from her teaching, B quit his job to care for her, because she had, according to both B and the psychiatrist, become very depressed. The couple were in very modest circumstances. On the day she changed her retirement plan, B drove her to the Retirement Board, but he said that he did not know why she was going and did not ask for fear she would "begin crying hysterically."

B now brings suit against the Retirement Board to revoke his deceased wife's actions in changing her retirement benefits so as to exclude him from benefits as her beneficiary. What result?

Answer to Problem I

Since there was no evidence of fraud or illegality in the final contract between A and the retirement system only two issues must be considered in deciding whether contract signed by her is voidable.

The first issue is whether A was mentally ill and thus without legal capacity to incur contractual duties. Since A had been diagnosed as mentally ill by the psychiatrist who took care of her, and had been forced by that illness to take a leave of absence from her teaching, there seems no doubt that she comes under this classification. Furthermore, her very action of changing her retirement plan two months before her death so as to cut her husband, B, off from benefits as her beneficiary may be considered additional proof of her mental illness. She and her husband had been happily married for many years, he had quit his own job so as to care for her during her final illness, and she was well aware of their "modest" financial condition. The conclusion may therefore be that had she been mentally competent, she would hardly have elected to change her retirement plan so as to greatly reduce the amount paid from the funds she had contributed to for 40 years and at the same time deprive her husband of all beneficiary rights on her death. If A is found to have been mentally ill when she signed the final contract with the retirement system, the contract will be held void and her earlier option will prevail, reinstating her husband as beneficiary.

But it is at least arguable that despite the diagnosis of involutional psychosis, A was mentally competent at the time she entered into her final transaction with the board. One indication that she was mentally competent is that at the same time she wrote a letter to the board, lucidly listing eight specific questions about alternatives available to her. Her letter reflected substantial understanding of the retirement system.

A second indication that A was mentally competent during her final transaction with the board is that her choice of the new option is rationally explicable in view of the new circumstances in which A found herself. Her decision to receive the maximum payments seems reasonable, based upon the greater needs of support for herself and her husband, since he had quit his job to take care of her. There is no evidence in the facts that A had any premonition of impending death, so her election of the maximum retirement benefits may well have been made to provide the greatest possible returns during her lifetime. Her borrowing of the maximum amount from the retirement fund ($8760) also seems reasonable in this context.

If the court finds that A's acts in her final transaction with the retirement system were unaffected by her mental illness, despite her physician's diagnosis of involutional psychosis, the final contract will be held enforceable and B's claim that A's previous contract be enforced instead will probably be denied.

There is, however, one other issue that may result in a decision favorable to B. If the transaction between A and the retirement board two months before A's death resulted in an unconscionable contract, the court may refuse to enforce it. The court may consider it unconscionable to enforce a contract made by a person presumably mentally ill, two months before her death, effectively nullifying 40 years of participation in a system established for the protection of its participating teachers and their heirs.

Problem II *

A married couple, who were recent immigrants and spoke no English, visited an appliance store in New York City. While they were looking at a refrigerator-freezer, they were approached by a salesman who spoke their native language and who attempted to sell them the appliance. The husband explained that they could not buy the refrigerator-freezer because he was about to lose his job the following week. In response, the salesman explained that the appliance would actually be free; they would be paid $25.00 in commission for each similar appliance that they sold friends and neighbors, who were poor people like themselves.

Following this sales talk, the husband signed a contract, printed in English, for $1,145.88: $900.00, the cash price of the refrigerator-freezer, and $245.88 in credit charges. The cost of the refrigerator-freezer to the dealer was $348.00.

The refrigerator-freezer is now in the possession of the purchasers. The only payment the purchasers made was in the amount of $32.00. The appliance store owner (plaintiff) brings action for a total of $1,364.10: $1,145.88, for the original purchase price; $227.35 for attorney fees; and $22.87 for late charges. What result?

Answer to Problem II

In order to determine the probable result, two issues need to be resolved: (1) whether the contract between the seller and the purchaser was fraudulent;

---

* This is a paraphrase of an actual court case. For the decision, see Frostifresh   Corp. v. Reynoso, N.Y.Dist.Ct., 52 Misc.2d 26, 274 N.Y.S.2d 757 (1966).

and (2) if not, whether the contract was unconscionable. An affirmative answer to either question would make the contract voidable.

With regard to possible fraud on the seller's part, since the buyers could understand no English, they were completely dependent upon the salesman, who, speaking their native language, seems to have improperly influenced them by convincing them that they would not need to pay for the appliance. Since their friends and neighbors were poor like themselves, there was almost no possibility that the purchasers could sell enough similar appliances to avoid paying for the appliance they purchased. If the salesman knew that such a possibility was so remote as hardly to exist, the seller may be deemed to have committed fraud.

Fraud might also have existed in the signing of the sales contract. Had the contract been written in the purchasers' native language, the purchasers might have detected the exorbitant credit cost of the purchase. Since it was not, and the seller knew the purchasers understood no English, fraud by the seller may be suggested. If the court finds that the purchaser was fraudulently induced to sign the contract, the court will refuse to enforce it.

If the court finds no fraud, however, it may still consider the contract unconscionable. The credit charge of $245.88 was almost equal to the plaintiff's cost of the appliance. There is no indication that the purchasers were told of these exorbitant credit costs, and they were unable to discover this fact for themselves because the contract was printed in a language they could not read. If the court finds that the contract was unconscionable, it may refuse to enforce it and to elect one of the following options: (1) The defendant-purchaser might be required to reimburse the plaintiff-seller only for the plaintiff's cost of the appliance ($348.00); (2) the defendant might be required to pay for the plaintiff's cost of the appliance, plus a reasonable markup and installment cost; or (3) the defendant-purchaser may be offered the alternative of returning the appliance to the plaintiff-seller at no cost to the purchaser or at a charge covering the amount of use the defendant has had of the appliance.

Problem III *

A, who is sixteen years old, purchased from B, an automobile dealer, a used car. B was aware that A was a minor. A at first put $50.00 down toward the price of the car, then returned two days later accompanied by his grandmother and aunt. During this second visit, A's aunt drove the car around the lot several times. Then A paid the remaining $90.00 due on the car, with money his aunt had lent him for this purpose. The dealer gave A a receipt, naming A as the purchaser.

A kept the car for a week. The car then broke down and he took it back to the dealer and was told by the dealer's mechanic that the main bearing was

---

* These facts are substantially the same as those of Bowling v. Sperry, 133 Ind.App. 692, 184 N.E.2d 901 (1962). You may wish to read the decision of the court in its entirety.

burned out and repairs would cost from $45.00 to $95.00. He refused to pay this amount and left the car on the dealer's lot. Then he wrote a letter to the dealer disaffirming the sales contract and demanding the return of his purchase price.

The dealer states that he "understood" that A needed the car for transportation to and from his summer job at a restaurant eight miles from his home. A said, however, that he never drove it to work, and used it only for recreational purposes. A stated that his usual method of getting to work was with the restaurant cook, and that sometimes he "bummed" rides. The dealer further stated that an inference could be drawn from the evidence that the burned-out bearing was caused by A's operation of the car without putting oil in the crankcase.

Is A legally entitled to a refund?

Answer to Problem III

Since A paid for the car in cash and received a receipt from B, the dealer, and since there seems to be no evidence of fraud or other illegality in the sale, a legal sales contract exists. It is not relevant that A borrowed money from his aunt for part of the purchase price of the car or that his aunt apparently approved the purchase after driving the car around the dealer's lot. The contract, signed by the dealer, contained A's name as purchaser.

As a minor, however, A has no legal capacity to incur contractual duties, and he may therefore choose to disaffirm any contract he has signed unless the article purchased was for a necessity of life. The dealer says he understood that A needed the car to drive back and forth to his employment. Even if A did make such a statement, the car was in fact not used for that purpose, but only for recreational purposes, during the week that A owned it. Thus, although to a teenager, a car might seem a necessity, the dealer has no ground for claiming "necessity" as a means of holding A to the contract.

The question of whether the burned-out bearing was due to an inherent defect in the car or to A's failure to put oil in the crankcase need not be considered. Whichever the case, A is legally within his rights as a minor to disaffirm the contract.

The court will probably force the dealer to refund A's purchase price of $140.00, minus a charge to A for whatever benefit he received from the use of the car for one week.

Chapter Nine

Questions Lawyers Ask About Language

For a number of years I have written columns on language for legal publications. The columns are based on questions lawyers submit. Some of the questions lawyers ask have already been answered in the pages of this book.

Lawyers ask questions ranging from the subject of general English usage to the propriety of certain terms of art and legal abbreviations, and to the way lawyers ought to refer to themselves and other lawyers. The questions have been listed below, divided for convenience into categories: style, correctness, meaning, and punctuation and spelling.

I. Style

Question: Should lawyers identify themselves and address others as *Esquire (Esq.)*?

Answer: Because this question was asked by a woman lawyer who wanted to know whether she could use *Esquire* to refer to herself or whether it was reserved to men, I checked the etymology of the honorific. I found that *Esquire* was derived from Latin *scutarius,* meaning "shield-bearer," and that when it came into English during the middle ages from French, it meant "squire," and was used to denote a country gentleman who, aspiring to knighthood, apprenticed himself to a knight.

When the title arrived in this country, however, our egalitarian society rejected the connotation of social rank that it held in England, and used the honorific to denote occupation. By the 19th century it denoted a justice of the peace or an associate judge. Later it was expanded to include lawyers. The only reason the title implied male-ness was that almost all lawyers were male. So I wrote that there seems no reason for women lawyers to forgo using the title. And I asked readers to share their views on the subject.

There followed a flood of mail. Most lawyers strongly opposed using *Esquire* to refer to themselves. A small number were opposed to using it in any circumstance. A very few favored using *Esquire (Esq.)* to refer both to other lawyers and to themselves.

Those lawyers and judges who deplored the use of *Esquire* argued heatedly that it conveys the very image lawyers are trying to avoid—that the legal profession is officious and self-serving. A significant minority of correspondents, however, believed that instead of *Esquire* lawyers should add *J.D.* after their signatures and to their letterheads.

As to addressing other lawyers as *Esquire,* most lawyers and judges agreed that the title is "to be given, but not taken." It should be added to the name of the lawyer to whom a letter is addressed, but not appended to the sender's name when he or she signs the letter. Most lawyers said that they are not offended when others apply the title to them. One lawyer wrote that it should be used regularly because it "connotes that measure of respect traditionally accorded members of the legal profession."

But almost all lawyers strongly opposed the practice of calling themselves *Esquire.* One lawyer wrote, "I have nothing but contempt for this offensive practice." Another wrote that the attempt to "legitimize self-aggrandizement" by calling oneself *Esquire* is "absolute nonsense." The consensus was best expressed by a lawyer who wrote, "Anyone who calls himself a gentleman probably isn't."

Question: What salutation should be substituted when *Gentlemen* is inappropriate?

Answer: (The writer was referring to a situation in which the recipients of a letter were of both sexes or their sex was unknown.) The problem is easily solved when the profession or role of the recipients is known. *Dear Lawyers* or *Dear Committee Members* might substitute, or (as a reader suggested) *Dear Colleagues.* Alternatively, one might substitute *Dear Recipients* or the more aloof *To Whom This May Concern.*

Other readers contributed suggestions. By far the most popular was *Gentlepeople* or *Gentlepersons,* or those words preceded by *Dear.* (Some readers objected to *Gentle* in those salutations on the ground that it was insincere.) Also popular was *Dear Ladies and Gentlemen,* or simply *Ladies and Gentlemen.* Several readers said that they preferred to put *Ladies* first because women had been ignored in salutations for many years.

A number of readers submitted *Dear Sirs and Madams* or, if the sex of the addressees was unknown, *Dear Sirs or Madams.* (A few readers objected to *Madams* because of its unfortunate connotation in other contexts.)

Finally, not a few readers argued for the abandonment of the salutation in letters altogether. And one reader concluded that the best salutation for southern correspondents is *Dear Y'all.*

Question: Is it proper to use the abbreviation *Ms.* to address a woman?

Answer: Yes, though not all authorities agree with that answer. But the prestigious *Oxford English Dictionary* lists *Ms* (no period) in its 1987 Supplement, defining it as "[a] compromise between Mrs. and Miss, a title prefixed to the surname of a woman, regardless of her marital status."

And that seems to be the chief advantage to *Ms.,* for there seems to be no justification for distinguishing between women according to marital status. If a reason to do so becomes evident, we shall have to create a title to distinguish between married and unmarried men as well.

The approved plural for *Ms.* is *Mss.* Although that plural is also an abbreviation for Manuscripts, the double usage is unlikely to cause ambiguity.

A related question was whether a woman should be addressed as *Mrs. Mary Jones* or *Ms. Mary Jones.* Etiquette consultants advise that the latter is correct. With *Mrs.,* they say, the surname of the woman's husband should be used (*Mrs. John Jones*).

Finally, it should be noted that a few persons (usually male and over forty years old) vehemently object to the title *Ms.* You may recall that a federal judge informed a woman attorney that he did not permit anyone to "use that *Ms.*" in his courtroom. He also told her, "Do what I tell you or you're going to sleep in the county jail tonight." (Later he apologized to the attorney.)

Question: Please comment on the use of the subjunctive after the word *if.* Couldn't we get along without subjunctive verbs?

Answer: We could, and many persons do, but the loss would be to fine distinctions in meaning. For the subjunctive form of the verb is used after the word *if* to express ideas that the speaker or writer knows to be contrary to fact or about which he is doubtful. For example:

- If the weather were favorable, I would play golf. (But the weather is not favorable.)
- He acts as if he were a child. (But he is not.)

In both of these contexts, many persons now use the indicative verb form, although that usage is still considered substandard. The following are therefore unacceptable:

- * If the weather was favorable, I would play golf.
- * He acts as if he was a child.

Because so many persons use the indicative form in sentences like those above, the subjunctive is moribund in English (and is no longer taught to foreign students in most English language classes). One reason for the coming demise of the subjunctive is that the plural subjunctive forms are exactly like the indicative forms. For example:

- If prices were higher, I would sell. (Compare the singular subjunctive: If the market were higher, I would sell.)

The subjunctive mood is also properly used after clauses that express a demand, a resolution, a motion, a recommendation, a wish, or a request, when the following clause is introduced by the word *that.* For example:

- The court ordered that the defendant desist from harassing the plaintiff.
- The committee chairman recommended that each member familiarize herself with the subject.
- I move that the meeting be adjourned.
- She demands that there be an investigation.

Notice that in each of these sentences the second verb (which follows *that*) is in the subjunctive. The indicative form of the same verbs would be *desists, familiarizes,* and *is.* You probably already use the subjunctive in contexts like these without thinking about it. You also automatically use the subjunctive in idioms like "God bless you," "Come what may," "So be it," and "Heaven forbid."

So, although the subjunctive may be on its last legs, it is not yet deceased, and because it makes possible nice distinctions in meaning, it is advisable to use it.

Question: Please discuss which of the forms in the two following pairs is stylistically preferable: *pled/pleaded* and *proved/proven.*

Answer: Both forms in the two pairs are correct. There are, however, some differences of opinion about them among authorities. Regarding *pled* and *pleaded, Words & Phrases* lists only *pleaded* as the past tense of *plead,* but the *American Heritage Dictionary (AHD)* lists both, with *pleaded* as preferred. That form is the older. It was used as early as 1305. By 1820, Noah Webster was denouncing the form *pled,* though he admitted that many New Englanders were using it "colloquially." An informal survey of modern American legal usage reveals a preference for *pled,* and since both past tenses are well established and neither will confuse anyone, use the form you prefer.

As to *proved* and *proven,* again, take your choice. The form *proved* is the older, having appeared as early as 1175. *Proven* arrived more than three centuries later, in 1536. The *AHD*'s panel of experts suggests that *proved* be used as the past participle (e.g., in "a proven record"). Current legal usage, however, seems to favor the use of *proven* both as past participle and as adjective.

Question: Please discuss the term *oxymoron.* Are oxymorons ever appropriate in legal usage?

Answer: Oxymorons are frequently and appropriately used in court opinions and elsewhere by the legal profession. By definition an oxymoron is a two-word term, the first word of which contradicts the second. Its name exemplifies its meaning, since it is composed of the Greek words *oxy* ("sharp") and *moron* ("foolish").

Legal terms that could be considered oxymorons are combinations like *negative pregnant, active and affirmative negligence, deliberate speed,* and *substantive due process.* A legal writing colleague, after reading his students briefwriting assignment, added *legal brief* to the list.

But the use of oxymorons is by no means confined to the legal profession. A local librarian submitted her list of favorites. It included *man child, firewater, horsefly,* and *night light. Lea and Febiger,* medical book publishers, recently sponsored an oxymoron contest for enthusiastic collectors. Among the winners were *exquisite pain* and *irregular rhythm.* Some of the other entries were *idiot savant, ill health, medicinal cigarettes, static flow, sanitary sewer, negative impact,* and *intense apathy.*

You may not consider all these pairs to be true oxymorons. That is because a person's bias sometimes decides whether a word combination should be included in the list. Do you consider, for example, that a "delicious low-calorie dinner" is possible? If not, that term would seem to you to be an oxymoron. Other selections that indicate the selector's bias are *Internal Revenue Service, clean bomb, painless dentistry, social security,* and *family vacation.*

Oxymorons are an ancient literary device. They are also as modern as today's newspaper. A wellknown columnist (and frequent critic of others' literary efforts) chose an infelicitous oxymoron in a recent column. Speaking against the legalization of drugs, he wrote: "What legalization advocates seek is a heavy mitigation of the concomitant consequences of the war on drugs." ("Heavy mitigation"?)

II. Correctness

Question: Why should business letters use *reference* as a verb when there is a perfectly good verb (*referred to*)?

Answer: This question addresses the characteristic practice of English speakers to change words from one category to another. Recently the phrase "the above referenced matter" has replaced the earlier "the above-referred-to matter" in legal and commercial usage.

It is hard to analyze why people who write on business or legal matters prefer *referenced* to *referred to,* but the newer usage has caught on and has practically driven out the old. The point is that when English speakers perceive that a change of word category is useful, they do not hesitate to change into verbs words that were formerly nouns, nouns into adjectives, adjectives into nouns, et cetera.

In the case of *referenced,* that one word replaces two, and may therefore be considered preferable. Other recent noun-to-verb forms include *instance, evidence, critique,* and *stonewall.* One example of a noun that is often currently used as a verb in legal writing despite a perfectly good verb being available is *garnishee,* which is really a noun though legal drafters mistakenly use it as a verb. The actual verb form is *to garnish,* which is derived from the French *garnir,* as are the nouns *garnishee* (one who garnishes) and *garnish-ment* (the process of garnishing).

When words change categories, their new forms sound strange at first, but once they become generally used, they are accepted as normal. It hasn't been long since *instance* was only a noun; now it is also a verb. You may recall the time when *fun* was only a noun; now it serves as an adjective too, as in *fun-time.*

This process of word change from one category of speech to another is usually painful when it is occurring. Benjamin Franklin voiced his concern about new words in a letter to Noah Webster:

- During my late absence in France, I find that several new words have been introduced. From the noun *notice* a new verb *noticed* was produced. Also *advocate* led to *advocated,* and *progress* to *progressed* . . . the most awkward and abominable of the three.

Franklin added, "If you should happen to be of my opinion with respect to these innovations, you will use your authority in reprobating them." The reporter of this correspondence adds, "If Webster *advocated* such action it is unlikely it *progressed* very far, for little effect can be *noticed.*" (S. Block, in *Benjamin Franklin, His Wit, Wisdom & Women,* Hastings House, 1975, at 372.)

It has not been many years since *breach* was only a noun, so one could only *break* a contract. And only forty years ago grammarians frowned on the use of *contact* as a verb. Lawyers have written protesting the use of *negative* as a verb, but it seems to be firmly ensconced in the language. Others complain about the new verbs *gifted* and *motioned,* which are on their way to replacing *given* and *moved.* There have also been queries about whether *nolle prosequi* and *praecipe* can be used as verbs.

The answer to all questions of this type is the same: if there is a need for the new usage, it will become a part of the language. Therefore though it is not wise to adopt (or coin) new words, don't resist the usage after it has settled into the language of the legal profession.

Question: How do you decide whether to add *er* to an adjective or to precede it with *more?*

Answer: Although all one-syllable adjectives add *er* to form the comparative, you can add *more* instead. For example, you can say *sweeter, finer,* and *sadder,* or *more sweet, more fine,* and *more sad.* Adjectives of more than two syllables always add *more;* for example, *beautiful, eccentric,* and *capable.* The exception to that rule is three-syllable adjectives formed by adding *un* to some two-syllable adjectives like *unhappy* and *unworthy.*

Two-syllable adjectives, especially those that end in *y* (like *pretty, friendly,* and *cozy*), can add *er.* With respect to other two-syllable adjectives, make your own decision based on current usage. I add *er* to *narrow, clever,* and *subtle,* but not to *often.* Your choices may differ, but are "wrong" only if they are idiosyncratic.

Question: Please comment on the use of *and/or* in legal writing.

Answer: My advice is to avoid *and/or.* The reason for that advice is that judges dislike the term, their disapproval ranging from mild to violent. Judges have written in their opinions that the term is misleading and confusing, that it leads to uncertainty, ambiguity, and multiplicity, that it is a linguistic abomination and a verbal monstrosity.

Judges have had to construe the meaning of *and/or* in numerous cases, in affidavits, ballots, contracts, motions, ordinances, pleadings, statutes, and verdicts. That list should cause lawyers to think twice before using *and/or* in their legal writing.

Question: Now that carbon copies are no longer used, what should be substituted for *cc.* to indicate copies?

Answer: Although almost nobody uses carbon copies, the abbreviation is still in use. You may wish to use a single *c.* to indicate one copy, two *cc.* to indicate more than one. The addition of the names of those to whom copies are being sent provides helpful additional information.

Question: A recent news item quoted a state prosecutor as saying: "In this state, there's not enough judges, there's not enough juries, and there's not enough courtrooms." Is this usage correct?

Answer: No. The word *there* (called a grammatical expletive) is number-neutral. It takes the number of the real subject, which follows, so it should be *there is* (*there's*) when it is followed by a singular subject and *there are* when it is followed by a plural subject. In the sentence cited above, all of the nouns are plural, so the sentence should read "in this state, there aren't enough judges, there aren't enough juries, and there aren't enough courtrooms."

To be sure, this rule is currently violated, even by people who should know better, but violation indicates sloppy usage and lawyers ought to be careful to attach the correct number (*is/are; was/were*) to *there*. On the other hand, consider omitting the grammatical expletive in your writing whenever it is not necessary. Although legal professionals seem to dote on expletive constructions, they often have two unfortunate results: they reduce clarity and usually create wordiness. Consider the following sentences from law students' writing:

- There is a cause of action on behalf of the passenger, who suffered from the reckless conduct of the driver.
- As soon as the victim's purse was grabbed there was battery, there was certainly no consent.

These sentences would be clearer if the expletives were deleted, and the actual subject of the sentence were stated:

- The passenger has a cause of action against the driver because of the driver's reckless conduct.
- As soon as the defendant grabbed the victim's purse, the defendant committed a battery; the victim had certainly not consented.

Question: What is the correct usage of the words *between* and *among?*

Answer: In exact usage, *between* refers to only two persons or objects. Its root is Anglo–Saxon *be tweonum* ("by the two"). In the Middle English period (about 1000 to 1500) *tweonum* evolved to *'twain* (as in Kipling's "Never the 'twain shall meet").

But *between* is now often used to refer to more than two persons or objects. Although "a debate among three opponents" follows the grammatical "rule," you might prefer "a debate between three opponents" as better conveying your meaning of controversy.

But one rule is still in effect, though often ignored. For correct usage, be sure to use the objective form of the personal pronoun after both *between* and *among.* The ungrammatical "between you and I" is a mistaken effort at elegance. Correct are the following:

- between you and me
- among (between) us
- between him and her
- between (among) them and us

Another fairly prevalent error that should be avoided is the redundant and ungrammatical: "He took a 30–minute lunch break between each and every appointment." Substitute instead one of the following:

- He took a 30–minute lunch break between appointments.
- He took a 30–minute lunch break after each appointment.

Question: What is correct in the following construction, *is* or *are?* "If your name, address or title (is/are) correct . . ."

Answer: The correct choice is *is.* The key word is *or.* Had that word been *and,* the plural verb *are* would have been correct. When you use *and,* you indicate that the listed items are to be considered as a total; *or* indicates that the listed items are to be considered separately.

When all of the listed items are either singular or plural, the rule causes no problem, but when the items are mixed in number, the principle of grammatical attraction takes over, and you choose for the verb the number of the closest noun. For example, the following are correct:

- A raincoat, an umbrella, or galoshes are advisable.
- Galoshes, an umbrella, or a raincoat is advisable.

Question: I hear television reporters using the construction "The reason is because. . . ." Is that considered correct now?

Answer: No. Grammars and dictionaries still label it redundant and unacceptable. For example, one grammar calls it "an informal redundancy" and advises that you use *that* ("the reason is that"). Another authority on usage comments that although "the reason is because" often appears, especially in speech, "the reason is that" is preferable. Similarly, *the reason why* is redundant, although it is used so frequently by educated speakers that it has gained currency and can be considered as correct.

III. Meaning

Question: Which is correct, *conclusionary* or *conclusory?*

Answer: Both words are in current use, and they have the same meaning: a conclusion reached without adequate proof or evidence. In about 3,000 recent federal and court opinions, however, *conclusory* appeared 2,840 times and *conclusionary* only 160 times. Therefore it would seem wise to use *conclusory* instead of *conclusionary.*

Question: What is the difference in meaning between *therefore* and *therefor?*

Answer: Although current dictionaries usually brand *therefor* "archaic," it is still in legal use in phrases like "just cause therefor," and "payment therefor." The word *therefor* means "for that." The word *therefore* is widely and currently used, both legally and generally. It means "for that reason."

Question: What does [*sic*] mean, and how should it be used?

Answer: [*Sic*], which is Latin for "thus," "so," or "in the same manner," is used to indicate that the writer is using exactly the same language as the person being quoted. Why not let quotation marks indicate this fact? Because the quoted matter followed by [*sic*] usually represents unorthodox or unusual usage—or more often because the word is misspelled in the quotation. Put elegantly, [*sic*] is an orthographical disclaimer. More bluntly, [*sic*] says, "I know this word is misspelled, but the person I am quoting didn't."

Question: What is the origin of the word *bar,* as used in "members of the bar"?

Answer: The origin of the word *bar* is uncertain, but it came into Middle English from Middle French *barre,* meaning "barrier," probably from Vulgar Latin *barra,* though the Latin word is unattested. In England, the bar was a railing separating the judge's seat from the rest of the courtroom. In the Inns of Court, the *barristers* (persons qualified to practice "at the bar") debated their case before the judges. (As counsel to the king, the barrister was called "within the bar.")

Another *bar* separated students, who observed the proceedings and would eventually take their places "at the bar." Later the word *bar* expanded to include the entire body of barristers or lawyers qualified to practice law, and to denote the legal profession. Thus the term, "members of the bar."

Question: What is the difference in the meaning of the following pairs of words: *previous* and *prior; subject* and *object;* and *in front of* and *before?*

Answer: Dictionaries list the two adjectives, *previous* and *prior,* as essentially synonymous. However, each has a meaning not in common with the other. *Previous* can mean "the next prior" or "the next preceding," and *prior* can mean "having precedence." For that meaning of *prior,* compare the word *priority,* from which it probably obtains that meaning. For the differences in meaning, see the following illustrations:

- the photograph on the previous page (i.e., the next prior)

- a responsibility prior to all others (i.e., having precedence over).

Although dictionaries do not distinguish between *subject* and *object,* when you examine the contexts in which the words are used, you do find that they are not completely interchangeable.

Subject means "topic," and is used to describe non-human nouns, as in "the subject of the course," "the subject under discussion." *Object* means "focus" and is often used to refer to human beings in phrases like "the object of pity," "the object of admiration," and "the object of contempt." If you switch the two words in the illustrative phrases, you will see that they don't "fit."

Finally, there is a difference in the two words *in front of* and *before* in one important context that legal writers should be aware of. A law professor complained to me that young attorneys were mistakenly using *in front of* when they should be using *before* in sentences like, "*Jones v. Smith* involved an action for damages tried before a jury." In that context, *before* means "in the presence of."

Question: What is the correct form of the verb: *recur* or *re-occur*? Is *re-occur* correct in the following sentence: "These problems should not re-occur."

Answer: The verb *re-occur* is not yet dead, but it is probably dying. The reason: an inexorable rule of usage is that when two words have the same meaning, they either differentiate in meaning or one disappears. Because *re-occur* and *recur* mean the same thing—and *recur* is shorter—*re-occur* is now in the process of disappearing.

We now have two verbs with the same meaning: *administer* and a backformation from the noun *administration, administrate*. Unless these two synonymous verbs differentiate in meaning, one (probably the original form, *administer*) will disappear. This process is also occurring with *preventive* and *preventative*. The shorter form almost always wins out, so that is why *re-occur* will probably disappear.

Question: Is the word *premises* singular or plural? Would you use a singular or plural verb in referring to *premises,* and what personal pronoun should be used?

Answer: Standard usage requires the use of a plural verb and a plural pronoun (*they*) to refer to *premises,* even though the word often conveys a singular meaning. Appellate court opinions regularly use plurals in reference to *premises;* for example, "The premises referred to were not the various buildings . . .," and "Premises are entitled to constitutional protection. . . ."

Question: In referring to a book title, should one say, "The book is titled," or "The book is entitled"?

Answer: Either word is correct. The two words are cognates, that is, they are derived from the same Latin root, *titulus,* meaning "title." Both words carry the meaning, "have a name," or "give a name or title to," but *entitle* has a second meaning, not shared by *title:* "have or bestow the right (sometimes legal) to do something." The slang expression, "You're entitled," illustrates that second meaning.

With the meanings, "have a title" or "give a title to," the verb *title* will probably eventually replace the longer form, *entitle.*

Question: Do the two phrases, *in behalf of* and *on behalf of* have different meanings?

Answer: Some dictionaries say they do, but few courts distinguish the two phrases in their opinions. For example, *Ballentine's Law Dictionary (3rd edition, 1969)* lists for *behalf* the meanings "in the name of; on account of; for the benefit, advantage, interest, profit or vindication of." Under a separate listing, *Ballentine's* defines *on his behalf* as meaning "for him and as authorized by him." *The American Heritage Dictionary,* 1973, quoted its Usage Panel as noting that the two phrases have distinct senses and cannot be used interchangeably. The Usage Panel's majority (58%) restricts *in behalf of* to the meanings "in the interest of, for the benefit of," and *on behalf of* to the meanings "as the agent of, on the part of." These definitions seem consistent with those listed by *Ballentine's.*

In portions of opinions cited in *Words and Phrases,* courts differ as to the meanings of *on behalf of* and *in behalf of.* While one court said that *on behalf of* means "for" a person, as agent, another said that "on behalf of does not indicate agency," and still another court said that *on behalf of* did mean "represented."

In 1988 Florida appellate court decisions, *on behalf of* occurred 31 times, *in behalf of* only 7 times. Some courts maintained a distinction between agency (*on behalf of*) and interest (*in behalf of*), but in some contexts, the phrases seemed to indicate either agency or interest—or both. For example, in the following contexts, *on behalf of* seems to indicate both agency and interest:

- Attorney's fees shall not be awarded against a party who is insolvent or poverty-stricken. Before initiating such a civil action on behalf of a client, it shall be the duty of the attorney to inform his client, in writing, of the provisions of this section.

- On behalf of the defendant . . ., I believe the moral thing to do is add the five years probation, but I think when you appointed me on this case you wanted me to represent the defendant [as well as possible].

And in the following contexts, *in behalf of* seems to indicate agency as well as interest:

- [F]or a period of two years following the termination of said employment . . ., he will not, for himself or in any capacity for or in behalf of any other person. . . .

- An application for writ of habeas corpus in behalf of a prisoner who is authorized to apply for relief by motion

Because those who act as agents for others also act in their interest, it is not surprising that the meanings of the two phrases have merged, nor that *on behalf of* is used more often and with both meanings. Under the rule of economy (when two words mean the same thing, one will probably disappear), it is likely that *in behalf of* is on its way out of the English language.

Question: Have you noticed the redundant *is?*

Answer: Indeed I have. It appears more often in speech than in writing, and distracts attention from what the speaker is saying to the way he is saying it. When you hear a person use it once you can be sure he will use it again— and again. I have listed below some of the contexts in which one speaker recently used the redundant *is:*

- The thought is is that the evidence has little probative value.
- The determining factor is is that the statement was hearsay.
- The problem is is that the defendant did not make the necessary repairs.
- I think that what he said is is that he was out of town.

In all of the sentences listed, the second *is* is both redundant and ungrammatical. Why does the speaker put it in? A possible explanation is that he is analogizing these constructions to one in which the second *is* is both grammatical and semantically necessary.

For example, take the phrase "What it is is a well-known fact." Here you need the second *is* because *what it is* is a noun phrase, although the noun phrase is composed of a pronoun/subject plus the verb (*is*). To prove that *what it is* is a noun phrase, substitute a noun or pronoun for it:

- The disappearance of smallpox is a well-known fact.
- That is a well-known fact.

But in all those sentences in which the second *is* was redundant, the subject of the sentence was a noun and the verb was *is.* For example, in the first sentence listed, "The thought is that the evidence has little probative value," *thought* is the subject noun, and *is* is the verb. The speaker who mistakenly adds the second *is* does so on the mistaken and probably subconscious assumption that all subject nouns and pronouns, when they are followed by a form of the verb *be* are similar to the *what it is* construction.

Redundancy often occurs when one stops considering what the language means. A chancellor of a western university recently sent out a memo creating an "ad hoc task force." But because all task forces are by their nature "ad hoc," that statement is redundant. Common redundant verb/adverb combinations are *return back, repeat again,* and *on-load* which seems to have replaced the older *load* and created *off-load* to replace *unload.*

Question: Does the word *none* require a singular or a plural verb. For example, would you use *is* or *are* in the sentence, "The clients have all left; none (is/are) in the waiting room"?

Answer: Either choice is appropriate. If you want to emphasize the singular meaning of *none,* use the singular verb, as in:

- None of us is without sin.
- There should be some alternatives, but none is available.

In its singular meaning, *none* means "not one." It is derived from Old English *ne* ("not") plus *an* ("one"). Grammarians used to insist, therefore, that *none* be followed by a singular verb. But that is no longer true; even the most conservative grammarians agree that *none* can be either singular or plural. Thus in the sentence the reader cited above, use either *is* or *are*.

IV. Punctuation and Spelling

Question: Which punctuation, of the two choices below, is correct?

- The Real Estate Company, Inc., (hereinafter referred to as "Company") . . .
- The Real Estate Company, Inc. (hereinafter referred to as "Company"), . . .

Answer: The second example is correct. The rule is that when the sentence requires other marks of punctuation along with the parenthetical material, you place the marks after the closing parenthesis. For example:

- During Herbert Hoover's presidency (1929–1933), this country suffered its worst financial depression.
- The term *liberum tenementum* means a "freehold estate" (as in a plea brought by one in actual possession of land, asserting title to the property and the right to possession, but admitting possession and a color of right to the property by another).

Question: Is a comma necessary after *etc.,* when it appears in the middle of a sentence?

Answer: Yes. The abbreviation of *et cetera* (which means "other unspecified things of the same class") substitutes for additional items in a list and should be set off by commas, just as are the other listed items. When *etc.* ends a sentence, you use only one period after it. For example, "*The Lonely Crowd* deals with social values, human relationships, etc.

Question: What do the initials LL.B., LL.M., and J.S.D. stand for?

Answer: LL.B. stands for "Legum Baccalaureus," Latin for "Bachelor of Laws," LL.M. stands for "Legum Magister," Latin for "Master of Laws," and J.S.D. stands for "Doctor of Judicial (or Juridical) Science." The doubling of the *L* in *LL.B.* and *LL.M.* indicates the plural of *Law*. *Legum* is the genitive (possessive) plural of *lex,* Latin for "law."

Question: Is there any rule for deciding whether to add *ible* or *able* to form adjectives meaning "capable of" to verbs?

Answer: There is a handy rule that should help you choose the right spelling. Examine the pairs of adjectives below and see if you can formulate a rule to govern your choice of either *able* or *ible*.

eatable	—	edible
detectable	—	visible
readable	—	legible
believable	—	credible

As you probably have noticed, all the adjectives in the lefthand column were formed by adding the suffix to a Modern English verb (*eat, detect, read,* and *believe*). In the case of *believe,* the final *e* was deleted, just as it is before *ed* and *ing.* The *y* in *apply* also changes to *i* in *applicable,* as it does in *applies* and *applied.*

The rule, then, is that whenever you add a suffix to a recognizable Modern English verb, spell it *able.* However, when the base word is not a Modern English verb, but a Latin borrowing, like the base verbs in the righthand column (*ed, vis, leg,* and *cred*), add *ible.* Applying the rule, you would spell *receivable* and *responsible* as shown.

Question: In a legal motion or brief, when one directly quotes a source and sets off the quotation by indenting and single-spacing, should one use quotation marks?

Answer: Some authorities agree that long quotations should be indented at both margins, without quotation marks. But not all authorities agree about the fifty-word limit. One authority permits up to 100 words to be quoted in the text itself. Other authorities do not count words, but say that more than nine lines should be indented. These authorities require indentation of five spaces from both margins, except for the first line of each paragraph, which is indented ten spaces.

On one point, however, all authorities I consulted agree: when the material is indented, quotation marks should be omitted. But court reporters often ignore this part of the rule, and one sees material both indented and enclosed with quotation marks. This practice has been defended on the argument that it makes the quotation unmistakable. That may be, but it seems to me that the necessity of using both double quotation marks (") and single quotation marks (') to distinguish quoted material within the quotation would cause more ambiguity and confusion than the omission of the double quotation marks in indented, single-spaced material.

Question: How does the spelling of a word decide when you should use *a* and when you should use *an?*

Answer: You decide according to the initial sound, not the spelling, of the word that follows *a* or *an.* If the word begins with a vowel sound, like *honest* or *hour,* even though it begins with a consonant, use *an.* On the other hand, words that begin with vowels, if they have the sound of consonants, use *a.* For example, before *union* and *eulogy,* use *a.*

The lawyer who sent the question was especially curious about the phrase *an historic question.* She wanted to know why the speaker had used *an* instead of *a.* The speaker did so because he pronounces *historic* with a silent *h,* as in *hour.* That is typically British; in this country, most speakers retain the *h* sound in *historic.* And even British speakers retain the *h* sound in *history,* probably because in the noun, the first syllable is stressed. The *h* sound tends to disappear only in unstressed syllables, as in the phrase (with the British dropped *h*), "An humble and a contrite heart."

Question: I have been taught that periods and commas are placed within quotation marks, regardless of context. Yet I often see this rule violated. Will you explain the rule?

Answer: In American usage, the rule is that periods and commas are invariably placed within quotation marks. Thus you do not have to decide where to put these two marks. When the punctuation mark is either a colon or a semi-colon, it is always placed outside the quotation marks. For example:

- The buyer purchased the "specified model"; under the U.C.C., he is therefore entitled to damages when the seller repudiated the contract.
- The New York cases "applied the profit test": contract price less cost of manufacture.

When the punctuation mark is a dash, a question mark, or an exclamation point, place it inside the quotation marks when the material quoted requires the punctuation; when the punctuation mark applies to the sentence as a whole, put it outside the quotation marks:

- The crowd shouted, "Free the Phillipines!"
- Did you hear him say, "I am guilty"?
- Did the witness say, "I was there"?

As you can see in the last example, when a period would otherwise be placed before the final quotation mark, omit it when the entire sentence ends with a question mark. The same rule applies when the sentence ends with an exclamation point.

INDEX

References are to Pages

†